READINGS IN GLOBAL HISTORY
Volume 2

Third Edition

Anthony Snyder
Sherri West
Brookdale Community College

KENDALL/HUNT PUBLISHING COMPANY
4050 Westmark Drive   P.O. Box 1840   Dubuque, Iowa 52004-1840

Copyright © 1993, 1997, 2007 by Kendall/Hunt Publishing Company

Library of Congress Catalog Card Number: 97-74031

ISBN 978-0-7575-4666-2

Printed in the United States of America
10   9   8   7   6   5   4   3   2   1

Contents

Acknowledgments

We would like to thank Jess Le Vine, Laura Neitzel, George Reklaitis, and Jane Scimeca, our colleagues in world history at Brookdale, for sharing their suggestions for this new edition. Also, our adjunct instructors have been helpful in advising us on various aspects of this reader. Finally, our thanks go to our students for whom we have labored on this book and from whom we have received invaluable information as to its strengths and weaknesses—we owe them a debt of gratitude.

Anthony W. Snyder
Sherri L. West

1

Europe and the World: The Spice Trade

Anthony Esler, the author of a well-known text on World History, describes the pre-modern world of 1500 as a "world in balance … a world of separate zones of culture … a tidy little world (where) regional societies, great empires, and some of the most impressive civilizations the world has seen shared the earth." While some have argued that the major cultures were never as separate, the world never as tidy as Esler suggests, it was from this world that Columbus and da Gama set forth, shattering whatever balance existed, and setting in motion forces that would lead to the emergence of a "single human story." The result has been the globalization of history, "binding the peoples of the world in more and more elaborate nets of interdependence," a hallmark of the modern world. In this selection, the author provides a brief history of the spice trade in the Indian Ocean up to today, the role that Europeans would play in that trade, and the impact of that trade on European nations, on Asian states, as well as the cultivators of the spices "worth their weight in gold."

Discussion Questions

1. Why does the author state that the "modern age" begins with da Gama's travels to Asia?

2. What is the "Muslim Curtain" and what is its connection with European voyages of exploration?

3. Why do you suppose that Europeans were eventually successful in establishing commercial ties in Asia, and, ultimately, how successful were they?

4. What similarities between the spice trade of yesterday and the spice trade of today are referred to in the reading?

5. Why were spices "worth their weight in gold," and what were Europeans willing to do to claim some of them as their own? What impact would it have on the farmers cultivating spices, or the local leaders that controlled the trade? Are there commodities today that are as priceless as nutmeg and pepper of yesterday?

A Taste of Adventure
Kerala, India, and the Molucca Islands, Indonesia
The History of Spices Is the History of Trade

Soon after dawn on May 21st 1498, Vasco da Gama and his crew arrived at Calicut after the first direct sea voyage from Europe to Asia. If history's modern age has a beginning, this is it. Europe's ignorance of, and isolation from, the cosmopolitan intellectual and commercial life of Asia were ended forever. With ships, weaponry and a willingness to use them both, the countries of Europe were about to colonize the rest of the world. To support this expansion, its merchant classes would invent new forms of commercial credit and the first great corporations, vital parts of capitalism's operating system, and spread their trading networks across the seven seas. And what did the men shout as they came ashore? "For Christ and spices!"

The proselytizing part turned out to be disappointingly unnecessary: there were already plenty of Christians living on the Malabar coast, following the arrival of a Syrian contingent many centuries earlier. But as far as spice went, Da Gama and his crew were right on the money. Then, as now, Calicut was a gateway to the world's greatest peppergrowing region—indeed this was why the Syrians had moved there in the first place. As such it was at the heart of the spice trade, a network of sea routes and entrepôts in the making for Millennia: the world economy's oldest, deepest, most aromatic roots.

For thousands of years before Da Gama and hundreds of years afterwards, the secret of the spice trade was simple: great demand and highly controlled supply. Some of that control was enforced through political power or contrived through mercantile guile. Some was simply a gift from the gods of climate and botany. Legend has it that, before leaving, Da Gama dared to ask the zamorin of Calicut whether he could take a pepper stalk with him for replanting. His courtiers were outraged, but the potentate stayed calm. "You can take our pepper, but you will never be able to take our rains." He knew how important the region's unusual twin monsoon, both phases of which bring heavy rain, was to its fickle crop. To this day, though regions elsewhere grow pepper, Kerala reigns supreme in its quality, dominating the high end of the market.

If those vital downpours have not washed away what passes for the road, a few days travel into Kerala's rolling Western Ghats, where waterfalls roar and herds of wild elephants loom from soft mist, brings you to the ancestral home of *Piper nigrum*. High up in the middle of nowhere, Iddicki produces the finest pepper in the world, its peppercorns always dark and heavy, bursting with flavor. Its vines wind their way around almost every tree in sight, climbing ten meters or more into the sky.

After such a journey you might expect Iddicki to be a sleepy backwater. In its own idyllic way, though, it is a boomtown worthy of the Wild West. Fancy jeeps clog the narrow streets; shops overflow with the latest necessities of rural life, like washing machines and stereos. Giant satellite dishes shove their expensive snouts at the heavens from every other house. One of the world's largest stashes of gold is in rural India, and to judge by its glittering jewelry shops this town has considerably more than its fair share. "Black gold," explains one pepper farmer with a broad grin, is fetching top prices on the world market.

Until you talk to them about that world market, Iddicki's residents seem much like farmers anywhere else in the developing world—scraping a living at the margins of the market economy. Thomas Thomas, one of the several hundred thousand small-holders who grow Kerala's pepper, is a good example. A humble man of the earth, he speaks softly and still wears his *dhothi*, a traditional loincloth, when he tills his soil. But with a little prompting

he will give you an analysis of the pepper market sophisticated enough to make a Chicago commodities trader blush: current prices, the direction of the futures market, the costs versus benefits of holding stocks. A local spice dealer explains over a feast of fiery snapper and spiced tapioca at his spacious bungalow that "there is full price-discovery in this market." The farmers who sell their crops to him (for resale at the big market in Jewtown, which has replaced Calicut as the hub of Kerala's pepper trade) do so with the latest New York and Rotterdam prices in hand. One particularly sharp farmer, he moans, is cutting out the middlemen altogether and shipping his stocks directly to Europe.

The global aspect of the dealer's trade is nothing new. As far back as 2600BC, there are records of the Egyptians feeding spices obtained from Asia to laborers building the great pyramid of Cheops, to give them strength. Archeological evidence suggests that cloves were quite popular in Syria not long after, despite the fact that, like nutmeg and mace, they came only from the spice islands of what is now Indonesia. Long before the 6th century BC, when Confucius advocated the use of ginger, the Chinese were obtaining spices from the tropics. Europe imported them before Rome was founded.

Today spices are chiefly flavorings for food, but a hundred other uses have contributed to the demand through history. In ancient Egypt cassia and cinnamon fetched a high price because they were essential for embalming; so too were anise, marjoram and cumin, used to rinse out the innards of the worthy dead. Hammurabi's legal code, which called for severe punishment of sloppy or unsuccessful surgeons, did much to encourage the use of medicinal spices in Sumeria.

Particularly in Europe, though, food came to matter most. Spices preserve, and they also make the poorly preserved palatable, masking the appetite-killing stench of decay. After bad harvests and in cold winters the only thing that kept starvation at bay was heavily salted meat—

with pepper. And there was never enough of it. Thus pepper began the association with gold it still has in the streets of Iddicki, often at a one-to-one exchange rate. In order to call off their siege of Rome in 408AD, the Visigoths demanded a bounty in gold, silver and pepper. In the Middle Ages plague added to the demand for medicinal spices; a German price table from the 14th century sets the value of a pound of nutmeg at seven fat oxen. At the same time "peppercorn rents" were a serious way of doing business. When the *Mary Rose*, an English ship that sank in 1545, was raised from the ocean floor in the 1980s, nearly every sailor was found with a bunch of peppercorns on his person—the most portable store of value available.

The great beneficiaries of Europe's need were the Arabs. Spices could change hands a dozen times between their source and Europe, soaring in value with each transaction, and the Arabs were the greatest of the middlemen. Keen to keep it that way, they did everything possible to confuse consumers about the spices' origins. As early as the 5th century BC an Arab cover story fooled Herodotus into believing that cinnamon was found only on a mountain range somewhere in Arabia. The spices were jealously guarded by vicious birds of prey, he wrote, which made their nests of the stuff on steep mountain slopes. Arabs would leave out large chunks of fresh donkey meat for the birds to take back to their nests, which would crash to the ground under the weight The brave Arabs then grabbed the nests, from under the talons of their previous owners.

Not everyone was fooled. In the 1st century AD the Roman historian Pliny grew concerned at the way the empire's gold flowed ever to the east, and set out to expose the truth and undercut the Arab monopolists, who he reckoned to be selling pepper at prices a hundred times what they paid for it in India. It did not help that the gluttonous Romans were, in the words of Frederic Rosengarten, a spice historian, "the most

extravagant users of aromatics in history." They used spices in every imaginable combination for their foods, wines and fragrances. Legionaries headed off to battle wearing perfume. The rich slept on pillows of saffron in the belief that it would cure hangovers.

Resentment against the Arab stranglehold had led Rome to launch an invasion of Arabia in 24BC, an ill-fated expedition that ended in humiliation. But where military means failed, market intelligence prevailed. In 40AD, Hippalus, a Greek merchant, discovered something the Arabs had long tried to obscure: that the monsoons which nourish India's pepper vines reverse direction midyear, and that trips from Egypt's Red Sea coast to India and back could thus be shorter and safer than the empire had imagined. Roman trade with India boomed: the Arab monopoly broke.

Early in the 7th century, an obscure spice merchant named Muhammad re-established Arab dominance of the spice trade by introducing an aggressive, expansionary Islam to the world. When the muslims took Alexandria in 641AD, they killed the trade which had long flourished between Rome and India. As they tightened their grip on the business over the next few centuries, prices in Europe rose dramatically. During the Middle Ages, spices became a luxury that only a few in Europe could afford. This was bad news for the poor and good news for Venice. Its shrewd merchants struck a deal with the Arabs that made them the trade's preferred—indeed almost exclusive—European distributors. Even during the crusades, the relationship bought wealth to all concerned.

The rest of Europe did not care at all for the Muslim Curtain, as the Islamic empire separating west from east came to be called, or for the Venetians. The final blow came in 1453 when the Ottoman Turks took Constantinople, shutting down the small overland trade that had previously evaded the Arab-Venetian monopoly. The Egyptians, gatekeepers of the trade with

Venice, felt confident enough to impose a tariff amounting to a third of the value of spices passing through their fingers.

Salvation for the palates and exchequers of Europe's kings lay in finding a sea route to the Indies. In particular, the hunt was on for Malacca, the most important entrepôt in the spice trade and the fabled gateway to the Spice Islands. Spain and Portugal financed dozens of exploration parties in its general direction; half would never make it back home. The rationale for this expense and danger was simple: "He who is lord of Malacca has his hand on the throat of Venice."

It was as part of Portugal's *Drang nach Osten* that Vasco da Gama rounded Africa's Cape of Good Hope to reach India in 1498. As waves of Portuguese explorers returned to Lisbon with their loads of spices, the Venetians and the Egyptians were stunned: the price of pepper in Lisbon fell to one-fifth that in Venice.

The Spaniards, too, were less than happy. They had sent Christopher Columbus to find a route to the Indies via the west, but he had failed, hitting upon the previously unknown Americas instead. In his zeal to convince his paymasters and himself that he had succeeded, he named the new world's natives as Indians and their sacred *chiles* "red" pepper—two unpardonable obfuscations that have confused people to this day.

Pope Alexander VI was drafted in to keep the two expansionist powers apart; the result was the treaty of Tordesillas, which granted all discoveries west of a mid-Atlantic meridian to Spain, and those east of it to Portugal. But the Spanish clung to the possibility of a western end-run to the Spice Islands, and financed Ferdinand Magellan on what would become the first circumnavigation of the earth. Magellan himself was killed in the Philippines, but his sidekick, Sebastian del Cano, completed the momentous journey—with a landfall at the Spice Islands en route. In 1522 his *Victoria*

returned to Europe with a tonne of spices on board. The king awarded him a coat of arms embellished with two cinnamon sticks, three nutmegs and twelve cloves.

But the Portuguese had pipped Spain to the post. They had captured the vibrant free-trading port of Malacca, in what is now Malaysia, in 1511. Using the intelligence they gathered there, they made it to the promised land: the tiny Banda islands, the world's only source of nutmeg and mace, which they reached the following year. Nutmeg is the pit of the nutmeg tree's fruit, and mace, which commanded and still commands a higher price, is the delicate red aril which comes between the pit and the fruit's husky exterior. Chaucer extolled "nutemuge put in ale . . ." and it remains an essential part of Coca-Cola's secret formula.

After filling their holds, the Portuguese began their return. One ship ran aground, stranding its crew on a remote island. Hearing of a strange race of white men in his parts, the sultan of Ternate, the most powerful of the clove isles, sent for them—and so the Europeans found the last secret source of spice.

Look out from the expansive verandah of the sultan's palace in Ternate and one of history's great microcosms lies before you. Dominating one side is Gamalama, the island's temperamental volcano. Opposite it stands its equally fickle twin on the island of Tidore. The two spits of land, not a mile apart, are now almost unknown beyond their immediate vicinity. But five centuries ago their names were uttered with breathless excitement across Europe as their rulers, ancient rivals, played the new great powers off against each other with promises of limitless wealth.

Dark, husky aromas swirl through the palace as incense made specially of local spices finds its way into the thick tropical air. The place is overflowing with gifts from distant customers: priceless Chinese vases, exquisitely carved Indian daggers, fine Venetian glassware, all of them evidence of the influence these rulers once wielded. Ask politely, and you might be allowed to gaze—from a respectful distance, and only after much ceremony—at the sultan's magical crown, its hundred sparkling gemstones hanging heavy like ripe peaches. You are not the first impressionable tourist here. Francis Drake gushed about the palace, especially its 400-strong harem. And it seems that it's still good to be the king: one of the gifts on display is an enormous modern settee, helpfully labelled "Lazy chair: for the sultan to take naps."

For much of the 16th century, Spain and Portugal tried to win control of the trade in cloves that made such a lifestyle possible. This meant entangling themselves in the long-running rivalry between the rulers of the two islands, who were in-laws. The European powers would build alliances and forts in one place and then the other, only to find themselves kicked out or caught up in endless intrigues and feuds. After decades of this Machiavellian palaver the Portuguese emerged as the top European player in the clove market, but they never really made it a monopoly. Indeed, they allowed the Dutch, who were growing increasingly anxious for a piece of the action, to be their chief distributors in the north and west of Europe. After Spain gobbled up Portugal in 1580, though, the trade changed again. The Spanish tightened control of the market to which they now had exclusive access, cutting the Dutch out of the picture and raising prices across the continent.

Convinced that they had to find a way to control the source of the spices, the Dutch got their act together. In 1602 they formed the Dutch East India Company (the *Vereenigde Oost-Indische Compagnie,* VOC), an association of merchants meant to reduce competition, share risk and realize economies of scale. Other European countries also formed East India companies—everyone from Portugal to Sweden to Austria had a go—but none was ever as successful in the spice trade as the VOC. By 1670 it was the richest corporation in the world, paying its shareholders an annual dividend of 40% on their investment despite financing 50,000 employees, 30,000 fighting men and 200 ships, many of them armed. The secret of this success was simple. They had no scruples whatsoever.

The VOC's first conquest was the Banda archipelago. Unlike the sultans of the clove islands, who relished the attention lavished upon them by their European suitors and the opportunities for mischief that came with it, the fiercely independent Islamic merchants of the Bandas had never allowed Spain or Portugal to build forts on their islands: they insisted on their freedom to trade with all nations. This independence proved their undoing, since it encouraged the VOC to put the nutmeg trade first on its order of business.

For a taste of Banda's romance nothing beats a trip to Run, an explosion of nutmeg trees in the middle of a turquoise sea. Reaching it after a night aboard ship is a magical experience; scores of dolphins dart about your bow-wave as the first glints of sunrise streak across the sky. It feels much as it must have done when English adventurers first claimed the place, making it the country's first colony anywhere. Not much of a colony, it must be said: the island is so small that even a modest fishing vessel can come ashore only at high tide. Yet this seemingly insignificant toe-hold in nutmeg-land so exercised the Dutch that they traded away a promising young colony on the other side of the world to secure it. That island was New Amsterdam, now better known as Manhattan.

The purchase of Run demonstrates the VOC's persistence; it does not do justice to the company's cruelty (normally, but not exclusively, meted out to non-Europeans). Its most successful head, Jan Pieterszoon Coen, had earlier convinced the reluctant Bandanese of his firm's God-given right to monopolize the nutmeg trade in a more typical style: he had had

---

Hot Chile

"Oh Blessed Incomparable Chile, ruler of all things … I give thee thanks for my digestive health, I give thee thanks for my very life!" Thus the Transcendental Capsaicinophilic Society, one of the worrying number of cults devoted to *capsicum*: chiles or "red" pepper.

If it sounds as if they are on drugs then so, in a way, they are. Paul Bosland of the Chile Pepper Institute in New Mexico reckons they and all chileheads are high on endorphins, painkillers released by the body to block the sting of the capsaicin which gives chiles their bite.

The addicts are spread all over the world. Travelling on the back of the European spice trade, America's chiles have since colonized every corner of the earth so thoroughly that everyone thinks they have always been around. Even the top man at the Indian Spices Board refuses to accept that chiles are an import, pulling dubious sanskrit references from the Vedas to bolster his point. His clinching argument? "Indians can go months without touching black pepper. but not a day goes by that we don't eat chile peppers,"

This is fast becoming true everywhere else, too, Americans' consumption of chile has doubled over the past two decades; they now use the spice in almost everything. Salsa now outsells ketchup as America's top condiment. But black pepper still gets all the glory as the world's most important traded spice. Unlike its fickle namesake, red pepper grows like mad all over the place. So though there may be a great demand for it, no one makes much money out of trading it. Bad news for traders, good news for foodies.

---

every single male over the age of fifteen that he could get his hands on butchered. Coen brought in Japanese mercenaries to torture, quarter and decapitate village leaders, displaying their heads on long poles. The population of the isles was 15,000 before the VOC arrived; 15 years later it was 600.

When they turned to the clove trade the Dutch had no time for the squabbling politics of Ternate and Tidore. The VOC uprooted all the Sultans' clove trees and concentrated production on Ambon, an island where its grip was tight. By 1681, it had destroyed threequarters of all nutmeg trees in unwanted areas and reorganized farming into plantations. It imposed the death penalty on anyone caught growing, stealing or possessing nutmeg or clove plants without authorization. It drenched every nutmeg with lime before export, to ensure that not one fertile seed escaped its clutches. Yet high on its hillside Afo lives to tell its tale.

Climb through the dense, aromatic forests that cover the steep slopes of Ternate's volcano, and you will find this living testament to the ultimate futility of monopoly. Nearly 40 meters tall and over 4 meters round, Afo is the world's oldest clove tree, planted in defiance of the Dutch ban nearly four centuries ago. Despite the VOC's extreme precautions, Afo's sister seedlings, stolen in 1770 by an intrepid Frenchman (curiously, named Poivre), ended up flourishing on the Seychelles, Réunion and especially Zanzibar, which later became the world's largest producer of cloves. By the end of the 18th century the emergence of these rivals had broken the Dutch monopoly for good.

By that time the VOC was already a hollow mockery of its original ghastly self. As early as the end of the 17th century, careful analysis of the books shows that its volume of trade was reducing every year. Even a monopoly so ruthlessly enforced could not help but leak, and the VOC's overheads were huge—tens of thousands of employees, garrisons, warships. Decades of easy rents had created a corrupt and inefficient beast. By 1735, dwindling spice income had been overtaken by textiles in the company's profit column. In 1799, the most vicious robber baron of them all met its final end. The VOC went bankrupt.

The demise of the VOC was not just a pleasing comeuppance. It was evidence that, in just two centuries, Europeans had changed the spice trade forever. The spices that were once limited to tiny islands in hidden archipelagoes were being grown around the world and in large quantities. Trade routes that spanned oceans were becoming commonplace and, as such, competitive. The Dutch did their best to buck the trend, destroying their stocks so blatantly that, according to one observer, the streets of Amsterdam were "flooded with nutmeg butter." But it was all in vain. Spices were no longer that hard to come by. Monopolies gave way to markets.

Those markets remained rich in romance; the allure of the trade, its role as a cultural crossroads, its many rival players, its uncertainties and its opportunities for smuggling (even relatively cheap spices carry a lot of value for a given weight) kept the spice bazaars of Kerala, Ambon and Rotterdam fascinating. And lucrative, too; though no one could control the overall flow of spice any more, information could still be rushed ahead fast enough—or sequestered behind long enough—for people in the know to make a killing. Now, though, the information itself has started to flow freely. "There just aren't so many secrets anymore," reflects a spice trader in Rotterdam. "The farmers in Vietnam are walking around with mobile phones. They know the market price as soon as I do."

Such traders are now caught in a trap. Their space for bargaining and trade, opened up with the end of monopoly production, is being hemmed in by ever more powerful purchasers—the food giants and spice multinationals. In an age of free-flowing information these buyers can bypass the markets and go directly to the source. From Jewtown, still the key pepper entrepôt, to Rotterdam, London and New York, the main international markets, spice traders are a dying breed. One industry veteran reckons that only a fifth of the trading concerns that flourished 30 years ago are still in business.

Their problems stem from men like Al Goetze. Meet him in his office near Baltimore, at the staid headquarters of McCormick, the world's largest spice firm, and his conservative suit and dry manner might lead you to mistake him for a stuffy corporate type. But to his admiring colleagues he is "a modern day Marco Polo."

Procurement managers at food-processing firms were once content to purchase spices through brokers, never leaving the comfort of their air-conditioned offices. Mr. Goetze hits the road. He and his men have travelled to nearly every country on earth that grows spices, again and again. McCormick has set up joint-ventures or wholly owned subsidiaries in over a dozen key spice-producing countries in recent years.

Once the reason for going to the source was price. Now, Mr. Goetze says, quality is what matters. Both American and European regulators, prompted by increasing consumer awareness of food safety, have been cracking down hard on impurities. Mr. Goetze points to an unlikely assortment of objects in a display case: stones, rusty nails, giant cockroaches, plastic beach sandals. All were crammed into bursting burlap bags and sold to McCormick with its spice. Big processing firms and marketers, frightened that such stuff—or worse, microscopic impurities that come with it—might make it to the dinner plates of litigious customers, are going straight to the source to clean things up.

Alfons van Gulick, the head of Rotterdam's Man Producten, the world's biggest and most influential spice-trading firm, is understandably unimpressed: "McCormick should stick to polishing its brand and selling, rather than telling countries how to produce spice." But the people for whose products McCormick and Man Producten compete have an interest in Mr. Goetze's strategy. The Indian Spices Board is already helping members improve standards and obtain seals of approval such as ISO certification. The hope is that, over time, producers can go downstream and capture more of the fat margins that come with the "value-added" processing now done in rich countries.

Industry analysts are skeptical about vertical integration. In other commodities it has not been much of a success. Cutting out the middleman may pose unexpected problems for conservative multinationals, unfamiliar with the culture and risks involved in going upstream. And then there is volatility, on which middlemen thrive and which farmers and multinationals dislike. Asked whether the trade has lost its mystery, one animated trader replies "Mystery? I experience it every day when I try to figure out what is going on with prices in this market!"

Producers hate this, and have made various attempts to iron out the market's ups and downs. The International Pepper Community—which includes India, Indonesia and Brazil among its members—has tried for decades to form a producers' cartel to boost prices, without any success. Price fixing by vanilla growers in Madagascar succeeded for a while, but then Uganda flooded the market with cheaper beans. Indonesia and Grenada, the top producers of nutmeg, managed to boost prices for a few years by limiting supply, but cheating quickly scuppered the arrangement. Quiet talks are underway between top cardamom producers in India and Guatemala, who produce nearly all the world's output, to restrict supply; it may work for a while, but not for long.

Every decade or so, an ambitious individual trader tries to do with money what the producers cannot do by agreement. To corner the pepper market would offer huge riches, and so people regularly have a go. Half a century ago, it was an Armenian; a decade ago, an American. Now it appears that a shadowy Indonesian tycoon may be making a play for at least the white pepper market. But history teaches that such grandiose efforts at monopoly face an uphill struggle. And though it may be possible to milk them for a while, the modern day economics of the trade ensure that they cannot last. The spice trade, once the stuff of legends, has become a market much like any other. And a taste of luxury beyond the dreams of almost every human in history is available to almost everyone, almost everywhere.

2

Transition to the Modern Era

From:

Traditionalism and Stability

Religion and Faith

Church

Agriculture

Rigid Social Structure

Monarchy

To:

Change, Revolution, Progress

Science and Reason

State

Industry

Mobility

Democracy and Dictatorship

Two Basic Currents in Western Civilization

1. Ancient, Pagan, Rational, Secular, Humanistic

2. Medieval, Christian, Faith-Based, Other-Worldly, Spiritualistic

3

The Scientific Revolution: Galileo

Written exactly midway between Copernicus' *On the Revolutions of the Heavenly Spheres* (1543) and Newton's *Mathematical Principles of Natural Philosophy* (1687), Galileo's letter to Christina, Grand Duchess of Tuscany, presents the conflicts involved in the Scientific Revolution. Most scientists remained committed to the Medieval-Ptolemaic geocentric worldview until after Newton's work was published and they did so for mostly scientific but also religious reasons. (In fact there was no proof that the earth moved until 1729.) Galileo, therefore, found himself in the midst of conflicts of faith (both scientific and religious) as well as of fact. The issues of the day involved not only what the truth was but also how it was to be ascertained. It was in the latter respect that Galileo raised the most important questions and made his most important contributions.

Discussion Questions

1. What motives does Galileo attribute to his critics? Does he think their chief objections to his opinions are religious?

2. Why doesn't he think the Bible should be the foundation of scientific knowledge? What does he think should be?

3. In the Middle Ages, theology was called "the Queen of the Sciences." Why does Galileo question that title? What are the differences he draws between religion and science?

Some years ago, as Your Serene Highness well knows, I discovered in the heavens many things that had not been seen before our own age. The novelty of these things, as well as some consequences which followed from them in contradiction to the physical notions commonly held among academic philosophers, stirred up against me no small numbers of professors—as if I had placed these things in the sky with my own hands in order to upset nature and overturn the sciences. They seemed to forget the increase of known truths stimulates the investigation, establishment, and growth of the arts; not their diminution or destruction.

Showing a greater fondness for their own opinions than for truth, they sought to deny and disprove the things which, if they had cared to look for themselves, their own senses would have demonstrated to them. To this end they hurled various charges and published numerous writings filled with vain arguments, and they made the grave mistake of sprinkling these with passages taken from places in the Bible which they had failed to understand properly, and which were ill suited to their purposes... .

Persisting in their original resolve to destroy me and everything mine by any means they can think of, these men are aware of my views in astronomy and philosophy. They know that as to the arrangement of the parts of the universe, I hold the sun to be situated motionless in the center of the revolution of the celestial orbs while the earth rotates on its axis and revolves about the sun. They know also that I support this position not only by refuting the arguments of Ptolemy and Aristotle, but by producing many counterarguments; in particular, some which relate to physical effects whose causes can perhaps be assigned in no other way. In addition there are astronomical arguments derived from many things in my new celestial discoveries that plainly confute the Ptolemaic system while admirably agreeing with and confirming the contrary hypothesis. Possibly because they are disturbed by the known truth of other propositions of mine which differ from those commonly held, and therefore mistrusting their defense so long as they confine themselves to the field of philosophy, these men have resolved to fabricate a shield for their fallacies out of the mantle of pretended religion and the authority of the Bible. These they apply, with little judgement, to the refutation of arguments that they do not understand and have not even listened to.

First they have endeavored to spread the opinion that such propositions in general are contrary to the Bible and are consequently damnable and heretical... . [And] they have had no trouble in finding men who would preach the damnability and heresy of the new doctrine from their very pulpits with unwonted confidence, thus doing impious and inconsiderate injury not only to that doctrine and its followers but to all mathematicians in general... .

Now as to the false aspersions which they so unjustly seek to cast upon me, I have thought it necessary to justify myself in the eyes of all men, whose judgement in matters of religion and of reputation I must hold in great esteem. I shall therefore discourse of the particulars which these men produce to make this opinion detested and to have it condemned not merely as false but as heretical. To this end they make a shield of their hypocritical zeal for religion. They go about invoking the Bible, which they would have minister to their deceitful purposes. Contrary to the sense of the Bible and the intention of the holy Fathers, if I am not mistaken, they would extend such authorities until even in purely physical matters—where faith is not involved—they would have us altogether abandon reason and the evidence of our senses in favor of some biblical passage, though under the surface meaning of its words this passage may contain a different sense… .

…I think that in discussions of physical problems we ought to begin not from the authority of scriptural passages, but from sense-experiences and necessary demonstrations; for the holy Bible and the phenomena of nature proceed alike from the divine Word, the former as the dictate of the Holy Ghost and the latter as the observant executrix of God's commands. It is necessary for the Bible, in order to be accommodated to the understanding of every man, to speak many things which appear to differ from the absolute truth so far as the bare meaning of the words is concerned. But Nature, on the other hand, is inexorable and immutable; she never transgresses the laws imposed upon her, or cares a whit whether her abstruse reasons and methods of operation are understandable to men. For that reason it appears that nothing physical which sense-experience sets before our eyes, or which necessary demonstrations prove to us, ought to be called in question (much less condemned) upon the testimony of biblical passages which may have some different meaning beneath their words. For the Bible is not chained in every expression to conditions as strict as those which govern all physical effects; nor is God any less excellently revealed in Nature's actions than in the sacred statements of the Bible… .

I do not wish to place in the number of such lay writers some theologians whom I consider men of profound learning and devout behavior, and who are therefore held by me in great esteem and veneration. Yet I cannot deny that I feel some discomfort which I should like to have removed, when I hear them pretend to the power of constraining others by scriptural authority to follow in a physical dispute that opinion which they think best agrees with the Bible, and then believe themselves not bound to answer the opposing reasons and experiences. In explanation and support of this opinion they say that since theology is queen of all the sciences, she need not bend in any way to accommodate herself to the teachings of less worthy sciences which are subordinate to her; these others must rather be referred to her as to their supreme empress, changing and altering their conclusions according to her statues and decrees… .

First, I question whether there is not some equivocation in failing to specify the virtues which entitle sacred theology to the title of "queen." It might deserve that name by reason of including everything that is learned from all the other sciences and establishing everything by better methods and with profounder learning. It is thus, for example, that the rules for measuring fields and keeping accounts are much more excellently contained in arithmetic and in the geometry of Euclid than in the practices of surveyors and accountants. Or theology might be queen because of being occupied with a subject which excels in dignity all the subjects which compose the other sciences, and because her teachings are divulged in more sublime ways.

That the title and authority of queen belongs to theology in the first sense, I think will not be affirmed by theologians who have any skill in the other sciences. None of these, I think, will say that geometry, astronomy, music, and medicine are much more excellently contained in the Bible than they are in the books of Archimedes, Ptolemy, Boethius, and Galen. Hence it seems likely that regal pre-eminence is given to theology in the second sense; that is, by reason of its subject and the miraculous communication of divine revelation of conclusions which could not be conceived by men in any other way, concerning chiefly the attainment of eternal blessedness.

Let us grant then that theology is conversant with the loftiest divine contemplation, and occupies the regal throne among sciences by dignity. But acquiring the highest authority in this way, if she does not descend to the lower and humbler speculations of the subordinate sciences and has no regard for them because they are not concerned with blessedness, then her professors should not arrogate to themselves the authority to decide on controversies in professions which they have neither studied nor practiced. Why, this would be as if an absolute despot, being neither a physician nor an architect but knowing himself free to command, should undertake to administer medicines and erect buildings according to his whim—at grave peril of his poor patients' lives, and the speedy collapse of his edifices.

Again, to command that the very professors of astronomy themselves see to the refutation of their own observations and proofs as mere fallacies and sophisms is to enjoin something that lies beyond any possibility of accomplishment. For this would amount to commanding that they must not see what they see and must not understand what they know, and that in searching they must find the opposite of what they actually encounter. Before this could be done they would have to be taught how to make one mental faculty command another, and the inferior powers the superior, so that the imagination and the will might be forced to believe the opposite of what the intellect understands. I am referring at all times to merely physical propositions, and not to supernatural things which are matters of faith.

* * *

Besides, I question the truth of the statement that the church commands us to hold as matters of faith all physical conclusions bearing the stamp of harmonious interpretation by all the Fathers…. So far as I can find, all that is really prohibited is the "perverting into senses contrary to that of the holy Church or that of the concurrent agreement of the Fathers those passages, and those alone, which pertain to faith or ethics, or which concern the edification of Christian doctrine." … But the mobility or stability of the earth or sun is neither a matter of faith nor one contrary to ethics.

4

The Scientific Revolution: Newton

In 1998, Michael H. Hart issued the second edition of his book *The 100: A Ranking of the Most Influential Persons in History.* As in the first edition, he ranked Isaac Newton as the second most influential person in history behind Muhammad and ahead of Jesus. The following selection is his chapter on Newton in which he explains the choice he made. That Newton is the leading scientist of all time was seconded by a Nobel physicist at the University of Chicago who, on the 300th anniversary of the publication of Newton's *Principia Mathematica* in 1987, said that among scientists Einstein ranks "a very distant second" behind Newton.

Discussion Questions

1. What are the major fields in which Newton made his most important contributions?

2. What does Hart think is the most significant overall contribution Newton made to science?

3. In what ways does Hart think that Newton's contributions extend beyond science?

4. Do you think that Hart makes his case that Newton ought to rank number 2?

Isaac Newton (1642–1727)

Isaac Newton, the greatest and most influential scientist who ever lived, was born in Woolsthorpe, England, on Christmas Day, 1642, the same year that Galileo died. Like Muhammad, he was born after the death of his father. As a child, he showed considerable mechanical aptitude, and was very clever with his hands. Although a bright child, he was inattentive in school and did not attract much attention. When he was a teenager, his mother took him out of school, hoping that he would become a successful farmer. Fortunately, she was persuaded that his principal talents lay elsewhere, and at eighteen, he entered Cambridge University. There, he rapidly absorbed what was then known of science and mathematics, and soon moved on to his own independent research. Between his twenty-first and twenty-seventh years, he laid the foundations for the scientific theories that subsequently revolutionized the world.

The middle of the seventeenth century was a period of great scientific ferment. The invention of the telescope near the beginning of the century had revolutionized the entire study of astronomy. The English philosopher Francis Bacon and the French philosopher René Descartes had both urged scientists throughout Europe to cease relying on the authority of Aristotle and to experiment and observe for themselves. What Bacon and Descartes had preached, the great Galileo had practiced. His astronomical observations, using the newly invented telescope, had revolutionized the study of astronomy, and his mechanical experiments had established what is now known as Newton's first law of motion.

Other great scientists, such as William Harvey, who discovered the circulation of the blood, and Johannes Kepler, who discovered the laws describing the motions of the planets around the sun, were bringing new basic information to the scientific community. Still, pure science was largely a plaything of intellectuals, and as yet there was no proof that when applied to technology, science could revolutionize the whole mode of human life, as Francis Bacon had predicted.

Although Copernicus and Galileo had swept aside some of the misconceptions of ancient science and contributed to a greater understanding of the universe, no set of principles had been formulated that could turn this collection of seemingly unrelated facts into a unified theory with which to make scientific predictions. It was Isaac Newton who supplied that unified theory and set modern science on the course which it has followed ever since.

Newton was always reluctant to publish his results, and although he had formulated the basic ideas behind most of his work by 1669, many of his theories were not made public until much later. The first of his discoveries to be published was his groundbreaking work on the nature of light. In a series of careful experiments, Newton had discovered that ordinary white light is a mixture of all the colors of the rainbow. He had also made a careful analysis of the consequences of the laws of the reflection and refraction of light. Using these laws, he had in 1668 designed and actually built the first reflecting telescope, the type of telescope that is used in most major astronomical observatories today. These discoveries, together with the results of many other optical experiments which he had performed, were presented by Newton before the British Royal Society when he was twenty-nine years old.

Newton's achievements in optics alone would probably entitle him to a place on this list; however, they are considerably less important than his accomplishments in pure mathematics and mechanics. His major mathematical contribution was his invention of integral calculus, which he probably devised when he was twenty-three or twenty-four years old. That invention, the most important achievement of modern mathematics, is not merely the seed out of which much of modern mathematical theory has grown, it is also the essential tool without which most of the subsequent progress in modern science would have been impossible. Had Newton done nothing else, the invention of integral calculus by itself would have entitled him to a fairly high place on this list.

Newton's most important discoveries, however, were in the field of mechanics, the science of how material objects move. Galileo had discovered the first law of motion, which describes the motion of objects if they are not subjected to any exterior forces. In practice, of course, all objects are subjected to exterior forces, and the most important question in mechanics is how objects move under such circumstances. This problem was solved by Newton in his famous second law of motion, which may rightly be considered the most fundamental law of classical physics. The second law (described mathematically by the equation $F = ma$) states that the acceleration of an object (i.e., the rate at which its velocity changes) is equal to the net force on the object divided by the object's mass. To those first two laws, Newton added his famous third law of motion

(which states that for each action—i.e., physical force—there is an equal and opposite reaction), and the most famous of his scientific laws, the law of universal gravitation. This set of four laws, taken conjointly, form a unified system by means of which virtually all macroscopic mechanical systems, from the swinging of a pendulum to the motion of the planets in their orbits around the sun, may be investigated, and their behavior predicted. Newton did not merely state these laws of mechanics; he himself, using the mathematical tools of the calculus, showed how these fundamental laws could be applied to the solution of actual problems.

Newton's laws can be and have been applied to an extremely broad range of scientific and engineering problems. During his lifetime, the most dramatic application of his laws was made in the field of astronomy. In this area, too, Newton led the way. In 1687, he published his great work, the *Mathematical Principles of Natural Philosophy* (usually referred to simply as the *Principia*), in which he presented his law of gravitation and laws of motion. Newton showed how these laws could be used to predict precisely the motions of the planets around the sun. The principal problem of dynamical astronomy—that is, the problem of predicting exactly the positions and motions of the stars and planets—was thereby completely solved by Newton in one magnificent sweep. For this reason, Newton is often considered the greatest of all astronomers.

What, then, is our assessment of Newton's scientific importance? If one looks at the index of an encyclopedia of science, one will find more references (perhaps two or three times as many) to Newton and to his laws and discoveries than to any other individual scientist. Furthermore, one should consider what other great scientists have said about Newton. Leibniz, no friend of Sir Isaac's, and a man with whom he engaged in a bitter dispute, wrote: "Taking mathematics from the beginning of the world to the time when Newton lived, what he has done is much the better part." The great French scientist Laplace wrote: "The *Principia* is preeminent above any other production of human genius." Lagrange frequently stated that Newton was the greatest genius who ever lived, while Ernst Mach, writing in 1901, said: "All that has been accomplished in mathematics since his day has been a deductive, formal, and mathematical development of mechanics on the basis of Newton's laws." This, perhaps, is the crux of Newton's great accomplishment: he found science a hodgepodge of isolated facts and laws, capable of describing some phenomena but of predicting only a few; he left us a unified system of laws, which were capable of application to an enormous range of physical phenomena, and which could be used to make exact predictions.

In a brief summary like this, it is not possible to detail all of Newton's discoveries; consequently, many of the lesser ones have been omitted, although they were important achievements in their own right. Newton made significant contributions to thermodynamics (the study of heat) and to acoustics (the study of sound); he enunciated the extremely important physical principles of conservation of momentum and conservation of angular momentum; he discovered the binomial theorem in mathematics; and he gave the first cogent explanation of the origin of the stars.

Now, one might grant that Newton was by far the greatest and most influential scientist who ever lived but still ask why he should be ranked higher than such major political figures as Alexander the Great or George Washington, and ahead of such major religious figures as Jesus Christ and Gautama Buddha. My own view is that even though political changes are of significance, it is fair to say that most people in the world were living the same way 500 years after Alexander's death as their forebears had lived five centuries before his time. Similarly, in most of their daily activities, the majority of human beings were living the same way in 1500 A.D. as human beings had been living in 1500 B.C. In the last five centuries, however, with the rise of modern science, the everyday life of most human beings has been completely revolutionized. We dress differently, eat different foods, work at different jobs, and spend our leisure time a great deal differently than people did in 1500 A.D. Scientific discoveries have not only revolutionized technology and economics; they have also completely changed politics, religious thinking, art, and philosophy. Few aspects of human activity have remained unchanged by this scientific revolution, and it is for this reason that so many scientists and inventors are to be found on this list. Newton was not only the most brilliant of all scientists; he was also the most influential figure in the development of scientific theory, and therefore well merits a position at or near the top of any list of the world's most influential persons.

Newton died in 1727, and was buried in Westminster Abbey, the first scientist to be accorded that honor.

5

The Age of Enlightenment

The Norwegian author, Jostein Gaarder, has combined in her book, *Sophie's World: A Novel About the History of Philosophy*, what one book reviewer called, "a short history of Western philosophy … embedded in the wrapping of a suspense novel." In a series of exchanges between Sophie, a 14-year-old Norwegian girl, and her teacher, the mysterious Alberto, some two thousand years of philosophy is imparted in bits and pieces, and its meanings used to unravel a strange set of circumstances. Suspense aside, this excerpt highlights the key concepts of the late 18th century intellectual movement known as the Enlightenment. Inspired by the scientific and rational theories of Newton, Galileo, Locke and Hobbes, a group of French writers known as the philosophes, not only popularized the new thinking of the day, but also sought to apply those principles to human society. The leaders of the movement, Voltaire, Rousseau and Montesquieu, attacked the so-called "unenlightened" institutions of monarchy, organized religion, mercantilism and class hierarchy presently existing in France, and advocated their reform. They reasoned that human society must, like the physical world, be governed by natural, universal laws that humans could employ to correct the abuses of the past and present. Modeling the institutions of government, the economy, social classes, the church and the schools, on the principles described in the following passage, would, so the philosophes believed, lead humankind into an era of unparalleled progress, indeed, would create a paradise on earth.

Discussion Questions

1. What similarities do the ideas in this passage share with those contained in Galileo's letter or in the sentiments of Tom Paine?

2. What meaning did the philosophes give to nature? Progress? Do they have the same meaning today?

3. Reason, or rationalism, is a key component of enlightenment thought. How was it used to support the arguments of the philosophes? Do you think it is as important in justifying present day institutions and policies as in the 18th century?

4. Would you consider yourself a philosophe, or do you think that too many of their ideas are wrong?

5. What was the long-term effect of the Enlightenment on Western values and society? Have the key ideas of the Enlightenment thinkers been discredited, or do they still apply to today's world?

Jostein Gaarder

❝ After Hume, the next great philosopher was the German, Immanuel Kant. But France also had many important thinkers in the eighteenth century. We could say that the philosophical center of gravity in Europe in the eighteenth century was in England in the first half, in France in the middle, and in Germany toward the end of it."

"A shift from west to east, in other words."

"Precisely. Let me outline some of the ideas that many of the French Enlightenment philosophers had in common. The important names are *Montesquieu, Voltaire, and Rousseau,* but there were many, many others. I shall concentrate on seven points."

"Thanks, that I am painfully aware of."

Sophie handed him the card from Hilde's father. Alberto sighed deeply, "He could have saved himself the trouble . . . the first key words, then, are *opposition to authority.* Many of the French Enlightenment philosophers visited England, which was in many ways more liberal than their home country, and were intrigued by the English natural sciences, especially Newton and his universal physics. But they were also inspired by British philosophy, in particular by Locke and his political philosophy. Once back in France, they become increasingly opposed to the old authority. They thought it was essential to remain skeptical of all inherited truths, the idea being that the individual must find his own answer to every question. The tradition of Descartes was very inspiring in this respect."

"Because he was the one who built everything up from the ground."

"Quite so. The opposition to authority was not least directed against the power of the clergy, the king, and the nobility. During the eighteenth century, these institutions had even more power in France than they had in England."

"Then came the French Revolution."

"Yes, in 1789. But the revolutionary ideas arose much earlier. The next key word is *rationalism.*"

"I thought rationalism went out with Hume."

"Hume himself did not die until 1776. That was about twenty years after Montesquieu and only two years before Voltaire and Rousseau, who both died in 1778. But all three had been to England and were familiar with the philosophy of Locke. You may recall that Locke was not consistent in his empiricism. He believed, for example, that faith in God and certain moral norms were inherent in human reason. This idea is also the core of the French Enlightenment."

"You also said that the French have always been more rational than the British."

"Yes, a difference that goes right back to the Middle Ages. When the British speak of 'common sense,' the French usually speak of 'evident.' The English expression means 'what everybody knows,' the French means 'what is obvious'—to one's reason, that is."

"I see."

"Like the humanists of antiquity—such as Socrates and the Stoics—most of the Enlightenment philosophers had an unshakable faith in human reason. This was so characteristic that the French Enlightenment is often called the Age of Reason. The new natural sciences had revealed that nature was subject to reason. Now the Enlightenment philosophers saw it as their duty to lay a foundation for morals, religion, and ethics in accordance with man's immutable reason. This led to the *enlightenment movement."*

"The third point."

"Now was the time to start 'enlightening' the masses. This was to be the basis for a better society. People thought that poverty and oppression were the fault of ignorance and superstition. Great attention was therefore focused on the education of children and of the people. It is no accident that the science of pedagogy was founded during the Enlightenment."

"So schools date from the Middle Ages, and pedagogy from the Enlightenment."

"You could say that. The greatest monument to the enlightenment movement was characteristically enough a huge encyclopedia. I refer to the Encyclopedia in 28 volumes published during the years from 1751 to 1772. All the great philosophers and men of letters contributed to it. 'Everything is to be found here,' it was said, 'from the way needles are made to the way cannons are founded.'"

"The next point is *cultural optimism,*" Sophie said... .

"The Enlightenment philosophers thought that once reason and knowledge became widespread, humanity would make great progress. It could only be a question of time before irrationalism and ignorance would give way to an 'enlightened' humanity. This thought was dominant in Western Europe until the last couple of decades. Today we are no longer so convinced that all 'developments' are to the good.

"But this criticism of 'civilization' was already being voiced by French Enlightenment philosophers."

"Maybe we should have listened to them."

"For some, the new catchphrase was *back to nature.* But 'nature' to the Enlightenment philosophers meant almost the same as 'reason,' since human reason was a gift of nature rather than of religion or of 'civilization.' It was observed that the so-called primitive peoples were frequently both healthier and happier than Europeans, and this, it was said, was because they had not been 'civilized.' Rousseau proposed the catchphrase, 'We should return to nature.' For nature is good, and man is 'by nature' good; it is civilization which ruins him. Rousseau also believed that the child should be allowed to remain in its 'naturally' innocent state as long as possible. It would not be wrong to say that the idea of the intrinsic value of childhood dates from the Enlightenment. Previously, childhood had been considered merely a preparation for adult life. But we are all human beings—and we live our life on this earth, even when we are children."

"I should think so!"

"Religion, they thought, had to be made natural."

"What exactly did they mean by that?"

"They meant that religion also had to be brought into harmony with 'natural' reason. There were many who fought for what one could call *a natural religion,* and that is the sixth point on the list. At the time there were a lot of confirmed materialists who did not believe in a God, and who professed to atheism. But most of the Enlightenment philosophers thought it was irrational to imagine a world without God. The world was far too rational for that. Newton held the same view, for example. It was also considered rational to believe in the immortality of the soul. Just as for Descartes, whether or not man has an immortal soul was held to be more a question of reason than of faith."

"That I find very strange. To me, it's a typical case of what you believe, not of what you know."

"That's because you don't live in the eighteenth century. According to the Enlightenment philosophers, what religion needed was to be stripped of all the irrational dogmas or doctrines that had got attached to the simple teachings of Jesus during the course of ecclesiastical history."

"I see."

"Many people consequently professed to what is known as *Deism.*"

"What is that?"

"By Deism we mean a belief that God created the world ages and ages ago, but has not revealed himself to the world since. Thus God is reduced to the 'Supreme Being' who only reveals himself to mankind through nature and natural laws, never in any 'supernatural' way. We find a similar 'philosophical God' in the writings of Aristotle. For him, God was the 'formal cause' or 'first mover.'"

"So now there's only one point left, *human rights.*"

"And yet this is perhaps the most important. On the whole, you could say that the French Enlightenment was more practical than the English philosophy."

"You mean they lived according to their philosophy?"

"Yes, very much so. The French Enlightenment philosophers did not content themselves with theoretical views on man's place in society. They fought actively for what they called the 'natural rights' of the citizen. At first, this took the form of a campaign against censorship—for the freedom of the press. But also in matters of religion, morals, and politics, the individual's right to freedom of thought and utterance had to be secured. They also fought for the abolition of slavery and for a more humane treatment of criminals."

"I think I agree with most of that."

"The principle of the 'inviolability of the individual' culminated in the Declaration of the Rights of Man and Citizen adopted by the French National Assembly in 1789. This Declaration of Human Rights was the basis for our own Norwegian Constitution of 1814."

"But a lot of people still have to fight for these rights."

"Yes, unhappily. But the Enlightenment philosophers wanted to establish certain rights that everybody was entitled to simply by being born. That was what they meant by natural rights.

"We still speak of a 'natural right' which can often be in conflict with the laws of the land. And we constantly find individuals, or even whole nations, that claim this 'natural right' when they rebel against anarchy, servitude, and oppression."

"What about women's rights?"

"The French Revolution in 1787 established a number of rights for all 'citizens.' But a citizen was nearly always considered to be a man. Yet it was the French Revolution that gave us the first inklings of feminism."

"It was about time!"

"As early as 1787 the Enlightenment philosopher *Condorcet* published a treatise on the rights of women. He held that women had the same 'natural rights' as men. During the Revolution of 1789, women were extremely active in the fight against the old feudal regime. For example, it was women who led the demonstrations that forced the king away from his palace at Versailles. Women's groups were formed in Paris. In addition to the demand for the same political rights as men, they also demanded changes in the marriage laws and in women's social conditions."

"Did they get equal rights?"

"No. Just as on so many subsequent occasions, the question of women's rights was exploited in the heat of the struggle, but as soon as things fell into place in a new regime, the old male-dominated society was reintroduced."

"Typical!"

"One of those who fought hardest for the rights of women during the French Revolution was *Olympe de Gouges*. In 1791—two years after the revolution—she published a declaration on the rights of women. The declaration on the rights of the citizen had not included any article on women's natural rights. Olympe de Gouges now demanded all the some rights for women as for men.

"What happened?"

"She was beheaded in 1793. And all political activity for women was banned."

"How shameful!"

"It was not until the nineteenth century that feminism really got under way, not only in France but also in the rest of Europe. Little by little this struggle began to bear fruit. But in Norway, for example, women did not get the right to vote until 1913. And women in many parts of the world still have a lot to fight for."

"They can count on my support." …

6

The Enlightenment: Deism

Some historians describe the European Enlightenment of the 18th century as the first fully modern worldview in history. The agents of this movement, whom we usually call the *philosophes* (men like Voltaire, Diderot and Montesquieu), believed that earlier thinkers like Descartes, Locke and Newton had opened up an entirely new, and true, view of man, society and nature. They believed that using reason to understand the laws of nature would lead inevitably to progress and the universal improvement of the human condition. But they also recognized that progress could only be achieved through the destruction of what they called the *ancien regime* (essentially a combination of absolutism, the church and mercantilism). Believing that the liberation of the mind was the first step toward progress, they leveled their guns at institutionalized religion and created what they thought would be a benign "natural" religion, deism.

Among the first full-scale attacks against institutionalized Christianity was Thomas Paine's *Age of Reason*, written in 1794, a selection from which follows.

Discussion Questions

1. What does Paine say he believes in? What doesn't he believe in?

2. For what reasons does he reject most institutionalized religions like Christianity?

3. What is Paine's standard of evidence?

4. Why does he consider Christianity to be a "contrivance?"

5. What are the foundations on which he thinks we can build a "true" religion?

The Age of Reason

To My Fellow Citizens of the United States of America

I put the following work under your protection. It contains my opinion upon religion. You will do me the justice to remember that I have always strenuously supported the right of every man to his opinion however different that opinion might be to mine. He who denies to another this right makes a slave of himself to his present opinion, because he precludes himself the right of changing it.

The most formidable weapon against errors of every kind is reason. I have never used any other, and I trust I never shall.

Your affectionate friend and fellow citizen,

Thomas Paine
Luxembourg (Paris), 8th Pluvôise.
Second year of the French Republic, one and indivisible,
January 27th, O. S. 1791.

It has been my intention, for several years past, to publish my thoughts upon religion. I am well aware of the difficulties that attend the subject and, from that consideration, had reserved it to a more advanced period of life. I intended it to be the last offering I should make to my fellow Citizens of all nations, and that at a time when the purity of the motive that induced me to it could not admit of a question, even by those who might disapprove the work.

The circumstance that has now taken place in France of the total abolition of the whole national order of priesthood, and of everything appertaining to compulsive systems of religion, and compulsive articles of faith, has not only precipitated my intention, but rendered a work of this kind exceedingly necessary, lest in the general wreck of superstition, of false systems of government and false theology, we lose sight of morality, of humanity, and of the theology that is true.

As several of my colleagues, and others of my fellow citizens of France, have given me the example of making their voluntary and individual profession of faith, I also will make mine; and I do this with all that sincerity and frankness with which the mind of man communicates with itself.

I believe in one God, and no more; and I hope for happiness beyond this life.

I believe in the equality of man; and I believe that religious duties consist in doing justice, loving mercy, and endeavoring to make our fellow creatures happy.

But, lest it should be supposed that I believe in many other things in addition to these, I shall, in the progress of this work, declare the things I do not believe, and my reasons for not believing them.

I do not believe in the creed professed by the Jewish church, by the Roman church, by the Greek church, by the Turkish church, by the Protestant church, nor by any church that I know of. My own mind is my own church.

All national institutions of churches, whether Jewish, Christian, or Turkish, appear to me no other than human inventions, set up to terrify and enslave mankind, and monopolize power and profit.

I do not mean by this declaration to condemn those who believe otherwise; they have the same right to their belief as I have to mine. But it is necessary to the happiness of man that he be mentally faithful to himself. Infidelity does not consist in believing or in disbelieving; it consists in professing to believe what he does not believe.

It is impossible to calculate the moral mischief, if I may so express it, that mental lying has produced in society. When a man has so far corrupted and prostituted the chastity of his mind as to subscribe his professional belief to things he does not believe, he has prepared himself for the commission of every other crime. He takes up the trade of a priest for the sake of gain, and in order to qualify himself for that trade he begins with a perjury. Can we conceive anything more destructive to morality than this? …

Every national church or religion has established itself by pretending some special mission from God, communicated to certain individuals. The Jews have their Moses; the Christians their Jesus Christ, their apostles and saints; and the Turks their Mohammed, as if the way to God was not open to every man alike.

Each of those churches show certain books which they call "revelation," or the word of God. The Jews say that their word of God was given by God to Moses, face to face; the Christians say their word of God came by divine inspiration; and the Turks say that their word of God (the Koran) was brought by an angel from heaven. Each of those churches accuse the other of unbelief; and for my part I disbelieve them all… .

When Moses told the children of Israel that he received the two tables of the Commandments from the hands of God, they were not obliged to believe him, because they had no other authority for it than his telling them so; and I have no other authority for it than some historian telling me so. The Commandments carry no internal evidence of divinity with them; they contain some good moral precepts, such as any man qualified to be a lawgiver, or a legislator, could produce himself without having recourse to supernatural intervention.*

When I am told that the Koran was written in heaven and brought to Mohammed by an angel, the account comes too near the same kind of hearsay evidence and secondhand authority as the former. I did not see the angel myself, and therefore I have a right not to believe it.

When also I am told that a woman called the Virgin Mary said, or gave out, that she was with child without any cohabitation with a man, and that her betrothed husband, Joseph, said that an angel told him so, I have a right to believe them or not; such a circumstance required a much stronger evidence than their bare word for it; but we have not even this—for neither Joseph nor Mary wrote any such matter themselves; it is only reported by others that they said so—it is hearsay upon hearsay, and I do not choose to rest my belief upon such evidence… .

Nothing that is here said can apply, even with the most distant disrespect, to the real character of Jesus Christ. He was a virtuous and an amiable man. The morality that he preached and practiced was of the most benevolent kind; and though similar systems of morality had been preached by Confucius and by some of the Greek philosophers many years before, by the Quakers since, and by many good men in all ages, it has not been exceeded by any.

---

* It is, however, necessary to except the declaration which says that God visits *the sins of the fathers upon the children; it is contrary to every principle of moral justice.*

Jesus Christ wrote no account of himself, of his birth, parentage, or anything else; not a line of what is called the New Testament is of his own writing. The history of him is altogether the work of other people; and as to the account of his resurrection and ascension, it was the necessary counterpart to the story of his birth. His historians, having brought him into the world in a supernatural manner, were obliged to take him out again in the same manner, or the first part of the story must have fallen to the ground.

The wretched contrivance with which the latter part is told exceeds everything that went before it. The first part, that of the miraculous conception, was not a thing that admitted of publicity; and therefore the tellers of this part of the story had this advantage that, though they might not be credited, they could not be detected. They could not be expected to prove it because it was not one of those things that admitted of proof, and it was impossible that the person of whom it was told could prove it himself.

But the resurrection of a dead person from the grave, and his ascension through the air, is a thing very different, as to the evidence it admits of, to the invisible conception of a child in the womb. The resurrection and ascension, supposing them to have taken place, admitted of public and ocular demonstration like that of the ascension of a balloon or the sun at noonday, to all Jerusalem at least. A thing which everybody is required to believe requires that the proof and evidence of it should be equal to all and universal; and as the public visibility of this last related act was the only evidence that could give sanction to the former part, the whole of it falls to the ground because that evidence never was given. Instead of this, a small number of persons, not more than eight or nine, are introduced as proxies for the whole world, to say they saw it, and all the rest of the world are called upon to believe it. But it appears that Thomas did not believe the resurrection and, as they say, would not believe without having ocular and manual

demonstration himself. So *neither will I,* and the reason is equally as good for me and for every other person as for Thomas.... .

But some, perhaps, will say: Are we to have no word of God—no revelation? I answer, Yes; there is a word of God; there is a revelation.

The word of God is the creation we behold: and it is in this word, which no human invention can counterfeit or alter, that God speaketh universally to man.... .

It is only in the *Creation* that all our ideas and conceptions of a *word of God* can unite. The Creation speaks a universal language, independently of human speech or human language, multiplied and various as they may be. It is an ever-existing original, which every man can read. It cannot be forged; it cannot be counterfeited; it cannot be lost; it cannot be altered; it cannot be suppressed. It does not depend upon the will of man whether it shall be published or not; it publishes itself from one end of the earth to the other. It preaches to all nations and to all worlds; and this *word of God* reveals to man all that is necessary for man to know of God.... .

It has been by rejecting the evidence that the word or works of God in the creation afford to our senses, and the action of our reason upon that evidence, that so many wild and whimsical systems of faith and of religion have been fabricated and set up. There may be many systems of religion that, so far from being morally bad, are in many respects morally good; but there can be but one that is true; and that one necessarily must, as it ever will, be in all things consistent with the everexisting word of God that we behold in his works. But such is the strange construction of the Christian system of faith that every evidence the Heavens afford to man either directly contradicts it or renders it absurd.... .

It is certain that in one point all nations of the earth and all religions agree—all believe in a God; the things in which they disagree are the redundancies annexed to that belief; and, therefore, if ever a universal religion should prevail, it will not be by believing anything new, but in getting rid of redundancies and believing as man believed at first. Adam, if ever there were such a man, was created a Deist; but in the meantime, let every man follow, as he has a right to do, the religion and the worship he prefers.

7

The Declaration of Independence

One of the earliest and most profound statements reflecting the Enlightenment values of natural law, reason and progress is found in the Declaration of Independence, issued on the eve of the American Revolution in 1776. Most of the ideas contained in the *Declaration* did not originate with Jefferson, but can be traced back to various English political philosophers of the 17th century, chief among them, John Locke (1632–1704). In his *Two Treatises of Government*, Locke set forth the view that all humans were born with certain natural rights, which no government could abridge. Government itself was to be the instrument of the people's will, its powers restricted by a social contract, or constitution, that the people could alter, as they could elect their officials, thus preventing tyranny and abuse of power. If a tyranny did develop, the people had the right of rebellion. Thus, Locke's views, as well as those of Jefferson's, are thought to be classic statements associated with the liberal state—popular sovereignty, representative government and constitutionalism.

Discussion Questions

1. What are natural rights? Do you think they exist today? What natural rights does Jefferson identify in the *Declaration*? Do you think Americans accept the premises and values of the document today?

2. The *Declaration of Independence* is a rationale for the American revolution as much as it is a statement of colonial values. What was the rationale used by the Americans, and is similar justification used by revolutionaries today?

3. What do you think Jefferson meant by his statement that "all men are created equal?" Is there a contradiction between the liberty and equality of which Jefferson speaks?

4. Peoples around the world, from Mao to Meiji Japan to Bolivar to Mandela to Gandhi to Gorbachev have been inspired by the *Declaration of Independence*. How do you account for its universal appeal?

The American Declaration of Independence

In Congress, July 4, 1776 the Unanimous Declaration of the Thirteen United States of America

When in the course of human events it becomes necessary for one people to dissolve the political bands which have connected them with another, and to assume among the powers of the earth, the separate and equal station to which the Laws of Nature and of Nature's God entitle them, a decent respect to the opinions of mankind requires that they should declare the causes which impel them to the separation.

We hold these truths to be self-evident, that all men are created equal, that they are endowed by their Creator with certain unalienable Rights, that among these are Life, Liberty and the pursuit of Happiness.—That to secure these rights, Governments are instituted among Men, deriving their just powers from the consent of the governed.—That whenever any Form of Government becomes destructive of these ends, it is the Right of the People to alter or to abolish it, and to institute new Government, laying its foundation on such principles, and organizing its powers in such form, as to them shall seem most likely to effect their Safety and Happiness. Prudence, indeed, will dictate that Governments long established should not be changed for light and transient causes; and accordingly all experience hath shewn, that mankind are more disposed to suffer, while evils are sufferable, than to right themselves by abolishing the forms to which they are accustomed. But when a long train of abuses and usurpations, pursuing invariably the same Object, evinces a design to reduce them under absolute Despotism, it is their right, it is their duty to throw off such Government, and to provide new Guards for their future security.—Such has been the patient sufferance of these Colonies, and such is now the necessity which constrains them to alter their former Systems of Government. The history of the present King of Great Britain is a history of repeated injuries and usurpations, all having in

Thomas Jefferson, The Declaration of Independence, July 2, 1776.

direct object the establishment of an absolute Tyranny over these States. To prove this, let Facts be submitted to a candid world.

He has refused his Assent to Laws, the most wholesome and necessary for the public good.

He has forbidden his Governors to pass Laws of immediate and pressing importance, unless suspended in their operation till his Assent should be obtained; and when so suspended, he has utterly neglected to attend to them.

He has refused to pass other Laws for the accommodation of large districts of people, unless those people would relinquish the right of Representation in the Legislature, a right inestimable to them and formidable to tyrants only.

He has called together legislative bodies at places unusual, uncomfortable, and distant from the depository of their public Records, for the sole purpose of fatiguing them into compliance with his measures.

He has dissolved Representative Houses repeatedly, for opposing with manly firmness his invasions on the rights of the people.

He has refused for a long time, after such dissolutions, to cause others to be elected; whereby the Legislative powers, incapable of Annihilation, have returned to the People at large for their exercise; the State remaining in the mean time exposed to all the dangers of invasion from without, and convulsions within.

He has endeavored to prevent the population of these States; for that purpose obstructing the Laws for Naturalization of Foreigners, refusing to pass others to encourage their migrations hither, and raising the conditions of new Appropriations of Lands.

He has obstructed the Administration of Justice, by refusing his Assent to Laws for establishing judiciary powers.

He has made judges dependent on his will alone, for the tenure of their offices, and the amount of payment of their salaries.

He has erected a multitude of New Offices, and sent hither swarms of Officers to harrass our people, and eat out their substance.

He has kept among us, in times of peace, Standing Armies without the Consent of our legislatures.

He has affected to render the Military independent of and superior to the Civil power.

He has combined with others to subject us to a jurisdiction foreign to our constitution, and unacknowledged by our laws; giving his Assent to their Acts of pretended Legislation:

For quartering large bodies of armed troops among us:

For protecting them, by a mock Trial, from punishment for any Murders which they should commit on the Inhabitants of these States:

For cutting off our Trade with all parts of the world:

For imposing Taxes on us without our Consent:

For depriving us in many cases, of the benefits of Trial by Jury:

For transporting us beyond Seas to be tried for pretended offences:

For abolishing the free System of English Laws in a neighbouring Province, establishing therein an Arbitrary government, and enlarging its Boundaries so as to render it at once an example and fit instrument for introducing the same absolute rule into these Colonies:

For taking away our Charters, abolishing our most valuable Laws, and altering fundamentally the Forms of our Governments:

For suspending our own Legislatures, and declaring themselves invested with power to legislate for us in all cases whatsoever.

He has abdicated Government here, by declaring us out of his Protection and waging War against us.

He has plundered our seas, ravaged our Coasts, burnt our towns, and destroyed the lives of our people.

He is at this time transporting large Armies of foreign Mercenaries to compleat the works of death, desolation and tyranny, already begun with circumstances of Cruelty & perfidy scarcely paralleled in the most barbarous ages, and totally unworthy the Head of a civilized nation.

He has constrained our fellow Citizens taken Captive on the high Seas to bear Arms against their Country, to become the executioners of their friends and Brethren, or to fall themselves by their Hands.

He has excited domestic insurrections amongst us, and has endeavored to bring on the inhabitants of our frontiers; the merciless Indian Savages, whose known rule of warfare, is an undistinguished destruction of all ages, sexes and conditions.

In every stage of these Oppressions We have Petitioned for Redress in the most humble terms: Our repeated Petitions have been answered only by repeated injury. A Prince, whose character is thus marked by every act which may define a Tyrant, is unfit to be the ruler of a free people.

Nor have We been wanting in attentions to our British brethren. We have warned them from time to time of attempts by their legislature to extend an unwarrantable jurisdiction over us. We have reminded them of the circumstances of our emigration and settlement here. We have appealed to their native justice and magnanimity, and we have conjured them by the ties of our common kindred to disavow these usurpations, which would inevitably interrupt our connections and correspondence. They too have been deaf to the voice of justice and of consanguinity. We must, therefore, acquiesce in the necessity, which denounces our Separation, and hold them, as we hold the rest of mankind, Enemies in War, in Peace Friends.

We, therefore, the Representatives of the united States of America, in General Congress, Assembled, appealing to the Supreme Judge of the world for the rectitude of our intentions, do, in the Name, and by Authority of the good People of these Colonies solemnly publish and declare, That these United Colonies are, and of Right ought to be Free and Independent States; that they are Absolved from all Allegiance to the British Crown, and that all political connection between them and the State of Great Britain, is and ought to be totally dissolved; and that as Free and Independent States, they have full Power to levy War, conclude Peace, contract Alliances, establish Commerce, and to do all other Acts and Things which Independent States may of right do.

And for the support of this Declaration, with a firm reliance on protection of divine Providence, we mutually pledge to each other our Lives, our Fortunes and our sacred Honor.

8

The Dust Never Settled

As North Americans continued the process of nation-building with the establishment of the United States of America under the Constitution, their example also served to inspire revolutions in South and Central America in the late 18th and early 19th century. In addition to the example set by the North Americans, the French Revolution of 1789, and, particularly Napoleon's intervention in Spain and Portugal provided an opportunity for those influenced by Enlightenment ideas to act. A generation of revolutionary leaders in the late 18th and early 19th century, including Toussaint L'Ouverture who helped to free Haiti from the French in 1801; Simon Bolivar, "The Liberator," who won his title by creating the modern states of Colombia, Venezuela, Bolivia, Peru and Ecuador; Father Miguel Hildalgo, who pioneered in the independence of Mexico; and Jose de San Martin, whose work led to revolutions in Argentina and Chile by the early 1820's, would usher in a new era in American politics. Yet, as the title of this selection, published anonymously in an Ecuadorian newspaper in 1829 suggests, "the dust never settled."

Discussion Questions

1. To what is the author referring when he writes that "the dust never settled?" What went wrong in the Latin American wars for independence?

2. Compare the American, French and Latin American revolutions? What similarities in goals, ideologies, personalities and events can you identify? What differences existed?

3. Does the same pattern exist in Central and South America today? If not, what has changed?

The Dust Never Settled

Anonymous

On May 25, 1810, the city of Buenos Aires began its political existence. As its example was not followed by the other provinces, it was necessary to use force in order to compel them to espouse the revolutionary cause. While so engaged, the troops of Buenos Aires set a precedent for their subsequent harsh and ignorant behavior by killing the Viceroy Liniers, who had earlier freed that country from the British troops. At the same time they began to persecute the pastors of the Church, in the person of a bishop who was guilty of nothing more than obedience to his vows... .

The Rio de la Plata [Buenos Aires and vicinity] has had but one man who proved capable of serving his country nobly and well, Saavedra quickly proved himself capable of presiding over the destinies of that Republic, but his death soon deprived the country of its one remaining hope. Since that time there has been no order or pattern in Argentine affairs. The federal government took possession of the land, and the land became its victim. Every province recovered its individual sovereignty, which God has given to every man, but that every man tacitly relinquishes to society, which thereupon assumes responsibility for the individual's safety. Nothing is so perilous as inconsistency between a political system and natural law. Each province governed itself, and every military expedition sent against them went down in humiliating defeat. The towns armed and fought each other like enemies. As a result of federation, the nation fell heir to blood, death, and crime of every description, due to the unleashing of the passions of a people who, although they had broken their chains, were devoid of the concepts of right and duty, and could only avoid enslavement by becoming tyrannical themselves.

Elections were characterized by riots and intrigue. Many times, armed soldiers marched to the polls in formation, something unknown even in ancient Rome or in the island of Haiti. Force, faction, and bribery determine everything. And to what purpose?—momentary control amidst times of trouble, battle, and sacrifice. Virtually every government official has been replaced by a blood-stained victor, and those who are removed are made to suffer the misfortune of banishment, proscription, or violent death. Rare are the elections that are free of terrible crimes, and fewer still are the government leaders who have held their posts for the term provided by law or have been succeeded by legally elected leaders... .

However, let us be fair to the Rio de la Plata. What we have just described is not peculiar to that country: its history is that of all Spanish America. We shall again see these same principles, these same processes, these same consequences in every republic, one country differing from another only incidentally, and modified only by circumstances and regional variations.

Throughout America we shall see but a single trend in public affairs. The cycles are

---

From an anonymous editorial in an Equadorian newspaper, 1829.

similar, varying at most according to time and conditions, but otherwise paralleling the stages and the events in the other newborn states.

Nowhere are there legal elections; nowhere do those elected come to office according to the law... . If a Dorrego has been assassinated, assassinations are also being committed in Mexico, Bolivia, and Colombia—September 25 is too recent a date to be forgotten. If Pueyrredon plunders the public treasury [of Buenos Aires], there are those in Colombia who do the same. If [the Argentine province of] Cordoba and Paraguay are ruled by bloody hypocrites, Peru has its General La Mar in a donkey-skin, with the claws of a tiger and an insatiable lust for American blood. If anarchic movements occur in every Argentine province, Chile and Guatemala set such horrible examples that we can scarcely hope for peace. In the Argentine provinces, Sarratea, Rodriguez, and Alvear have compelled their country to house, in the capital, bandits who call themselves liberators... . The lawful authorities have been removed; the provinces have rebelled against the capital; brother wars upon brother—a horror which the Spaniards had prevented—and this war is to the death. Town fights town; city stands against city, each with its own government, and every street is a self-constituted nation. In Central America all is bloodshed and terror!

Though it is true that a government in Buenos Aires lasts scarcely a week, it is equally certain that Bolivia has now followed this monstrous example. No sooner had the illustrious Sucre left that unfortunate country than the traitor Blanco seized, through intrigue, the government which legally belonged to General Santa Cruz. Yet Blanco did not hold it five days before he was captured and killed by a dissatisfied faction, to be followed by a legitimate head, Velazco, who was in turn succeeded by Santa Cruz. Thus, hapless Bolivia has had four different leaders in less than two weeks! Only the Kingdom of Hell could offer so appalling a picture discrediting humanity!

We are amazed at the almost infinite number of subdivisions in the territory of the Argentine, whose condition resembles that of the baronies of old, so that this federation under freedom is like the feudal estates under monarchy. The barons imposed levies, built castles, and ruled as they pleased; they thus defied their sovereign, and on occasion they even fought him. Buenos Aires, Chile, and Guatemala imitate and surpass the practices and doctrines of those barons; thus, extremes clash, and, for the same reasons, personal ambition... .

...From one end to the other, the New World is an abyss of abominations, and, were anything lacking to complete this terrible chaos, Peru could more than supply it. A partisan of the tyrannical Spaniards during the war for independence, Peru, with her liberty not yet fully won, in the very first days of her existence, was the scene of a fraticidal struggle. The country had been cleared of Spaniards from Trujillo to Ica by valorous General San Martin, at the head of the Chileans and Argentines. In the eyes of the people of Lima there was no more of Peru to liberate; thereupon, some promptly undertook to rid the country of San Martin, whose services were most urgently needed. This act of ingratitude interrupted all political progress in Peru... .

There is no good faith in America, nor among the nations of America. Treaties are scraps of paper; constitutions, printed matter; elections, battles; freedom, anarchy; and life, a torment. Such, Fellow-Americans, is our deplorable situation. Unless we change it, death is to be preferred. Anything is better than endless conflict, the indignity of which appears to increase with the violence and the duration of the movement. Let us not delude ourselves— this evil, which increases revolts and mutinies in the armed forces, will eventually compel us to reject the very first constructive principles of political life. We lost all individual rights when, in an effort to obtain them in perfect form, we sacrificed our blood and all that we cherished most, prior to the war—for, if we look back at that time, who will deny that our rights were then more respected? Never were we as badly off as we are at present. At that time we enjoyed positive and tangible benefits, whereas today we have dreams bordering upon illusion, hope feeding upon the future, and disillusionment forever tortured with the bitterness of reality.... .

9

The Age of Romanticism

This selection from Jostein Gaarder's *Sophie's World* discusses the Romantic movement of the late eighteenth and early nineteenth centuries. The emphasis is on some of the key thinkers of the era, their main ideas and how they differed from the Enlightenment of the eighteenth century.

Discussion Questions

1. In what ways did the Romantics challenge the ideas of the Enlightenment?

2. What were the most important Romantic ideas concerning nature, art and human beings?

3. What are the differences between universal and national Romanticism?

4. In what specific ways did Romanticism contribute to the new ideology of nationalism?

Sophie's World

Jostein Gaarder

Alberto Knox was sitting on the step again when Sophie arrived.

"Have a seat," he said, getting straight down to work.

"Previously we spoke of the Renaissance, the Baroque period, and the Enlightenment. Today we are going to talk about *Romanticism,* which could be described as Europe's last great cultural epoch. We are approaching the end of a long story, my child."

"Did Romanticism last that long?"

"It began toward the end of the eighteenth century and lasted till the middle of the nineteenth. But after 1850 one can no longer speak of whole 'epochs' which comprise poetry, philosophy, art, science, and music."

"Was Romanticism one of those epochs?"

"It has been said that Romanticism was Europe's last common approach to life. It started in Germany, arising as a reaction to the Enlightenment's unequivocal emphasis on reason. After Kant and his cool intellectualism, it was as if German youth heaved a sigh of relief."

"What did they replace it with?"

"The new catchwords were 'feeling,' 'imagination,' 'experience,' and 'yearning.' Some of the Enlightenment thinkers had drawn attention to the importance of feeling—not least Rousseau—but at that time it was a criticism of the bias toward reason. What had been an undercurrent now became the mainstream of German culture."

"So Kant's popularity didn't lost very long?"

"Well, it did and it didn't. Many of the Romantics saw themselves as Kant's successors, since Kant had established that there was a limit to what we can know of 'das Ding an sich.' On the other hand, he had underlined the importance of the ego's contribution to knowledge, or cognition. The individual was now completely free to interpret life in his own way. The Romantics exploited this in an almost unrestrained 'ego-worship,' which led to the exaltation of artistic genius."

"Were there a lot of these geniuses?"

"*Beethoven* was one. His music expresses his own feelings and yearnings. Beethoven was in a sense a 'free' artist—unlike the Baroque masters such as Bach and Handel, who composed their works to the glory of God, mostly in strict musical forms."

"I only know the Moonlight Sonata and the Fifth Symphony."

"But you know how romantic the Moonlight Sonata is, and you can hear how dramatically Beethoven expresses himself in the Fifth Symphony."

"You said the Renaissance humanists were individualists too."

"Yes. There were many similarities between the Renaissance and Romanticism. A typical one was the importance of art to human cognition. Kant made a considerable contribution here as well. In his aesthetics he investigated what happens when we are overwhelmed by beauty—in a work of art, for instance. When we abandon ourselves to a work of art with no other intention than the aesthetic experience itself, we are brought closer to an experience of 'das Ding an sich.'"

"So the artist can provide something philosophers can't express?"

"That was the view of the Romantics. According to Kant, the artist plays freely on his faculty of cognition. The German poet *Schiller* developed Kant's thought further. He wrote that the activity of the artist is like playing, and man is only free when he plays, because then he makes up his own rules. The Romantics believed that only art could bring us closer to 'the inexpressible.' Some went as far as to compare the artist to God."

"Because the artist creates his own reality the way God created the world."

"It was said that the artist had a 'universecreating imagination.' In his transports of artistic rapture he could sense the dissolving of the boundary between dream and reality.

"*Novalis,* one of the young geniuses, said that 'the world becomes a dream, and the dream becomes reality.' He wrote a novel called *Heinrich von Ofterdingen* set in Medieval times. It was unfinished when he died in 1801, but it was nevertheless a very significant novel. It tells of the young Heinrich who is searching for the 'blue flower' that he once saw in a dream and has yearned for ever since. The English Romantic poet *Coleridge* expressed the same idea; saying something like this:

> What if you slept? And what if, in your sleep, you dreamed? And what if, in your dream, you went to heaven and there plucked a strange and beautiful flower? And what if, when you awoke, you had the flower in your hand? Ah, what then?"

"How pretty!"

"This yearning for something distant and unattainable was characteristic of the Romantics. They longed for bygone eras, such as the Middle Ages, which now become enthusiastically reappraised after the Enlightenment's negative evaluation. And they longed for distant cultures like the Orient with its mysticism. Or else they would feel drawn to Night, to Twilight, to old ruins and the supernatural. They were preoccupied with what we usually refer to as the dark side of life, or the murky, uncanny, and mystical."

"It sounds to me like an exciting period. Who were these Romantics?"

"Romanticism was in the main an urban phenomenon. In the first half of the last century there was, in fact, a flourishing metropolitan culture in many parts of Europe, not least in Germany. The typical Romantics were young men, often university students, although they did not always take their studies very seriously. They had a decidedly antimiddle class approach to life and could refer to the police or their landladies as philistines, for example, or simply as the enemy."

"I would never have dared rent a room to a Romantic!"

"The first generation of Romantics were young in about 1800, and we could actually call the Romantic Movement Europe's first student uprising. The Romantics were not unlike the hippies a hundred and fifty years later."

"You mean flower power and long hair, strumming their guitars and lying around?"

"Yes. It was once said that 'idleness is the ideal of genius, and indolence the virtue of the Romantic.' It was the duty of the Romantic to experience life—or to dream himself away from it. Day-to-day business could be taken care of by the philistines."

"Byron was a Romantic poet, wasn't he?"

"Yes, both Byron and Shelley were Romantic poets of the so-called Satanic school. Byron, moreover, provided the Romantic Age with its idol, the Byronic hero—the alien, moody, rebellious spirit—in life as well as in art. Byron himself could be both willful and passionate, and being also handsome, he was besieged by women of fashion. Public gossip attributed the romantic adventures of his verses to his own life, but although he had numerous liaisons, true love remained as illusive and as unattainable for him as Novalis's blue flower. Novalis became engaged to a fourteen-year-old girl. She died four days after her fifteenth birthday, but Novalis remained devoted to her for the rest of his short life."

"Did you say she died four days after her fifteenth birthday?"

"Yes . . ."

"I am fifteen years and four days old *today*."

"So you are."

"What was her name?"

"Her name was Sophie."

"What?"

"Yes, it was

"You scare me. Could it be a coincidence?"

"I couldn't say, Sophie. But her name was Sophie."

"Go on!"

"Novalis himself died when he was only twenty-nine. He was one of the 'young dead.' Many of the Romantics died young, usually of tuberculosis. Some committed suicide. . ."

"Ugh!"

"Those who lived to be old usually stopped being Romantics at about the age of thirty. Some of them went on to become thoroughly middle-class and conservative."

"They went over to the enemy, then."

"Maybe. But we were talking about romantic love. The theme of unrequited love was introduced as early as 1774 *by Goethe* in his novel *The Sorrows of Young Werther*. The book ends with young Werther shooting himself when he can't have the woman he loves."

"Was it necessary to go that far?"

"The suicide rate rose after the publication of the novel, and for a time the book was banned in Denmark and Norway. So being a Romantic was not without danger. Strong emotions were involved."

"When you say 'Romantic,' I think of those great big landscape paintings, with dark forests and wild, rugged nature ... preferably in swirling mists."

"Yes, one of the features of Romanticism was this yearning for nature and nature's mysteries. And as I said, it was not the kind of thing that arises in rural areas. You may recall Rousseau, who initiated the slogan 'back to nature.' The Romantics gave this slogan popular currency. Romanticism represents not least a reaction to the Enlightenment's mechanistic universe. It was said that Romanticism implied a renaissance of the old *cosmic consciousness*."

"Explain that, please."

"It means viewing nature as a whole; the Romantics were tracing their roots not only back to Spinoza, but also to Plotinus and Renaissance philosophers like Jakob Böhme and Giordano Bruno. What all these thinkers had in common was that they experienced a divine 'ego' in nature."

"They were Pantheists then…"

"Both Descartes and Hume had drawn a sharp line between the ego and 'extended' reality. Kant had also left behind him a sharp distinction between the cognitive 'I' and nature 'in itself.' Now it was said that nature is nothing but one big 'I.' The Romantics also used the expressions 'world soul' or 'world spirit.'"

"I see."

"The leading Romantic philosopher was *Schelling*, who lived from 1775 to 1854. He wanted to unite mind and matter. All of nature—both the human soul and physical reality—is the expression of one Absolute, or world spirit, he believed."

"Yes, just like Spinoza."

"Nature is visible spirit, spirit is invisible nature, said Schelling, since one senses a 'structuring spirit' everywhere in nature. He also said that matter is slumbering intelligence."

"You'll have to explain that a bit more clearly."

"Schelling saw a 'world spirit' in nature, but he saw the same 'world spirit' in the human mind. The natural and the spiritual are actually expressions of the some thing."

"Yes, why not?"

"World spirit can thus be sought both in nature and in one's own mind. Novalis could therefore say 'the path of mystery leads inwards.' He was saying that man bears the whole universe within himself and comes closest to the mystery of the world by stepping inside himself."

"That's a very lovely thought."

"For many Romantics, philosophy, nature study, and poetry formed a synthesis. Sitting in your attic dashing off inspired verses and investigating the life of plants or the composition of rocks were only two sides of the some coin because nature is not a dead mechanism, it is one living world spirit."

"Another word and I think I'll become a Romantic."

"The Norwegian-born naturalist *Henrik Steffens*—whom Wergeland called 'Norway's departed laurel leaf' because he had settled in Germany—went to Copenhagen in 1801 to lecture on German Romanticism. He characterized the Romantic Movement by saying, 'Tired of the eternal efforts to fight our way through raw matter, we chose another way and sought to embrace the infinite. We went inside ourselves and created a new world...'"

"How can you remember all that?"

"A bagatelle, child."

"Go on, then."

"Schelling also saw a development in nature from earth and rock—to the human mind. He drew attention to very gradual transitions from inanimate nature to more complicated life forms. It was characteristic of the Romantic view in general that nature was thought of as an organism, or in other words, a unity which is constantly developing its innate potentialities. Nature is like a flower unfolding its leaves and petals. Or like a poet unfolding his verses."

"Doesn't that remind you of Aristotle?"

"It does indeed. The Romantic natural philosophy had Aristotelian as well as Neoplatonic overtones. Aristotle had a more organic view of natural processes than the mechanical materialists..."

"Yes, that's what I thought..."

"We find similar ideas at work in the field of history. A man who came to have great significance for the Romantics was the historical philosopher Johann Gottfried von *Herder,* who lived from 1744 to 1803. He believed that history is characterized by continuity, evolution, and design. We say he had a 'dynamic' view of history because he saw it as a process. The Enlightenment philosophers had often had a 'static' view of history. To them, there was only one universal reason which there could be more or less of at various periods. Herder showed that each historical epoch had its own intrinsic value and each nation its own character or 'soul.' The question is whether we can identify with other cultures."

"So, just as we have to identify with another person's situation to understand them better, we have to identify with other cultures to understand them too."

"That is taken for granted nowadays. But in the Romantic period it was a new idea. Romanticism helped strengthen the feeling of national identity. It is no coincidence that the Norwegian struggle for national independence flourished at that particular time—in 1814."

"I see."

"Because Romanticism involved new orientations in so many areas, it has been usual to distinguish between two forms of Romanticism. There is what we call *Universal Romanticism,* referring to the Romantics who were preoccupied with nature, world soul, and artistic genius. This form of Romanticism flourished first, especially around 1800, in Germany, in the town of Jena."

"And the other?"

"The other is the so-called *National Romanticism,* which become popular a little later, especially in the town of Heidelberg. The National Romantics were mainly interested in the history of 'the people,' the language of 'the people,' and the culture of 'the people' in general. And 'the people' were seen as an organism unfolding its innate potentiality— exactly like nature and history."

"Tell me where you live, and I'll tell you who you are."

"What united these two aspects of Romanticism was first and foremost the key word 'organism.' The Romantics considered both a plant and a nation to be a living organism. A poetic work was also a living organism. Language was an organism. The entire physical world, even, was considered one organism. There is therefore no sharp dividing line between National Romanticism and Universal Romanticism. The world spirit was just as much present in the people and in popular culture as in nature and art."

"I see."

"Herder had been the forerunner, collecting folk songs from many lands under the eloquent title *Voices of the People.* He even referred to folktales as 'the mother tongue of the people.' The *Brothers Grimm* and others began to collect folk songs and fairy tales in Heidelberg. You must know of *Grimm's Fairy Tales.*"

"Oh sure, Snow White and the Seven Dwarfs, Rumpelstiltskin, The Frog Prince, Hansel and Gretel..."

"And many more. In Norway we had *Asbøjørnsen and Moe,* who traveled around the country collecting 'folks' own tales.' It was like harvesting a juicy fruit that was suddenly discovered to be both good and nourishing. And it was urgent—the fruit had already begun to fall. Folk songs were collected; the Norwegian language began to be studied scientifically. The old myths and sagas from heathen times were rediscovered, and composers all over Europe began to incorporate folk melodies into their compositions in an attempt to bridge the gap between folk music and art music."

"What's art music?"

"Art music is music composed by a particular person, like Beethoven. Folk music was not written by any particular person, it came from the people. That's why we don't know exactly when the various folk melodies date from. We distinguish in the same way between folktales and art tales."

"So art tales are . . .?"

"They are tales written by an author, like *Hans Christian Andersen.* The fairy tale genre was passionately cultivated by the Romantics. One of the German masters of the genre was *E.T.A. Hoffmann.*"

"I've heard of The Tales of Hoffmann."

"The fairy tale was the absolute literary ideal of the Romantics—in the same way that the absolute art form of the Baroque period was the theater. It gave the poet full scope to explore his own creativity."

"He could play God to a fictional universe."

"Precisely. And this is a good moment to sum up."

"Go ahead."

"The philosophers of Romanticism viewed the 'world soul' as an 'ego' which in a more or less dreamlike state created everything in the world. The philosopher *Fichte* said that nature stems from a higher, unconscious imagination. Schelling said explicitly that the world is 'in God.' God is aware of some of it, he believed, but there are other aspects of nature which represent the unknown in God. For God also has a dark side."

"The thought is fascinating and frightening. It reminds me of Berkeley."

"The relationship between the artist and his work was seen in exactly the same light. The fairy tale gave the writer free rein to exploit his 'universe-creating imagination.' And even the creative act was not always completely conscious. The writer could experience that his story was being written by some innate force. He could practically be in a hypnotic trance while he wrote."

"He could?"

"Yes, but then he would suddenly destroy the illusion. He would intervene in the story and address ironic comments to the reader, so that the reader, at least momentarily, would be reminded that it was, after all, only a story."

"I see."

"At the some time the writer could remind his reader that it was he who was manipulating the fictional universe. This form of disillusion is called 'romantic irony.' *Henrik Ibsen,* for example, lets one of the characters in *Peer Gynt* say: 'One cannot die in the middle of Act Five.'"

"That's a very funny line, actually. What he's really saying is that he's only a fictional character."

"The statement is so paradoxical that we can certainly emphasize it with a new section."

10

Romanticism: Wordsworth

The Romantic movement of the early nineteenth century emerged as a reaction to the Enlightenment. In almost every respect, the Romantics contradicted the basic assumptions of the *philosophes* of the eighteenth century. One of the most obvious points of disagreement was in their respective approaches toward nature. The *philosophes* had emphasized the rational, scientific analysis of the physical universe as a path to progress in human society—to them nature was a thing, an entity, to be observed and studied with the goal of discovering the laws that govern it and are embedded within it.

In the following poem from 1798, William Wordsworth (1770–1850) presents the Romantic approach to nature.

Discussion Questions

1. What passages show that Wordsworth rejects the Enlightenment assessment of nature?

2. What, according to Wordsworth, is the value of nature to human beings?

3. What human qualities does Wordsworth emphasize? How do they differ from those emphasized by the *philosophes*?

The Tables Turned
An Evening Scene on the Same Subject

William Wordsworth (1770–1850)

UP! up! my Friend, and quit your books;
Or surely you'll grow double:
Up! up! my Friend, and clear your looks;
Why all this toil and trouble?

The sun, above the mountain's head,
A freshening lustre mellow
Through all the long green fields has spread,
His first sweet evening yellow.

Books! 'tis a dull and endless strife:
Come, hear the woodland linnet,   10
How sweet his music! on my life,
There's more of wisdom in it.

And hark! how blithe the throstle sings!
He, too, is no mean preacher:
Come forth into the light of things,
Let Nature be your teacher.

She has a world of ready wealth,
Our minds and hearts to bless—
Spontaneous wisdom breathed by health,
Truth breathed by cheerfulness.   20

One impulse from a vernal wood
May teach you more of man,
Of moral evil and of good,
Than all the sages can.

Sweet is the lore which Nature brings;
Our meddling intellect
Mis-shapes the beauteous forms of things:—
We murder to dissect.

Enough of Science and of Art;
Close up those barren leaves;   30
Come forth, and bring with you a heart
That watches and receives.

                    1798.

11

A Definition of Nationalism

Modern nationalism emerged out of the dual revolutions of the 18th century, the French and the Industrial Revolutions. Along with the liberty and equality that were rallying cries of French citizens, were also those of "La Patrie!," the nation, conveying a sense of patriotic community. As Napoleon's armies poured throughout Europe, they carried these inflammatory ideas with them, awakening many to the cause of revolution. The Industrial Revolution created national markets, with railroads and other forms of transportation and communication knitting together heretofore autonomous regions to form a national economic community. Another influence in the emergence of nationalism came from the Romantic Movement, whose championing of individual freedom, emphasis on the emotions rather than reason, and love of nature, encouraged people to "find their roots." Thus, cultural or romantic nationalism was born, particularly among the Germans, whose search for their past led them to conclude that each culture had a heritage and a destiny that was unique to it. In this selection, the contemporary political scientist, Hans Kohn, offers a definition of nationalism that incorporates the earliest expressions of nationalism, with those that developed later in the 19th century, linking nationality with creation of the nation-state.

Discussion Questions

1. Is nationalism a liberal idea, like that of liberty and equality? Did the Liberals of the 19th century advocate nationalism? To whom would nationalism appeal?

2. Has the definition of nationalism changed over time? Is nationalism like religion?

3. What does national or ethnic identity have to do with the creation of a nation-state? Does every nationality or ethnic group that can identify itself as such have the right to a separate, sovereign state?

4. Has nationalism been a largely positive or negative force in world history? What is its present role?

The Roots of Nationalism

What is Nationalism? Nationalism is a state of mind, in which the supreme loyalty of the individual is felt to be due the national-state. A deep attachment to one's native soil, to local traditions and to established territorial authority has existed in varying strength throughout history. But it was not until the end of the eighteenth century that nationalism in the modern sense of the word became a generally recognized sentiment increasingly molding all public and private life. Only very recently has it been demanded that each nationality should form a state, its own state, and that the state should include the whole nationality. Formerly, man's loyalty was due not to the nation-state, but to differing other forms of social authority, political organization and ideological cohesion such as the tribe or clan, the city-state or the feudal lord, the dynastic state, the church or religious group. Throughout many centuries the political ideal was not the nation-state but the, at least, theoretically world-wide empire comprising various nationalities and ethnic groups on the basis of a common civilization and for the assurance of a common peace.

Nationalities are the products of the living forces of history, and therefore fluctuating and never rigid. They are groups of the utmost complexity and defy exact definition. Most of them possess certain objective factors distinguishing them from other nationalities like common descent, language, territory, political entity, customs and traditions, or religion. But it is clear that none of these factors is essential to the existence or definition of nationality. Thus the people of the United States do not claim common descent to form a nationality, and the people of Switzerland speak three or four languages and yet form one well-defined nationality. Although objective factors are of great importance for the formation of nationalities, the most essential element is a living and active corporate will. It is this will which we call nationalism, a state of mind inspiring the large majority of a people and claiming to inspire all of its members. It asserts that the nationstate is the ideal and the only legitimate form of political organization and that the nationality is the source of all cultural creative energy and of economic well-being.

12

Aspects of Nationalism

1. Feeling of uniqueness identified with a "nationality" group as seen in:
   a. Common language, culture, territory, history and ethnic background (*"Ethnic Nationalism"*)
   b. Common institutions and interests (economic, political, social)
   c. Pride in achievements and sorrow in tragedies (victimization)

2. **Leads to:**
   a. Preference for fellow nationals and indifference or hostility to others
   b. Desire for political self-determination (independent, sovereign state)
   c. Devotion to the nation and nationality

3. **Four types of nationalism**
   a. *Traditional Nationalism ("Civic Nationalism")*
      - People identify with their country (loyalty)
      - Symbols: flag, holidays, national anthems, heroes
      - Education in the nation's history and greatness
      - "We-they" sentiments
   b. *Striving Nationalism*
      - Nationality group ruled by others
      - Desire for self-determination
   c. *Protective Nationalism*
      - Nation under severe threat from within or without
      - Plea for national unity expressed by leadership
   d. *Imperialistic Nationalism*
      - National mission requires control over others
      - Conquest of others shows national greatness/superiority
      - Make other people accept one's nation's values and way of life

13

Working Conditions in the Industrial Revolution

British public policy during the nineteenth century was under the sway of the principle of laissez faire. Unquestionably it contributed to tremendous advances in the economy as a whole, but also led to terrible working conditions. Several parliamentary committees gathered information from both the working and manufacturing classes in order to make recommendations for reform. The selections below come from the Sadler Committee and Lord Ashley's Mines Commission.

Discussion Questions

1. What view of children did English industrial society apparently have?

2. Do you think the conditions they had to endure were much different from the children of farmers?

3. What forms of discipline were employed in factories?

4. What position did Thomas Wilson take on the question of governmental regulation of working conditions?

5. Would any governmental reform be consistent with laissez faire doctrine?

The Sadler Report

VENERIS, 18° DIE MAII, 1832

Michael Thomas Sadler, Esquire, in the chair

* * *

MR. MATTHEW CRABTREE, *called in; and Examined.*

What age are you?_____Twenty-two.

What is your occupation?_____A blanket manufacturer.

Have you ever been employed in a factory?_____Yes.

At what age did you first go to work in one?_____Eight.

How long did you continue in that occupation?_____ Four years.

Will you state the hours of labour at the period when you first went to the factory, in ordinary times?_____From 6 in the morning to 8 at night.

Fourteen hours?_____Yes.

With what intervals for refreshment and rest?_____An hour at noon.

Then you had no resting time allowed in which to take your breakfast, or what is in Yorkshire called your "drinking"?_____No.

When trade was brisk what were your hours?_____From 5 in the morning to 9 in the evening.

Sixteen hours?_____Yes.

With what intervals at dinner?_____An hour.

How far did you live from the mill?_____ About two miles.

Was there any time allowed for you to get your breakfast in the mill?_____No.

Did you take it before you left your home?_____generally.

During those long hours of labour could you be punctual; how did you awake?_____ I seldom did awake spontaneously; I was most generally awoke or lifted out of bed, sometimes asleep, by my parents.

Were you always in time?_____No.

What was the consequence if you had been too late?_____I was most commonly beaten.

Severely?_____Very severely, I thought.

In whose factory was this?_____Messrs. Hague & Cook's, of Dewsbury.

Will you state the effect that those long hours had upon the state of your health and feelings?_____I was, when working those long hours, commonly very much fatigued at night, when I left my work; so much so that I sometimes should have slept as I walked if I had not stumbled and started awake again; and so sick often that I could not eat, and what I did eat I vomited.

Did this labour destroy your appetite?_____ It did.

In what situation were you in that mill?_____I was a piecener.

Will you state to this Committee whether piecening is a very laborious employment for children, or not?_____

It is a very laborious employment. Pieceners are continually running to and fro, and on their feet the whole day.

Reports from the Sadler Committee, *Parliamentary Papers* (1831–1832) and Lord Ashley's Mines Commission, *Parliamentary Papers* (1842).

The duty of the piecener is to take the cardings from one part of the machinery, and to place them on another?_____Yes.

So that the labour is not only continual, but it is unabated to the last?_____It is unabated to the last.

Do you not think, from your own experience, that the speed of the machinery is so calculated as to demand the utmost exertions of a child supposing the hours were moderate?_____It is as much as they could do at the best; they are always upon the stretch, and it is commonly very difficult to keep up with their work.

State the condition of the children toward the latter part of the day, who have thus to keep up with the machinery._____It is as much as they can do when they are not very much fatigued to keep up with their work, and toward the close of the day, when they come to be more fatigued, they cannot keep up with it very well, and the consequence is that they are beaten to spur them on.

Were you beaten under those circumstances _____Yes.

Frequently?_____Very frequently.

And principally at the latter end of the day? _____Yes.

And is it your belief that if you had not been so beaten, you should not have got through the work?_____I should not if I had not been kept up to it by some means.

Does beating then principally occur at the latter end of the day, when the children are exceedingly fatigued?_____It does at the latter end of the day, and in the morning sometimes, when they are very drowsy, and have not got rid or the fatigue of the day before.

What were you beaten with principally? _____A strap.

Anything else?_____Yes, a stick sometimes; and there is a kind of roller which runs on the top of the machine called a billy, perhaps two or three yards in length, and perhaps an inch and a half,

or more in diameter; the circumference would be four or five inches; I cannot speak exactly.

Were you beaten with that instrument? _____Yes.

Have you yourself been beaten, and have you seen other children struck severely with that roller?_____I have been struck very severely with it myself, so much so as to knock me down, and I have seen other children have their heads broken with it.

You think that it is a general practice to beat the children with the roller?_____It is.

You do not think then that you were worse treated than other children in the mill?_____ No, I was not, perhaps not so bad as some were.

In those mills is chastisement towards the latter part of the day going on perpetually? _____Perpetually.

So that you can hardly be in a mill without hearing constant crying?_____Never an hour, I believe.

Do you think that if the overlooker were naturally a humane person it would be still found necessary for him to beat the children, in order to keep up their attention and vigilance at the termination of those extraordinary days of labour?_____Yes, the machine turns off a regular quantity of cardings, and of course they must keep as regularly to their work the whole of the day; they must keep with the machine, and therefore however humane the slubber may be, as he must keep up with the machine or be found fault with, he spurs the children to keep up also by various means but that which he commonly resorts to is to strap them when they become drowsy.

At the time when you were beaten for not keeping up with your work, were you anxious to have done it if you possibly could?_____ Yes; the dread of being beaten if we could not keep up with our work was a sufficient impulse to keep us to it if we could.

When you got home at night after this labour, did you feel much fatigued?_____Very much so.

Had you any time to be with your parents, and to receive instruction from them?_____ No.

What did you do?_____All that we did when we got home was to get the little bit of supper that was provided for us and go to bed immediately. If the supper had not been ready directly, we should have gone to sleep while it was preparing.

Did you not, as a child, feel it a very grievous hardship to be roused so soon in the morning? _____I did.

Were the rest of the children similarly circumstanced?_____Yes, all of them; but they were not all of them so far from their work as I was.

And if you had been too late you were under the apprehension of being cruelly beaten? _____I generally was beaten when I happened to be too late; and when I got up in the morning the apprehension of that was so great, that I used to run, and cry all the way as I went to the mill.

That was the way by which your punctual attendance was secured?_____Yes.

And you do not think it could have been secured by any other means?_____No.

Then it is your impression from what you have seen, and from your own experience, that those long hours of labour have the effect of rendering young persons who are subject to them exceedingly unhappy?_____Yes.

You have already said it had a considerable effect upon your health?_____Yes.

Do you conceive that it diminished your growth?_____I did not pay much attention to that; but I have been examined by some persons who said they thought I was rather stunted, and that I should have been taller if I had not worked at the mill.

What were your wages at that time?_____ Three shillings [per week].

And how much a day had you for overwork when you were worked so exceedingly long? _____A halfpenny a day.

Did you frequently forfeit that if you were not always there to a moment?_____Yes; I most frequently forfeited what was allowed for those long hours.

You took your food to the mill; was it in your mill, as is the case in cotton mills, much spoiled by being laid aside?_____It was very frequently covered by flues from the wool; and in that case they had to be blown off with the mouth, and picked off with the fingers before it could be eaten.

So that not giving you a little leisure for eating your food, but obliging you to take it at the mill, spoiled your food when you did get it? _____Yes, very commonly.

And that at the same time that this overlabour injured your appetite?_____Yes.

Could you eat when you got home?_____ Not always.

What is the effect of this piecening upon the hands?_____It makes them bleed; the skin is completely rubbed off, and in that case they bleed in perhaps a dozen parts.

The prominent parts of the hand?_____Yes, all the prominent parts of the hand are rubbed down till they bleed; every day they are rubbed in that way.

All the time you continue at work?_____All the time we are working. The hands never can be hardened in that work, for the grease keeps them soft in the first instance, and long and continual rubbing is always wearing them down, so that if they were hard they would be sure to bleed.

Is it attended with much pain?_____Very much.

Do they allow you to make use of the back of the hand?_____No; the work cannot be so well done with the back of the hand, or I should have made use of that.

Is the work done as well when you are so many hours engaged in it, as it would be if you were at it a less time?_____I believe it is not done so well in those long hours; toward the latter end of the day the children become completely bewildered, and know not what they are doing, so that they spoil their work without knowing.

Then you do not think that the masters gain much by the continuance of the work to so great a length of time?_____I believe not.

Were there girls as well as boys employed in this manner?_____Yes.

Were they more tenderly treated by the overlookers, or were they worked and beaten in the same manner?_____There was no difference in their treatment.

Were they beaten by the overlookers, or by the slubber?_____By the slubber.

But the overlooker must have been perfectly aware of the treatment that the children endured at the mill?_____Yes; and sometimes the overlooker beat them himself; but the man that they wrought under had generally the management of them.

Did he pay them their wages?_____No; their wages were paid by the master.

But the overlooker of the mill was perfectly well aware that they could not have performed the duty exacted from them in the mill without being thus beaten?_____I believe he was.

You seem to say that this beating is absolutely necessary, in order to keep the children up to their work; is it universal throughout all factories?_____I have been in several other factories, and I have witnessed the same cruelty in them all.

Evidence Before Lord Ashley's Mines Commission

THOMAS WILSON, Esq., OF THE BANKS, SILKSTONE, OWNER OF THREE COLLIERIES

I object on general principles to government interference in the conduct of any trade, and I am satisfied that in the mines it would be productive of the greatest injury and injustice. The art of mining is not so perfectly understood as to admit of the way in which a colliery shall be conducted being dictated by any person, however experienced, with such certainty as would warrant an interference with the management of private business. I should also most decidedly object to placing collieries under the present provisions of the Factory Act with respect to the education of children employed therein. First, because, if it is contended that coalowners, as employers of children, are bound to attend to their education, this obligation extends equally to all other employers, and therefore it is unjust to single out one class only; secondly, because, if the legislature asserts a right to interfere to secure education, it is bound to make that interference general; and thirdly, because the mining population is in this neighborhood so intermixed with other classes, and is in such small bodies in any one place, that it would be impossible to provide separate schools for them.

14

An Industrial Town

Charles Dickens' *Hard Times,* Written in 1854, is one of the most evocative novels about England's industrial age. Few writers could describe the sights, sounds and even smells of factory work and life as well as he did for his avid readers. England had just celebrated its progress at the Crystal Palace Exposition, but Dickens finds in Coketown greedy capitalists like Bounderby and "efficiency experts" like Gradgrind who see none of life's beauty. In the following selection, Dickens describes Coketown, the model of an industrial town.

Discussion Questions

1. What does Dickens mean by saying Coketown was "a triumph of fact?"

2. Why didn't the laboring people go to church?

3. Why does Dickens say that the millers of Coketown were as fragile as China-ware?

4. How would a modern environmentalist describe Coketown?

5. What connections could you make between the testimony before the Sadler committee and Dickens' description of Coketown?

Coketown, to which Messrs. Bounderby and Gradgrind now walked, was a triumph of fact; it had no greater taint of fancy in it than Mrs. Gradgrind herself. Let us strike the keynote, Coketown, before pursuing our tune.

It was a town of red brick, or of brick that would have been red if the smoke and ashes had allowed it; but as matters stood it was a town of unnatural red and black like the painted face of a savage. It was a town of machinery and tall chimneys, out of which interminable serpents of smoke trailed themselves forever and ever, and never got uncoiled. It had a black canal in it, and a river that ran purple with ill-smelling dye, and vast piles of building full of windows where there was a rattling and a trembling all day long, and where the piston of the steam-engine worked monotonously up and down like the head of an elephant in a state of melancholy madness. It contained several large streets all very like one another, and many small streets still more like one another, inhabited by people equally like one another, who all went in and out at the same hours, with the same sound upon the same pavements, to do the same work, and to whom every day was the same as yesterday and tomorrow; and every year the counterpart of the last and the next.

These attributes of Coketown were in the main inseparable from the work by which it was sustained; against them were to be set off comforts of life which found their all over the world, and elegancies of life which made, we will not ask how much of the fine-lady, who could scarcely bear to hear the place mentioned. The rest of its features were voluntary, and they were these.

You saw nothing in Coketown but what was severely workful. If the members of a religious persuasion built a chapel there—as the members of eighteen religious persuasions had done—they made it a pious warehouse of red brick, with sometimes (but this is only in highly ornamental examples) a bell in a bird-cage on the top of it. The solitary exception was the New Church; a stuccoed edifice with a square steeple over the door, terminating in four short pinnacles like florid wooden legs. All the public inscriptions in the town were painted alike, in severe characters of black and white. The jail might have been the infirmary, the infirmary might have been the jail, the townhall might have been either, or both, or anything else, for anything that appeared to the contrary in the graces of their construction. Fact, fact, fact, everywhere in the material aspect of the town; fact, fact, fact, everywhere in the immaterial. The McChoakum child school was all fact, and the school of design was all fact, and the relations between master and man were all fact, and everything was fact between the lying in hospital and the cemetery, and what you couldn't state in figures, or show to be purchasable in the cheapest market and saleable in the dearest, was not, and never should be, world without end, Amen.

A town so sacred to fact, and so triumphant in its assertion, of course got on well? Why no, not quite well. No? Dear me!

No. Coketown did not come out of its own furnaces in all respects like gold that had stood the fire. First, the perplexing mystery of the place was, Who belonged to the eighteen denominations? Because, whoever did, the labouring people did not. It was very strange to walk through the streets on a Sunday morning and note how few of *them*; the barbarous jangling of bells that was driving the sick and nervous mad called away from their own quarter, from their own close rooms, from the comers of their own streets, where they lounged listlessly, gazing at all the church- and chapel-going, as at a thing with which they had no manner of concern. Nor was it merely the stranger who noticed this, because there was a native organization in Coketown itself whose members were to be heard of in the House of Commons every session, indignantly petitioning for acts of Parliament that should make these people religious by main force. Then—came the Teetotal Society, who complained that these same people *would* get drunk, and showed in tabular statements that they did get drunk, and proved at tea parties that no inducement, human or divine (except a medal), would induce them to forgo their custom of getting drunk. Then came the chemist and druggist, with other tabular statements, showing that when they didn't get drunk they took opium. Then came the experienced chaplain of the jail, with more tabular statements, outdoing all the previous tabular statements, and showing that the same people *would* resort to low haunts, hidden from the public eye, where they heard low singing and saw low dancing, and mayhap joined in it; and where A.B., aged twenty-four next birthday, and committed for eighteen months' solitary, had himself said—not that he had ever shown himself particularly worthy of belief—his ruin began, as he was perfectly sure and confident that otherwise he would have been a tip-top moral specimen.

* * *

I entertain a weak idea that the English people are as hard-worked as any people upon whom the sun shines. I acknowledge to this ridiculous idiosyncrasy as a reason why I would give them a little more play.

In the hardest working part of Coketown; in the innermost fortifications of that ugly citadel, where Nature was as strongly bricked out as killing airs and gases were bricked in; at the heart of the labyrinth of narrow courts upon courts, and close streets upon streets, which had come into existence piecemeal, every piece in a violent hurry for some one man's purpose, and the whole an unnatural family, shouldering, and trampling, and pressing one another to death; in the last close nook of this great exhausted receiver, where the chimneys, for want of air to make a draught, were built in an immense variety of stunted and crooked shapes, as though every house put out a sign of the kind of people who might be expected to be born in it; among the multitude of Coketown, generically called "the Hands"—a race who would have found more favour with some people if Providence had seen fit to make them only hands, or, like the lower creatures of the seashore, only hands and stomachs—lived a certain Stephen Blackpool, forty years of age.

Stephen looked older, but he had had a hard life. It is said that every life has its roses and thorns; there seemed, however, to have been a misadventure or mistake in Stephen's case, whereby somebody else had become possessed of his roses, and he had become possessed of the same somebody else's thorns in addition to his own. He had known, to use his words, a peck of trouble. He was usually called Old Stephen, in a kind of rough homage to the fact.

A rather stooping man, with a knitted brow, a pondering expression of face, and a hard-looking head sufficiently capacious on which his iron-grey hair lay long and thin, Old Stephen might have passed for a particularly intelligent man in his condition. Yet he was not. He took no place among those remarkable "Hands," who, piecing together their broken intervals of leisure through many years, had mastered difficult sciences and acquired a knowledge of most unlikely things. He held no station among the Hands who could make speeches and carry on debates. Thousands of his compeers could talk much better than he, at any time. He was a good power-loom weaver, and a man of perfect integrity. What more he was, or what else he had in him, if anything, let him show for himself.

The lights in the great factories, which looked, when they were illuminated, like Fairy Palaces—or the travellers by expresstrain said so—were all extinguished; and the bells had rung for knocking off for the night, and had ceased again; and the Hands, men and women, boy and girl, were clattering home. Old Stephen was standing in the street with the old sensation upon him which the stoppage of the machinery always produced—the sensation of its having worked and stopped in his own head.

* * *

A sunny midsummer day. There was such a thing sometimes, even in Coketown.

Seen from a distance in such weather, Coketown lay shrouded in a haze of its own, which appeared impervious to the sun's rays. You only knew the town was there, because you knew there could have been no such sulky blotch upon the prospect without a town. A blur of soot and smoke, now confusedly tending this way, now that way, now aspiring to the vault of Heaven, now murkily creeping along the earth, as the wind rose and fell, or changed its quarter: a dense formless jumble, with sheets of cross light in it, that showed nothing but masses of darkness—Coketown in the distance was suggestive of itself, though not a brick of it could be seen.

The wonder was, it was there at all. It had been ruined so often that it was amazing how it had borne so many shocks. Surely there never was such fragile china-ware as that of which the millers of Coketown were made. Handle them never so lightly and they fell to pieces with such ease that you might suspect them of having been flawed before. They were ruined when they were required to send labouring children to school; they were ruined when inspectors were appointed to look into their works; they were ruined when

such inspectors considered it doubtful whether they were quite justified in chopping people up with their machinery; they were utterly undone when it was hinted that perhaps they need not always make quite so much smoke. Besides Mr. Bounderby's gold spoon which was generally received in Coketown, another prevalent fiction was very popular there. It took the form of a threat. Whenever a Coketowner felt he was ill-used—that is to say, whenever he was not left entirely alone, and it was proposed to hold him accountable for the consequences of any of his acts—he was sure to come out with the awful menace that he would "sooner pitch his property into the Atlantic." This had terrified the Home Secretary within an inch of his life on several occasions.

However, the Coketowners were so patriotic, after all, that they never had pitched their property into the Atlantic yet, but, on the contrary, had been kind enough to take mighty good care of it. So there it was, in the haze yonder, and it increased and multiplied.

The streets were hot and dusty on the summer day, and the sun was so bright that it even shone through the heavy vapour drooping over Coketown, and could not be looked at steadily. Stokers emerged from low underground doorways into factory yards, and sat on steps, and posts, and palings, wiping their swarthy visages, and contemplating coals. The whole town seemed to be frying in oil. There was a stifling smell of hot oil everywhere. The steam-engines shone with it, the dresses of the Hands were soiled with it, the mills throughout their many stories oozed and trickled it. The atmosphere of those Fairy Palaces was like the breath of the simoom, and their inhabitants, wasting with heat, toiled languidly in the desert. But no temperature made the melancholy mad elephants more mad or more sane. Their wearisome heads went up and down at the same rate, in hot weather and cold, wet weather and dry, fair weather and foul. The measured motion of their shadows on the walls was the substitute

Coketown had to show for the shadows of rustling woods; while, for the summer hum of insects, it could offer, all the year round, from the dawn of Monday to the night of Saturday, the whirr of shafts and wheels.

Drowsily they whirred all through this sunny day, making the passenger more sleepy and more hot as he passed the humming walls of the mills. Sun-blinds, and sprinklings of water, a little cooled the main streets and the shops, but the mills, and the courts and alleys, baked at a fierce heat. Down upon the river that was black and thick with dye, some Coketown boys who were at large—a rare sight there—rowed a crazy boat, which made a spumous track upon the water as it jogged along, while every dip of an oar stirred up vile smells. But the sun itself, however beneficent generally, was less kind to Coketown than hard frost, and rarely looked intently into any of its closer regions without engendering more death than life. So does the eye of Heaven itself become an evil eye, when incapable or sordid hands are interposed between it and the things it looks upon to bless... .

15

Industrialization and Women

In the following selection the authors Louise Tilly and Joan Scott review the complex changes that industrialization has had on the roles of women in the family and in society at large since about 1700.

Discussion Questions

1. What was the nature of what the authors call the "family economy" in the pre-industrial era and how did women fit into it?

2. How did the new "family wage economy" differ? How were productive and reproductive activities related to each other?

3. As industrialism proceeded, what role did consumption come to play? What was the new position of women and children?

4. What do the authors mean by a "U-shaped pattern of female productive activity?"

5. What factors influenced the supply of and the demand for women as workers?

6. What role did the family play in the various periods of transition from around 1700 to around 1900?

What was the impact of industrialization on women's work? There is no simple or single answer. Changes in the mode of production did not immediately or automatically transform women's work. Nor did they directly alter reproductive strategies and family organization, both of which influenced women's productive activities. Yet important changes have occurred. We can best answer the question about the impact of industrialization by conceiving of a process of change which affected the economy, demography and family organization in different ways and which also changed the relationships among them.

Let us review briefly the changing relationships among the economic, demographic and family influences on the work of women of the popular classes in Britain and France since 1700. In the household mode of production typical of the preindustrial economy, the unit of production was small and productivity was low. All household members worked at productive tasks, differentiated by age and sex. We have called this form of organization the *family economy*. Within marriage, fertility was high. High mortality was, however, an involuntary check on net reproduction. Children were potential workers, but they were also potential heirs to limited resources. So households controlled the size of future generations by late marriage and enforced celibacy for some members. Parental control of limited resources limited the autonomy of children. High fertility, high mortality, a small-scale household organization of production, and limited resources meant that women's time was spent primarily in productive activity. Unmarried women worked in their parents' households or in other households if there was no need for their labor at home. Married women were both producers and mothers. The household setting of work facilitated the combination of productive and domestic activities. Married women adjusted their time to meet the demands of production in the interest of the family economy.

During industrialization, the size of productive units grew and productive activity moved out of the household to workshops and factories. Increasingly, people worked for wages. Early industrialization, particularly in the textile industry, relied heavily on the labor of women and children. Families adapted older expectations about work and strategies of reproduction to the new circumstances. The result was the *family wage economy*. Under this organization the family continued to allocate the labor of its members. Now the household's need for wages rather than for labor determined the productive activity, of women when they were daughters as well as wives and mothers. Families continued to bear many children, and infant mortality remained very high. This high mortality and the fact that surviving children were potential family wage earners made the continuation of earlier high fertility strategies feasible. Yet high fertility in the new circumstances created problems for married women. As in the past, they had to balance their time between productive and reproductive activities, but work now took them away from home. Under the family wage economy, married women worked when the household needed their wages. A woman's time was not invested exclusively in child care or domestic activity when subsistence had to be earned. But the domestic and reproductive needs of the household also claimed much of her time. So, her work tended to be episodic and irregular. If possible, she improvised cash-producing activities connected to her domestic work. When other family members, particularly children, were available to replace her as wage earners, the married woman withdrew from wage-earning activity. Over the course of her lifetime, a woman alternated productive and reproductive activity. Family needs determined when she worked. As a daughter, a woman was usually a family wage earner. As a mother and wife, the time she spent earning money depended on the need of the family for wages and therefore on the wages and work of other family members.

Technological change, the growth of heavy industry, and the increased scale of industrial organization led to increased productivity and greater prosperity by the end of the nineteenth century. The new organization of manufacturing required an adult male labor force primarily. In the tertiary sector, however, an increasing number of white-collar jobs were available for women. Men's wages in this period increased, and the standard of living of many working-class families rose above the subsistence level. The family economy became a *family consumer economy*, as households specialized in reproduction and consumption. Nonetheless, the family continued to allocate the labor of its members. Children of both sexes were family wage earners, usually after they had completed school. The state now required some schooling for all children and, increasingly, one's ability to find a regular, well-paying job depended on a minimum level of education. Married women, too, worked when their wages were needed, but increasingly this meant finding a temporary job during a family crisis. These crises of

unemployment, illness, or death of the primary wage earner tended more and more to cluster in old age. During most of her married life a woman served as a specialist in child rearing and consumer activities for her family. These tasks filled important and economically useful needs for the working-class family. Managing family finances and buying goods and services required time and skill. Moreover, new fertility strategies demanded that women spend more time nurturing children. By the end of the nineteenth century, families had begun to restrict fertility. New health measures and a decline in infant mortality developed only later—in the first decades of the twentieth century. As families bore fewer children it became important to invest more time in their care so they would survive to maturity. Family needs thus allocated the mother's time away from wage earning and toward domestic responsibilities and child care.

After World War II, economic conditions and family needs exerted a different influence on women's work. The tertiary sector expanded and the demand for women in white-collar jobs grew. More part-time work was also available, particularly in Britain. Fertility continued to decline, but new levels of health reduced the fragility of infant and child life. Children remained in school for longer periods of their lives and spent less time as family wage earners. The result was an increase in the time married women spent in wage-earning activity.

The historical record shows a U-shaped pattern of female productive activity—from relatively high in the preindustrial household economy to a lower level in industrial economies. Married women's productive work contributed to this pattern. The fact that married as well as single women worked in the household economy and work today in the consumer economy raises the level of female productive activity in these two time periods.

There is no neat complementary curve for reproductive activity. Reproductive patterns have changed in the following manner: from relatively low nuptiality, high marital fertility, and high infant and child mortality; to high nuptiality, lower fertility, and lower infant and child mortality (dependent on women's increased investment of time in child nurture); to low fertility and low infant mortality (no longer dependent exclusively on a mother's time). Yet at any point in time, patterns of female productive activity have influenced and been influenced by the prevailing family fertility strategies.

Determinants of Women's Productive Activity

In this book we have compared aggregate features of two nation-states over a 250-year period. We have compared several cities with special economic and ecological characteristics. We also have studied women in families in their roles as daughters, wives, and mothers. The comparative examination of women and work at several different levels permits us to offer some general explanations of changes in patterns of women's work.

At the most general level we conclude that the interplay between a society's productive and reproductive systems within the household influences the *supply* of women available for work. The characteristics of the economy and its mode of production, scale of organization, and technology influence the *demand* for women as workers.

Historically, the likelihood of women participating in production is strongly correlated with the household mode of production. The closer in time that a given household is to the experience of household production, the more likely it is that women will do productive work and that they will subordinate time spent in reproductive activity to that work. During the entire nineteenth century the French economy was marked by the continuing importance

of a small-scale, household organization of production. Britain, on the other hand, early developed a large-scale, factory-based system. As a result, French rates of female work-force participation were consistently higher than British rates.

Once the industrial mode of production predominates, once people work for wages outside of households, aggregate and local economic organization influence the demand for women in paid employment. An important constraint operates here: the almost universal segregation of occupations by sex. The degree of occupational segregation has varied somewhat over time, but there has been a continuing tendency for societies, employers, and workers to accept sex-typing of occupations. Women, then, are most likely to work when the demand for workers in female occupations is high. When there is a shortage of the supply of male workers (during or after a war, for example) more women will be drawn into nonfemale occupations. The analysis of the economic structure of the different cities demonstrated that levels of female employment were highest where female jobs were most numerous.

The supply of female workers, of course, is shaped in part by demographic, social, and economic factors. Single women are best able to work, since they have few other claims on their time. Married women, on the other hand, must adjust reproductive and domestic activity with paid employment. The difficulties of such an adjustment were evident during the early period of industrialization, particularly in textile towns. Then the economic need for women workers and the family's need for wages led to high levels of married women's employment at high costs to themselves and, even more, to their infants. Even in the textile towns, however, the demographic situation—the proportions in the population of married and single women—shaped the supply of women workers. In later periods, when demand for women was great and the supply of single women small, employers might change work conditions to accommodate the special needs of married women.

Household needs also influence the supply of women workers. The division of labor within the household is based on the family's economic needs. Under the household mode of production, the labor needs of the unit defined the work of all members. For wageearning families, subsistence requirements replaced labor needs. Poor households sent as many members as possible into wage-earning employment. When possible, however, the family division of labor allocated time for domestic and child care activity to married women. Increased productivity and higher male wages permitted a sharper division of labor and a differentiation of activity within the household. Single women became preferred wage earners, while married women were preferred as child-care and consumer specialists.

Of course, household needs were not simply economic. The emphasis placed on children and childcare also influenced the supply of women, particularly of married women, to the labor market. In the earliest period of high fertility and high mortality there was no notion that infants and children required special care. Beyond time spent in childbirth and suckling an infant, little time was spent on children. With the decline in fertility and improved prospects for children to survive to adulthood, there developed a new emphasis on the needs of children. Mothers were assumed to be responsible for children's physical, mental, and moral health. The time they spent caring for children was considered valuable by the family. Indeed the value of time spent at home began to outweigh time spent in wage-earning activity. After the Second World War, yet another change in conceptions of child care occurred. Continuing low fertility and dramatically improved prospects for infant and child survival mean that there are less demands on a mother's time for the nurture and care of young children. Not the physical survival, but the social and economic future of the child, his or her education and training, have become increasingly important. This kind of investment in children requires additional funds from the family and, increasingly, married women have sought paid employment to help earn those funds.

By looking not only at work, but at workers as members of households, we have been able to assess the role of the family. We have found that the family provided a certain continuity in the midst of economic change. Values, behavior, and strategies shaped under one mode of production continued to influence behavior as the economy changed. The older practices only slowly were adapted to the new circumstances. In the period we have examined, the family economy was modified from a productive unit to a wage unit. Yet membership in a family continued to define the work roles and relationships of parents and children. Our study challenges an older view which held that industrialization separated the family and work, isolating one sphere from another. We have found that industrialization did deprive the family unit of its productive activity. Nonetheless, the family continued to influence the productive activities of its members. That point was well understood by the three commentators we cited at the beginning of this book. Despite the vastly different conclusions they drew, Jules Simon, Jules Turgan, and Friedrich Engels all agreed that women's work had to be assessed in terms of the family.

Throughout this book we have described and analyzed changes in patterns of women's productive activity. Our analysis has been enriched by the insights of other disciplines, particularly economics, anthropology, and demography. Although we have focused on the history of women in Britain and France since 1700, our conclusions have wider applicability. In the past, as in the present, patterns of women's work are shaped by the intersection of economy, demography, and family. Specific historical contexts differ and so do the experiences, attitudes and choices women make in different situations. The excitement and interest of social history lies in exploring and specifying the differences. The use of an interdisciplinary perspective yields important insights both for those seeking to understand women's position in the past and for those seeking to change and improve it in the present and future.

16

Marxism: The Communist Manifesto

The *Communist Manifesto* is the most famous work, and its author Karl Marx the most famous figure, in the history of socialism. The *Manifesto* contains most of the key ideas we identify collectively today as "Marxism," an ideology that represents an entire worldview, though its focal point is the industrial revolution. In it we see Marx the historian, Marx the sociologist, Marx the economist and even Marx the scientist. Indeed, Marx called his version of socialism, "Scientific Socialism," and he is therefore in the mainstream of European thought in the 19th century, especially those currents which reflect the 18th century Enlightenment values of reason, natural law and progress. In summarizing his contributions, the eleventh edition of the Encyclopedia Britannica (1911) said:

> The great scientific achievement of Marx lies ... in the details and yet more in the method and principles of his investigations in his philosophy of history. Here he has, as is now generally admitted, broken new ground and opened new ways and new outlooks. Nobody before him had so clearly shown the role of the productive agencies in historical evolution; nobody so masterfully exhibited their great determining influence on the forms and ideologies of social organisms. The passages and chapters dealing with this subject form, notwithstanding occasional exaggerations, the crowning parts of his works. If he has been justly compared with Darwin, it is in these respects that he ranks with that great genius... . In the same year as Darwin's epoch-making work on the origin of species there also appeared Marx's work Critique of Political Economy, where he explains in concise sentences in the preface that philosophy of history which has for the theory of the transformation or evolution of social organisms the same significance that the argument of Darwin had for the transformation of biological organisms.

Discussion Questions

1. What is the significance of "class struggle" in Marx's view of history?

2. To what does Marx attribute the emergence of the bourgeoisie as the "ruling" class of Europe?

3. What is to be the historical role of the proletariat?

4. What aspect of the Manifesto might be called "scientific?"

5. Why does Marx want to get rid of private property?

6. Marx concludes the Manifesto with the exhortation "Working men of all countries, unite!" What did he mean by that? What about nationalism?

The Communist Manifesto

1

Bourgeois and Proletarians

The history of all hitherto existing society is the history of class struggles.

Freeman and slave, patrician and plebeian, lord and serf, guild-mastery and journeyman, in a word, oppressor and oppressed, stood in constant opposition to one another, carried on an uninterrupted, now hidden, now open fight, a fight that each time ended, either in a revolutionary reconstitution of society at large, or in the common ruin of the contending classes.

In the earlier epochs of history, we find almost everywhere a complicated arrangement of society into various orders, a manifold gradation of social rank. In ancient Rome we have patricians, knights, plebeians, slaves; in the Middle Ages, feudal lords, vassals, guild-masters, journeymen, apprentices, serfs; in almost all of these classes, again, subordinate gradations.

The modern bourgeois society that has sprouted from the ruins of feudal society has not done away with class antagonisms. It has

but established new classes, new conditions of oppression, new forms of struggle in place of the old ones.

Our epoch, the epoch of the bourgeoisie, possesses, however, this distinctive feature: it has simplified the class antagonisms. Society as a whole is more and more splitting up into two great hostile camps, into two great classes directly facing each other: Bourgeoisie and Proletariat.

From the serfs of the Middle Ages sprang the chartered burghers of the earliest towns. From these burgesses the first elements of the bourgeoisie were developed.

The discovery of America, the rounding of the Cape, opened up fresh ground for the rising bourgeoisie. The East-Indian and Chinese markets, the colonization of America, trade with the colonies, the increase in the means of exchange and in commodities generally, gave to commerce, to navigation, to industry, an impulse never before known, and thereby, to the revolutionary element in the tottering feudal society, a rapid development.

The feudal system of industry, under which industrial production was monopolized by closed guilds, now no longer sufficed for the growing wants of the new market. The manufacturing system took its place. The guild-masters were pushed on one side by the manufacturing middle class; division of labour between the different corporate guilds vanished in the face of division of labour in each single workshop.

Meantime the markets kept ever growing, the demand ever rising. Even manufacture no longer sufficed. Thereupon, steam and machinery revolutionized industrial production. The place of manufacture was taken by the giant, Modern Industry, the place of the industrial middle class, by industrial millionaires, the leaders of whole industrial armies, the modern bourgeois.

Modern industry has established the world market, for which the discovery of America paved the way. This market has given an immense development to commerce, to navigation, to communication by land. This development has, in its turn, reacted on the extension of industry; and in proportion as industry, commerce, navigation, railways extended, in the same proportion the bourgeoisie developed, increased its capital, and pushed into the background every class handed down from the Middle Ages.

We see, therefore, how the modern bourgeoisie is itself the product of a long course of development, of a series of revolutions in the modes of production and of exchange.... .

The bourgeoisie, historically, has played a most revolutionary part.

The bourgeoisie, wherever it has got the upper hand, has put an end to all feudal, patriarchal, idyllic relations. It has pitilessly torn asunder the motley feudal ties that bound man to his 'natural superiors.' and has left remaining no other nexus between man and man than naked self-interest, than callous 'cash payment.' It has drowned the most heavenly ecstasies of religious fervour, of chivalrous enthusiasm, of philistine sentimentalism, in the icy water of egotistical calculation. It has resolved personal worth into exchange value, and in place of the numberless indefeasible chartered freedoms, has set up that single, unconscionable freedom—Free Trade. In one word, for exploitation, veiled by religious and political illusions, it has substituted naked, shameless, direct, brutal exploitation.

The bourgeoisie has stripped of its halo every occupation hitherto honoured and looked up to with reverent awe. It has converted the physician, the lawyer, the priest, the poet, the man of science, into its paid wage-labourers.

The bourgeoisie has torn away from the family its sentimental veil, and has reduced the family relation to a mere money relation.... .

We see then: the means of production and of exchange, on whose foundation the bourgeoisie built itself up, were generated in feudal society. At a certain stage in the development of these means of production and of exchange, the conditions under which feudal society produced and exchanged, the feudal organization of agriculture and manufacturing industry, in one word, the feudal relations of property became no longer compatible with the already developed productive forces; they became so many fetters. They had to be burst asunder; they were burst asunder.

Into their place stepped free competition, accompanied by a social and political constitution adapted to it, and by the economical and political sway of the bourgeois class.

A similar movement is going on before our own eyes. Modern bourgeois society with its relations of production, of exchange and of property, a society that has conjured up such gigantic means of production and of exchange, is like the sorcerer, who is no longer able to control the powers of the nether world whom he has called up by his spells. For many a decade past the history of industry and commerce is but the history of the revolt of modern productive forces against modern conditions of production, against the property relations that are the conditions for the existence of the bourgeoisie and of its rule. It is enough to mention the commercial crises that by their periodical return put on its trial, each time more threateningly, the existence of the entire bourgeois society. In these crises a great part not only of the existing products, but also of the previously created productive forces, are periodically destroyed. In these crises there breaks out an epidemic that, in all earlier epochs, would have seemed an absurdity—the epidemic of overproduction… .

And how does the bourgeoisie get over these crises? On the one hand by enforced destruction of a mass of productive forces; on the other, by the conquest of new markets, and by the more thorough exploitation of the old ones, That is to say, by paving the way for more extensive and more destructive crises, and by diminishing the means whereby crises are prevented.

The weapons with which the bourgeoisie felled feudalism to the ground are now turned against the bourgeoisie itself.

But not only has the bourgeoisie forged the weapons that bring death to itself; it has also called into existence the men who are to wield those weapons—the modern working class—the proletarians… .

Modern industry has converted the little workshop of the patriarchal master into the great factory of the industrial capitalist. Masses of labourers, crowded into the factory, are organized like soldiers. As privates of the industrial army they are placed under the command of a perfect hierarchy of officers and sergeants. Not only are they slaves of the bourgeois class, and of the bourgeois State; they are daily and hourly enslaved by the machine, by the overlooker, and, above all, by the individual bourgeois manufacturer himself. The more openly this despotism proclaims gain to be its end and aim, the more petty, the more hateful and the more embittering it is… .

The lower strata of the middle class—the small tradespeople shopkeepers, and retired tradesmen generally, the handicraftsmen and peasants—all these sink gradually into the proletariat, partly because their diminutive capital does not suffice for the scale on which Modern Industry is carried on, and is swamped in the competition with the large capitalists, partly because their specialized skill is rendered worthless by new methods of production. Thus the proletariat is recruited from all classes of the population… .

But with the development of industry the proletariat not only increases in number; it becomes concentrated in greater masses, its strength grows, and it feels that strength more. The various interests and conditions of life within the ranks of the proletariat are more and more equalized, in proportion as machinery obliterates all distinctions of labour, and nearly everywhere reduces wages to the same low level. The growing competition among the bourgeois, and the resulting commercial crises, make the wages of the workers ever more fluctuating. The unceasing improvement of machinery, ever more rapidly developing, makes their livelihood more and more precarious; the collisions between individual workmen and individual bourgeois take more and more the character of collisions between two classes. Thereupon the workers begin to form combinations (Trades Unions) against the bourgeois; they club together in order to keep up the rate of wages; they found permanent associations in order to make provision beforehand for these occasional revolts. Here and there the contest breaks out into riots.

Now and then the workers are victorious, but only for a time. The real fruit of their battles lies, not in the immediate result, but in the ever-expanding union of the workers. This union is helped on by the improved means of communication that are created by modern industry and that place the workers of different localities in contact with one another. It was just this contact that was needed to centralize the numerous local struggles, all of the same character, into one national struggle between classes. But every class struggle is a political struggle. And that union, to attain which the burghers of the Middle Ages, with their miserable highways, required centuries, the modern proletarians, thanks to rail-ways, achieve in a few years.

This organization of the proletarians into a class, and consequently into a political party, is continually being upset again by the competition between the workers themselves. But it ever rises up again, stronger, firmer, mightier... .

Further, as we have already seen, entire sections of the ruling classes are, by the advance of industry, precipitated into the proletariat, or are at least threatened in their conditions of existence. These also supply the proletariat with fresh elements of enlightenment and progress.

Finally, in times when the class struggle nears the decisive hour, the process of dissolution going on within the ruling class, in fact within the whole range of old society, assumes such a violent, glaring character, that a small section of the ruling class cuts itself adrift, and joins the revolutionary class, the class that holds the future in its hands. Just as, therefore, at an earlier period, a section of the nobility went over to the bourgeoisie, so now a portion of the bourgeoisie goes over to the proletariat, and in particular, a portion of the bourgeois ideologists, who have raised themselves to the level of comprehending theoretically the historical movement as a whole... .

2

Proletarians and Communists

In what relation do the Communists stand to the proletarians as a whole?

The Communists do not form a separate party opposed to other working-class parties.

They have no interests separate and apart from those of the proletariat as a whole.

They do not set up any sectarian principles of their own, by which to shape and mould the proletarian movement.

The Communists are distinguished from the other working-class parties by this only: 1. In the national struggles of the proletarians of the different countries, they point out and bring to the front the common interests of the entire proletariat, independently of all nationality. 2. In the various stages of development which the struggle of the working class against the bourgeoisie has to pass through, they always and everywhere represent the interests of the movement as a whole.

The Communists, therefore, are on the one hand, practically, the most advanced and resolute section of the working-class parties of every country, that section which pushes forward all others; on the other hand, theoretically, they have over the great mass of the proletariat the advantage of clearly understanding the line of march, the conditions, and the ultimate general results of the proletarian movement.

The immediate aim of the Communists is the same as that of all the other proletarian parties: formation of the proletariat into a class, overthrow of the bourgeois supremacy, conquest of political power by the proletariat... .

The distinguishing feature of Communism is not the abolition of property generally, but the abolition of bourgeois property. But modern bourgeois private property is the final and most complete expression of the system of producing and appropriating products, that is based on class antagonisms, on the exploitation of the many by the few.

In this sense, the theory of the Communists may be summed up in the single sentence: Abolition of private property... .

You are horrified at our intending to do away with private property. But in your existing society, private property is already done away with for nine-tenths of the population; its existence for the few is solely due to its non-existence in the hands of those nine-tenths. You reproach us, therefore, with intending to do away with a form of property the necessary condition for whose existence is the non-existence of any property for the immense majority of society.

In one word, you reproach us with intending to do away with your property. Precisely so; that is just what we intend... .

The Communists are further reproached with desiring to abolish countries and nationality.

The working men have no country. We cannot take from them what they have not got... .

National differences and antagonisms between peoples are daily more and more vanishing, owing to the development of the bourgeoisie, to freedom of commerce, to the world market, to uniformity in the mode of production and in the conditions of life corresponding thereto.

The supremacy of the proletariat will cause them to vanish still faster. United action, of the leading civilized countries at least, is one of the first conditions for the emancipation of the proletariat.

In proportion as the exploitation of one individual by another is put an end to, the exploitation of one nation by another will also be put an end to. In proportion as the antagonism between classes within the nation vanishes, the hostility of one nation to another will come to an end.

The charges against Communism made from a religious, a philosophical, and, generally, from an ideological standpoint, are not deserving of serious examination.

Does it require deep intuition to comprehend that man's ideas, views and conceptions, in one word, man's consciousness, changes with every change in the conditions of his material existence, in his social relations and in his social life?

What else does the history of ideas prove, than that intellectual production changes in character in proportion as material production is changed? The ruling ideas of each age have ever been the ideas of its ruling class... .

...the first step in the revolution by the working class, is to raise proletariat to the position of ruling class, to win the battle of democracy.

The proletariat will use its political supremacy to wrest, by degrees, all capital from the bourgeoisie, to centralize all instruments of production in the hands of the State, i.e., of the proletariat organized as the ruling class; and to increase the total of productive forces as rapidly as possible.

Of course, in the beginning, this cannot be effected except by means of despotic inroads on the rights of property, and on the conditions of bourgeois production; by means of measures, therefore, which appear economically insufficient and untenable, but which, in the course of the movement, outstrip themselves, necessitate further inroads upon the old social order, and are unavoidable as a means of entirely revolutionizing the mode of production.

These measures will of course be different in different countries.

Nevertheless, in the most advanced countries, the following will be pretty generally applicable:

1. Abolition of property in land and application of all rents of land to public purposes.
2. A heavy progressive or graduated income tax.
3. Abolition of all right of inheritance.
4. Confiscation of the property of all emigrants and rebels.
5. Centralization of credit in the hands of the State, by means of a national bank with State capital and an exclusive monopoly.
6. Centralization of the means of communication and transport in the hands of the State.

7. Extension of factories and instruments of production owned by the State; the bringing into cultivation of wastelands, and the improvement of the soil generally in accordance with a common plan.
8. Equal liability of all to labour. Establishment of industrial armies, especially for agriculture.
9. Combination of agriculture with manufacturing industries; gradual abolition of the distinction between town and country, by a more equable distribution of the population over the country.
10. Free education for all children in public schools. Abolition of children's factory labour in its present form. Combination of education with industrial production, &c., &c.

When, in the course of development, class distinctions have disappeared, and all production has been concentrated in the whole nation, the public power will lose its political character. Political power, properly so called, is merely the organized power of one class for oppressing another. If the proletariat during its contest with the bourgeoisie is compelled, by the force of circumstances, to organize itself as a class, if, by means of a revolution, it makes itself the ruling class, and, as such, sweeps away by force the old conditions of production, then it will, along with these conditions, have swept away the conditions for the existence of class antagonisms and of classes generally, and will thereby have abolished its own supremacy as a class.

In place of the old bourgeois society, with its classes and class antagonisms, we shall have an association, in which the free development of each is the condition for the free development of all... .

17

Race and Nation

During the last third of the nineteenth century, in the wake of the emergence of Darwin's theory of natural selection, there appeared a series of efforts to put the study of human society, nations and race on a scientific biological basis. The first result of this was the concept of Social Darwinism proposed by Herbert Spencer, who had invented the phrase "survival of the fittest." Social Darwinism suggested that human society operated according to Darwinian evolutionary principles and that therefore competition showed that certain individuals were biologically superior to others—an idea very popular among the business classes and free market advocates. Before long some people were suggesting that certain nations were superior to other nations. From this a new "scientific" basis for racism emerged, with white Europeans at the top of the evolutionary scale—this idea became very popular among nationalists and imperialists. A "logical" deduction of these assumptions (because that is what they were) was the so-called science of eugenics which argued that superior races could be designed or preserved, especially by eliminating or isolating allegedly "inferior" persons from the human gene pool. This idea became particularly popular in the United States during the first half of the twentieth century (and was the one thing Hitler said he liked about the United States.)

Houston Stewart Chamberlain (1855–1926) was in this tradition. He was the son of a British admiral, son-in-law of the composer Richard Wagner and a professed Germanophile. His major work was *The Foundations of the Nineteenth Century* which he wrote in German in 1899. It sold well and was especially popular later with the Nazis. The following selections from his work illustrate his view of the importance of race in the history of nations and the world.

Discussion Questions

1. What is the link between nationality and race?

2. How is the consciousness of race a product of science?

3. Is racialism a valid science? Or is it a pseudo-science?

4. Is Chamberlain's comparison of breeds of dogs and human beings a valid one?

5. Does history demonstrate that Teutons are the superior race? Just who are the Teutons he refers to?

Ranke had prophesied that our century would be a century of nationality; that was a correct political prognostic, for never before have the nations stood opposed to each other so clearly and definitely as antagonistic unities. It has, however, also become a century of races, and that indeed is in the first instance a necessary and direct consequence of science and scientific thinking. I have already said at the beginning of this introduction that science does not unite but dissects. That statement has not contradicted itself here. Scientific anatomy has furnished such conclusive proofs of the existence of physical characteristics distinguishing the races from each other that they can no longer be denied; scientific philology has discovered between the various languages fundamental differences which cannot be bridged over; the scientific study of history in its various branches has brought about similar results, especially by the exact determination of the religious history of each race, in which only the most general of general ideas can raise the illusion of similarity, while the further development has always followed and still follows definite, sharply divergent lines. The so-called unity of the human race is indeed still honoured as a hypothesis, but only as a personal, subjective conviction lacking every material foundation. The ideas of the eighteenth century with regard to the brotherhood of nations were certainly very noble but purely sentimental in their origin; and in contrast to these ideas to which the Socialists still cling, limping on like reserves in the battle, stern reality has gradually asserted itself as the necessary result of the events and investigations of our time.

* * *

From Houston Stewart Chamberlain, *Foundations of the Nineteenth Century,* ranslated by John Lees, copyright © 1912 by John Lane Ltd., Volume I, pp. xciii–xciv, 256–257, 260–263, 269, 292, 297.

To this day these two powers—Jews and Teutonic races—stand, wherever the recent spread of the Chaos has not blurred their features, now as friendly, now as hostile, but always as alien forces face to face. If we look around, we see that the importance of each nation as a living power to-day is dependent upon the proportion of genuinely Teutonic blood in its population. Only Teutons sit on the thrones of Europe.

* * *

And as if the scientific rearing of animals and plants did not afford us an extremely rich and reliable material, whereby we may become acquainted not only with the conditions but with the importance of "race"! Are the so-called (and rightly so-called) "noble" animal races, the draught-horses of Limousin, the American trotter, the Irish hunter, the absolutely reliable sporting dogs, produced by chance and promiscuity? Do we get them by giving the animals equality of rights, by throwing the same food to them and whipping them with the same whip? No, they are produced by artificial selection and strict maintenance of the purity of the race. Horses and especially dogs give us every chance of observing that the intellectual gifts go hand in hand with the physical; this is especially true of the moral qualities: a mongrel is frequently very clever, but never reliable; morally he is always a weed. Continual promiscuity between two pre-eminent animal races leads without exception to the destruction of the pre-eminent characteristics of both. Why should the human race form an exception?... In spite of the broad common foundation, the human races are, in reality, as different from one another in character, qualities, and above all, in the degree of their individual capacities, as greyhound, bull-dog, poodle and Newfoundland dog. Inequality is a state towards which nature inclines in all spheres; nothing extraordinary is produced without "specialisation"; in the case of men, as of animals, it is this specialisation that produces noble races;

history and ethnology reveal this secret to the dullest eye. Has not every genuine race its own glorious, incomparable physiognomy? ...

* * *

Nothing is so convincing as the consciousness of the possession of Race. The man who belongs to a distinct, pure race, never loses the sense of it. The guardian angel of his lineage is ever at his side, supporting him where he loses his foothold, warning him like the Socratic Daemon where he is in danger of going astray, compelling obedience, and forcing him to undertakings which, deeming them impossible, he would never have dared to attempt. Weak and erring like all that is human, a man of this stamp recognises himself, as others recognise him, by the sureness of his character, and by the fact that his actions are marked by a certain simple and peculiar greatness, which finds its explanation in his distinctly typical and superpersonal qualities. Race lifts a man above himself: it endows him with extraordinary—I might almost say supernatural—powers, so entirely does it distinguish him from the individual who springs from the chaotic jumble of peoples drawn from all parts of the world: and should this man of pure origin be perchance gifted above his fellows, then the fact of Race strengthens and elevates him on every hand, and he becomes a genius towering over the rest of mankind, not because he has been thrown upon the earth like a flaming meteor by a freak of nature, but because he soars heavenward like some strong and stately tree, nourished by thousands and thousands of roots—no solitary individual, but the living sum of untold souls striving for the same goal.

* * *

There is one point which I have not expressly formulated, but it is self-evident from all that I have said; the conception of Race has nothing in it unless we take it in the narrowest and not in the widest sense: if we follow the usual custom and use the word to denote far remote hypothetical races, it ends by becoming little more than a colourless synonym for "mankind"—possibly including the long-tailed and short-tailed apes: Race only has a meaning when it relates to the experiences of the past and the events of the present.

Here we begin to understand what nation signifies for race. It is almost always the nation, as a political structure, that creates the conditions for the formation of race or at least leads to the highest and most individual activities of race.

* * *

...since race is not a mere word, but an organic living thing, it follows as a matter of course that it never remains stationary; it is ennobled or it degenerates, it develops in this or that direction and lets this or that quality decay. This is a law of all individual life. But the firm national union is the surest protection against going astray: it signifies common memory, common hope, common intellectual nourishment; it fixes firmly the existing bond of blood and impels us to make it ever closer.

18

The World Revolution
of Westernization

In this selection a contemporary author, Theodore H. Von Laue, offers a provocative view of what he feels has been the "central force" that has shaped the 20th century world—the world revolution of westernization. The West's expansion, beginning with Columbus' voyages in the late 15th century, led to a global revolution and transformation that eventually led to the "unification of the world," a phenomenon that has produced some surprising consequences. As you read, consider the evidence Von Laue uses to support his arguments, and the biases reflected in his views.

Discussion Questions

1. What does Von Laue mean by the "world revolution of Westernization." Has it been largely a success or a failure?

2. What changes have resulted from the unification of the world and its domination by the West? Do you accept his arguments, and, if not, why not?

3. When he speaks of a "cultural limbo," to what and whom is he referring?

4. Why does Von Laue state that all counterrevolutions have been futile, and do you agree?

This book offers a novel look at the conditions of the anarchic world community in which we live, a look reasonably free of the illusions buttressing liberal complacency. It aims at the detachment that allows true impartiality as well as a better sense of control over our destiny. It explains the 20th century, the most momentous and still largely uncomprehended age in all history, in terms of the central force that shaped it: the world revolution of Westernization. That gigantic, all-inclusive, and still incomplete historic process may be briefly outlined as follows.

The Expansion of the West

For the first time in all human experience the world revolution of Westernization brought together, in inescapably intimate and virtually instant interaction, all the peoples of the world, regardless of their prior cultural evolution or their capacity—or incapacity—for peaceful coexistence. Within a brief time, essentially within half a century, they were thrust into a common harness, against their will, by a small minority commonly called "The West"— the peoples of Western Europe and their descendants in North America. As a result, the human condition in the present and the future can only be understood within the framework of the Westernized world.

This massive confluence of the world's peoples, infinitely exceeding in intensity all previous interdependence and transforming the world's ecosystem on which human life depends, was started by irresistible force, by guns, supported by a vast and complex array of cultural skills, adding up to an overwhelming political presence that excelled also in the arts of peace. In creating an interdependent world through conquest, colonization, and expanded opportunities for all, that Western minority imposed its own accomplishments as a universal standard to which all others, however reluctantly, had to submit. Robbed of their past freedom to go their own ways politically and culturally, non-Western peoples were subjected to a world order that perpetuated or even deepened their helplessness. Henceforth equality could be attained only on the terms imposed by the West.

Western ascendancy was so complete that it left only one rational response: abject imitation as a condition of survival and self-affirmation. Decolonization and the formation of Western-inspired nation-states among the former colonial and semi-colonial peoples merely escalated the imitation and hardened the grip of Western institutions and values over the entire world. Even the most heated protests against Western power—and they were never lacking—were expressed in Western concepts and propagated by Western technology in Western languages. Yet inequality continued.

Submission and cultural imitation, however, were not without elemental advantage, individually and collectively. Overall material conditions improved, increasing individual welfare and tripling the volume of human life on earth within less than a century. Yet the survival of the ever growing and more demanding human multitudes led to yet greater dependence,

---

calling for a further copying of essential aspects of Western culture. For the sake of feeding, housing, transporting, educating, and employing the world's population, "Westernization" is now pressed forward by non-Westerners themselves. Culturally neutralized, it has become "modernization" or simply "development," the common goal of all peoples and governments no matter how handicapped in achieving it.

Seen in a superficial light, the unification of the world was the work of all humanity. In expanding their power around the world the Europeans freely drew on the ingenuity, riches, and labor of non-Europeans; all humanity gained as the achievements of its separate peoples became accessible to all. Yet, examined more closely, the Europeans merely copied on their own terms whatever strengthened their might; they exploited the world's resources, hitherto mostly dormant, for their own gain; they enlisted the prowess and resilience of people around the world to make themselves masters. The will to power and the capacity for taking advantage of all opportunities for their own aggrandizement—the initiative for the world revolution of Westernization—sprang from Europe, from the hothouse competition among the Europeans themselves. In expanding around the world and enlarging their base from Europe into the "the West," they foisted their singular qualities on the unwilling and unprepared majority of humanity, dynamically transforming the entire world in their own image and establishing a hierarchy of prestige defined by the success of imitation. In the world revolution of Westernization, Western political ambition and competitiveness became universal—and fiercer because of the fury born of persistent inequality.

The Consequences of Western Expansion

The major effect of the world revolution of Westernization—generally down-played in the West—has been to undermine and discredit all non-Western cultures. The victorious Westerners, their own ways and self-confidence boosted by their worldwide sway, left the rest of the world humiliated and in cultural limbo. Under the Western impact traditional authorities and local customs had no future; they crumbled away. Meanwhile the imported ways of the West remained superficial or even incomprehensible; they did not fit societies whose cultural sovereignty had been crushed.

The subversion of traditional cultures admittedly took different forms in different parts of the world. It was perhaps least painful in Japan, a unique case where native tradition proved miraculously compatible with Western imports. Elsewhere, among the majority of peoples around the world, the results were cultural chaos characterized by a loss of purpose, moral insensibility, and a penchant for violence; by social and political fragmentation, and by the psychological misery of knowingly belonging to a "backward" society. Never before had the extremes of inequality been so great. Now the Great Confluence carried the wealth and glory of the richest instantly into the presence and conscience of the poorest. Expectations were raised and crushed, opportunities advanced and denied in the same instant. No wonder that violence spread and turned more vicious.

Traditional culture and society in non-Western parts of the world were subverted just as the pace of political competition was accelerated to worldwide intensity. After World War I, and even more after World War II, Western democracy, with the United States in the lead, stood out as the universal model of power in the world, of good government, and of economic prosperity; however imperfect, unfinished, and vilified by its critics, it proved elementally persuasive by comparison. Who among the onlookers did not feel envious? Who among the envious did not feel morally entitled—and tempted—to make the world even safer by their own ideals? Equality in political power, though deftly omitted from the Western-inspired inventory of human rights, certainly was claimed as an entitlement by proud non-Westerners. Few states possessed the wherewithal to take up the challenge, yet the aspiration became embedded in the new competition for global power, a source of heightened instability and conflict. But how could ambitious leaders of polities caught in cultural disorientation and social fragmentation mobilize their peoples to match this mighty model on their own terms?

Futile Counterrevolutions

The search for answers among culturally subverted countries with political potential, so this book argues, led to the totalitarian experiments of communism and fascism in the wake of World War I; from them, after World War II, communist Russia emerged as the most powerful challenger to the Western model. Simultaneously, the totalitarian experiments inspired state-builders among the new states emerging from decolonization. What was wanted, it turned out, was not selfaffirmation but further Westernization through "reculturation" (to coin an ugly term for an ugly process), through an unnatural revamping of unsuitable indigenous institutions and human values under external pressure to meet alien goals. Leaving people to their own devices under these conditions, as tried by short-lived democratic regimes, merely enhanced the common disorientation and political weakness. Command and indoctrination had to be substituted for the lacking appropriate voluntary motivation, while a furious anti-Westernism covered up the blatant imitation.

In the West the experiments of totalitarianism have been castigated as outrages of inhumanity and terror; yet as counterrevolutions they merely carried the world revolution of Westernization one step further. Western-oriented indigenous leaders impressed by the fullness of Western power applied to their own peoples the violence that had characterized the elemental expansion of the West. They tried to convert their subjects by force into organization-minded citizens as disciplined, loyal, and cooperative as their counterparts in the Western democracies. They had to accomplish, in a hurry and by conscious design, what in the West had been achieved over centuries of largely invisible cultural conditioning (accompanied too, we should remember, by ferocious violence in war, civil war, and revolution). Seen in this light, communism and fascism were no more than idealized versions of Western (or "capitalist") society dressed up to inspire the humiliated and disadvantaged. Their statecraft was merely a disguised form of cultural colonialism creating, out of helpless and resentful people, a "new man" and a "new society" capable of competing with the West on more equal terms. Yet the results of all totalitarian experiments have refuted the high hopes for matching, let alone outpacing, the Western model. Inasmuch as they relied on compulsion, they remained tragically non-Western and inferior because compulsion can never match the cultural creativity of spontaneous civic cooperation.

Not all past experiments of Westernization (or modernization), fortunately, were as extreme in ambition or execution as Hitler's or Stalin's. Some were favored by newfound wealth, others by long association with Westerners or, as in the case of Japan (always the exception), by an element of cultural compatibility. Yet all of them suffered from intense partisanship, violence, and mismanagement; indigenous ways did not harmonize with the imported modern ways. Alienation and anger brooded under the surface (even in Japan, certainly in the twenty years before 1945), directed against Westernized natives or the ultimate source of all misery, the West itself. Tragic indeed is the record of state-building and development through the non-Western world in the past and in the present; ominous are the prospects for the future. The political competition and cultural disorientation of the Great Confluence continue to accelerate unabated, promoted in large part by Western ignorance of the consequences of Westernization.

Cultural Incomprehension and Confusion

The world's population is now organized in states patterned after the European nationstate. The relations between states are both cooperative and competitive within a common framework of an anarchic community governed by the rules of power; preparation for war and war itself characterize the new world system as much as it did the old European system of states. For better or worse, the whole world has now become a furnace of human creativity in intense competitive political and cultural interaction. The worldwide rivalry for wealth and power has stimulated an unprecedented rise in material prosperity; it has quickened the pace of scientific and technological discovery; it has advanced human mobility and built, on the surface, a global metropolis remarkably uniform in appearance and standards, glittering with the splendor of human ingenuity, forever eager to advance its vision of human rights in all lands.

Yet that global city is also crammed full with deadly fears and explosive anger. The larger the volume of life on earth, the greater also the common willingness to sacrifice human beings for the sake of power, as one can see from the rising casualty rates of two world wars and the projected carnage of nuclear conflict. The tensions, playing havoc with human rights, are constantly escalating—for obvious reasons.

To this day all-too-few people in the immensely privileged West realize the depths of despair, frustration, and fury to which the world revolution of Westernization has reduced its victims; public opinion, denying

all responsibility, still prefers to look only at its positive aspects. All-too-few observers admit the legitimacy of the counterrevolutions which, in bloody experiments, have tried to recreate the fullness of Western power from recalcitrant non-Western peoples—peoples gladly taking the latest fruits of modernity (including the pride of leadership in the world) yet unwilling or unable to submit to the demanding work routines and civic obligations which constitute the invisible aspects of effective power. In the old Europe cultural diversity was a source of tension and war. In a shrunken world the tensions are even greater. Incompatible cultures and historical traditions are compressed into even closer association among people utterly incapable of dealing constructively with cultural incompatibility. Their ignorance has raised hostility to hitherto unmatched ferocity.

The world revolution of Westernization, in short, has not created a peaceful world order guided by the ascetic and all-inclusive humane rationalism, the best quality in Western civilization. Universalizing the tensions inherent in its own dynamic evolution, it has rather produced a worldwide association of peoples compressed against their will into an inescapable but highly unstable interdependence laced with explosive tensions. Underneath the global universals of power and its most visible supporting skills—literacy, science and technology, large-scale organization—the former diversities persist. The traditional cultures, though in mortal peril, linger under the ground floors of life. Rival political ideologies and ambitions clash head-on. The world's major religions vie with each other as keenly as ever. Attitudes, values, lifestyles from all continents mingle freely in the global marketplace, reducing in the intensified invidious comparison all former absolute truths to questionable hypotheses.

Viewed in this manner, the global confluence thus far has produced not a shiny global city but a global Tower of Babel in which the superficial and ignorant comparison of everything with everything else is undermining all subtle distinctions between right and wrong, good and evil, worth and worthlessness. Even the centers of Western culture, whose traditions were until recently affirmed by their political power, are now inundated by alien ideas and practices, with subversive effects on the very convictions responsible for Western ascendance. An aimless cultural relativism threatens all moral energies; it encourages withdrawal into an illusory shelter of tradition while glorifying brute force perfected by sophisticated technology as the ultimate authority and source of security. Where in this global Babylon do we find the transcendent moral absolutes that can restrain the rising penchant for violence?...

19

European Expansion and Imperialism

	The Old Imperialism ca. 1400–1600	Free Trade Imperialism ca.1600–1830 [*]	The New Imperialism ca. 1870–1945
Chief Players:	Spain, Portugal	England, France, Holland	England, France, Germany, Italy, USA, Japan
Major Agents:	Explorers, Missionaries, Conquistadors	Chartered Monopolies, Merchants	Nations, Missions, Corporations
Main Areas of Activity:	Americas, Indian Ocean (periphery)	Americas, Indian Ocean and China (periphery)	Asia & Africa (Land empires)
Chief Commodities:	Gold, Spices, Slaves	Luxury goods (spices, silk, porcelain, gems, tea) Slaves	Raw materials
Motivations, Rationalizations:	Proselytizing, wealth, individual advancement ("God, Gold, Glory")	Dynastic competition, wealth; "Man-on-the-spot"	National Prestige; Social Darwinism (racism), Cultural & religious superiority, "Dual-Mandate," Humanitarianism; Markets
Relationships to Indigenous People:	Conquest, Trade, Accommodation	Accommodation, Trade, Conquest	Colonialism (pol. subjugation)
Approx % of World Land Area Ruled:	(ca. 1600) 16%	(ca. 1830) 25%	(ca. 1914) 85%

*ca. 1830–1880: The Industrial Revolution and nationalism begin to have major effects in transforming the relationships between Europe and the rest of the world:

1. Trade in luxury goods declines relative to bulk raw materials and the search for markets for European manufactured goods; the slave trade is abolished (1807 and after).
2. European accommodation gives way to educating indigenous peoples in European languages, religion, etc.; this was accompanied by growing disdain and contempt for non-Western cultures.
3. There is some additional territorial acquisition (esp. Britain in India, Australia and New Zealand and the United States to the Pacific Ocean).

20

"The White Man's Burden"

The famous English writer, Rudyard Kipling, composed this poem as a way of celebrating America's annexation of the Philippines after the Spanish-American War of 1898. Though the Americans would not only have to defeat the Spanish in order to lay claim to the Philippines, but also to suppress an independence movement by Filipinos under the leadership of Emiliano Aquinaldo, the acquisition of this strategic outpost in the Pacific, along with Hawaii, placed America in the ranks of a leading world power. As you read this selection, compare Kipling's view of the situation with those of Albert Beveridge, as well as Lugard and other European imperialists, and try to imagine how the Filipinos reacted, both to the event and to the poem.

Discussion Questions

1. What does Kipling mean by "the White Man's Burden?" How did the anti-imperialists respond? Was there a "Brown Man's Burden," and, if so, what was it?

2. How were the Filipinos characterized in this poem? What assumptions about the people of the Philippines, and the Westerners, does Kipling make?

3. How do you suppose the people of the Philippines reacted to the tone and message of this poem?

4. How are race, gender and class used by Kipling in his poem? Were his views typical of attitudes at that time? Do attitudes such as these still exist?

"The White Man's Burden"

Rudyard Kipling

Take up the White Man's burden—
Send forth the best ye breed—
Go, bind your sons to exile
To serve your captives' need;
To wait, in heavy harness,
On fluttered folk and wild—
Your new-caught sullen peoples,
Half devil and half child.

Take up the White Man's burden—
In patience to abide,
To veil the threat of terror
And check the show of pride;
By open speech and simple,
An hundred times made plain,
To seek another's profit
And work another's gain.

Take up the White Man's burden—
The savage wars of peace—
Fill full the mouth of Famine,
And bid the sickness cease;
And when your goal is nearest
(The end for others sought)
Watch sloth and heathen folly
Bring all your hope to nought.

Take up the White Man's burden—
No iron rule of kings,
But toil of serf and sweeper—
The tale of common things.

The ports ye shall not enter,
The roads ye shall not tread,
Go, make them with your living
And mark them with your dead.

Take up the White Man's burden,
And reap his own reward—
The blame of those ye better
The hate of those ye guard—
The cry of hosts ye humour
(Ah, slowly!) toward the light:—
"Why brought ye us from bondage,
Our loved Egyptian night?"

Take up the White Man's burden—
Ye dare not stoop to less—
Nor call too loud on Freedom
To cloke your weariness.
By all ye will or whisper,
By all ye leave or do,
The silent sullen peoples
Shall weigh your God and you.

Take up the White Man's burden!
Have done with childish days
The lightly-proffered laurel,
The easy ungrudged praise;
Comes now, to search your manhood
Through all the thankless years,
Cold, edged with dear-bought wisdom
The judgment of your peers.

Rudyard Kipling, "The White Man's Burden," *McClure's Magazine*, Volume XII, Number 4 (February 1899), pp. 290–291.

21

Social History of the Machine Gun—Imperialism

In this reading, Robert Ellis, a contemporary social historian, explains some of the connections between technology and racism as causal factors in the New Imperialism of the late 19th century.

Discussion Questions

1. What role did the machine gun play in the colonialization of Africa? How do Ellis' views compare with those of Headrick's in the "Legacy of Imperialism?" Did the machine gun facilitate Lugard's rule of thumb regarding imperialism, "to keep the peace and to make the colonies pay?"

2. What did the racism of the late 19th century have to do with the decision to use the machine gun against indigenous peoples in Africa, and throughout the world? Do you see similar attitudes today between the use of technology and the assumptions that are made about different cultures or subcultures?

3. What do you think was the African response to the introduction of the machine gun?

4. If the use of the machine gun was as effective as Ellis suggests, why did the "brass back home," consider it more a "tiresome gimmick," unsuitable for use on a European battlefield?

Making the Map Red

"And the white man had come again with his guns that spat bullets as the heavens sometimes spit hail, and who were the naked Matabele to stand up against these guns?"

A great gulf existed between the effectiveness of military firepower and the soldiers' total lack of respect for its potential. Their contemptuous attitude persisted, even in the teeth of mounting evidence of the unparalleled efficacy of modern firearms. Nor ha that evidence been manifested only in parts of the world not very familiar to European military establishments. The machine gun had also been put to use in an area of the world with which most European armies had close connections, and there its effectiveness had become shatteringly obvious.

In Africa automatic weapons were used to support the seizure of millions of square miles of land and to discipline those unfortunates who wished to eschew the benefits of European civilisation. With machine guns in their armoury, mere handfuls of white men, plunderers and visionaries, civilians and soldiers, were able to scoff at the objections of the Africans themselves and impose their rule upon a whole continent.

Without examining all the reasons for imperialist expansion it is certain that the search for markets, strategical considerations and the question of national prestige were all contributory factors, though historians have argued about the exact importance of each. But of one thing there is no doubt. Whatever the general causes, or the personal motives of the individual colonisers, the whole ethos of the of the imperialist drive was predicated upon racism. Attitudes to the Africans varied from patronising paternalism to contempt and outright hatred, but all assumed that the white man was inherently superior to the black.

A central strand of this racialism was the crude interpretation of Darwinian theories about "the survival of the fittest." Projected back into the past, such theories enabled people to put forward the relative superiority of Western civilisation as a reason for arguing that the white man was the dominant race. One could also extrapolate from them to predict that eventually this race would physically dominate the whole world. An extreme version of this prediction was given in 1881, by W. D. Hay, in a book called *Three Hundred Years Hence*. He described the future paradise:

> The old idea of universal fraternity had worn itself out; or rather it had become modified when elevated into the practical law of life. Throughout the Century of Peace ... men's minds had become opened to the truth, had become sensible of the diversity of species, had become conscious of Nature's law of development ... The stern logic of facts proclaimed the Negro and Chinaman below the level of the Caucasian, and incapacitated from advance towards his intellectual standard. To the development of the White Man, the Black Man and the Yellow must ever remain inferior, and as the former raised itself higher and yet higher, so did these latter seem to sink out of humanity and appear nearer and nearer to the

---

brutes.... It was now incontrovertible that the faculty of Reason was not possessed by them in the same degree as the White Man, nor could it be developed by them beyond a very low point. This was the essential difference that proved the worthlessness of the Inferior Races as contrasted with ourselves, and that therefore placed them outside the pale of Humanity and its brotherhood.

Clearly, working from such a theory of human development, it was easy, even natural, to go on to regard superior military technology as a God-given gift for the suppression of these inferior races. A popular history of science of 1876 offers a perfect example of such an attitude. In the chapter on firearms the author tells us:

We often hear people regretting that so much attention and ingenuity as are shown by the weapons of the present day should have been expended upon instruments of destruction. ...The wise and the good have in all ages looked forward to a time when sword and spear shall be everywhere finally superseded by the ploughshare and the reaping–hook.... Until that happy time arrives ... we may consider that the more costly and ingenious and complicated the instruments of war become, the more certain will be the extension and the permanence of civilisation. The great cost of such appliances as those we are about to describe, the ingenuity needed for their contrivance, the elaborate machinery required for their construction, and the skill implied in their use, are such that these weapons can never be the arms of other than wealthy and intelligent nations. We know that in ancient times opulent and civilised communities could hardly defend themselves against poor and barbarous races.... In our day it is the poor and barbarous tribes who are everywhere at the mercy of the wealthy and cultivated nations.

Europeans had superior weapons because they were the superior race. With regard to the machine gun, for example, one writer assured

his readers that "the tide of invention which has ... developed the 'infernal machine' of Fieschi into the mitrailleur (sic) and Gatling Battery of our own day—this stream took its rise in the God–like quality of reason."

Thus when the Europeans opened their bloody dialogue with the tribes of Africa it was only natural that they should make them see reason through the ineluctable logic of automatic fire. The British Army had decided to purchase twelve Gatlings in October 1869 but they were not sent on active service until 1874, on the occasion of the first campaign against the Ashantis. It was decided that Wolseley's small expeditionary force should take along some Gatlings to even up the odds. The Times heard of this decision in late 1873 and it prompted them to express some rather bloodthirsty hopes:

The Gatling guns ... we presume are mainly intended for the defence of stockaded positions. For fighting in the bush a Gatling would be as much use as a fire engine, but if by any lucky chance Sir Garnet Wolseley manages to catch a good mob of savages in the open, and at a moderate distance, he cannot do any better than treat them to a little Gatling music.... Altogether we cannot wish the Ashantees worse luck than to get in the way of a Gatling well served...

For men like Cecil Rhodes and Frederick Lugard, and organizations like the British South Africa Company and the Imperial East African Trading Company, the Maxim gun was an indispensable tool for the imposition of European control. Maxim himself was only too pleased that his invention should be used in such a role. In 1887 an expedition led by Stanley set off for Wadelai, near Lake Albert, to rescue Emin Pasha (Eduard Schnitzer), who had established a bizarre dominion among the natives of that region. This expedition of mercy attracted the imagination of Europe and Maxim donated one of his guns to help them on their way.

In 1890 the somewhat battered gun was taken up by Lugard when he left Mombasa to travel to Uganda. By the Anglo–German Treaty of that year Uganda had been recognised as falling within the British sphere of influence, and Lugard lost no time in revealing the reality of that influence. Missionaries had already exacerbated tribal tensions there and relations between Protestant and Catholic Africans became increasingly bitter. In 1892 open warfare broke out, with the Catholics demanding the expulsion of the British. Lugard immediately threw his support, which included his Maxims, behind the Protestant Ingleza tribe. This support was decisive, despite Catholic over–optimism. During the preparation for the uprising, Mwanga, its leader, had drawn some faulty conclusions from the tatty appearance of Lugard's much– travelled Maxim. One of his envoys "had circulated the most extraordinary reports, saying that we were cowards who dare not fight … that our Maxim was merely for show, and fired single bullets like a gun." Clearly the usual efficacy of such weapons had already been noised abroad in Africa. But even a battered Maxim was better than no Maxim at all. At the Battle of Mango Hill Lugard and his Sudanese mercenaries threw their weight behind the Protestants, the former taking charge of the machine gun: "Firing the Maxim hastily, Lugard scored a pair of freak hits on the legs of two Fransa chiefs. … He then traversed to cover an open potato patch that the attackers would have to cross. The Maxim was now jamming at almost every other shot . . . but the few rounds Lugard got off sufficed to hold the Fransa back."

Perhaps Mwanga's original concern with the potential of the Maxim gun had been aroused by events in Tanganyika. In 1890 certain German opportunists had established the German East African Company. They almost immediately encountered African opposition and in 1891 the Company was involved in a savage war with the Hehe tribe under their chief Mkwawa. At one stage Hehe warriors had ambushed a German column and massacred almost everyone. But it turned out to be a Pyrrhic victory at best. Towards the end of the battle, "the German officer–surgeon, helped by *askaris*, dragged two machine guns, with plenty of ammunition into a mud hut, and from there turned the tables on the Hehe. He is said to have killed about one thousand of them."

For the rest of the century, and into the twentieth, the use of machine guns was limited to consolidating the Europeans' hold on the African continent, and to the suppression of any native dissent. In 1897 Sir Arthur Hardinge gave a succinct definition of the true nature of European rule. His remarks referred to British policy in Kenya but they are applicable to all nations who had established a foothold on the "dark continent." As he said: "These people must learn submission by bullets—it is the only school. …In Africa to have peace you must first teach obedience and the only person who teaches the lesson properly is the sword." The choice of weapon is a little confused but the message is clear. The only adequate response to native discontent was violence. And despite Harding's rhetorical reference to the *arme blanche*, it was the machine gun that offered the most economical solution to the problem of keeping down the whole population of a continent with small bodies of police and soldiers.

Another group who were prepared to come out into the open about the harsh realities of imperialism were certain British poets of the turn of the century. Perhaps because it was 'only poetry' people felt that their words had less real significance. Nevertheless, the message sometimes came through loud and clear. Even Rudyard Kipling, usually so piously smug about the duties of Empire and the thankless self-sacrifice involved in them, gave at least one scathing definition of Christian civilisation. In 1897 he wrote a poem called "Pharaoh and the Sergeant," dedicated to the Sergeant–Instructors sent to Egypt to help train that country's ramshackle army. It begins thus:

> Said England unto Pharaoh, 'I must make a man of you,
> That will stand upon his feet and play the game;
> That will Maxim his oppressor as a Christian ought to do.'
> And she sent old Pharaoh Sergeant Whatsisname.

Hilaire Belloc was equally blunt in a poem called "The Modern Traveller." In it a typical, somewhat languid colonial figure utters the perfect motto for the triumph of British imperialism:

> I shall never forget the way
> That Blood stood upon this awful day
> Preserved us all from death.
> He stood upon a little mound
> Cast his lethargic eyes around,
> And said beneath his breath:
> "Whatever happens, we have got
> The Maxim Gun, and they have not."

So the slaughter continued. In 1900 the Ashanti had once again to bear the brunt of British displeasure. At first the British fared rather badly. One force was besieged by the Ashanti in the fort at Kumasi, and the relief column, under Captain Aplin, which was sent from Lagos, was continually harassed by the natives. The main reason for Aplin's plight was that the inevitable Maxims accompanying the column were of an old and unreliable model, and whenever they were brought into action they never failed to overheat and jam. But Aplin's force eventually reached the fort and found that the plight of its occupants was not as desperate as had at first been feared. Yet again Maxim guns had saved the day, for "at first the Ashantis had tried to attack the fort itself, but the machine guns on the bastions had proved too effective for them and they had settled down to a long and patient siege. More troops were thrown into the campaign as swiftly as possible, mainly from the

Gold Coast Constabulary and the West African Frontier Force, all these units possessing large numbers of Maxims. They were used to effect in the final battle of Aboasu in which Ashanti resistance was crushed for good.

As was common practice at this time, almost all the troops used in this campaign were African, only the officer being British. One of the most important duties of these officers was to operate the Maxim guns. It would clearly be too dangerous to teach natives, even though they might be wearing a British uniform, the secrets of the white man's ultimate weapon.

In 1898 the U.S. Government also took on colonial responsibilities of a sort when they annexed the Philippines, which had been under Spanish dominion for the preceding four centuries. In the following year they received the honour of having one of Kipling's poems addressed to them. In it he warned them of their heavy responsibilites:

> Take up the White Man's burden—
> Send forth the best ye breed—
> Go bind your sons to exile
> To serve your captives' need;
> To wait in heavy harness
> On fluttered folk and wild—
> Your new-caught, sullen peoples,
> Half devil and half child.

At the time few people in either Britain or the United States objected to such smug assumptions about the superiority of Western civilization. Theodore Roosevelt described it as "rather poor poetry, but good sense from the expansionist view point." But there was in England a small group of radical anti-imperialists, known as the Little Englanders, who did find such patronizing guff rather offensive. Their most prominent spokesperson was Henry Labouchere, who as well as being an emphatic opponent of imperialism in general, was also keenly aware of the intimate links between "paternal" British control and the power of automatic weapons. In a reply to Kipling's poem, published in *Truth*, a journal of which he was the editor, Labouchere banged his point home.

> Pile on the Brown Man's burden!
> And if ye rouse his hate
> Meet his old-fashioned reasons
> With Maxims—up to date,
> With shells and Dum–Dum bullets
> A hundred times make plain
> The Brown Man's loss must never
> Imply the White Man's gain.

In the same journal he also lampooned writing that was generally regarded as being even more sacred than Kipling's verse. His *Pioneers' Hymn* began thus:

> Onward Christian Soldiers, on to heathen lands,
> Prayer-books in your pockets, rifles in your hands,
> Take the glorious tidings where trade can be done:
> Spread the peaceful gospel—with a Maxim gun.

By now then, the picture should be clear. The machine gun was a vitally useful tool in the colonisation of Africa. Time and time again automatic fire enabled small groups of settlers and soldiers to stamp out any indigenous resistance of their activities and to extend their writ over vast areas the African continent. Yet, as has already been indicated, this gruesome test of the machine gun's efficiency had almost no effect upon the military High Command in Britain. For "brass" back home automatic fire was still a tiresome gimmick, not likely to play any significant role upon a European battlefield. The reasons for this complacency are not hard to find.

They are to be found in the ideology of British imperialism, whose very essence was an unquestioning belief in the innate superiority of the white race, and the British in particular. Without such beliefs it would have been impossible for the original colonisers to set such a low price on African lives. For only by holding them so cheap could the slaughter of the natives seem to be morally acceptable. The belief in white supremacy was the very bedrock of imperialist attitudes, and is evident in all their manifestations. At best the Europeans regarded those they slaughtered with little more than amused contempt. Thus Winston Churchill in a letter home from the Sudan:

> It is like a pantomime scene at Drury Lane. These extraordinary foreign figures… march one by one from the dark wings of Barbarism up to the bright footlights of civilisation … And the world audience clap their hands, amused yet impatient … and their conquerors, taking their possessions, forget even their names. Nor will history record such trash … Perhaps the time will come when the supply will be exhausted and there will be no more royal freaks to conquer . . . The good old times will have passed away, and the most cynical philosopher will be forced to admit that though the world may not be much more prosperous it can scarcely be so merry.

This feeling of contempt is obviously functional within a colonial situation. It dehumanises one's opponent and makes it easier to seize his lands and his labour, and to stamp ruthlessly on any sparks of resistance. Thus when it becomes necessary to kill those who stand in one's way, the problem is seen in technical rather than human terms. It is simply a matter of "bagging" as many natives as possible with the minimum effort. The machine gun filled these requirements admirably.

22

Belgian Congo: The Rubber Terror

At the Berlin Conference of 1884–85, the huge central African region of the Congo was accepted as King Leopold II of Belgium's personal possession (which it remained until 1908 when Leopold was pressured into granting it to the Belgian government.) Leopold, who never visited the Congo, exploited the region ruthlessly—making a fortune for his efforts—even though his well-honed publicity presented his goals as strictly benevolent and "civilizing."

The following selection from Adam Hochschild's *King Leopold's Ghost* shows the role of rubber harvesting in making the Congo pay dividends to Leopold and other private investors. (This sort of system was common in many imperialist possessions around the world.)

Glossary:

> Kuba—a kingdom deep in the Congo interior; the people are among the greatest artists in Africa; valued their isolation; had a sophisticated political system.
> William Sheppard—a black American Presbyterian missionary and explorer.
> Chicotte—a whip of raw, sun-dried hippopotamus hide, cut into a long, sharp-edged corkscrew strip; chicotte beatings were very common and sometimes fatal.
> Force Publique—formed in 1888 as an army for the Congo; composed of African mercenaries and European officers; the most powerful army in central Africa; often acted as a corporate labor police force.

Discussion Questions

1. Why was rubber such an important global commodity by the end of the nineteenth century?

2. What role did private corporations play in the Congo rubber trade and how were they related to Leopold and the Congo state?

3. What methods were used to encourage the inhabitants of the Congo to provide rubber to the companies?

4. Was the expansion of the rubber trade beneficial to the indigenous people of the Congo?

5. Can the global trade in commodities ever be beneficial to indigenous people?

The Rubber Terror

Adam Hochschild

Not surprisingly, the Kuba were happy with their existing way of life, and, despite their friendliness toward Sheppard, showed little interest in Christianity. The mission station Sheppard ran among them made few converts. But Sheppard had become so well known back home for his discoveries that the Presbyterians were afraid of an adverse public reaction if they closed his mission to the Kuba and stationed him elsewhere.

The entire Kasai region, like the rest of the Congo, in time succumbed to the tightening grip on the Congo state. Some eight years after Sheppard's historic visit, Leopold's forces finally reached and looted the Kuba capital.

The raid on the capital, like many other events in the Congo, was triggered by a discovery far away. One day a few years before William Sheppard first embarked for Africa, a veterinary surgeon with a majestic white beard was tinkering with his son's tricycle at his home in Belfast, Ireland. John Dunlop was trying to solve a problem that had bedeviled bicyclists for many years: how do you get a gentle ride without springs? Dunlop finally devised a practical way of making a long-sought solution, an inflatable rubber tire. In 1890 the Dunlop Company began making tires—setting off a bicycle craze and starting a new industry just in time, it turned out, for the coming of the automobile.

Europeans had known about rubber ever since Christopher Columbus noticed it in the West Indies. In the late 1700s, a British scientist gave the substance its English name when he noticed it could rub out pencil marks. The Scot Charles Macintosh contributed his name to the language in 1823 when he figured out a mass-production method for doing something long practiced by the Indians of the Americas: applying rubber to cloth to make it waterproof. Sixteen years later the American inventor Charles Goodyear accidentally spilled sulfur into some hot rubber on his stove. He discovered that the resulting mixture did not turn stiff when cold or smelly and gooey when hot—major problems for those trying to make rubber boots or raincoats before then. But it was not until the early 1890s, half a decade after Dunlop fitted the pneumatic tire onto his son's tricycle wheel, that the worldwide rubber boom began. The industrial world rapidly developed an appetite not just for rubber tires, but for hoses, tubing, gaskets, and the like, and for rubber insulation for the telegraph, telephone, and electrical wiring now rapidly encompassing the globe. Suddenly factories could not get enough of the magical commodity, and its price rose throughout the 1890s. Nowhere did the boom have a more drastic impact on people's lives than in the equatorial rain forest, where wild rubber vines snaked high into the trees, that covered nearly half of King Leopold's Congo.

For Leopold, the rubber boom was a godsend. He had gone dangerously into debt with his Congo investments, but he now saw that the return would be more lucrative than he had ever imagined. The world did not lose its desire for ivory, but by the late 1890s wild rubber had far surpassed it as the main source of revenue from the Congo. His fortune assured, the king eagerly grilled functionaries returning from the Congo about rubber harvests; he devoured a constant stream of telegrams and reports from the territory, marking them up in the margins and passing them on to aides for action. His letters from this period are filled with numbers: commodity prices from world markets, interest rates on loans, quantities of rifles to be shipped

to the Congo, tons of rubber to be shipped to Europe, and the exact dimensions of the triumphal arch in Brussels he was planning to build with his newfound profits. Reading the king's correspondence is like reading the letters of the CEO of a corporation that has just developed a profitable new product and is racing to take advantage of it before competitors can get their assembly lines going.

The competition Leopold worried about was from cultivated rubber, which comes not from a vine but a tree. Rubber trees, however, require much care and some years before they grow large enough to be tapped. The king voraciously demanded ever greater quantities of wild rubber from the Congo, because he knew that the price would drop once plantations of rubber trees in Latin America and Asia reached maturity. This did indeed happen, but by then the Congo had had a wildrubber boom nearly two decades long. During that time the search knew no bounds.

As with the men bringing in ivory, those supplying rubber to the Congo state and private companies were rewarded according to the amount they turned in. In 1903, one particularly "productive" agent received a commission eight times his annual salary. But the big money flowed directly back to Antwerp and Brussels, in the capital mostly to either side of the rue Bréderode, the small street that separated the back of the Royal Palace from several buildings holding offices of the Congo state and Congo business operations.

Even though Leopold's privately controlled state got half of concession-company profits, the king made vastly more money from the land the state exploited directly. But because the concession companies were not managed so secretively, we have better statistics from them. In 1897, for example, one of the companies, the Anglo-Belgian India Rubber and Exploration Company, or A.B.I.R., spent 1.35 francs per kilo to harvest rubber in the Congo and ship it to the company's headquarters at Antwerp—where it was sold for prices that sometimes reached 10 francs per kilo, a profit of more than 700 percent. By 1898, the price of A.B.I.R.'s stock was nearly thirty times what it had been six years earlier. Between 1890 and 1904, total Congo rubber earnings increased ninety-six times over. By the turn of the century, the État Indépendant du Congo had become, far and away, the most profitable colony in Africa. The profits came swiftly because, transportation costs aside, harvesting wild rubber required no cultivation, no fertilizers, no capital investment in expensive equipment. It required only labor.

How was this labor to be found? For the Congo's rulers, this posed a problem. They could not simply round up men, chain them together, and put them to work under the eye of an overseer with a *chicotte,* as they did with porters. To gather wild rubber, people must disperse widely through the rain forest and often climb trees.

Rubber is coagulated sap; the French word for it , *caoutchouc,* comes from a South American Indian word meaning "the wood that weeps" The wood that wept in the Congo was a long spongy vine of the *Landolphia* genus. Up to a foot thick at the base, a vine would twine upward around a tree to a hundred feet or more off the ground, where it could reach sunlight. There, branching, it might wind its way hundreds of feet through the upper limbs of another half-dozen trees. To gather the rubber, you had to slash the vine with a knife and hang a bucket or earthenware pot to collect the slow drip of thick, milky sap. You could make a small incision to tap the vine, or—officially forbidden but widely practiced—cut through it entirely, which produced more rubber but killed the vine. Once the vines near a village were drained dry, workers had to go ever deeper into the forest until, before long, most harvesters were traveling at least one or two days to find fresh vines. As the lengths of vine within reach of the ground were tapped dry, workers climbed high

into the trees to reach sap. "We ... passed a man on the road who had broken his back by falling from a tree while ... tapping some vines," wrote one missionary. Furthermore, heavy tropical downpours during much of the year turned large areas of the rain forest, where the rubber vines grew, into swampland.

No payments of trinkets or brass wire were enough to make people stay in the flooded forest for days at a time to do work that was so arduous—and physically painful. A gatherer had to dry the syrup-like rubber so that it would coagulate, and often the only way to do so was to spread the substance on his arms, thighs, and chest. "The first few times it is not without pain that the man pulls it off the hairy parts of his body," Louis Chaltin, a Force Publique officer, confided to his journal in 1892. "The native doesn't like making rubber. He must be compelled to do it."

How was he to be compelled? A trickle of news and rumor gradually made its way to Europe. "An example of what is done was told me up the Ubangi [River]," the British vice consul reported in 1899. "This officer[s]... method ... was to arrive in canoes at a village, the inhabitants of which invariably bolted on their arrival; the soldiers were then landed, and commenced looting, taking all the chickens, grain, etc., out of the houses; after this they attacked the natives until able to seize their women; these women were kept as hostages until the Chief of the district brought in the required number of kilogrammes of rubber. The rubber having been brought, the women were sold back to their owners for a couple of goats apiece, and so he continued from village to village until the requisite amount of rubber had been collected."

Sometimes the hostages were women, sometimes children, sometimes elders or chiefs. Every state or company post in the rubber areas had a stockade for hostages. If you were a male villager, resisting the order to gather rubber could mean death for your wife. She might die anyway, for in the stockades food was scarce and conditions were harsh. "The women taken during the last raid at Engwettra are causing me no end of trouble," wrote Force Publique officer Georges Bricusse in his diary on November 22, 1895. "All the soldiers want one. The sentries who are supposed to watch them unchain the prettiest ones and rape them."

Leopold, of course, never proclaimed hostage-taking as official policy; if anyone made such charges, authorities in Brussels indignantly denied them. But out in the field, far from prying eyes, the pretense was dropped. Instructions on taking hostages were even given in the semiofficial instruction book, the revealing *Manuel du Voyageur et du Résident au Congo,* a copy of which the administration gave to each agent and each state post. The manual's five volumes cover everything from keeping servants obedient to the proper firing of artillery salutes. Taking hostages was one more routine piece of work:

> In Africa taking prisoners is … an easy thing to do, for if the natives hide, they will not go far from their village and must come to look for food in the gardens which surround it. In watching these carefully, you will be certain of capturing people after a brief delay … When you feel you have enough captives, you should choose among them an old person, preferably an old woman. Make her a present and send her to her chief to begin negotiations. The chief, wanting to see his people set free, will usually decide to send representatives.

Seldom does history offer us a chance to see such detailed instructions for those carrying out a regime of terror. The tips on hostage-taking are in the volume of the manual called *Practical Questions,* which was compiled by an editorial committee of about thirty people. One member—he worked on the book during a two-year period following his stint as the head-

collecting station chief at Stanley Falls—was Léon Rom.

Hostage-taking set the Congo apart from most other forced-labor regimes. But in other ways it resembled them. As would be true decades later of the Soviet gulag, another slave labor system for harvesting raw materials, the Congo operated by quotas. In Siberia the quotas concerned cubic meters of timber cut or tons of gold ore mined by prisoners each day; in the Congo the quota was for kilos of rubber. In the A.B.I.R. concession company's rich territory just below the Congo River's great half-circle bend, for example, the normal quota assigned to each village was three to four kilos of dried rubber per adult male per fortnight which essentially meant full-time labor for those men. Elsewhere, quotas were higher and might be raised as time went on. An official in the Mongala River basin in the far north, controlled by another concession company, the Société Anversoise du Commerce au Congo, estimated that to fill their quota, rubber gatherers had to spend twenty-four days a month in the forest, where they built crude cages to sleep in for protection—not always successful—against leopards.

To get at parts of the vine high off the ground, men frantic to get every possible drop of rubber would sometimes tear down the whole vine, slice it into sections, and squeeze the rubber out. Although the Congo state issued strict orders against killing the vines this way, it also applied the *chicotte* to men who didn't bring in enough rubber. The *chicotte* prevailed. One witness saw Africans who had to dig up roots in order to find enough rubber to meet their quotas.

The entire system was militarized. Force Publique garrisons were scattered everywhere, often supplying their firepower to the companies under contract. In addition, each company had its own militia force, euphemistically called "sentries" In military matters as in almost everything else, the companies operated as an extension of the Congo state, and when hostages had to be taken or a rebellious village subdued, company sentries and Force Publique soldiers often took to the field together.

Wherever rubber vines grew, the population was tightly controlled. Usually you had to get a permit from the state or company agent in order to visit a friend or relative in another village. In some areas, you were required to wear a numbered metal disk, attached to a cord around your neck, so that company agents could keep track of whether you had met your quota. Huge numbers of Africans were conscripted into this labor army: in 1906, the books of A.B.I.R. alone, responsible for only a small fraction of the Congo state's rubber production, listed forty-seven thousand rubber gatherers.

All along the rivers, columns of exhausted men, carrying baskets of lumpy gray rubber on their heads, sometimes walked twenty miles or more to assemble near the houses of European agents, who sat on their verandas and weighed the loads of rubber. At one collection point, a missionary counted four hundred men with baskets. After the sap was turned in, it was formed into rough slabs, each the size of a small suitcase, and left to dry in the sun. Then it was shipped downriver, on a barge or scow towed by a steamboat, the first stage of the long journey to Europe.

The state and the companies generally paid villagers for their rubber with a piece of cloth, beads, a few spoonfuls of salt, or a knife. These cost next to nothing, and the knives were essential tools for gathering more rubber. On at least one occasion, a chief who forced his people to gather rubber was paid in human beings. A legal dispute between two white officials near Stanley Falls put the following exchange on record in 1901. The witness being questioned was Liamba, chief of a village named Malinda:

Question: Did M. Hottiaux [a company official] ever give you living women or children?

Answer. Yes, he gave me six women and two men.

Question: What for?

Answer. In payment for rubber which I brought into the station, telling me I could eat them, or kill them, or use them as slaves—as I liked.

The rain forest bordering the Kasai River was rich in rubber, and William Sheppard and the other American Presbyterians there found themselves in the midst of a cataclysm. The Kasai was also the scene of some of the strongest resistance to Leopold's rule. Armed men of a chief allied with the regime rampaged through the region where Sheppard worked, plundering and burning more than a dozen villages. Floods of desperate refugees sought help at Sheppard's mission station.

In 1899 the reluctant Sheppard was ordered by his superiors to travel into the bush, at some risk to himself, to investigate the source of the fighting. There he found bloodstained ground, destroyed villages, and many bodies; the air was thick with the stench of rotting flesh. On the day he reached the marauders' camp, his eye was caught by a large number of objects being smoked. The chief "conducted us to a framework of sticks, under which was burning a slow fire, and there they were, the right hands, I counted them, 81 in all." The chief told Sheppard, "See! Here is our evidence. I always have to cut off the right hands of those we kill in order to show the State how many we have killed." He proudly showed Sheppard some of the bodies the hands had come from. The smoking preserved the hands in the hot, moist climate, for it might be days or weeks before the chief could display them to the proper official and receive credit for his kills.

Sheppard had stumbled on one of the most grisly aspects of Leopold's rubber system. Like the hostage-taking, the severing of hands was deliberate policy, as even high officials would later admit. "During my time in the Congo I was the first commissioner of the Equator district," recalled Charles Lemaire after his retirement. "As soon as it was a question of rubber, I wrote to the government, 'To gather rubber in the district … one must cut off hands, noses and ears.'"

If a village refused to submit to the rubber regime, state or company troops or their allies sometimes shot everyone in sight, so that nearby villages would get the message. But on such occasions some European officers were mistrustful. For each cartridge issued to their soldiers they demanded proof that the bullet had been used to kill someone, not "wasted" in hunting or, worse yet, saved for possible use in a mutiny. The standard proof was the right hand from a corpse. Or occasionally not from a corpse. "Sometimes," said one officer to a missionary, soldiers "shot a cartridge at an animal in hunting; they then cut off a hand from a living man" In some military units there was even a "keeper of the hands"; his job was the smoking.

Sheppard was not the first foreign witness to see severed hands in the Congo, nor would he be the last. But the articles he wrote for missionary magazines about his grisly find were reprinted and quoted widely, both in Europe and the United States, and it is partly due to him that people overseas began to associate the Congo with severed hands. A half-dozen years after Sheppard's stark discovery, while attacking the expensive public works Leopold was building with his Congo profits, the socialist leader Émile Vandervelde would speak in the Belgian Parliament of "monumental arches which one will someday call the Arches of the Severed Hands." William Sheppard's outspokenness would eventually bring down the wrath of the authorities and one day Vandervelde, an attorney, would find himself defending Sheppard in a Congo courtroom. But that is getting ahead of our story.

As the rubber terror spread throughout the rain forest, it branded people with memories that remained raw for the rest of their lives. A Catholic priest who recorded oral histories half a century later quotes a man, Tswambe, speaking of a particularly hated state official named Léon Fiévez, who terrorized a district along the river three hundred miles north of Stanley Pool:

> All the blacks saw this man as the Devil of the Equator… . From all the bodies killed in the field, you had to cut off the hands. He wanted to see the number of hands cut off by each soldier, who had to bring them in baskets…. A village which refused to provide rubber would be completely swept clean. As a young man, I saw [Fiévezs] soldier Molili, then guarding the village of Boyeka, take a big net, put ten arrested natives in it, attach big stones to the net, and make it tumble into the river…. Rubber caused these torments; that's why we no longer want to hear its name spoken. Soldiers made young men kill or rape their own mothers and sisters.

A Force Publique officer who passed through Fiévez's post in 1894 quotes Fiévez himself describing what he did when the surrounding villages failed to supply his troops with the fish and manioc he had demanded: "I made war against them. One example was enough: a hundred heads cut off, and there have been plenty of supplies at the station ever since. My goal is ultimately humanitarian. I killed a hundred people … but that allowed five hundred others to live."

With "humanitarian" ground rules that included cutting off hands and heads, sadists like Fiévez had a field day. The station chief at M'Bima used his revolver to shoot holes in Africans' ear lobes. Raoul de Premorel, an agent working along the Kasai River, enjoyed giving large doses of castor oil to people he considered malingerers. When villagers, in a desperate attempt to meet the weight quota, turned in rubber mixed with dirt or pebbles to the agent Albéric Detiège, he made them eat it. When two porters failed to use a designated latrine, a district commissioner, Jean Verdussen, ordered them paraded in front of troops, their faces rubbed with excrement.

As news of the white man's soldiers and their baskets of severed hands spread through the Congo, a myth gained credence with Africans that was a curious reversal of the white obsession with black cannibalism. The cans of corned beef seen in white men's houses, it was said, did not contain meat from the animals shown on the label; they contained chopped-up hands.

23

American Imperialism

In his book, *The World Revolution of Westernization*, Theodore Von Laue, a contemporary historian, analyzes the relative success of the 19th century imperialists, as well as characterizing the motives, means and consequences of their colonization. Looking at America, which acquired an empire fairly late in the history of the "new" imperialism, with its victory in the Spanish-American War of 1898–1900, Von Laue explains the reasons for his conclusion that the Americans were the "most successful" of the expansionists. As you read, also compare his explanation of American imperialism with the others that we will examine—the Europeans and the Japanese.

Discussion Questions

1. What did American imperialism have in common with its European and Japanese counterparts? What were the differences?

2. Why does Von Laue conclude that the Americans were the most successful of the expansionists, and would you agree? If not, why not?

3. What ideals and institutions motivated the American imperialists? Would you agree with Emily Rosenberg, a contemporary diplomatic historian, who has characterized the American expansionists as "Capitalists, Christians and Cowboys" whose goal was to "spread the American Dream?"

4. What did Manifest Destiny mean to Americans, both before and after 1898? Did America's "bloody 'taste of empire,'" begin in 1898, or, as Von Laue suggests, from the beginning of the encounter between Europeans and the native Americans?

5. How would you answer the last questions Von Laue poses in this selection? How were they answered by Americans, and other expansionists, at the end of the 19th century?

American Imperialism

Americans—to put now their most characteristic qualities into this thumbnail sketch—certainly were the most successful expansionists in the world. From the start, expansion was an elemental necessity of self-preservation and self-affirmation, self-righteously viewed in moral terms. As the Rev. Increase Mather wrote in 1676: the "Lord God of our Fathers has given us for a rightful Possession" the land of "the heathen People amongst whom we live," to which he added his thanks for "... the wonderful Providence of God, who did ... lay the fear of the English and the dread of them upon all the Indians. The terror of God was upon them round about." In this spirit the white man claimed dominion over all lands from the eastern seaboard to the Rocky Mountains and beyond. Resenting the encroachment of arrogant strangers, the Indians fought back, sometimes in utter desperation, to no avail; in the ceaseless Indian wars the best Indian, as the saying went, was a dead Indian. Between the Indians and the frontiersmen backed up by the U.S. army, the contests of power were so unequal that by the end of the 19th century the Indians had ceased to be a political factor deserving recognition or serious attention; the Indian wars, while nurturing romantic fantasies, left no scars on the civic creed. In the process of fighting the Indians the seaboard settlers grew into proud Americans adding new states to the United States from the Atlantic to the Pacific.

In the westward thrust through the continent lateral security posed no problem. To the north the British in Canada offered few incentives for territorial expansion, although in one instance, over a border dispute in the Northwest, Americans threatened to fight if they did not get their way; through the 19th century Canada was eyed as a potential enemy. The temptations were greater to the south, towards the countries of Latin America. Here Americans, some decades after declaring independence, took a sweeping view, claiming to be the protectors of the entire hemisphere against European intervention. In the famous statement by President Monroe (1823), the American government declared that it would regard any attempt by European nations "to extend their system to any portion of this hemisphere as dangerous to [its] peace and safety." Much depended, of course, on the interpretation of "peace and safety," but the Monroe Doctrine projected a bold pretension to an American hegemony over the Western Hemisphere. How bold was shown not long afterwards, when trouble brewed over American settlers in Mexican Texas. For their sake Americans went to war with their southern neighbor, conquering Mexico City in 1847 and annexing California as well as Texas; all told, the Americans took two-fifths of Mexico's territory.

The Mexican war marked the culmination of a feverish expansionism in the name of an American "manifest destiny to overspread the continent allotted by Providence for the free development of our yearly multiplying millions." Its exultation was perhaps best expressed by a senator from New York in January 1848:

> Whoever will look back upon the past and forward to the present, must see that, allured by the justice of our institutions, before the

close of the present century, this continent will teem with a free population of a hundred million souls. Nor have we yet fulfilled the destiny allotted to us. New territory is spread out for us to subdue and fertilize; new races are presented for us to civilize, educate, and absorb; new triumphs for us to achieve in the cause of freedom.

Subsequently, however, Americans respected Mexico's territorial integrity (with minor infringements under President Wilson). Why fight a country when it posed no threat militarily, economically, or politically? By 1900 American capital dominated Mexican finance; Americans owned 78% of the mines, 72% of the smelters, 58% of the oil, 68% of the rubber plantations, and about two-thirds of the railroads. Almost as attractive as Canada, it offered opportunities for the peaceful expansion of American business.

Tempting opportunities also beckoned further afield. After the Mexican war Americans began looking across the Pacific. "Westward will the course of empire take its way," observed Commodore Perry after forcibly opening Japan to Western commerce in 1853, adding that "to me it seems that the people of America will, in some form or other, extend their dominion and their power until they shall have brought within their mighty embrace multitudes of the Islands of the great Pacific, and placed the Saxon race upon the eastern shores of Asia."

After the issue of slavery had been resolved and the West been settled, "Manifest Destiny" reemerged, encouraged by the final thrust of European colonial expansion at the end of the 19th century. "Whether they will or no, Americans must now begin to look outward," wrote Captain Mahan, the prophet of American seapower. And outwardly they looked, especially on their own continent and in the Pacific. As for the Americas, Secretary of State Olney in 1896 announced that "the United States is practically sovereign on this continent, and its fiat is law upon the subjects to which it confines its interpretations." It soon showed its strength by annexing Puerto Rico, exercising protectorates over Cuba, Panama, and Nicaragua, as well as by making the British government toe the American line in a South American border dispute. In the Pacific Admiral Perry's vision came closer to reality with the annexation of the islands of Hawaii, Midway, Guam, and Wake; after the war with Spain the Philippine islands were added. In West Africa Liberia, settled by American blacks, constituted a more inconspicuous (and often overlooked) outpost of American influence.

By 1900 the United States—now come of age, as it was said—had acquired colonial dependencies and become a world power. Reflecting a common sentiment and setting an American model for the great anti-Western challengers of the 20th century, the influential Senator Henry Cabot Lodge wrote, "Small states are of the past, and have no future. The great nations are rapidly absorbing for their future expansion and their present defence all the waste places of the earth. It is a movement which makes for civilization and the advancement of the race. As one of the great nations of the world the United States must not fall out of the line of march." The "advancement of the race" sometimes took rather uncivilized forms, as in an incident during the conquest of the Philippines when the people of a rebellious village, men, women, and children, were herded into an extinct crater and cold-bloodedly gunned to death from the rim. As the *Washington Post* in 1898 summed up the new American mood: "A new consciousness seems to have come upon us—the consciousness of strength, and with it a new appetite, a yearning to show our strength. … Ambition, interest, land-hunger, .pride, the mere joy of fighting, whatever it may be, we are animated by a new sensation. … The taste of empire is in the mouth of the people, even as the taste of blood is in the jungle."

That bloody "taste of empire" in all encounters with alien peoples and creeds had been an ingredient in the American character from the start nourished by the Indian wars, it was not channeled, especially under Theodore Roosevelt's New Nationalism, into global politics. It remained, however, subordinate to the idealism of the American civic creed, held in check by isolationist sentiments or even morally deplored. As compared with the urgency of foreign policy in European states, American foreign relations remained a peripheral issue in public awareness. In any case, territorially secure, the country could expand its sway more effectively in nonterritorial ways and more in line with its ideals.

In reaction against the blatant imperialism of the previous decade President Taft argued that dollars were better than bullets. In an increasingly interdependent world, one of his spokesmen asserted that "international commerce conduces powerfully to international sympathy." Aware of the rapidly growing strength of the American economy, American businessmen had long looked for opportunities abroad, in Europe, Latin America, the Far East, and the Middle East too. Now they worked hand in glove with the government as agents of American policy, eager to spread American influence and promote prosperity. Thus in the Progressive Era American expansionism took an economic turn, demanding an Open Door wherever it saw new opportunities. Thus began the age of the ubiquitous American multinational corporations, led by Standard Oil. Superior technology of mass production aided the process, introducing mechanican novelties like the telephone, phonograph, typewriter, sewing machine, electric streetcars, and, of course, the automobile.

Promoting American business in an interdependent world could easily be fitted into the door-opening American civic creed. American business would draw together the whole world in mutually advantageous relationships, as happened within the American polity. This vision contained even a pacifist strain. Traditional power politics impeded the peaceful flow of goods and people. For that reason President Taft advocated the settlement of international disputes by arbitration.

It was President Wilson, however, who completed the idealist reinterpretation of American expansionism, drawing together the best in the American experience as a model for global cooperation. Under the banner of making the world safe for democracy and guaranteeing lasting peace under the League of Nations (as told in an earlier chapter), he presided over the peace conference which ended World War I. Prompted by the current globalization of power politics, Wilson, the most high-minded among American presidents, projected the American ideal over the world at large. He annexed it to the American dream, holding out the vision of an Americanized humanity.

His initiative, as we have seen, impressed another idealist, Lenin, whose vision by contrast was based on theory rather than on an exceptional historic fate. But he raised a basic question: did the American vision, abstracted from its moorings, really possess universal validity or was its export merely another form of imperialist expansionism? Admittedly, Americans carried with them the benefits of their historical exceptionality and the fruits of their prosperity, in sharp contrast with Lenin's backward Russians. Yet, however attractive their gifts, did Americans in-fuse into international relations the equality so stressed at home? In their pride of global mission they let their ego grow large in 1917, ready to face the sacrifices of war. Yet, giving victory to the countries upholding the Western liberal-democratic tradition, were they aware at their moment of glory that they inspired others, who were outsiders to their traditions, to attempt the same preeminence? What they felt to be idealism might appear to the others merely as raw power disguised as moral righteousness. Who, for that matter, was morally entitled to reshape the world in their own image? Did there exist a universallyaccepted political morality?

24

The March of the Flag

Senator Albert Beveridge of Indiana (1862–1927) delivered the following speech during his campaign for office in 1898 at the time of the Spanish-American War. He was an enthusiastic advocate of American imperialism in which he was joined by many influential people such as Presidents McKinley and Theodore Roosevelt.

Discussion Questions

1. How does Beveridge demonstrate that Americans are God's chosen people?

2. Why does he argue that the consent of the governed should not be considered in the case of American imperialist expansion?

3. On what bases does he justify imperialism?

4. What duties does he imagine America has in the world? In this respect are his views the same as those of Rudyard Kipling in "The White Man's Burden?"

The March of the Flag

It is a noble land that God has given us; a land that can feed and clothe the world; a land whose coastlines would inclose half the countries of Europe; a land set like a sentinel between the two imperial oceans of the globe, a greater England with a nobler destiny.

It is a mighty people that He has planted on this soil; a people sprung from the most masterful blood of history; a people perpetually revitalized by the virile, man–producing working–folk of all the earth; a people imperial by virtue of their power, by right of their institutions, by authority of their Heaven–directed purposes the propagandists and not the misers of liberty.

It is a glorious history our God has bestowed upon His chosen people; a history heroic with faith in our mission and our future; a history of statesmen who flung the boundaries of the Republic out into unexplored lands and savage wilderness; a history of soldiers who carried the flag across blazing deserts and through the ranks of hostile mountains, even to the gates of sunset; a history of a multiplying people who overran a continent in half a century; a history of prophets who saw the consequences of evils inherited from the past and of martyrs who died to save us from them; a history divinely logical, in the process of whose tremendous reasoning we find ourselves today.

Therefore, in this campaign, the question is larger than a party question. It is an American question. It is a world question. Shall the American people continue their march toward the commercial supremacy of the world? Shall free institutions broaden their blessed reign as the children of liberty wax in strength, until the empire of our principles is established over the hearts of all mankind?

Have we no mission to perform, no duty to discharge to our fellow-man? Has God endowed us with gifts beyond our deserts and marked us as the people of His peculiar favor, merely to rot in our own selfishness, as men and nations must, who take cowardice for their companion and self for their deity—as China always has, as India has, as Egypt has?

Shall we be as the man who had one talent and hid it, or as he who had ten talents and used them until they grew to riches? And shall we reap the reward that waits on our discharge of our high duty; shall we occupy new markets for what our farmers raise, our factories make, our merchants sell-aye, and please God, new markets for what our ships shall carry?

Hawaii is ours; Puerto Rico is to be ours; at the prayer of her people Cuba finally will be ours; in the islands of the East, even to the gates of Asia, coaling stations are to be ours at the very least; the flag of a liberal government is to float over the Philippines, and may it be the banner that Taylor unfurled in Texas and Fremont carried to the coast.

The Opposition tells us that we ought not to govern a people without their consent. I answer, The rule of liberty that all just government derives its authority from the consent of the governed, applies only to those who are capable of self-government. We govern the Indians without their consent, we govern our territories without their consent, we govern our children without their consent. How do they know what our government would be without their consent?

By Senator Albert Beveridge. Delivered as a campaign speech on September 16, 1898.

Would not the people of the Philippines prefer the just, humane, civilizing government of this Republic to the savage, bloody rule of pillage and extortion from which we have rescued them?

And, regardless of this formula of words made only for enlightened, self–governing people, do we owe no duty to the world? Shall we turn these peoples back to the reeking hands from which we have taken them? Shall we abandon them, with Germany, England, Japan, hungering for them? Shall we save them from those nations, to give them a self–rule of tragedy?

They ask us how we shall govern these new possessions. I answer: Out of local conditions and the necessities of the case methods of government will grow. If England can govern foreign lands, so can America. If Germany can govern foreign lands, so can America. If they can supervise protectorates, so can America. Why is it more difficult to administer Hawaii than New Mexico or California? Both had a savage and an alien population; both were more remote from the seat of government when they came under our dominion than the Philippines are today.

Will you say by your vote that American ability to govern has decayed; that a century's experience in self–rule has failed of a result? Will you affirm by your vote that you are an infidel to American power and practical sense? Or will you say that ours is the blood of government; ours the heart of dominion; ours the brain and genius of administration? Will you remember that we do but what our fathers did—we but pitch the tents of liberty farther westward, farther southward—we only continue the march of the flag?

The march of the flag! In 1789 the flag of the Republic waved over 4,000,000 souls in thirteen states, and their savage territory which stretched to the Mississippi, to Canada, to the Floridas. The timid minds of that day said that no new territory was needed, and, for the hour, they were right. But Jefferson, through whose intellect the centuries marched; Jefferson, who dreamed of Cuba as an American state; Jefferson, the first Imperialist of the Republic—Jefferson acquired that imperial territory which swept from the Mississippi to the mountains, from Texas to the British possessions, and the march of the flag began!

The infidels to the gospel of liberty raved, but the flag swept on! The title to that noble land out of which Oregon, Washington, Idaho and Montana have been carved was uncertain; Jefferson, strict constructionist of constitutional power though he was, obeyed the Anglo-Saxon impulse within him, whose watchword then and whose watchword throughout the world to–day is, "Forward!": another empire was added to the Republic, and the march of the flag went on!

Those who deny the power of free institutions to expand urged every argument, and more, that we hear, to–day; but the people's judgment approved the command of their blood, and the march of the flag went on!

A screen of land from New Orleans to Florida shut us from the Gulf, and over this and the Everglade Peninsula waved the saffron flag of Spain; Andrew Jackson seized both, the American people stood at his back, and, under Monroe, the Floridas came under the dominion of the Republic, and the march of the flag went on! The Cassandras prophesied every prophecy of despair we hear, today, but the march of the flag went on!

Then Texas responded to the bugle calls of liberty, and the march of the flag went on! And, at last, we waged war with Mexico, and the flag swept over the southwest, over peerless California, past the Gate of Gold to Ore-gon on the north, and from ocean to ocean its folds of glory blazed.

And, now, obeying the same voice that Jefferson heard and obeyed, that Jackson heard and obeyed, that Monroe heard and obeyed, that

Seward heard and obeyed, that Grant heard and obeyed, that Harrison heard and obeyed, our President today plants the flag over the islands of the seas, outposts of commerce, citadels of national security, and the march of the flag goes on!

Distance and oceans are no arguments. The fact that all the territory our fathers bought and seized is contiguous, is no argument. In 1819 Florida was farther from New York than Puerto Rico is from Chicago today; Texas, farther from Washington in 1845 than Hawaii is from Boston in 1898; California, more inaccessible in 1847 than the Philippines are now. Gibraltar is farther from London than Havana is from Washington; Melbourne is farther from Liverpool than Manila is from San Francisco.

The ocean does not separate us from lands of our duty and desire—the oceans join us, rivers never to be dredged, canals never to be repaired. Steam joins us; electricity joins us—the very elements are in league with our destiny. Cuba not contiguous? Puerto Rico not contiguous! Hawaii and the Philippines not contiguous! The oceans make them contiguous. And our navy will make them contiguous.

But the Opposition is right—there is a difference. We did not need the western Mississippi Valley when we acquired it, nor Florida, nor Texas, nor California, nor the royal provinces of the far northwest. We had no emigrants to people this imperial wilderness, no money to develop it, even no highways to cover it. No trade awaited us in its savage fastnesses. Our productions were not greater than our trade. There was not one reason for the land–lust of our states-men from Jefferson to Grant, other than the prophet and the Saxon within them. But, to–day, we are raising more than we can consume, making more than we can use. Therefore we must find new markets for our produce.

And so, while we did not need the territory taken during the past century at the time it was acquired, we do need what we have taken in 1898, and we need it now. The resources and the commerce of these immensely rich dominions will be increased as much as American energy is greater than Spanish sloth. In Cuba, alone, there are 15,000,000 acres of forest unacquainted with the ax, exhaustless mines of iron, priceless deposits of manganese, millions of dollars' worth of which we must buy, to–day, from the Black Sea districts. There are millions of acres yet unexplored.

The resources of Puerto Rico have only been trifled with. The riches of the Philippines have hardly been touched by the finger–tips of modern methods. And they produce what we consume, and consume what we produce—the very predestination of reciprocity—a reciprocity "not made with hands, eternal in the heavens." They sell hemp, sugar, cocoanuts, fruits of the tropics, timber of price like mahogany; they buy flour, clothing, tools, implements, machinery and all that we can raise and make. Their trade will be ours in time. Do you endorse that policy with your vote?

Cuba is as large as Pennsylvania, and is the richest spot on the globe. Hawaii is as large as New Jersey; Puerto Rico half as large as Hawaii; the Philippines larger than all New England, New York, New Jersey and Delaware combined. Together they are larger than the British Isles, larger than France, larger than Germany, larger than Japan.

If any man tells you that trade depends on cheapness and not on government influence, ask him why England does not abandon South Africa, Egypt, India. Why does France seize South China, Germany the vast region whose port is Kaou–chou?

Our trade with Puerto Rico, Hawaii and the Philippines must be as free as between the states of the Union, because they are American territory, while every other nation on earth must pay our tariff before they can compete with us. Until Cuba shall ask for annexation, our trade with her will, at the very least, be like the preferential trade of Canada with England. That, and the excellence of our goods and products; that, and the convenience of traffic; that, and the kinship of interests and destiny, will give the monopoly of these markets to the American people.

The commercial supremacy of the Republic means that this Nation is to be the sovereign factor in the peace of the world. For the conflicts of the future are to be conflicts of trade struggles for markets—commercial wars for existence. And the golden rule of peace is impregnability of Position and invincibility of preparedness. So, we see England, the greatest strategist of history, plant her flag and her cannon on Gibraltar, at Quebec, in the Bermudas, at Vancouver, everywhere.

So Hawaii furnishes us a naval base in the heart of the Pacific; the Ladrones another, a voyage further on; Manila another, at the gates of Asia—Asia, to the trade of whose hundreds of millions American merchants, manufacturers, farmers, have as good right as those of Germany or France or Russia or England; Asia, whose commerce with the United Kingdom alone amounts to hundreds of millions of dollars every year; Asia, to whom Germany looks to take her surplus products; Asia, whose doors must not be shut against American trade. Within five decades the bulk of Oriental commerce will be ours.

No wonder that, in the shadows of coming events so great, free–silver is already a memory. The current of history has swept past that episode. Men understand, to–day, that the greatest commerce of the world must be conducted with the steadiest standard of value and most convenient medium of exchange human ingenuity can devise. Time, that unerring reasoner, has settled the silver question. The American people are tired of talking about money—they want to make it.

* * *

There are so many real things to be done—canals to be dug, railways to be laid, forests to be felled, cities to be builded, fields to be tilled, markets to be won, ships to be launched, peoples to be saved, civilization to be proclaimed and the flag of liberty flung to the eager air of every sea. Is this an hour to waste upon triflers with nature's laws? Is this a season to give our destiny over to word–mongers and prosperity–wreckers? No! It is an hour to remember our duty to our homes. It is a moment to realize the opportunities fate has opened to us. And so it is an hour for us to stand by the Government.

Wonderfully has God guided us. Yonder at Bunker Hill and Yorktown His providence was above us. At New Orleans and on ensanguined seas His hand sustained us. Abraham Lincoln was His minister and His was the altar of freedom the Nation's soldiers set up on a hundred battle–fields. His power directed Dewey in the East and delivered the Spanish fleet into our hands, as He delivered the elder Armada into the hands of our English sires two centuries ago [in 1588—ed.]. The American people can not use a dishonest medium of exchange; it is ours to set the world its example of right and honor. We can not fly from our world duties; it is ours to execute the purpose of a fate that has driven us to be greater than our small intentions. We can not retreat from any soil where Providence has unfurled our banner; it is ours to save that soil for liberty and civilization.

25

Qianlong's Letter to George III

When the Chinese emperor Qianlong wrote this letter to George III, he was writing as a well-established monarch of a powerful, prosperous dynasty, the Manchu, or Qing, established in 1644. Two long-reigning emperors, Qianlong (1726–1795) and his predecessor and considered to be China's ideal leader, Kangxi (1661–1722), would bring China to its peak of greatness, with increases in economic prosperity, population, agricultural innovations and foreign conquests. Yet this dynasty, founded by non-Chinese Manchurians, won respect from the Chinese by sinifying, that is, adopting Chinese values and institutions, in essence, trying to be more Chinese than the Chinese. This sinification included an especially conservative Confucianism that placed importance on self-sufficiency and, in terms of the outside world, a culture-centrism that viewed China as superior to all other cultures. The Chinese had had little contact with other nations, and those in East Asia with whom China had contact, were seen as inferior and expected to pay tribute in the form of regular missions which included the performance of the kowtow to the Chinese emperor. The Tribute System, as these missions were called, was applied to the Europeans when they came to call. In light of their worldview, perhaps it is not surprising that the Manchu (Qing) Dynasty was to be China's last, its decline beginning in 1800, soon after Qianlong's abdication.

Discussion Questions

1. What were the English demands, and what arguments does Qianlong make in refusing those demands? Which position, the English or the Chinese, seems the most rational to you? The most fair?

2. How do you think Qianlong viewed the English? How do you think the English reacted to Qianlong's letter?

3. From Qianlong's letter, how do you think the Tribute System worked? What Chinese attitudes did it reflect? How did it differ from Western views of the relations between nations?

Y ou, O King, live beyond the confines of many seas, nevertheless, impelled by your humble desire to partake of the benefits of our civilisation, you have dispatched a mission respectfully bearing your memorial. Your Envoy has crossed the seas and paid his respects at my Court on the anniversary of my birthday. To show your devotion, you have also sent offerings of your country's produce.

"I have perused your memorial: the earnest terms in which it is couched reveal a respectful humility on your part, which is highly praiseworthy. In consideration of the fact that your Ambassador and his deputy have come a long way with your memorial and tribute, I have shown them high favour and have allowed them to be introduced into my presence. To manifest my indulgence, I have entertained them at a banquet and made them numerous gifts. I have also caused presents to be forwarded to the Naval Commander and six hundred of his officers and men, although they did not come to Peking, so that they too may share in my all-embracing kindness.

"As to your entreaty to send one of your nationals to be accredited to my Celestial Court and to be in control of your country's trade with China, this request is contrary to all usage of my dynasty and cannot possibly be entertained. It is true that Europeans, in the service of the dynasty, have been permitted to live at Peking, but they are compelled to adopt Chinese dress, they are strictly confined to their own precincts and are never permitted to return home. You are presumably familiar with our dynastic regulations. Your proposed Envoy to my Court could not be placed in a position similar to that of European officials in Peking who are forbidden to leave China, nor could be, on the other hand, be allowed liberty of movement and the privilege of corresponding with his own country; so that, you would gain nothing by his residence in our midst.

"Moreover, Our Celestial dynasty possesses vast territories, and tribute missions from the dependencies are provided for by the Department for Tributary States, which ministers to their wants and exercises strict control over their movements. It would be quite impossible to leave them to their own devices. Supposing that your Envoy should come to our Court, his language and national dress differ from that of our people, and there would be no place in which to bestow him. It may be suggested that he might imitate the Europeans permanently resident in Peking and adopt the

From The Emperor Qianlong's "Mandates" in *Annals and Memoirs of the Court of Peking*, by E. Backhouse and J. P. P. Bland, London, 1914, pp. 322–334.

dress and customs of China, but, it has never been our dynasty's wish to force people to do things unseemly and inconvenient. Besides, supposing I sent an Ambassador to reside in your country, how could you possibly make for him the requisite arrangements? Europe consists of many other nations besides your own: if each and all demanded to be represented at our Court, how could we possibly consent? The thing is utterly impracticable. How can our dynasty alter its whole procedure and system of etiquette, established for more than a century, in order to meet your individual views? If it be said that your object is to exercise control over your country's trade, your nationals have had full liberty to trade at Canton for many a year, and have received the greatest consideration at our hands. Missions have been sent by Portugal and Italy, proffering similar requests. The Throne appreciated their sincerity and loaded them with favours, besides authorising measures to facilitate their trade with China. You are no doubt aware that, when my Canton merchant, Wu Chao-ping, was in debt to the foreign ships, I made the Viceroy advance the monies due, out of the provincial treasury, and ordered him to punish the culprit severely. Why then should foreign nations advance this utterly unreasonable request to be represented at my Court? Peking is nearly two thousand miles from Canton, and at such a distance what possible control could any British representative exercise?

"If you assert that your reverence for Our Celestial dynasty fills you with a desire to acquire our civilisation, our ceremonies and code of laws differ so completely from your own that, even if your Envoy were able to acquire the rudiments of our civilisation, you could not possibly transplant our manners and customs to your alien soil. Therefore, however adept the Envoy might become, nothing would be gained thereby.

"Swaying the wide world, I have but one aim in view, namely, to maintain a perfect governance and to fulfil the duties of the state: strange and costly objects do not interest me. If I have commanded that the tribute offerings sent by you, O King, are to be accepted, this was solely consideration for the spirit which prompted you to dispatch them from afar. Our dynasty's majestic virtue has penetrated unto every country under Heaven, and Kings of all nations have offered their costly tribute by land and sea. As your Ambassador can see for himself, we possess all things. I set no value on objects strange or ingenious, and have no use for your country's manufactures. This then is my answer to your request to appoint a representative at my Court, a request contrary to our dynastic usage, which would only result in inconvenience to yourself. I have expounded my wishes in detail and have commanded your tribute Envoys to leave in peace on their homeward journey. It behooves you, O King, to respect my sentiments and to display even greater devotion and loyalty in future, so that, by perpetual submission to our Throne, you may secure peace and prosperity for your country hereafter. Besides making gifts (of which I enclose an inventory) to each member of your Mission, I confer upon you, O King, valuable presents in the number usually bestowed on such occasions, including silks and curios—a list of which is likewise enclosed. Do you reverently receive them and take note of goodwill towards you! A special mandate."

A further mandate to King George III dealt in detail with the British Ambassador's proposals and the Emperor's reasons for declining them: "You, O King, from afar have yearned after the blessings of our civilisation, and in your eagerness to come into touch with our converting influence have sent an Embassy across the sea bearing a memorial. I already taken note of your respectful spirit of submission, have treated your mission with extreme favour and loaded it with gifts, besides issuing a mandate to you, O King, and honouring with the bestowal of valuable presents. Thus has my indulgence been manifested.

"Yesterday your Ambassador petitioned my Ministers to memorialise me regarding your trade with China, but his proposal is not consistent with our dynastic usage and cannot be entertained. Hitherto, all European nations, including your own country's barbarian merchants, have carried on their trade with Our Celestial Empire at Canton. Such has been the procedure for many years, although Our Celestial Empire possesses all things in prolific abundance and lacks no product within its own borders. There was therefore no need to import the manufactures of outside barbarians in exchange for our own produce. But as the tea, silk and porcelain which the Celestial Empire produces, are absolute necessities to European nations and to yourselves, we permitted, as a signal mark of favour, that foreign *hongs* should be established at Canton, so that your wants might be supplied and your country thus participate in our beneficence. But your Ambassador has now put forward new requests which completely fail to recognise the Throne's principle to 'treat strangers from afar with indulgence,' and to exercise a pacifying control over barbarian tribes, the world over. Moreover, our dynasty, swaying the myriad races of the globe, extends the same benevolence towards all. Your England is not the only nation trading at Canton. If other nations, following your bad example, wrongfully importune my ear with further impossible requests, how will it be possible for me to treat them with easy indulgence? Nevertheless, I do not forget the lonely remoteness of your island, cut off from the world by intervening wastes of sea, nor do I overlook your excusable ignorance of the usages of Our Celestial Empire. I have consequently commanded my Ministers to enlighten your Ambassador on the subject, and have ordered the departure of the mission. But I have doubts that, after your Envoy's return he may fail to acquaint you with my view in detail or that he may be lacking in lucidity, so that I shall now proceed to take your requests *seriatim* and to issue my mandate on each question separately. In this way you will, I trust, comprehend my meaning... .

[The emperor then lists the seven requests of the British; only the seventh is included here—Ed.]

"(7) Regarding your nation's worship of the Lord of Heaven, it is the same religion as that of other European nations. Ever since the beginning of history, sage Emperors and wise rulers have bestowed on China a moral system and inculcated a code, which from time immemorial has been observed by the myriads of my subjects. There has been no hankering after heterodox doctrines. Even the European (missionary) officials in my capital are forbidden to hold intercourse with Chinese subjects; they are restricted within the limits of their appointed residences, and may not go about propagating their religion. The distinction between Chinese and barbarian is most strict, and your Ambassador's request that barbarians shall be given full liberty to disseminate religion is utterly unreasonable.

"It may be, O King, that the above proposals have been wantonly made by your Ambas-sador on his shown responsibility, peradventure you yourself are ignorant of our dynastic regulations and had no intention of transgressing them when you expressed these wild ideas and hopes. I have ever shown the greatest condescension to the tribute missions of all States which sincerely yearn after the blessings of civilization, so as to manifest my kindly indulgence. I have even gone out of my way to grant any requests which were in any way consistent with Chinese usage. Above, all, upon you, who live in a remote and inaccessible region, far across the spaces of ocean, but who have shown your submissive loyalty by sending this tribute mission, I have heaped benefits far in excess of those accorded to other nations. But the demands presented by your Embassy are not only a contravention of dynastic tradition, but would be utterly unproductive of good result to yourself, besides being quite impracticable. I have accordingly stated the facts to you in detail, and it is your bounden duty reverently to appreciate my feelings and to obey these instructions henceforward for all time, so that you may enjoy the blessings of perpetual peace. If, after the receipt of this explicit decree, you lightly give ear to the representations of your subordinates and allow your barbarian merchants to proceed to Chêkiang and Tientsin, with the object of landing and trading there, the ordinances of my Celestial Empire are strict in the extreme, and the local officials, both civil and military, are bound reverently to obey the law of the land. Should your vessels touch the shore, your merchants will assuredly never be permitted to land or to reside there, but will be subject to instant expulsion. In that event your barbarian merchants will have had a long journey for nothing. Do not say that you were not warned in due time! Tremblingly obey and show no negligence! A special mandate!

26

Lord Palmerston

This brief selection contains a suggested way to ease the growing tensions over the opium trade. Lord Palmerston, the British Foreign Secretary is writing to the British Envoy in China.

Discussion Questions

1. Do you think Palmerston's suggestion would have removed the tensions between the English and the Chinese? Would the Chinese have accepted it?

2. Do you agree with Palmerston's statement that it was impossible for the English to help the Chinese prevent the importation of opium? What do you think is his underlying message?

3. How did Palmerston view the role and the power of the Chinese government?

May, 1841

Experience has shown that it is entirely beyond the power of the Chinese Government to prevent the introduction of opium into China; and many reasons render it impossible that the British Government can give the Chinese Government any effectual aid toward the accomplishment of that purpose. But while the opium trade is forbidden by law it must inevitably be carried on by fraud and violence; and hence must arise frequent conflicts and collisions between the Chinese preventive service and the parties who are engaged in carrying on the opium trade. These parties are generally British subjects, and it is impossible to suppose that this private war can be carried on between British opium smugglers and the Chinese authorities, without events happening which must tend to put in jeopardy the good understanding between the Chinese and British Governments.

H. M. Government makes no demand in this matter; for they have no right to do so. The Chinese Government is fully entitled to prohibit the importation of opium, if it pleases; and British subjects who engage in a contraband trade must take the consequences of doing so. But it is desirable that you should avail yourself of every favorable opportunity to strongly impress upon the Chinese Plenipotentiary, and through him upon the Chinese Government how much it would be for the interest of the Chinese Government itself to alter the law of China on this matter, and to legalize, by a regular duty, a trade which they cannot prevent.

From Lord Palmerston's Instructions to Sir Henry Pottinger respecting Opium, May, 1841, from S. Couling, *Encyclopedia Sinica*, London, 1917, p. 406.

27

Commissioner Lin's Letter

Lin Zexu, appointed to be the customs inspector at Canton shortly before the outbreak of the Opium War, addressed this letter to Queen Victoria as part of his campaign to eradicate opium from Chinese society. As the governor-general of the two central provinces of Hupei and Hunan, he had earlier distinguished himself by dealing with the opium menace through a policy of confiscating smoking equipment and the drug itself, as well as helping addicts overcome their addiction. He had never dealt with foreigners, however, and this is perhaps apparent in his entreaties to Queen Victoria, as well as in his actions in Canton. His confiscation of Westerners' opium and his blockading of Western enclaves would increase Chinese-British tensions that eventually led to war.

Discussion Questions

1. What is Commissioner Lin's view of the Westerners? Of Chinese?

2. What arguments does he make regarding the reasons that the English should stop the opium trade immediately? Do you find his arguments convincing?

3. How do Lin's views compare with those of the Emperor Qianlong in his letter to George III? Can you detect any differences in attitude or values in the two letters?

4. Besides stopping the trade of opium, what other changes in the Chinese-Western relationship do you think Lin would have welcomed?

A communication: magnificently our great emperor smoothes and pacifies China and the foreign countries, regarding all with the same kindness. If there is profit, then he shares it with the peoples of the world; if there is harm, then he removes it on behalf of the world. This is because he takes the mind of Heaven and earth as his mind.

The kings of your honorable country by a tradition handed down from generation to generation have always been noted for their politeness and submissiveness. We have read your successive tributary memorials saying: "In general our countrymen who go to trade in China have always received His Majesty the Emperor's gracious treatment and equal justice," and so on. Privately we are delighted with the way in which the honorable rulers of your country deeply understand the grand principles and are grateful for the Celestial grace. For this reason the Celestial Court in soothing those from afar has redoubled its polite and kind treatment. The profit from trade has been enjoyed by them continuously for two hundred years. This is the source from which your country has become known for its wealth.

But after a long period of commercial intercourse, there appear among the crowd of barbarians both good persons and bad, unevenly. Consequently there are those who smuggle opium to seduce the Chinese people and so cause the spread of the poison to all provinces. Such persons who only care to profit themselves, and disregard their harm to others, are not tolerated by the laws of Heaven and are unanimously hated by human beings. His Majesty the Emperor, upon hearing of this, is in a towering rage. He has especially sent me, his commissioner, to come to Kwangtung, and together with the governor-general and governor jointly to investigate and settle this matter... .

We find that your country is sixty or seventy thousand *li* from China. Yet there are barbarian ships that strive to come here for trade for the purpose of making a great profit. The wealth of China is used to profit the barbarians. That is to say, the great profit made by barbarians is all taken from the rightful share of China. By what right do they then in return use the poisonous drug to injure the Chinese people? Even though the barbarians may not necessarily intend to do us harm, yet in coveting profit to an extreme, they have no regard for injuring others. Let us ask, where is your conscience? I have heard that the smoking of opium is very strictly forbidden by your country; that is because the harm caused by opium is clearly understood. Since it is not permitted to do harm to your own country, then even less should you let it be passed on to the harm of other countries—how much less to China! Of all that China exports to foreign countries, there is not a single thing which is not beneficial to people; they are of benefit when eaten, or of benefit when used, or of benefit when resold: all are beneficial. Is there a single article from China which has done any harm to foreign countries? Take tea and rhubarb, for example; the foreign countries cannot get along for a single day without them. If China cuts off these benefits with no sympathy for those who are to suffer, then what can the barbarians rely upon to keep themselves alive? Moreover the woolens, camlets, and longells [i.e., textiles] of foreign countries cannot be woven unless they

From *International Relations of the Chinese Empire* (Shanghai, 1910), Volume I, pp. 138–144.

obtain Chinese silk. If China, again, cuts off this beneficial export, what profit can the barbarians expect to make? As for other foodstuffs, beginning with candy, ginger, cinnamon, and so forth, and articles for use, beginning with silk, satin, chinaware, and so on, all the things that must be had by foreign countries are innumerable. On the other hand, articles coming from the outside to China can only be used as toys. We can take them or get along without them. Since they are not needed by China, what difficulty would there be if we closed the frontier and stopped the trade? Nevertheless our Celestial Court lets tea, silk, and other goods be shipped without limit and circulated everywhere without begrudging it in the slightest. This is for no other reason but to share the benefit with the people of the whole world.

The goods from China carried away by your country not only supply your own consumption and use, but also can be divided up and sold to other countries, producing a triple profit. Even if you do not sell opium, you still have this threefold profit. How can you bear to go further, selling products injurious to others in order to fulfill your insatiable desire?...

We have further learned that in London, the capital of your honorable rule, and in Scotland (Ssu-ko-lan), Ireland (Ai-lun), and other places, originally no opium has been produced. Only in several places of India under your control such as Bengal, Madras, Bombay, Patna, Benares, and Malwa has opium been planted from hill to hill, and ponds have been opened for its manufacture. For months and years work is continued in order to accumulate the poison. The obnoxious odor ascends, irritating Heaven and frightening the spirits. Indeed you, O King, can eradicate the opium plant in these places, hoe over the fields entirely, and sow in its stead the five grains [i.e., millet, barley, wheat, etc.}. Anyone who dares again attempt to plant and manufacture opium should be severely punished. This will really be a great, benevolent government policy that

will increase the common weal and get rid of evil. For this, Heaven must support you and the spirits must bring you good fortune, prolonging your old age and extending your descendants. All will depend on this act.....

Now we have set up regulations governing the Chinese people. He who sells opium shall receive the death penalty and he who smokes it also the death penalty. Now consider this: if the barbarians do not bring opium, then how can the Chinese people resell it, and how can they smoke it? The fact is that the wicked barbarians beguile the Chinese people into a death trap. How then can we grant life only to these barbarians? He who takes the life of even one person still has to atone for it with his own life; yet is the harm done by opium limited to the taking of one life only? Therefore in the new regulations, in regard to those barbarians who bring opium to China, the penalty is fixed at decapitation or strangulation. This is what is called getting rid of a harmful thing on behalf of mankind.

Moreover we have found that in the middle of the second month of this year [April 9] Consul [Superintendent] Elliot of your nation, because the opium prohibition law was very stern and severe, petitioned for an extension of the time limit. He requested a limit of five months for India and its adjacent harbors and related territories, and ten months for England proper, after which they would act in conformity with the new regulations. Now we, the commissioner and others, have memorialized and have received the extraordinary Celestial grace of His Majesty the Em-peror, who has redoubled his consideration and compassion. All those who within the period of the coming one year (from England) or six months (from India) bring opium to China by mistake, but who voluntarily confess and completely surrender their opium, shall be exempt from their punishment. After this limit of time, if there are still those who bring opium to China then they will plainly have committed a willful violation and shall at once be executed according to law, with absolutely no clemency or pardon. This may be called the height of kindness and the perfection of justice.

Our Celestial Dynasty rules over and supervises the myriad states, and surely possesses unfathomable spiritual dignity. Yet the Emperor cannot bear to execute people without having first tried to reform them by instruction. Therefore he especially promulgates these fixed regulations. The barbarian merchants of your country, if they wish to do business for a prolonged period, are required to obey our statutes respectfully and to cut off permanently the source of opium. They must by no means try to test the effectiveness of the law with their lives. May you, O King, check your wicked and sift out your vicious people before they come to China, in order to guarantee the peace of your nation, to show further the sincerity of your politeness and submissiveness, and to let the two countries enjoy together the blessings of peace. How fortunate, how fortunate indeed! After receiving this dispatch will you immediately give us a prompt reply regarding the details and circumstances of your cutting off the opium traffic. Be sure not to put this off. The above is what has to be communicated. [Vermilion endorsement:] This is appropriately worded and quite comprehensive (*Te-t'i chou-tao*).

28

The English and the Opium Trade

This selection, written by a contemporary Chinese scholar, is an historical account of the issues, events and personalities involved in the opium trade, one of the contentious issues that would eventually lead to the Opium War (1839–1842) and China's first defeat. In the words of one western historian, these events for the West constituted "imperialism begun in a pipe dream."

Discussion Questions

1. How was the opium trade conducted, and how did the trade change between the reign of Qianlong and the beginning of the war in 1839? What were the reasons for these changes?

2. What did the Chinese offer as solutions to the problems caused by the opium trade? Do you see similarities in the Chinese recommendations, and those of Americans today? Were any of the Chinese proposals successful, and if not, why not?

3. What response did the Westerners make to the attempts by the Chinese government to eradicate opium? What do you think of the Western position, and is it in any way similar to the views of those countries involved in the present drug trade? What underlying attitudes, even principles, motivated the Western response?

4. The writer calls the Chinese view of opium "hypocritical." Why, and would you agree? Is this view similar to our contemporary attitude towards drugs?

5. Do you think Commissioner Lin's policies were the only ones available to the Chinese at the time? Was Lin a hero or a fool? Did Captain Elliot, who controlled the British trade in China, handle his role effectively?

Before the eighteenth century England produced no major product marketable in China, and for the most part her ships carried silver rather than goods to China. Economists at that time, whether Chinese or foreign, appreciated the fact that a steady drain of gold and silver was detrimental to a nation's economy, and each nation sought to increase exports, thereby increasing the inflow of gold and silver. After many years in the China trade the British discovered that opium was an extremely lucrative item; thus the British East India Company encouraged the cultivation of opium in India while controlling its transport to China. During the first few years of the Ch'ien-lung Emperor's reign (1736–1795) the Chinese imported only about four hundred chests annually (each chest was about a hundred *chin*; a *chin* is about a kilo). The Ch'ien-lung Emperor had forbidden Chinese merchants to sell opium, but his efforts came to nought. By the time of the Chia-ch'ing Emperor (1796–1820) the import of opium had increased to almost four thousand chests a year. Finally, the Chia-ch'ing Emperor prohibited further imports, but because of corruption among the official class, the enforcement of inspection and prohibition proved to be extremely difficult. The opium trade continued to expand.

The Tao-kuang Emperor was more concerned than all his predecessors over the opium problem. He proved the most determined to suppress its use, and upon ascending the throne, he issued ordinances strictly prohibiting opium smoking. But opium imports increased faster than ever before. During the first year of the Tao-kuang Emperor's reign (1821) the amount of opium coming into China was still quite low, only five thousand chests, but by 1850 it had jumped to over thirty thousand chests (worth about eighteen million Chinese *yuan*). The result was that Chinese silver was rapidly drained away in return for opium which was of no benefit to her whatsoever. The whole country regarded this as a calamity, but officials in Kwangtung felt that the prohibition on opium was utterly impractical in view of the fact that the opium trade was in the interest of those who gave the orders to suppress it. This group suggested instead that the tax on foreign opium be increased, and that local product ion in China be stepped up simultaneously to compete with the foreign opium trade, thus rendering it no longer profitable for foreign merchants to bring opium from India and thereby halting importation.

By the fourteenth year of the Tao-kuang Emperor's reign (1834) the advocates of this policy were in ascendancy, but no one except Hsu Nai-chi dared publicly speak in its favor. In the eighteenth year of the Tao-kuang Emperor's reign (1838) Huang Chueh-tzu memorialized the Emperor, clamoring angrily for prohibition and advocating summarily stamping out all opium smoking. He claimed that if no one smoked opium, no one would buy opium, and he suggested that those who smoked opium might be cured by capital punishment.

After Huang Chueh-tzu's memorial had reached the Emperor, the Emperor asked that each provincial governor present his view on the subject. Although no one came forward and directly opposed Huang Chueh-tzu, they felt that his policy was obviously too extreme, maintaining that opium smokers harmed only themselves while the merchants who dealt in opium harmed many. Were not the merchants' crimes much graver than the addicts? They concluded that since Canton was the main port of entry and sale of opium, outlawing its use should begin there.

Lin Tse-hsu, Viceroy for Hunan and Hupei, agreed with Huang Chueh-tzu's proposal and advised that all measures be taken to enforce them. The Tao-kuang Emperor decided that the prohibition of the sale and use of opium ought to be enforced with greater severity; thus he sent Lin Tse-hsu to Canton as his High Commissioner to look into the problem. Lin, a Fukienese and one of the most renowned and capable officials in political circles of his time, and greatly respected by the scholar-official class, was a tremendously self-confident and arrogant man. He had no real experience handling "barbarians," but he recklessly announced that, "I am intimately acquainted with the wily ways of the barbarian from my sojourn in Fukien."

Actually, people at that time were rather hypocritical about the whole opium problem. They admitted in private correspondence to the difficulties of suppressing opium, but in their official memorials they toed the line with ceremonious ostentation. This sort of lack of candor was a great problem among the scholar-official class.

In reality, opium suppression was an extremely complicated and difficult problem, and it would have been no easier without foreign interference. But how much more difficult it was during the Tao-kuang reign, when the English were totally unwilling to allow us to carry out the policy of suppression. Opium was not only commercially very profitable then, it also constituted the greater part of the revenues earned by the Indian government, and in view of this, the English were uneasy about our policy of trying to close the country to free trade. They were eager to settle matters once and for all, and

had we given them the slightest pretext over the opium problem, they would not have hesitated to deal with us by force of arms.

We call the war that followed the Opium War; the English call it the Trade War. Both sides had their own reasons. In regard to the opium problem—we tried to get rid of the curse altogether, while the English hoped to maintain the situation as it was; we were the ones who wished to alter the status quo. In regard to the trade problem—the English sought new opportunities and freedom, and it was we who wished to maintain the status quo. Under these circumstances, war was unavoidable.

Clash Between East and West

On March 10 of the nineteenth year of the Tao-kuang Emperor's reign (1839), Lin Tsehsu arrived at Canton. He spent a week pondering the situation and settling himself before he made his first move. He then issued a proclamation to all foreigners, saying that it was not right to harm others for the sake of one's own profit: "How dare you bring your country's vile opium into China, cheating and harming our people?"

Lin made two demands of the foreigners: first, he asked that they take all the unsold opium and "hand it all over to Chinese officials"; second, he asked that the foreigners pledge not to import any more opium into China. If they continued, said Lin, "the opium will be confiscated and those involved will be decapitated." Unfortunately, the foreigners did not understand that Lin meant business, thinking that he was just another ordinary official who, as a matter of course, had issued a pious proclamation as a formality at the beginning of his term of office. But after all, they thought, would not Lin be willing to sell out like all the other officials after they got around to settling the price of the squeeze and, would not trade then be able to continue as usual? They did not realize that Lin was not this sort of man. Lin said, "If the opium trade does not cease, I, the Imperial High Commissioner, will not leave my post. I will persevere in this matter until the end."

By the end of March the foreigners were still unwilling to hand over their opium stocks. Lin Tse-hsu then issued an order forbidding any movement to and from Canton, and sent troops to encircle the thirteen foreign factories (foreign trading establishments). He ordered all Chinese to leave the factories and he later forbade anyone at all from entering or leaving. In short, Lin turned the thirteen factories into foreign prisons and prohibited the sale of foodstuffs to the inmates.

At that time there were roughly three hundred and fifty foreigners inside the thirteen factories, among whom was the English Superintendent of Trade, Captain Charles Elliot. Naturally, those inside did suffer a certain amount of privation—they had to do chores, like boil their own water, wash their own dishes, and do their own housework—but there was enough food, since the foreigners had previously stored up a large quantity and were also being clandestinely supplied.

Captain Elliot had originally hoped to compromise, but Lin stood firmly to his two demands. At that time the English, unfortunately, happened to have only two small gunboats in Chinese waters, and the troops on board had no chance of landing at Canton. Captain Elliot had no means by which to protest, and to yield was his only alternative. But the way in which he chose to yield is worth our attention: instead of simply ordering the English merchants to hand over their opium to Lin, he ordered them to hand the opium over to him; in his capacity as Superintendent of Trade, he gave each merchant a receipt, and by one quick maneuver all British opium became the property of the British crown.

Captain Elliot then handed over 20,280 chests of opium to the Chinese. This was a great victory for Lin, who, with one toss of the net, had trapped a million *chin* of opium, The Tao-kuang Emperor was indeed pleased, and he commended Lin, saying, "Your great loyalty to the throne and your unbounded love of your country are unequaled and unmatched by any within or without the Empire."

But still the foreigners did not quite believe that Lin was genuinely determined to suppress the opium trade, and they thought that he must be in some way profiting. They soon learned otherwise.

At Hu-men, on the Pearl River Delta, Lin ordered two huge pools to be dug in the sandy banks. He later wrote:

> First I had a series of trenches dug and then I dug ditches to connect them. After this was completed, I had water diverted into the trenches through the ditches. Then I had salt sprinkled on the pools. Finally, I had the unprocessed opium thrown into the pools and added lime to boil the opium. The opium was thereby turned into ashes and completely destroyed. The nauseating odor was more than we could bear. When the tide finally receded we opened the trenches and let the residue flow away. We then used brushes to clean the bottom of the pools so that nothing remained. The process took twenty-three days. Every bit of opium was completely destroyed. Each day civilian and military officials were there to supervise. Even the foreigners came to watch and to record the events in detail. They lavishly praised the Commissioner's integrity.

Meanwhile Captain Elliot had made thorough report to London and was quietly awaiting further orders. After his apparent success, Lin was greatly relieved. The Emperor was so pleased that he offered Lin a new position—Viceroy to Kwangtung and Kwangsi—but Lin humbly turned down the offer, claiming that "although all the opium in the factories had been completely destroyed, there is still the possibility that more may be smuggled in." Lin wanted to do the job thoroughly, and thus subsequently demanded that all foreign merchants sign a bond committing themselves thenceforth to observe the Chinese regulations prohibiting opium trade. Captain Elliot refused to sign thereby stirring up the simmering conflict once again. But by this time Lin was swelled with new confidence, and claimed that the English power was nowhere near as menacing as in fact it was. In addition, he believed that the English were utterly dependent on the Chinese since they needed Chinese *tea* and *rhubarb!* He thought that if he simply cut off their supply of tea and rhubarb he could bring about their ruination.

The forts at Hu-men were repaired and overhauled. Lin also took a huge iron chain and stretched it across the entrance of Humen harbor as a blockade.

That winter Chinese junks clashed on numerous occasions with British ships in the waters around Canton. Each time Lin memorialized the Emperor claiming smashing victories, putting the whole country in a very optimistic mood.

When the British government finally received Elliot's letter, they dispatched Admiral George Elliot as plenipotentiary in charge of an expeditionary force to China.

29

Treaties of Nanjing and Wang-hea

Key provisions of the treaties ending the Opium War are presented in this selection. The Treaty of Nanjing was the first of four treaties that were signed with China by the Western nations, ending formal hostilities. As if these assaults to China's sovereignty were not enough, two years later, the Treaty of Wanghea, signed by the United States and China, provided additional humiliation to a China humbled by their loss, and, for that reason, they have been called the "unequal treaties." These treaties also established a pattern in the West's dealing with other nations in Asia and throughout the world, where similar negotiations led to the establishment of a relationship favorable to the West's interests. In addition to the economic and territorial provisions of the treaties, the sections dealing with diplomatic conduct between nations, which contains the concept of "most favored nation," is also important. Article XXI of the Treaty of Wang-hea introduced the right of extraterritoriality, or the right for foreigners to be governed by western judicial standards.

Discussion Questions

1. Based on the reasons that the Opium War was fought, how successful were the victors in achieving their objectives in these treaties? What price did the Chinese have to pay for defeat?

2. Do you think the treaties were fair to China? Given the earlier arguments of Qianlong and Commissioner Lin, with which provisions would the Chinese find most difficult to comply? Which of the provisions was most injurious to China's view of itself? Which was most injurious to the West's view of itself?

3. If you were a member of the Chinese government at this time (1840s), what course of action would you now recommend to your emperor?

Treaty of Nanjing, 1842

Victoria, by the Grace of God, Queen of the United Kingdom of Great Britain and Ireland, Defender of the Faith, etc., etc., etc. To all and Singular to whom these Presents shall come. Greetings! Whereas a Treaty between Us and Our Good Brother the Emperor of China, was concluded and signed, in the English and Chinese Languages, on board Our Ship the *Cornwallis*, at Nanjing, on the Twenty-ninth day of August, in the Year of Our Lord One Thousand Eight Hundred and Forty-two, by the Plenipotentiaries of Us and of Our said Good Brother, duly and respectively authorized for that purpose; which Treaty is hereunto annexed in Original:—

ARTICLE I.

There shall henceforward be Peace and Friendship between Her Majesty the Queen of the United Kingdom of Great Britain and Ireland, and His Majesty the Emperor of China, and between their respective Subjects, who shall enjoy full security and protection for their persons and property within the Dominions of the other.

ARTICLE II.

His Majesty the Emperor of China agrees, that British Subjects, with their families and establishments, shall be allowed to reside, for the purpose of carrying on their Mercantile pursuits, without molestation or restraint at the Cities and Towns of Canton, Amoy, Foochow-fu, Ningpo, and Shanghai... .

ARTICLE III.

It being obviously necessary and desirable, that British Subjects should have some Port whereat they may careen and refit their ships, when required, and keep Stores for that purpose, His Majesty the Emperor of China cedes to Her Majesty the Queen of Great Britain, etc., the Island of Hongkong... .

ARTICLE IV.

The Emperor of China agrees to pay the sum of Six Millions of Dollars as the value of Opium which was delivered up at Canton in the month of March 1839, as a Ransom for the lives of Her Britannic Majesty's Superintendent and Subjects, who had been imprisoned and threatened with death by the Chinese High Officers.

ARTICLE VI.

The Government of Her Britannic Majesty having been obliged to send out an Expedition to demand and obtain redress for the violent and unjust Proceedings of the Chinese High Authorities towards Her Britannic Majesty's Officers and Subjects, the Emperor of China agrees to pay the sum of Twelve Millions of Dollars on account of the Expenses incurred... .

From the Treaty of Nanjing, Vol. I, pp. 351–356, and "The Most-Favored Nation Clause: Article VIII, Treaty of the Bogue, p. 393, in *China: Treaties, Conventions, Etc., Between China and Foreign States*, published at the Statistical Department of the Inspectorate General of Customs, 2 vols., 1917.

ARTICLE XII.

On the assent of the Emperor of China to this Treaty being received and the discharge of the first instalment of money, Her Britannic Majesty's Forces will retire from Nanjing and he Grand Canal, and will no longer molest or stop the Trade of China. The Military Post at Chinhai will also be withdrawn, but the Islands of Koolangsoo and that of Chusan will continue to be held by Her Majesty's Forces until the money payments, and the arrangements for opening the Ports to British Merchants be completed.

Treaty of Wang-Hea, 1844

ARTICLE I.

There shall be a perfect, permanent, and universal peace and a sincere and cordial amity between the United States of America on the one part, and the Ta-Tsing Empire on the other part, and between their people respectively, without exception of persons or places.

ARTICLE II.

Citizens of the United States resorting to China for the purpose of commerce will pay duties of import and export prescribed by the Tariff which is fixed by and made a part of this Treaty. They shall in no case be subject to other or higher duties than are or shall be required of the people of any other nation whatever. ... If the Chinese Government desire to modify in any respect the said Tariff, such modifications shall be made only in consultation with Consuls or other functionaries thereto duly authorised in behalf of the United States, and with consent thereof. And if additional advantages or privileges of whatever description be conceded hereafter by China to any other nation, the United States and the citizens thereof shall be entitled thereupon to a complete, equal, and impartial participation in the same.

ARTICLE III.

The citizens of the United States are permitted to frequent the five ports of Quangchow, Amoy, Fuchow, Ningpo, and Shanghai, and to reside with their families and trade there, and to proceed at pleasure with their vessels and merchandise to or from any Foreign port and either of the said five ports, and from either of said five ports to any other of them; but the said vessels shall not unlawfully enter the other ports of China, nor carry on a clandestine and fraudulent trade along the coasts thereof; and any vessel belonging to a citizen of the United States which violates this provision shall, with her cargo, be subject to confiscation to the Chinese Government.

ARTICLE XIX.

All citizens of the United States in China peaceably attending to their affairs, being placed on a common footing of amity and goodwill with subjects of China, shall receive and enjoy, for themselves and everything appertaining to them, the special protect ion of the local authorities of Government, who shall defend them from all insult or injury of any sort on the part of the Chinese.

If their dwellings or their property be threatened or attacked by mobs, incendiaries, or other violent or lawless persons, the local officers, on requisition of the Consul, will immediately despatch a military force to disperse the rioters, and will apprehend the guilty individuals and punish them with the utmost rigour of the law.

ARTICLE XXI.

Subjects of China who may be guilty of any criminal act towards citizens of the United States shall be arrested and punished by the Chinese authorities according to the laws of China, and citizens of the United States who may commit any crime in China shall be subject to be tried and punished only by the Consul or other public functionary of the United States thereto authorised according to the laws of the United States; and in order to the prevention of all controversy and disaffection, justice shall be equitably and impartially administered on both sides.

30

The Reform Movement in China, 1898—Chang Chih-tung

A critical issue for the Chinese since their defeat in the Opium War in 1842 and the disastrous Taiping Rebellion, finally suppressed in 1864, was how to regain their loss of sovereignty and reestablish the stability they had once enjoyed. While most of those responsible for leading China preferred to continue the Confucian-oriented policies of the past, there were some officials who, in the 1870's, advocated reform in the form of a "self-strengthening" movement. With the slogan, "Learn the superior technology of the barbarian, in order to control him," the T'ung Chih Restoration led to new plans for a modern army and navy, industrialization and changes within the diplomatic corps, but the changes were slow for lack of government support. The "Hundred Days of Reform" would sprout in 1898, after China's shocking defeat in the Sino-Japanese War, with decrees issued by the dozens. The following selection presents a case for change in the form of a memorial written to Emperor Kuang Hse, a nephew of the Empress Dowager Cixi, the real power in China at the time. His essay was translated and published in English as *China's Only Hope*. Though the writer was one of China's leading officials at the time, and his memorial was praised by the emperor himself as a model of classical Chinese scholarship, few of the suggestions were adopted due to the opposition from the Empress, other conservative officials and the coming of the Boxer Rebellion. As you read, consider why, given all of the humiliations that China had suffered, there would not have been a greater impetus for change at this time.

Discussion Questions

1. In one of his statements, the writer suggests, "Know what is important." What was that and do you think the suggestions he made would have saved China further humiliation? What additional proposals would you have made?

2. When he refers to the parable of Confucius, what do you think his purpose and his intended audience were?

3. What aspects of Western values and institutions does the writer admire and how does he suggest China make use of them? What is his opinion of China? Of its values?

In no period of China's history has there arisen an emergency like the present. It is a time of change, and His Imperial Highness, the Emperor of China, has accepted the situation by altering somewhat the system of civil and military examinations and by establishing schools... . The Conservatives are evidently off their food from inability to swallow, whilst Liberals are like a flock of sheep who have arrived at a road of many forks and do not know which to follow. The former do not understand what international intercourse means, the latter are ignorant of what is radical in Chinese affairs. The Conservatives fail to see the utility of modern military methods and the benefits of successful change, while the Progressionists, zealous without knowledge, look with contempt upon our widespread doctrines of Confucius. Thus those who cling to the order of things heartily despise those who even propose any innovation, and they in turn cordially detest the Conservatives with all the ardor of their liberal convictions. It thus falls out that those who really wish to learn are in doubt as to which course to pursue, and in the meantime error creeps in, the enemy invades our coast, and, consequently, there is no defence and no peace.

The present condition of things is not due to outside nations, but to China herself. It has ever been true that the number of our able men has been proportioned to the good qualities of the government, and that morals are gauged by the conduct of the schools. In view of many facts, and with the hope of relieving our country from her present embarrassments, We, the Viceroy of the Liang Hu, have prepared this work especially for the Chinese under our jurisdiction, and generally for our countrymen in the other provinces... .

The corollaries of these Twenty Chapters may be briefly Comprehended in Five Objects of Knowledge.

1. Know the shame of not being like Japan, Turkey, Siam, and Cuba.
2. Know the fear that we will become India, Annam, Burmah, Korea, Egypt, and Poland.
3. Know that if we do not change our customs we cannot reform our methods, and if we do not reform our methods we cannot utilize the modern implements of war, etc.
4. Know what is important. The study of the old is not urgent; the call for men of attainments in useful knowledge is

---

From Chang Chih-tung, *China's Only Hope: An Appeal*, trans. by Samuel I. Woodbridge, New York, 1900, pp. 19–21, 25, 26.

pressing. Foreign education is of different kinds. Western handicraft is not in demand, but a knowledge of the methods of foreign governments is a consummation devoutly to be wished.

5. Know what is radical. When abroad, do not forget your own native country; when you see strange customs, do not forget your parents; and let not much wisdom and ingenuity make you forgot the holy sages.

It will be seen then that the purport of what we have written accords well with the Doctrine of the Mean. Long ago, when the kingdom of Lu was in a weak condition, Duke Ai (B. C. 550) inquired of Confucius about government. He replied: "To he fond of learning is the next thing to knowledge. To be up and doing comes near to perfection. Know what shame is, and you will not be far from heroism." Finally the sage said: "If these principles can be carried out, although one may be stupid, yet he will become clever; although weak, he will attain to strength." These maxims were spoken in the time of Lu. How much more urgent are they now when China has become great, with her almost limitless territory and her teeming population of four hundred millions!... .

Chapter 1. United Hearts

How circumscribed would be the responsibility of one graduate, the altruism of one official, or the duty of a single individual! But if by one determined purpose the heart's of *all* the graduates, the officials, and the men of China were united, our country world rest upon a great rock and we could defy the world to overthrow us. To attain this object it is necessary first that every man should fulfill his duty to his parents and elders. The country would then be at peace. And if every Chinese would but exercise his wisdom and courage the Empire would become strong... .

We would here state that there are now three things necessary to be done in order to save China from revolution. The first is to *maintain the reigning dynasty*; the second is to *conserve the Holy Religion*; and the third is to *protect the Chinese race*. These are inseparably connected; in fact they constitute one... .

Under the present circumstances there is nothing for it but to arouse ourselves to the situation. Let us display our loyalty and love and embrace every opportunity to become wealthy and strong; let our first object be the veneration of the Imperial Court which vouchsafes its protection to the Commonwealth, and let those who hold the reins of government consider the general good... .

Chapter III. The Three Moral Obligations

The Sovereign is the head of the Subject, the Father is the head of the Son, and the Husband is the head of the Wife. These tenets have been handed down from the sages, and as Heaven does not change, so they never change. They constitute the first of the Five Relations and the mainspring of every act... . Know then, that the obligation of subject to sovereign is incompatible with republicanism.... .

Now, we have examined somewhat into the methods of Western Governments. They have their Lords and Commons, their Senates and Representatives, which hold their prerogatives in State matters. But we have noticed that the Sovereign, or the President, retains the power of dissolving these assemblies; and in case one assembly does not suit him he exercises this power, dismisses the obnoxious body and convenes another. A Constitutional Government with a Sovereign, and a Republic are about the same. In the West the intercourse of Sovereign, Ministers, and People is easy, the rules of deportment meagre, and the needs of the people are communicated to the sovereign with rapid facility; but the bearing or dignity of the Western

Prince is not to be compared with that of the Chinese Emperor. Western people, however, love their sovereigns more than the Chinese do theirs, and, although they may leave home and live abroad thousands of miles from their native land they do not disobey their country's laws or defraud their rulers. ... It is a mistake, then, to suppose that Western countries do not maintain the doctrine of the Relation of Subject to Sovereign... .

Chapter IV. The Recognition of Class

The highest degree of culture was reached in the Chow (B. C. 1122–255) Dynasty. Then began the decline about which Confucius grieved. The Dynasties following had no powerful neighbors to strive against, but heaped up large treasures of literary lore at the expense of power. This accumulation produced the hollowness of forms, and this, in turn begat weakness.

Not so all the countries of Europe. These were opened up at a late period in history, fresh and vigorous. Surrounded by strong neighbors, they were always in circumstances of desperate competition, stripped for a fight and ever striving to escape destruction. Continual apprehension produced determination, and determination begat strength. Of all countries China alone has for these fifty years proved herself almost irreclaimably stupid and not awake. Many of the officials and people are proud and indolent.

They contentedly rest in the belief that the old order of things will suffice for those dangerous times, and in the end become the easy prey of outsiders... .

Chapter IX. Cast Out the Poison

The Custom's Returns for the past few years give the value of our imports at 80,000,000 Tae ls, and the exports at 50,000,000 Taels. The balance of *thirty million Taels* represents what has been consumed in smoking the pernicious opium pipe!. Assuredly it is not foreign intercourse that is ruining China, but his dreadful poison. Oh, the grief and desolation it has wrought to our people! ... Opium has spread with frightful rapidity and heart-rending results through the provinces. Millions upon millions have been struck down by the plague. To-day it is running like wildfire. In its swift, deadly course it is spreading devastation everywhere, wrecking the minds and eating away the strength of its victims. The ruin of the mind is the most woeful of its many deleterious effects... .

Therefore we say, bring learning to the front in order to remedy the opium evil! ... All the countries of the world recoil with disgust at the idea of smoking this vile, illsmelling, poisonous stuff. Only our Chinese people love to sleep and eat with the deadly drug, and in the deadly drug we arc selfsteeped, seeking poverty, imbecility, death, destruction... .

31

Japan: The Charter Oath of the Five Articles

The Charter Oath of 1868 was a statement of general principles meant to appeal to the broadest possible support for the Meiji Restoration. Its vagueness left room for adjustment in a rapidly changing situation and attempted to alienate as few people and groups as possible.

Discussion Questions

1. Why do you think the Oath called for the wide establishment of deliberative assemblies?

2. What elements in the Oath advocate change and what elements might appeal to more conservative interests in Japanese society?

By this oath we set up as our aim the establishment of the national weal on a broad basis and the framing of a constitution and laws.

1. Deliberative assemblies shall be widely established and all matters decided by public discussion.
2. All classes, high and low, shall unite in vigorously carrying out the administration of affairs of state.
3. The common people, no less than the civil and military officials, shall each be allowed to pursue his own calling so that there may be no discontent.
4. Evil customs of the past shall be broken off and everything based upon the just laws of Nature.
5. Knowledge shall be sought throughout the world so as to strengthen the foundations of imperial rule.

From *Sources of Japanese Tradition* by William Theodore de Bary. Copyright © 1980 by Columbia University Press. Reprinted with permission of the publisher.

32

Japan: Overenthusiasm for Westernization

Many Japanese became enthusiastic about the Westernization of their country by the 1880's, often acting as if they wished to have no part of their past. Copying the dress, manners and social relations of Westerners became very popular in some quarters. In the following case, one Robun Kanagaki uses eating beef (which had been forbidden by Buddhist law) as an occasion to praise many other aspects of Western culture.

Discussion Questions

1. What justification does Kanagaki give for violating traditional Japanese Buddhist customs?

2. What does he admire about the West and what does he think is the secret of their progress?

A man about thirty-five, rather swarthy it is true, but of clear complexion, thanks apparently to the daily use of soap, which purges all impurities. His hair, not having been cut for some hundred days, is long and flowing, and looks as if it is in the process of being let out altogether, in the foreign style. Naturally enough, he uses that scent called Eau de Cologne to give a sheen to his hair. He wears a padded silken kimono beneath which a calico undergarment is visible. By his side is his Western-style umbrella, covered in *gingham. From time to time he removes from his sleeve with a painfully contrived gesture a cheap watch, and consults the time. As a matter of fact this is merely so much display to impress others, and the chain is only gold-plate. He turns to his neighbor, who is also eating beef, and speaks:*

Excuse me, but beef is certainly a most delicious thing, isn't it? Once you get accustomed to its taste, you can never go back to deer or wild boar again. I wonder why we in Japan haven't eaten such a clean thing before? For over 1620—or is it 1630—years people in the West have been eating huge quantities of beef. Before then, I understand, beef and mutton were considered the king's exclusive property, and none ever entered the mouth of a commoner, unless he happened to be something on the order of a daimyo's chief retainer. We really should be grateful that even people like ourselves can now eat beef, thanks to the fact that Japan is steadily becoming a truly civilized country. Of course, there are some unenlightened boors who cling to their barbaric superstitions and say that eating meat defiles you so much that you can't pray any more before Buddha and the gods. Such nonsense shows they simply don't understand natural philosophy. Savages like that should be made to read Fukuzawa's article on eating beef. In the West they're free of superstitions. There it's the custom to do everything scientifically, and that's why they've invented amazing things like the steamship and the steam engine. Did you know that they engrave the plates for printing newspapers with telegraphic needles? And that they bring down wind from the sky with balloons? Aren't they wonderful inventions! Of course, there are good reasons behind these inventions. If you look at a map of the world you'll see some countries marked "tropical," which means that's where the sun shines closest. The people in those countries are all burnt black by the sun. The king of that part of the world tried all kinds of schemes before he hit on what is called a balloon. That's a big round bag they fill with air high up in the sky. They bring the bag down and open it, causing the cooling air inside the bag to spread out all over the country. That's a great invention. On the other hand, in Russia, which is a cold country where the snow falls even in summer and the ice is so thick that people can't move, they invented the steam engine. You've got to admire them for it. I understand that they modeled the steam engine after the flaming chariot of hell, but anyway, what they do is to load a crowd of people on a wagon and light a fire in a pipe underneath. They keep feeding the fire inside the pipe with coal, so that the people riding on top can travel a great distance completely oblivious to the cold. Those people in the West can think up inventions like that, one after the other.... You say you must be going? Well, good-bye. Waitress! Another small bottle of sake. And some pickled onions to go with it!

33

Japan: The Imperial Rescript on Education

During the Meiji period the leaders understood the importance of education. The establishment of public schools was a high priority and by 1905, 95% of the children were in schools. These schools were meant to instill values as well as skills. A concerted effort was made to inculcate values of nationalism, loyalty to the emperor and respect for authority. An important part of this was the Imperial Rescript on Education which was issued in 1890 and was dutifully read in the schools on a regular basis.

Discussion Questions

1. What view of Japan is presented in the Rescript?

2. What personal qualities are advocated in the document?

3. What is the purpose of education as seen here?

4. Do you think the Rescript encourages independence and initiative in students?

Know ye, Our Subjects!

Our Imperial Ancestors have founded Our Empire on a basis broad and everlasting and have deeply and firmly implanted virtue; Our subjects, ever united in loyalty and filial piety, have from generation to generation illustrated the beauty thereof. This is the glory of the fundamental character of Our Empire, and herein also lies the source of Our education. Ye, Our subjects, be filial to your parents, affectionate to your brothers and sisters; as husbands and wives be harmonious, as friends true; bear yourselves in modesty and moderation; extend your benevolence to all; pursue learning and cultivate arts, and thereby develop your intellectual faculties and perfect your moral powers; furthermore, advance the public good and promote common interests; always respect the Constitution and observe the laws; should any emergency arise, offer yourselves courageously to the State; and thus guard and maintain the prosperity of Our Imperial Throne, coeval with heaven and earth. So shall ye not only be Our good and faithful subjects, but render illustrious the best traditions of your forefathers.

The way here set forth is indeed the teaching bequeathed by Our Imperial Ancestors, to be observed alike by Their Descendants and subjects, infallible for all ages and true in all places. It is Our wish to lay it to heart in all reverence, in common with you. Our subjects, that we may all thus attain to the same virtue.

The 30th day of the 10th month of the 23rd year Meiji.

34

Japan Observes the West

The Japanese policy of isolation under the Tokugawa vanished with the appearance of Commodore Perry's ships in 1853 and 1854. Subsequently the Japanese were forced to submit to a series of "unequal treaties" similar to those imposed on China. Since no Japanese wanted to become another China or India, the samurai responsible for the overthrow of the shogun in 1868 determined that Japan should be able to stand up to the Western powers on equal terms. Yukichi Fukuzawa (1834–1901), who had made several trips the the United States and Europe, supported Western learning so this could be brought about. (Later in life he became a fervent nationalist and promoter of Japanese expansion.)

The following selections are from his *Autobiography* and *Good-bye Asia* in which he recalls his impressions of the West, and his views on education and his concept of Japan's relationship to Asia.

Discussion Questions

1. In what ways does Fukuzawa show his pride in Japan's accomplishments?

2. What aspects of American and British life surprised him? Did he seem to think Japan was superior or just different?

3. What does he think Japan should learn from the West?

4. In the past Japan had been an ardent admirer of Chinese civilization, from which Japan had borrowed much; does Fukuzawa still seem to have that admiration?

5. Why does Fukuzawa think Japan should say "good-bye" to Asia?

I am willing to admit my pride in this accomplishment for Japan. The facts are these: It was not until the sixth year of Kaei (1853) that a steamship was seen for the first time; it was only in the second year of Ansei (1855) that we began to study navigation from the Dutch in Nagasaki; by 1860, the science was sufficiently understood to enable us to sail a ship across the Pacific. This means that about seven years after the first sight of a steamship, after only about five years of practice, the Japanese people made a trans-Pacific crossing without help from foreign experts. I think we can without undue pride boast before the world of this courage and skill... .

As I consider all the other peoples of the Orient as they exist today, I feel convinced that there is no other nation which has the ability or the courage to navigate a steamship across the Pacific after a period of five years of experience in navigation and engineering. Not only in the Orient would this feat stand as an act of unprecedented skill and daring. Even Peter the Great of Russia, who went to Holland to study navigation, with all his attainments could not have equalled this feat of the Japanese. Without doubt, the famous emperor was a man of genius, but his people did not respond to his leadership in the practice of science as did our Japanese in this great adventure.

As soon as our ship came into the port of San Francisco, we were greeted by many important personages who came on board from all over the country. Along the shores thousands of people were lined up to see the strange newcomers.

* * *

Our hosts in San Francisco were very considerate in showing us examples of modern industry. There was as yet no railway laid to the city, nor was there any electric light in use. But the telegraph system and also Galvani's electroplating were already in use. Then we were taken to a sugar refinery and had the principle of the operation explained to us quite minutely. I am sure that our hosts thought they were showing us something entirely new, namely looking for our surprise at each new device of engineering. But on the contrary, there was really nothing new, at least to me. I knew the principle of the telegraphy even if I had not seen the actual machine before; I knew that sugar was bleached by straining the solution with bone-black, and that in boiling down the solution, the vacuum was used to better effect than heat. I had been studying nothing else but such scientific principles ever since I had entered Ogata's school.

Rather, I was surprised by entirely different things in American life. First of all, there seemed to be an enormous waste of iron everywhere. In garbage piles, on the seashores—everywhere—I found lying old oil tins, empty cans, and broken tools. This was remarkable to us, for in Yedo, after a fire, there would appear a swarm of people looking for nails in the ashes.

Then too, I was surprised at the high cost of daily commodities in California. We had to pay a half-dollar for a bottle of oysters, and there were only twenty or thirty in the bottle at that.

In Japan the price of so many would be only a cent or two.

Things social, political, and economic proved most inexplicable. One day, on a sudden thought, I asked a gentleman where the descendants of George Washington might be. He replied, "I think there is a woman who is directly descended from Washington. I don't know where she is now, but I think I have heard she is married." His answer was so very casual that it shocked me.

Of course, I knew that America was a republic with a new president every four years, but I could not help feeling that the family of Washington would be revered above all other families. My reasoning was based on the reverence in Japan for the founders of the great lines of rulers—like that for Ieyasu of the Tokugawa family of Shoguns, really deified in the popular mind. So I remember the astonishment I felt at receiving this indifferent answer about the Washington family. As for scientific inventions and industrial machinery, there was no great novelty in them for me. It was rather in matters of life and social custom and ways of thinking that I found myself at a loss in America... .

Before we sailed, the interpreter, Nakahama, and I each bought a copy of Webster's dictionary. This, I know, was the very first importation of Webster's into Japan. Once I had secured this valuable work, I felt no disappointment on leaving the new world and returning home again.

* * *

When I asked a gentleman [in England] what the "election law" was and what kind of a bureau the Parliament really was, he simply replied with a smile, meaning I suppose that no intelligent person was expected to ask such a question. But these were the things most difficult of all for me to understand. In this connection, I learned that there were bands of men called political parties—the Liberals and the Conservatives—who were always fighting against each other in the government.

For some time it was beyond my comprehension to understand what they were fighting for, and what was meant, anyway, by "fighting" in peace time. "This man and that man are enemies in the House," they would tell me. But these "enemies" were to be seen at the same table, eating and drinking with each other. I felt as if I could not make much out of this. It took me a long time, with some tedious thinking, before I could gather a general notion of these separate mysterious facts. In some of the more complicated matters, I might achieve an understanding five or ten days after they were explained to me. But all in all, I learned much from this initial tour of Europe.

* * *

In my interpretation of education, I try to be guided by the laws of nature and I try to coordinate all the physical actions of human beings by the very simple laws of "number and reason." In spiritual or moral training, I regard the human being as the most sacred and responsible of all orders, unable in reason to do anything base. Therefore, in self-respect, a man cannot change his sense of humanity, his justice, his loyalty or anything belonging to his manhood even when driven by circumstances to do so. In short, my creed is that a man should find his faith in independence and self-respect.

From my own observations in both Occidental and Oriental civilizations, I find that each has certain strong points and weak points bound up in its moral teachings and scientific theories. But when I compare the two in a general way as to wealth, armament, and the greatest happiness for the greatest number, I have to put the Orient below the Occident. Granted that a nation's destiny depends upon the education of its people, there must be some fundamental differences in the education of Western and Eastern peoples.

In the education of the East, so often saturated with Confucian teaching, I find two things lacking; that is to say, a lack of studies in number and reason in material culture, and a lack of the idea of independence in spiritual culture. But in the West I think I see why their statesmen are successful in managing their national affairs, and the businessmen in theirs, and the people generally ardent in their patriotism and happy in their family circles.

I regret that in our country I have to acknowledge that people are not formed on these two principles, though I believe no one can escape the laws of number and reason, nor can anyone depend on anything but the doctrine of independence as long as nations are to exist and mankind is to thrive. Japan could not assert herself among the great nations of the world without full recognition and practice of these two principles. And I reasoned that Chinese philosophy as the root of education was responsible for our obvious shortcomings.

With this as the fundamental theory of education, I began and, though it was impossible to institute specialized courses because of lack of funds, I did what I could in organizing the instructions on the principles of number and reason. And I took every opportunity in public speech, in writing, and in casual conversations, to advocate my doctrine of independence. Also I tried in many ways to demonstrate the theory in my actual life. During my endeavor I came to believe less than ever in the old Chinese teachings... .

The true reason of my opposing the Chinese teaching with such vigor is my belief that in this age of transition, if this retrogressive doctrine remains at all in our young men's minds, the new civilization cannot give its full benefit to this country. In my determination to save our coming generation, I was prepared even to face single-handed the Chinese scholars of the country as a whole.

Gradually the new education was showing its results among the younger generation; yet men of middle age or past, who held responsible positions, were for the most part uninformed as to the true spirit of Western culture, and whenever they had to make decisions, they turned invariably to their Chinese sources for guidance. And so, again and again I had to rise up and denounce the all important Chinese influence before this weighty opposition. It was not altogether a safe road for my reckless spirit to follow.

Good-bye Asia

Transportation has become so convenient these days that once the wind of Western civilization blows to the East, every blade of grass and every tree in the East follow what the Western wind brings. Ancient Westerners and present-day Westerners are from the same stock

From *Japan: A Documentary History.* Volume II: *The Late Tokugawa Period to the Present*, ed. and trans. by David J. Lu (Armonk, NY: M.E. Sharpe, 1997), pp. 351-353. Translation copyright © 1997 by David J. Lu. Reprinted with permission of M.E. Sharpe, Inc.

and are not much different from one another. The ancient ones moved slowly, but their contemporary counterparts move vivaciously at a fast pace. This is possible because present-day Westerners take advantage of the means of transportation available to them. For those of us who live in the Orient, unless we want to prevent the coming of Western civilization with a firm resolve, it is best that we cast our lot with them. If one observes carefully what is going on in today's world, one knows the futility of trying to prevent the onslaught of Western civilization. Why not float with them in the same ocean of civilization, sail the same waves, and enjoy the fruits and endeavors of civilization?

The movement of a civilization is like the spread of measles. Measles in Tokyo start in Nagasaki and come eastward with the spring thaw. We may hate the spread of this communicable disease, but is there any effective way of preventing it? I can prove that it is not possible. In a communicable disease, people receive only damages. In a civilization, damages may accompany benefits, but benefits always far outweigh them, and their force cannot be stopped. This being the case, there is no point in trying to prevent their spread. A wise man encourages the spread and allows our people to get used to its ways.

The opening to the modern civilization of the West began in the reign of Kaei (1848–58). Our people began to discover its utility and gradually and yet actively moved toward its acceptance. However, there was an old-fashioned and bloated government that stood in way of progress. It was a problem impossible to solve. If the government were allowed to continue, the new civilization could not enter. The modern civilization and Japan's old conventions were mutually exclusive. If we were to discard our old conventions, that government also had to be abolished. We could have prevented the entry of this civilization, but it would have meant loss of our national independence. The struggles taking place in the world civilization were such that they would not allow an Eastern island nation to slumber in isolation. At that point, dedicated men (*shijin*) recognized the principle of "the country is more important than the government," relied on the dignity of the Imperial Household, and toppled the old government to establish a new one. With this, public and the private sectors alike, everyone in our country accepted the modern Western civilization. Not only were we able to cast aside Japan's old conventions, but we also succeeded in creating a new axle toward progress in Asia. Our basic assumptions could be summarized in two words: "Good-bye Asia (*Datsu-a*)."

Japan is located in the eastern extremities of Asia, but the spirit of her people have already moved away from the old conventions of Asia to the Western civilization. Unfortunately for Japan, there are two neighboring countries. One is called China and another Korea. These two peoples, like the Japanese people, have been nurtured by Asiatic political thoughts and mores. It may be that we are different races of people, or it may be due to the differences in our heredity or education; significant differences mark the three peoples. The Chinese and Koreans are more like each other and together they do not show as much similarity to the Japanese. These two peoples do not know how to progress either personally or as a nation. In this day and age with transportation becoming so convenient, they cannot be blind to the manifestations of Western civilization. But they say that what is seen or heard cannot influence the disposition of their minds. Their love affairs with ancient ways and old customs remain as strong as they were centuries ago. In this new and vibrant theater of civilization when we speak of education, they only refer back to Confucianism. As for school education, they can only cite [Mencius's] precepts of humanity, righteousness, decorum, and knowledge. While professing their abhorrence to ostentation, in reality they show their ignorance of truth and principles. As for their morality, one only has to observe their unspeakable acts of cruelty and shamelessness. Yet they remain arrogant and show no sign of self-examination.

In my view, these two countries cannot survive as independent nations with the onslaught of Western civilization to the East. Their concerned citizens might yet find a way to engage in a massive reform, on the scale of our Meiji Restoration, and they could change their governments and bring about a renewal of spirit among their peoples. If that could happen they would indeed be fortunate. However, it is more likely that would never happen, and within a few short years they will be wiped out from the world with their lands divided among the civilized nations. Why is this so? Simply at a time when the spread of civilization and enlightenment (*bummei kaika*) has a force akin to that of measles, China and Korea violate the natural law of its spread. They forcibly try to avoid it by shutting off air from their rooms. Without air, they suffocate to death. It is said that neighbors must extend helping hands to one another because their relations are inseparable. Today's China and Korea have not done a thing for Japan. From the perspectives of civilized Westerners, they may see what is happening in China and Korea and judge Japan accordingly, because of the three countries' geographical proximity. The governments of China and Korea still retain their autocratic manners and do not abide by the rule of law. Westerners may consider Japan likewise a lawless society. Natives of China and Korea are deep in their hocus pocus of nonscientific behavior. Western scholars may think that Japan still remains a country dedicated to the *yin* and *yang* and five elements. Chinese are mean-spirited and shameless, and the chivalry of the Japanese people is lost to the Westerners. Koreans punish their convicts in an atrocious manner, and that is imputed to the Japanese as heartless people. There are many more examples I can cite. It is not different from the case of a righteous man living in a neighborhood of a town known for foolishness, lawlessness, atrocity, and heartlessness. His action is so rare that it is always buried under the ugliness of his neighbors' activities. When these incidents are multiplied, that can affect our normal conduct of diplomatic affairs. How unfortunate it is for Japan.

What must we do today? We do not have time to wait for the enlightenment of our neighbors so that we can work together toward the development of Asia. It is better for us to leave the ranks of Asian nations and cast our lot with civilized nations of the West. As for the way of dealing with China and Korea, no special treatment is necessary just because they happen to be our neighbors. We simply follow the manner of the Westerners in knowing how to treat them. Any person who cherishes a bad friend cannot escape his bad notoriety. We simply erase from our minds our bad friends in Asia.

35

Macauley's Minute on Education

Perhaps the most important single act of British policy in India was the decision in 1835 to support education in the English language and curriculum. In the 18th century the East India Company had been cautious not to disturb traditional Indian society and culture and therefore sponsored Persian, Arabic and Sanskritic studies—this was known as the Orientalist approach. But in the early 19th century, as the Company became the paramount power in India, both the British and some Indians such as Ram Mohun Roy, who had a good knowledge of Western as well as Eastern learning, pressed for a new educational system that would allow Indians to get jobs in the new government. The British were slow to respond, but in 1834 Thomas Babington Macauley became president of the Committee on Public Instruction in India and broke the deadlock between the Orientalists and the Anglicists in favor of the latter.

The introduction of English education had deep and lasting significance for India. One result was the creation of a new class of Indians who could act as intermediaries between the British and the Indian population they ruled. Another was the spread of European values throughout India which challenged Indians to rethink their own past and either reject, accept or compromise with what the West represented. In addition, the English language acted to provide a common tongue in a country traditionally divided by caste, region, culture and numerous languages. Indian Muslims, by contrast, tended to be alienated by the new education since it did not include Koranic studies which they considered a prerequisite to any further education.

The following selection comes from Macaulay's famous Minute on Education in which he argued for the Anglicist position in 1835.

Discussion Questions

1. Do you think Macauley was in a position to pass judgment on "Oriental" studies?

2. Why did he think English education was so superior to that already being offered?

3. What kind of Indians did he wish to create and what role did he see them playing?

4. How do you think such "Macaulay-type" Indians would be received by the British and the Indians?

We have to educate a people who cannot at present be educated by means of their mother-tongue. We must teach them some foreign language. The claims of our own language it is hardly necessary to recapitulate. It stands preeminent even among the languages of the West. It abounds with works of imagination not inferior to the noblest which Greece has bequeathed to us; with models of every species of eloquence; with historical compositions, which, considered merely as narratives, have seldom been surpassed, and which, considered as vehicles of ethical and political instruction, have never been equaled; with just and lively representations of human life and human nature; with the most profound speculations on metaphysics, morals, government, jurisprudence, and trade; with full and correct information respecting every experimental science which tends to preserve the health, to increase the comfort, or to expand the intellect of man. Whoever knows that language has ready access to all the vast intellectual wealth, which all the wisest nations of the earth have created and hoarded in the course of ninety generations. It may safely be said that the literature now extant in that language is of far greater value than all the literature which three hundred years ago was extant in all the languages of the world together.

The question now before us is simply whether, when it is in our power to teach this language, we shall teach languages in which, by universal confession, there are no books on any subject which deserve to be compared to our own; whether, when we can teach European science, we shall teach systems which, by universal confession, whenever they differ from those of Europe, differ for the worse; and whether, when we can patronize sound philosophy and true history, we shall countenance, at the public expense, medical doctrines which would disgrace an English farrier, astronomy which would move laughter in girls at an English boarding school, history abounding with kings thirty feet high and reigns thirty thousand years long, and geography, made up of seas of treacle and seas of butter.

To sum up what I have said, I think it clear that we are not fettered by the Act of Parliament of 1813; that we are not fettered by any pledge expressed or implied; that we are free to employ our funds as we choose; that we ought to employ them in teaching what is best worth knowing; that English is better worth knowing than Sanscrit or Arabic; that the natives are desirous to be taught English, and are not desirous to be taught Sanscrit or Arabic; that neither as the languages of law, nor as the languages of religion, have the Sanscrit and Arabic any peculiar claim to our engagement; that it is possible to make natives of this country thoroughly good English scholars; and that to this end our efforts ought to be directed.

In one point I fully agree with the gentlemen to whose general views I am opposed. I feel with them, that it is impossible for us, with our limited means, to attempt to educate the body of the people. We must at present do our best to form a class who may be interpreters between us and the millions whom we govern; a class of persons, Indian in blood and color, but English in taste, in opinions, in morals, and in intellect. To that class we may leave it to refine the vernacular dialects of the country, to enrich those dialects with terms of science borrowed from the Western nomenclature, and to render them by degrees fit vehicles for conveying knowledge to the great mass of the population.

36

India and the West

Swami Vivekananda (1863–1902) was originally planning to study law in Britain and return to India to achieve success as many in his generation had. But his interviews with the mystic and spiritual teacher Sri Ramakrishna turned his life around and he gave up worldly pursuits to become an ascetic; twelve years later he became a missionary of Vedantic Hinduism to the world. In 1893 he addressed the First World Parliament of Religions in Chicago and spent four years lecturing in America and England. He returned home a national hero and, although he died at 39, deeply impressed his fellow Indians with the greatness of Hinduism and gave them a new-found sense of pride and confidence in their own culture. His interest in helping the masses of the population was very influential on Gandhi, who gladly recognized his debt to Vivekananda. Both Vivekananda and Gandhi believed India could achieve greatness by living up to her own high ideals.

The following selection is from a speech given by Vivekananda in New York in which he evaluates and compares East and West.

Discussion Questions

1. Why did Vivekananda believe that the world of his day needed a spiritual "adjustment?"

2. What does he think is wrong with the idea of progress as the West defined it?

3. What can the Occident and the Orient learn from each other?

Whenever virtue subsides and vice prevails, I come down to help mankind," declares Krishna, in the *Bhagavad-Gita*. Whenever this world of ours, on account of growth, on account of added circumstances, requires a new adjustment, a wave of power comes, and as man is acting on two planes, the spiritual and the material, waves of adjustment come on both planes. On the one side, of the adjustment on the material plane, Europe has mainly been the basis during modern times, and of the adjustment on the other, the spiritual plane, Asia has been the basis throughout the history of the world. Today, man requires one more adjustment on the spiritual plane; today when material ideas are at the height of their glory and power, today when man is likely to forget his divine nature, through his growing dependence on matter, and is likely to be reduced to a mere money-making machine, an adjustment is necessary; the voice has spoken, and the power is coming to drive away the clouds of gathering materialism. The power has been set in motion which, at no distant date, will bring unto mankind once more the memory of its real nature, and again the place from which this power will start will be Asia. This world of ours is on the plan of the division of labor. It is vain to say that one man shall possess everything. Yet how childish we are! The baby in its ignorance thinks that its doll is the only possession that is to be coveted in this whole universe. So a nation which is great in the possession of material power thinks that that is all that is to be coveted, that that is all that is meant by progress, that that is all that is meant

by civilization, and if there are other nations which do not care for possession, and do not possess that power, they are not fit to live, their whole existence is useless! On the other hand, another nation may think that mere material civilization is utterly useless. From the Orient came the voice which once told the world, that if a man possesses everything that is under the sun and does not possess spirituality, what avails it? This is the Oriental type; the other is the Occidental type.

Each of these types has its grandeur, each has its glory. The present adjustment will be the harmonizing, the mingling of these two ideals. To the Oriental, the world of spirit is as real as to the Occidental is the world of senses. In the spiritual, the Oriental finds everything he wants or hopes for; in it he finds all that makes life real to him. To the Occidental he is a dreamer; to the Oriental, the Occidental is a dreamer, playing with ephemeral toys, and he laughs to think that grown-up men and women should make so much of a handful of matter which they will have to leave sooner or later. Each calls the other a dreamer. But the Oriental ideal is as necessary for the progress of the human race as is the Occidental, and I think it is more necessary. Machines never made mankind happy, and never will make. He who is trying to make us believe this, will claim that happiness is in the machine, but it is always in the mind. The man alone who is the lord of his mind can become happy, and none else.

And what, after all, is power of machinery? Why should a man who can send a current of electricity through a wire be called a very great man, and very intelligent man? Does not Nature do a million times more than that every moment? Why not then fall down and worship Nature? What avails it if you have power over the whole of the world, if you have mastered every atom in the universe? That will not make you happy unless you have the power of happiness in yourself, until you have conquered yourself. Man is born to conquer Nature, it is true, but the Occidental means by "Nature" only the physical or external Nature. It is true that external Nature is majestic, with its mountains, and oceans, and rivers, and with the infinite powers and varieties. Yet there is a more majestic internal Nature of man, higher than the sun, moon, and

the stars, higher than this earth of ours, higher than the physical universe, transcending these little lives of ours; and it affords another field of study. There the Orientals excel, just as the Occidentals excel in the other. Therefore it is fitting that, whenever there is a spiritual adjustment, it should come from the Orient. It is also fitting that when the Oriental wants to learn about machinemaking, he should sit at the feet of the Occidental and learn from him. When the Occident wants to learn about the spirit, about God, about the soul, about the meaning and the my of this universe, he must sit at the feet of the Orient to learn.

37

The Case for India

In 1930 Will Durant went to India to do research for the first volume of *The Story of Civilization*. While there he was shocked by what he saw and decided to write a book presenting the Indian side of the growing debate with England over Indian independence.

The selections below illustrate how he thought England had worked to India's disadvantage, especially in the 19th century.

Discussion Questions

1. Why did Durant blame England for India's condition as he himself observed it?

2. Do you think his evidence supports his assertion that India's poverty was caused by British imperialism?

3. By what techniques does Durant say that England deprived India of its native wealth?

4. How was India transformed into "a purely agricultural country?"

5. Durant supports the "economic drain theory of empire." What do you think that is, according to the reading?

A Note to the Reader*

I went to India to help myself visualize a people whose cultural history I had been studying for The Story of Civilization. I did not expect to be attracted by the Hindus, or that I should be swept into a passionate interest in Indian politics. I merely hoped to add a little to my material, to look with my own eyes upon certain works of art, and then to return to my historical studies, forgetting this contemporary world.

But I saw such things in India has made me feel that study and writing were frivolous things in the presence of a people—one–fifth of the human race—suffering poverty and oppression bitterer than any to be found elsewhere on the earth. I was horrified. I had not thought it possible that any government could allow its subjects to sink to such misery.

I came away resolved to study living India as well the India with the brilliant past; to learn more of this unique Revolution that fought with suffering, accepted but never returned; to read the Gandhi of today as well as the Buddha of long ago.

And the more I read the more I was filled with astonishment and indignation at the apparently conscious and deliberate bleeding of India by England throughout a hundred and fifty years. I began to feel that I had come upon the greatest crime in all history.

And so I ask the reader's permission to abandon for a while my researches into the past, so that I may stand up and say a word for India. I know how weak words are in the face of guns and blood; how irrelevant mere truth and decency appear beside the might of empires and gold. But if even one Hindu, fighting for freedom far off there on the other side of the globe, shall hear this call of mine and be a trifle comforted, then these months of work on this little book will seem sweet to me. For I know of nothing in the world that I would rather do today than to be of help to India.

Will Durant
October 1, 1930.

With a government responsible to England, not to India, it is natural that the power of taxation should be freely used. Though before the coming of the English the land was private property, the Government made itself the sole owner of the soil and charged for it a land tax or rental now equal to one–fifth of the produce. In many cases in the past this land tax has amounted to half the gross produce, in some cases to more than the entire gross produce; in general it is two to three times as high as under pre–English rule. The Government has the exclusive right to manufacture salt, and adds to its sale–price a tax amounting to one–half a cent per pound.

A member of parliament, Cathcart Wilson, says: "The percentage of taxes in India, as related to the gross produce, is more than that of any other country." Until recently the rate was twice as high as in England, three times as

* Note. This book has been written without the knowledge or co–operation in any form, of any Hindu, or of any person acting for India.

high as in Scotland. Herbert Spencer protested against "the pitiless taxation which wrings from the poor Indian ryots nearly half the product of their soil." Another Englishman, the late H.M. Hyndman, after detailing the proof that taxation in India was far heavier than in any other country, though its population is poorer, entitled his book *The Bankruptcy of India*. Sir William Hunter, former member of the Viceroy's Council, said in 1875: "The government assessment does not leave enough food to the cultivator to support himself and his family throughout the year."

The result is a pitiful crushing of the Hindu spirit, a stifling of its pride and growth, a stunting of genius that once flourished in every city of the land. Have we felt that the Hindu character is degraded, that it lacks virility and initiative? But what people could have retained these qualities under such ruthless alien rule? "Subjection to a foreign yoke," says Professor Ross, "is one of potent causes of the decay of nations." Said Charles Francis Adams before the American Historical Association in 1901: "There is not an instance in all recorded history … where a so–called inferior race or community has been elevated in its character, or made self–sustaining, or self-governing, or even put on the way to that result through a condition of dependency or tutelage. I might, without much danger, assert that the condition of dependency, even for communities of the same race and blood, always exercises an emasculating and deteriorating influence. I would undertake, if called upon, to show that this rule is invariable." "The foreign system under which India is governed today." says Gandhi, "has reduced India to pauperism and emasculation. We have lost self–confidence."

The British charge the Hindu with lack of manliness; but it is the British who have driven it out of him by the accident of superior guns and the policy of merciless rule. If there is rebellion in India to–day let every true Briton be glad; for it means that India is not quite dead,

that the spirit of liberty is risen again, and that the Hindu can be a man after all.

The economic condition of India is the inevitable corollary of its political exploitation.

Even the casual traveler perceives the decay of agriculture (which absorbs 85% of the people), and the destitution of the peasant. He sees the Hindu ryot in the rice–fields, wading almost naked in the mud of a foreign tyrant's land; his loin-cloth is all the finery that he has. In 1915 the Statistical Department of Bengal, the most prosperous of India's provinces, calculated the average wage of the able–bodied agricultural laborer to be $3.60 per month. His hut is of branches often open at the sides, and loosely roofed with straw; or it is a square of dried mudadorned with a cot of dried mud, and covered with mud and sticks and leaves. The entire house and furnishings of a family of six including all their clothing, are worth $10. The peasant cannot afford newspapers or books, entertainment, tobacco, or drink. Almost half his earnings go to the Government and if he cannot pay the tax, his holding, which may have been in his family for centuries, is confiscated by the State.

If he is fortunate he escapes from the overtaxed land and takes refuge in the cities. Provided there are not too many other applicants, he may get work in Delhi the capital of India, carrying away the white master's excrement; sanitary facilities are unnecessary when slaves are cheap. Or he can go to the factory, and become, if he is very lucky, one of the 1,409,000 "hands" of India. He will find difficulty in getting a place, for 33% of the factory workers are women, and 8% are children. In the mines 34% of the employees are women, of whom one–half work underground; 16% of the miners are children. In the cotton mills of Bombay the heat is exhausting, and the lungs are soon destroyed by the fluff–laden air; men work there until they reach a subsistence factories use their employees fifty–four hours a week. The average wage of the factory workers is sixty to seventy cents a day; though allowance must be made for the inferior skill and strength of the Hindu as compared with the European or American laborer long trained in the ways of machines. In Bombay, in 1922, despite the factory acts of that year, the average wage of the cotton workers was 33 cents. In that same year the profit of the owners of those mills was 125%. This was an "off-year"; in better years, the owners said, the profits were 200%. The work–man's home is like his wage; usually it consists of one room, shared by the family with various animals; Zimand found one room with thirty tenants. Such is the industrial revolution that a British government has allowed to develop under its control, despite the example of enlightened legislation in America and England.

The people flock to the factories because the land cannot support them; and the land cannot support them because it is overtaxed, because it is overpopulated, and because the domestic industries with which the peasants formerly eked out in winter their gleanings from the summer fields, have been destroyed by the British control of Indian tariffs and trade. For of old the handicrafts of India were known throughout the world; it was *manufactured*—i.e., hand–made—goods which European merchants brought from India to sell to the West. In 1680, says the British historian Orme, the manufacture of cotton was almost universal in India, and the busy spinning–wheels enabled the women to round out the earnings of their men.

But the English in India objected to this competition of domestic industry with their mills at home; they resolved that India should be reduced to a purely agricultural country, and be forced in consequence to become a vast market for British machine–made goods. The Directors of the East India Company gave orders that the production of raw silk should be encouraged, and the manufacture of silk fabrics discouraged; that silk–winders should be compelled to work in the Company's factories, and be prohibited, under severe penalties, from working outside. Parliament discussed ways and means of replacing Hindu by British industries. A tariff of 70–80% was placed upon Hindu textiles imported into free–trade England, while India was compelled, by foreign control of her government, to admit English textiles almost duty free. Lest Indian industries should nevertheless continue somehow to exist, an excise tax was placed on the manufacture of cotton goods in India. As a British historian puts it:

> It is a melancholy instance of the wrong done to India by the country on which she has become dependent. ... Had India been independent, she would have retaliated, would have imposed prohibitive duties upon British goods, and would thus have preserved her own productive industry from annihilation. This act of self–defense was not permitted her; she was at the mercy of the stranger. British goods were forced upon her without paying any duty, and the foreign manufacturer employed the arm of political injustice to keep down and ultimately strangle a competitor with whom he could not have contended on equal terms.

And another Englishman wrote:

> We have done everything possible to impoverish still further the miserable beings subject to the cruel selfishness of English commerce... . Under the pretense of free trade, England has compelled the Hindus to receive the products of the steam–looms of Lancashire, Yorkshire, Glasgow, etc., at merely nominal duties; while the handwrought manufactures of Bengal and Behar, beautiful in fabric and durable in wear, have heavy and almost prohibitive duties imposed on their importation into England.

The result was that Manchester and Paisley flourished, and Indian industries declined; a country well on its way to prosperity was forcibly arrested in its development and compelled to be only a rural hinterland for industrial England. The mineral wealth abounding in India's soil was not explored, for no competition with England was to be allowed. The millions of skilled artisans whom Indian handicrafts had maintained were added to the hundreds of millions who sought support from the land. "India," says Kohn, "was transformed into a purely agricultural country, and her people lived perpetually on the verge of starvation" The vast population which might have been comfortably supported by a combination of tillage and industry, became too great for the arid soil; and India was reduced to such penury that to–day nothing is left of her men, her women and her children but empty stomachs and fleshless bones.

To this ruining of the land with taxation, this ruining of industry with tariffs, and this ruining of commerce with foreign control, add the drainage of millions upon millions of dollars from India year after year—and the attempt to explain Indian poverty as the result of her superstitions becomes a dastardly deception practised upon a world too busy to be well informed. This drain having been denied, it is only necessary to state the facts, and to introduce them with a quotation from a document privately addressed by the British government in India to the Parliament of England.

> Great Britain, in addition to the tribute which she makes India pay her through the customs, derives benefits from the savings of the service of the three presidencies (the provinces of Calcutta, Madras and Bombay) being spent in England instead of in India; and in addition to these savings, which probably amount to $500,000,000, she derives benefit from the fortunes realized by the European mercantile community, which are all remitted to England.

This is a general statement; let us fill it in.

Consider first the drain on India through trade. Not merely is this carried in British ships; far worse than that, there is an astounding surplus of exports over imports. In 1927, e.g., imports were $651,600,000, exports were $892,800,000; the excess of exports, $241,200,000. Where goes the money that pays for this excess? But it is the officials, the merchants and the manufacturers (most of whom are British) who take the great bulk of this profit, and return it to their countries in one form or another. As an East Indian merchant said in a Parliamentary report in 1853, when this process of bleeding was on a comparatively modest scale: "Generally up to 1847, the imports were about $30,000,000 and the exports about $47,500,000. The difference is the tribute which the Company received from the country.

Consider, second, the drain through fortunes, dividends and profits made in India and spent broad. The British come as officials or soldiers or traders; they make their money and return to Great Britain.

Consider, third, the drain through salaries and pensions derived from India and spent abroad. In 1927 Lord Winterton showed, in the House of Commons, that there were then some 7500 retired officials in Great Britain drawing annually $17,500,000 in pensions from the Indian revenue; Ramsay MacDonald put the figure at $20,000,000 a year. When England, which is almost as over–populated as Bengal, sends its sons to India, she requires of them twenty–four years of service, reduced by four years of furloughs; she then retires them for life on a generous pension, paid by the Hindu people. Even during their service these officials send their families or their children to live for the most part in England; and they support them there with funds derived from India.

Almost everything bought by the British in India, except the more perishable foods, is purchased from abroad. A great proportion of the funds appropriated for supplies by the Government of India is spent in England.

As early as 1783 Edmund Burke predicted that the annual drain of Indian resources to England without equivalent return would eventually destroy India. From Plassey to

Waterloo, fifty–seven years, the drain of India's wealth to England is computed by Brooks Adams at two–and–a–half to five billion dollars. He adds, what Macaulay suggested long ago, that it was this stolen wealth from India which supplied England with free capital for the development of mechanical inventions, and so made possible the Industrial Revolution.

Though it may seem merely spectacular to juggle such figures, it is highly probable that the total wealth drained from India since 1757, if it had an been left and invested in India, would now amount, at a low rate of interest, to $400,000,000,000. Allow for money reinvested in India, and a sum remains easily equivalent to the difference between the poorest and the richest nations in the world. The same high rate of taxation which has bled India to perhaps a mortal weakness, might have done her no permanent injury if the wealth so taken had all been returned into the economy and circulation of the country; but bodily withdrawn from her as so much of it was, it has acted like a long–continued transfusion of vital blood. "So great an economic drain out of the resources of the land," says Dutt, "would impoverish the most prosperous countries on earth; it has reduced India to a land of famines more frequent, more widespread and more fatal, than any known before in the history of India, or of the world."

Sir Wilfred Scawen Blunt sums it up from the point of view of a true Englishman:

India's famines have been severer and more frequent, its agricultural poverty has deepened, its rural population has become more hopelessly in debt, their despair more desparate. The system of constantly enhancing the land values (i.e. raising the valuation and assessment) has not been altered. The salt tax … still robs the very poor… . What was bad twenty–five years ago is worse now. At any rate there is the same drain of India's food to alien mouths. Endemic famines and endemic plagues are facts no official statistics can explain away… . Though myself a good Conservative … I own to being shocked at the bondage in which the Indian people are held; … and I have come to the conclusion that if we go on developing the country at the present rate, the inhabitants, sooner or later, will have to resort to cannibalism, for there will be nothing left for them to eat.

And now, having quoted authorities sufficiently to guard against relying on my own too brief experience, I may be permitted, despite that limitation, to express my own judgment and feeling. I came to India admiring the British, marveling at their imperial capacity for establishing order and peace, and thankful for the security which their policing of the world's waters has given to every traveler. I left India feeling that its awful poverty is an unanswerable indictment of its alien government, that so far from being an excuse for British rule, it is overwhelming evidence that the British ownership of India has been a calamity and a crime. For this is quite unlike the Mohammedan domination: those invaders came to stay, and their descendants call India their home; what they took in taxes and tribute they spent in India, developing its industries and resources, adorning its literature and art. If the British had done likewise, India would to–day be a flourishing nation. But the present plunder has now gone on beyond bearing; year by year it is destroying one of the greatest and gentlest peoples of history.

The terrible thing is that this poverty is not a beginning, it is an end; it is not growing less, it is growing worse; England is not "preparing India for self-government," she is bleeding it to death. "Even as we look on," said another loyal Englishman, H. M. Hyndman, "India is becoming feebler and feebler. The very life–blood of the great multitude under our rule is slowly, yet ever faster ebbing away."

Any man who sees this crime, and does not speak out, is a coward. Any Englishman or any American, seeing it and not revolted by it, does not deserve his country or his name.

38

Xhosa Freedom Fighters

Among the most vigorous resisters to the expansion of the Dutch and British in South Africa, the Bantu-speaking Xhosa stand out. They were the first to clash with the whites and proved more than capable of holding their own against the Dutch in the last decades of the 18th century. An influential Xhosa spiritual leader and warrior named Makana proclaimed that his mission was to annihilate all white men and in 1819, after a number of attacks by the whites, led his army into the Cape Colony (which had come under British control in 1795.) They were repulsed and the British pushed them back in a brutal fashion, murdering and plundering as they went. To make peace, Makana turned himself over to the British; he was imprisoned for life. To secure his release, several prominent Xhosa offered themselves in exchange for Makana. The following selection is a speech made by one of them at a parley with the British. (The British refused to make peace or release Makana, who died in 1820 while trying to escape.)

Discussion Questions

1. How did the Xhosa justify their resistance to the Europeans?

2. Were the Xhosa united in their efforts?

3. Do the Xhosa appear to have been peace-loving people?

The war, British chiefs, is an unjust one. You are striving to extirpate a people whom you forced to take up arms. When our fathers and the fathers of the Boers first settled in the Suurveld [an area west of the Fish River], they dwelt together in peace. Their flocks grazed on the same hills: there herdsmen smoked together out of the same pipes; they were brothers ... until the herds of the Xhosas increased so as to make the hearts of the Boers sore. What those covetous men could not get from our fathers for old buttons, they took by force. Our fathers were *men*; they loved their cattle; their wives and children lived upon milk; they fought for their property. They began to hate the colonists who coveted their all, and aimed at their destruction.

Now, their kraals and our fathers' kraals were separate. The Boers made commandos on our fathers. Our fathers drove them out of the Suurveld; and we dwelt there because we had conquered it. There we were circumcised; there we married wives; and there our children were born. The white men hated us, but could not drive us away. When there was war we plundered you. When there was peace some of our bad people stole; but our chiefs forbade it. Your treacherous friend, Gaika [the Xhosa chief who was an ally of the British] always had peace with you; yet, when his people stole, he shared in the plunder. Have your patrols ever found cattle taken in time of peace, runaway slaves or deserters, in the kraals of our chiefs? Have they ever gone into Gaika's country without finding such cattle, such slaves, such deserters, in Gaika's kraals? But he was your friend; and you wished to possess the Suurveld. You came

at last like locusts [in attack of 1818]. We stood; we could do no more. You said, "Go over the Fish River ... that is all we want." We yielded and came here.

We lived in peace. Some of our bad people stole, perhaps; but the nation was quiet ... the chiefs were quiet. Gaika stole ... his chiefs stole ... his people stole. You sent him copper; you sent him beads; you sent him horses, on which he rode to steal more. To us you sent only commandos.

We quarreled with Gaika about grass ... no business of yours. You sent a commando ... you took our last cow ... you left only a few calves, which died for want, along with our children.... You gave half of what you took to Gaika; half you kept yourselves. Without milk ... our corn destroyed ... we saw our wives and children perish ... we saw that we must ourselves perish, we followed, therefore, the tracks of our cattle into the Colony. We plundered and we fought for our lives. We found you weak; we destroyed your soldiers. We saw that we were strong; we attacked your headquarters, Grahamstown ... and if we had succeeded, our right was good, for you began the war. We failed ... and you are here.

We wish for peace; we wish to rest in our huts; we wish to get milk for our children; our wives wish to till the land. But your troops cover the plains, and swarm in the thickets, where they cannot distinguish the man from the woman and shoot all.

You want us to submit to Gaika. That man's face is fair to you, but his heart is false. Leave him to himself. Make peace with us. Let him fight for himself ... and we shall not call on you

---

for help. Set Makana at liberty; and Islambi, Dushani, Kongo and the rest will come to make peace with ou at any time we fix. But if you will still make war, you may indeed kill the last man of us ... but Gaika shall not rule over the followers of those who think him a woman.

39

"Things Fall Apart"

If asked which groups were most active in the European imperialism of Africa, most would identify business interests and traders, and, perhaps, government officials. Few would readily mention missionaries, whose connections to either business activities or government policy seem distant. However, the missionary played an important role in colonizing efforts throughout the world, and a study of the way they perceived their role, the policies they helped to implement, the assumptions that guided their actions, and their interaction with both business and political institutions allows us to explore the cultural impact of imperialism. For just as there were profound political and economic changes resulting from the imperial policies of the European powers, there were equally startling cultural and social transformations that influenced traditional cultures. Likewise the interactions between the missionaries and the peoples among whom they worked, provide us with a personal window into the process of colonization, and give us an opportunity to explore the various responses of those who were the missionaries' intended converts. The following selection is from a widely acclaimed novel, *Things Fall Apart*, by Chinua Achebe, set around the year 1900, whose main character, Okonkwo, is faced with the coming of the missionaries and its ramifications within his own family. Though a fictional account, the selection highlights the interactions between the missionaries and the Africans, and reveals the turmoil created by this new force in their presence.

Discussion Questions

1. What was the initial reaction of most of the Africans to the missionaries? Why did some of the Africans change their minds about the Europeans, and why did others refuse to change?

2. What assumptions guided the missionaries in their work? Was there any attempt to understand African culture and religion?

3. Would you consider the missionary to be as much of an imperialist as a merchant or government official?

4. Why do you think Okonkwo acted as he did? What do you think happened to him as a result?

5. If you were an African living at that time, what would your response to the missionaries have been?

The missionaries spent their first four or five nights in the marketplace, and went into the village in the morning to preach the gospel. They asked who the king of the village was, but the villagers told them that there was no king. "We have men of high title and the chief priests and the elders," they said.

It was not very easy getting the men of high title and the elders together after the excitement of the first day. But the missionaries persevered, and in the end they were received by the rulers of Mbanta. They asked for a plot of land to build their church.

Every clan and village had its "evil forest." In it were buried all those who died of the really evil diseases, like leprosy and smallpox. It was also the dumping ground for the potent fetishes of great medicine men when they died. An "evil forest" was, therefore, alive with sinister forces and powers of darkness. It was such a forest that the rulers of Mbanta gave to the missionaries. They did not really want them in their clan, and so they made them that offer which nobody in his right senses would accept.

"They want a piece of land to build their shrine," said Uchendu to his peers when they consulted among themselves. "We shall give them a piece of land." He paused, and there was a murmur of surprise and disagreement. "Let us give them a portion of the Evil Forest. They boast about victory over death. Let us give them a real battlefield in which to show their victory." They laughed and agreed, and sent for the missionaries, whom they had asked to leave them for a while so that they might "whisper together." They offered them as much of the Evil Forest as they cared to take. And to their greatest amazement the missionaries thanked them and burst into song.

"They do not understand," said some of the elders. "But they will understand when they go to their plot of land tomorrow morning." And they dispersed.

The next morning the crazy men actually began to clear a part of the forest and to build their house. The inhabitants of Mbanta expected them all to be dead within four days. The first day passed and the second and third and fourth, and none of them died. Everyone was puzzled. And then it became known that the white man's fetish had unbelievable power. It was said that he wore glasses on his eyes so that he could see and talk to evil spirits. Not long after, he won his first three converts.

Although Nwoye had been attracted to the new faith from the very first day, he kept it secret. He dared not go too near the missionaries for fear of his father. But whenever they came to preach in the open marketplace or the village playground, Nwoye was there. And he was already beginning to know some of the simple stories they told.

"We have now built a church," said Mr. Kiaga, the interpreter, who was now in charge of the infant congregation. The white man had gone back to Umuofia, where he built his headquarters and from where he paid regular visits to Mr. Kiaga's congregation at Mbanta.

"We have now built a church," said Mr. Kiaga, "and we want you all to come in every seventh day to worship the true God."

On the following Sunday, Nwoye passed and repassed the little red-earth and thatch building without summoning enough courage to enter. He heard the voice of singing and although it came from a handful of men it was loud and confident. Their church stood on a circular clearing that looked like the open mouth of the Evil Forest. Was it waiting to snap its teeth together? After passing and re-passing by the church, Nwoye returned home.

It was well known among the people of Mbanta that their gods and ancestors were sometimes long-suffering and would deliberately allow a man to go on defying them. But even in such cases they set their limit at seven market weeks or twenty-eight days. Beyond that limit no man

was suffered to go. And so excitement mounted in the village as the seventh week approached since the impudent missionaries built their church in the Evil Forest. The villagers were so certain about the doom that awaited these men that one or two converts thought it wise to suspend their allegiance to the new faith.

At last the day came by which all the missionaries should have died. But they were still alive, building a new red-earth and thatch house for their teacher, Mr. Kiaga. That week they won a handful more converts. And for the first time they had a woman. Her name was Nneka, the wife of Amadi, who was a prosperous farmer. She was very heavy with child.

Nneka had had four previous pregnancies and childbirths. But each time she had borne twins, and they had been immediately thrown away. Her husband and his family were already becoming highly critical of such a woman and were not unduly perturbed when they found she had fled to join the Christians. It was a good riddance.

One morning Okonkwo's cousin, Amikwu, was passing by the church on his way from the neighboring village, when he saw Nwoye among the Christians. He was greatly surprised, and when he got home he went straight to Okonkwo's hut and told him what he had seen. The women began to talk excitedly, but Okonkwo sat unmoved.

It was late afternoon before Nwoye returned. He went into the *obi* and saluted his father, but he did not answer. Nwoye turned round to walk into the inner compound when his father, suddenly overcome with fury, sprang to his feet and gripped him by the neck.

"Where have you been?" he stammered. Nwoye struggled to free himself from the choking grip.

"Answer me," roared Okonkwo, "before I kill you!" He seized a heavy stick that lay on the dwarf wall and hit him two or three savage blows.

"Answer me!" he roared again. Nwoye stood looking at him and did not say a word. The women were screaming outside, afraid to go in.

"Leave that boy at once!" said a voice in the outer compound. It was Okonkwo's uncle, Uchendu. "Are you mad?"

Okonkwo did not answer. But he left hold of Nwoye, who walked away and never returned.

He went back to the church and told Mr. Kiaga that he had decided to go to Umuofiawhere the white missionary had set up a school to teach young Christians to read and write.

Mr. Kiaga's joy was very great. "Blessed is he who forsakes his father and his mother for my sake," he intoned. "Those that hear my words are my father and my mother."

Nwoye did not fully understand. But he was happy to leave his father. He would return later to his mother and his brothers and sisters and convert them to the new faith.

As Okonkwo sat in his hut that night, gazing into a log fire, he thought over the matter. A sudden fury rose within him and he felt a strong desire to take up his machete, go to the church and wipe out the entire vile and miscreant gang. But on further thought he told himself that Nwoye was not worth fighting for. Why, he cried in his heart, should he, Okonkwo, of all people, be cursed with such a son? He saw clearly in it the finger of his personal god or *chi*. For how else could he explain his great misfortune and exile and now his despicable son's behavior? Now that he had time to think of it, his son's crime stood out in its stark enormity. To abandon the gods of one's father and go about with a lot of effeminate men clucking like old hens was the very depth of abomination. Suppose when he died all his male children decided to follow Nwoye's steps and abandon their ancestors? Okonkwo felt a cold shudder run through him at the terrible prospects, like the prospect of annihilation. He saw himself and his fathers crowding round their ancestral shrine waiting in vain for worship and sacrifice

and finding nothing but ashes of bygone days, and his children the while praying to the white man's god. If such a thing were ever to happen, he, Okonkwo, would wipe them off the face of the earth.

Okonkwo was popularly called the "Roaring Flame." As he looked into the log fire he recalled the name. He was a flaming fire. How then could he have begotten a son like Nwoye, degenerate and effeminate? Perhaps he was not his son. No! he could not be. His wife had played him false. He would teach her! But Nwoye resembled his grandfather, Unoka, who was Okonkwo's father. He pushed the thought out of his mind. He, Okonkwo, was called a flaming fire. How could he have begotten a woman for a son? At Nwoye's age Okonkwo had already become famous throughout Umuofia for his wrestling and his fearlessness.

He sighed heavily, and as if in sympathy the smoldering log also sighed. And immediately Okonkwo's eyes were opened and he saw the whole matter clearly. Living fire begets cold, impotent ash. He sighed again, deeply.

The young church in Mbanta had a few crises early in its life. At first the clan had assumed that it would not survive. But it had gone on living and gradually becoming stronger. The clan was worried, but not over-much. If a gang of *efulefu* decided to live in the Evil Forest it was their own affair. When one came to think of it, the Evil Forest was a fit home for such undesirable people. It was true they were rescuing twins from the bush, but they never brought them into the village. As far as the villagers were concerned, the twins still remained where they had been thrown away. Surely the earth goddess would not visit the sins of the missionaries on the innocent villagers?

But on one occasion the missionaries had tried to overstep the bounds. Three converts had gone into the village and boasted openly that all the gods were dead and impotent and that they were prepared to defy them by burning all their shrines.

"Go and burn your mothers' genitals," said one of the priests. The men were seized and beaten until they streamed with blood. After that nothing happened for a long time between the church and the clan.

But stories were already gaining ground that the white man had not only brought a religion but also a government. It was said that they had built a place of judgment in Umuofia to protect the followers of their religion. It was even said that they had hanged one man who killed a missionary.

"Does the white man understand our custom about land?"

"How can he when he does not even speak our tongue? But he says that our customs are bad; and our own brothers who have taken up his religion also say that our customs are bad. How do you think we can fight when our own brothers have turned against us? The white man is very clever. He came quietly and peaceably with his religion. We were amused at his foolishness and allowed him to stay. Now he has won our brothers, and our clan can no longer act like one. He has put a knife on the things that held us together and we have fallen apart."

There were many men and women in Umuofia who did not feel as strongly as Okonkwo about the new dispensation. The white man had indeed brought a lunatic religion, but he had also built a trading store and for the first time palm-oil and kernel became things of great price, and much money flowed into Umuofia.

And even in the matter of religion there was a glowing feeling that there might be something in it after all, something vaguely akin to method in the overwhelming madness.

This growing feeling was due to Mr. Brown, the white missionary, who was very firm in restraining his flock from provoking the wrath of the clan. Mr. Brown learned a good deal about the religion of the clan and he came to the conclusion that a frontal attack on it would not succeed. And so he built a school and a little hospital in Umuofia. He went from family to family begging people to send their children to his school. But at first they only sent their slaves or sometimes their lazy children. Mr. Brown begged and argued and prophesied. He said that the leaders of the land in the future would be men and women who had learned to read and write. If Umuofia failed to send her children to the school, strangers would come from other places to rule them. They could already see that happening in the Native Court, where the D.C. was surrounded by strangers who spoke his tongue. Most of these strangers came from the distant town of Umuru on the bank of the Great River where the white man first went.

In the end Mr. Brown's arguments began to have an effect. More people came to learn in his school, and he encouraged them with gifts of singlets and towels. They were not all young, these people who came to learn. Some of them were thirty years old or more. They worked on their farms in the morning and went to school in the afternoon. And it was not long before the people began to say that the white man's medicine was quick in working. Mr. Brown's school produced quick results. A few months in it were enough to make one a court messenger or even a court clerk. Those who stayed longer became teachers; and from Umuofia laborers went forth into the Lord's vineyard. New churches were established in the surrounding villages and a few schools with them. From the very beginning religion and education went hand in hand.

Okika sprang to his feet and also saluted his clansmen four times. Then he began to speak:

"You all know why we are here, when we ought to be building our barns or mending our huts, when we should be putting our compounds in order. My father used to say to me: 'Whenever you see a toad jumping in broad daylight, then know that something is after its life.' When I saw you all pouring into this meeting from all the quarters of our clan so early in the morning,

I knew that something was after our life." He paused for a brief moment and then began again:

"All our gods are weeping. Idemili is weeping, Ogwugwu is weeping, Agbala is weeping, and all the others. Our dead fathers are weeping because of the shameful sacrilege they are suffering and the abomination we have all seen with our eyes." He stopped again to steady his trembling voice.

"This is a great gathering. No clan can boast of greater numbers or greater valor. But are we all here? I ask you: Are all the sons of Umuofia with us here?" A deep murmur swept through the crowd.

"They are not," he said. "They have broken the clan and gone their several ways. We who are here this morning have remained true to our fathers, but our brothers have deserted us and joined a stranger to soil their fatherland. If we fight the stranger we shall hit our brothers and perhaps shed the blood of a clansman. But we must do it. Our fathers never dreamed of such a thing, they never killed their brothers. But a white man never came to them. So we must do what our fathers would never have done. Eneke the bird was asked why he was always on the wing and he replied: 'Men have learned to shoot without missing their mark and I have learned to fly without perching on a twig.' We must root out this evil. And if our brothers take the side of evil must root them out too. And we must do it now. We must bale this water now that it is only ankle-deep... .

At this point there was a sudden stir in the crowd and every eye was turned in one direction. There was a sharp bend in the road that led from the marketplace to the white man's court, and to the stream beyond it. And so no one had seen the approach of the five court messengers until they had come round the bend, a few paces from the edge of the crowd. Okonkwo was sitting at the edge.

"What do you want here?"

"The white man whose power you know too well has ordered this meeting to stop."

In a flash Okonkwo drew his machete. The messenger crouched to avoid the blow. It was useless. Okonkwo's machete descended twice and the man's head lay beside his uniformed body.

The waiting backcloth jumped into tumultuous life and the meeting was stopped. Okonkwo stood looking at the dead man. He knew that Umuofia would not go to war. He knew because they had let the other messengers escape. They had broken into tumult instead of action. He discerned fright in that tumult. He heard voices asking: "Why did he do it?"

He wiped his machete on the sand and went away.

40

The Dual Mandate in Africa

Sir F.D. Lugard, a famous British colonial soldier and governor, offers a justification of colonization in Africa and sees it as a two-way process.

Discussion Questions

1. What does Lugard mean by the "dual mandate?"

2. What are the major contributions of Europe to Africa, as he sees them?

3. What does Lugard mean when he says that "their very discontent is a measure of their progress?

4. Are Lugard's arguments convincing?

The Dual Mandate

In accepting responsibility for the control of these new lands, England obeyed the tradition of her race. British Africa was acquired not by groups of financiers, nor yet … by the efforts of her statesmen, but in spite of them. It was the instinct of the British democracy which compelled us to take our share… .

The fundamental character of British official policy in West Africa, [a Labour leader] says, has primarily been influenced by a desire to promote the welfare and advancement of the native races. England, he points out, led the way in the suppression of the overseas slave trade, paying enormous sums in compensation to slave-owners … and in patrolling the seas [to intercept slave ships]. She [took up] the cause of Congo reform, and of the indentured labor [labor bound to colonists by contract] in Portuguese West Africa. The extension of British control in the Gold Coast hinterland was (he adds) to … [protect] the natives, and in southern Nigeria to suppress war and human sacrifice… .

Let it be admitted at the outset that European brains, capital, and energy have not been, and never will be, expended in developing the resources of Africa from motives of pure philanthropy; that Europe is in Africa for the mutual benefit of her own industrial classes, and of the native races in their progress to a higher plane; that the benefit can be made reciprocal, and that it is the aim and desire of civilized administration to fulfill this dual mandate.

By railways and roads, by reclamation of swamps and irrigation of deserts, and by a system of fair trade and competition, we have added to the prosperity and wealth of these lands, and [have] checked famine and disease. We have put an end to the awful misery of the slave trade and intertribal war, to human sacrifice, and the ordeals of the witch doctor. Where these things survive, they are severely suppressed. We are endeavoring to teach the native races to conduct their own affairs with justice and humanity, and to educate them alike in letters and in industry.

When I recall the state of Uganda at the time I made the treaty in 1890 which brought it under British control, or the state of Nigeria ten years later, and contrast them with the conditions of today [late 1920's], I feel the British effort—apart from benefits to British trade—has not been in vain. In Uganda a triangular civil war was raging: Protestants, Roman Catholics, and Muslims—representing the rival political factions of British, French, and Arabs—were murdering each other. Only a short time previously, triumphant paganism had burned Christians at the stake… . Today there is an ordered government with its own native parliament. Liberty and justice have replaced chaos, bloodshed, and war. The wealth of the country steadily increases… .

In Nigeria in 1902 slave-raiding armies of 10,000 or 15,000 men laid waste the country, and wiped out its population annually in the quest for slaves. Hundreds of square miles of rich will-watered land were depopulated…. Nowhere was there security for life and property. Today the native emirs [(chiefs) compete] with each other in the progress of their schools; the native courts administer justice and themselves have liberated over 50,000 slaves.

The … emirs are keenly interested in such questions as afforestation, artesian wellboring, and vaccination. The native prisons have been pronounced by the medical authority to be a model for government to imitate; the leper settlement in Bornu under purely native control is the most successful I know of.

I refer to these two countries because I happen to have personally witnessed their condition prior to the advent of British control, but similar results may be seen in every other British dependency in tropical Africa.

As Roman imperialism laid the foundations of modern civilization, and led the wild barbarians of [the British Isles] along the path of progress, so in Africa today we are repaying the debt, and bringing to the dark places of the earth—the abode of barbarism and cruelty—the torch of culture and progress, while ministering to the material needs of our own civilization. In this task the nations of Europe have pledged themselves to cooperation…. Towards the common goal each will advance by the methods most consonant with [suited to] its national genius. British methods have not perhaps in all cases produced ideal results, but I am profoundly convinced that there can be no question but that British rule has promoted the happiness and welfare of the primitive races. Let those who question it examine the results impartially. If there is unrest, and a desire for independence, as in India and Egypt, it is because we have taught the value of liberty and freedom, which for centuries these peoples had not known. Their very discontent is a measure of their progress.

We hold these countries because it is the genius of our race to colonize, to trade, and to govern. The task in which England is engaged in the tropics … has become part of her tradition, and she has ever given of her best in the cause of liberty and civilization. There will always be those who cry aloud that the task is being badly done, that it does not need doing, that we can get more profit by leaving others to do it, that it brings evil to subject races and breeds profiteers at home. These were not the principles which prompted our forefathers, and secured for us the place we hold in the world today in trust for those who shall come after us.

41

The Berlin Act, 1885

The Berlin West Africa Conference of 1884–5 gave international recognition to an already existing situation. Since 1880 the great powers had become increasingly suspicious of each others' designs on Africa, even though individually they had little interest in the continent. Fear of another power or powers gaining ascendency there impelled the powers to make adversarial claims. The European powers rushed to make treaties with various African rulers to lay claim to territory. Bismarck of Germany, who had said that "for Germany to acquire colonies would be like a poverty-stricken Polish nobleman providing himself with silks and sables, when he needed shirts," dropped his opposition to colonial ventures when Britain occupied Egypt in 1882. In 1884 he convened a conference in Berlin to set down rules to formalize the chaotic "scramble."

Every major power in Europe, plus the United States and the Ottoman Empire, attended and the formal act was promulgated in early 1885. The Act included the following provisions.

Discussion Questions

1. What clauses in the act were indicative of European imperialistic sentiments?

2. How did the powers expect to regularize the process of acquiring territories?

The Berlin Act, 1885

Article VI

Provisions Relative to Protection of the Natives, of Missionaries and Travellers, as well as Relative to Religious Liberty

Preservation and Improvement of Native Tribes; Slavery, and the Slave Trade

All the powers exercising sovereign rights or influence in the aforesaid territories bind themselves to watch over the preservation of the native tribes, and to care for the improvement of the conditions of their moral and material well-being, and to help in suppressing slavery, and especially the slave trade.

Religious and Other Institutions. Civilization of Natives

They shall, without distinction of creed or nation, protect and favour all religious, scientific, or charitable institutions, and undertakings created and organized for the above ends, or which aim at instructing the natives and bringing home to them the blessings of civilization.

Protection of Missionaries, Scientists, and Explorers

Christian missionaries, scientists, and explorers, with their followers, property, and collections, shall likewise be the objects of especial protection.

Religious Toleration

Freedom of conscience and religious toleration are expressly guaranteed to the natives, no less than to subjects and to foreigners.

Notification of Acquisitions and Protectorates on Coasts of African Continent

Article XXXIV

Any power which henceforth takes possession of a tract of land on the coasts of the African continent outside of its present possessions, or which, hitherto without such possessions, shall acquire them, as well as the Power which assumes a Protectorate there, shall accompany the respective act with a notification thereof, addressed to the other Signatory Powers of the present Act, in order to enable them, if need be, to make good any claims of their own.

Extracts from the General Appendices. Cited in Raymond Leslie Buell, *The Native Problem in Africa* (New York: The Macmillan Co., 1928) II, pp. 891–907.

42

The Social History of the Machine Gun—World War I

World War I was not only the first world war but also the first total war, involving civilians far-removed from the battlefields in a direct and significant way. In fact, there were more civilian casualties than combatant, a reflection of the stalemated military situation that developed early in August, 1914, at the Battle of the Marne. Each side tried, through any means possible, to destroy the other side's ability to wage war—the classic elements of a war of attrition. Thus, the symbols of World War I came to be the trench, no-man's land, barbed wire, and, above all, the machine gun. Yet this was not the scenario envisioned by the statesmen of the day, who were surprised by the very start of the war itself, nor the military leaders, whose contempt for technology and whose plans for the conduct of the war are highlighted in this selection. Most agreed with a British historian of the period who argued that modern weapons, if needed at all, would have a beneficial and deterrent effect on any future war in that "if any man could invent a means of destruction, by which two nations going to war with each other would see large armies destroyed … in a single campaign they would both hesitate at entering upon another… . In this sense the greatest destroyer is the greatest philanthropist." The reality of World War I destroyed this and many other illusions—about modern technology and modern warfare.

Discussion Questions

1. How did 19th century military leaders view war? What role did technology play in their definition of war, and why?

171

2. What do you see as the basic contradiction between the military's notions of war and the reality of the industrialized societies of which the military was a part? Why you think 19th century leaders were so wrong in their assessment of war, technology and human beings?

3. How did the role of the soldier change with World War I?

4. What lessons from this examination of the role of technology in World War I could we apply to our present situation? Does this selection reveal anything about the human potential for self-destruction?

(There was) a decided hardening of the arteries ... in the general staffs, evidenced in their reluctance to consider technological innovations; how utterly averse they were to changes in material was discovered to their great chagrin by industrialists like Colt, Krupp and Whitworth, and the military inventor and officer Werner Siemens grew so disgusted with the Prussian service that he gave it up to go into industry... . Especially in the first half of the nineteenth century ... the officer remained a romantic in the industrial age.

A. Vagts, *History of Militarism*

General Manteuffel gave a very clear example of this contempt for all things technical when he attacked the whole notion of schools "where often enough haughty teachers, as a rule full of hostility to war and the better classes, proud of their fancied scholarship, in brutal ways kill the feeling of honour and, saturated with the destructive tendencies of the time, almost exclusively rationalist, educate for everything else but character."

But there was more to the officers' attitude than a mere inability to comprehend technological progress. Because of their aristocratic origins many of the officers were, as Vagts put it, romantics in an industrial age. Their social isolation limited them to a conception of war as it had existed in a previous century. They still believed in the glorious cavalry charge and, above all, the supremacy of man as opposed to mere machines. Certainly they acknowledged that soldiers got killed by firearms, but they were never prepared to admit that advances in technology had reached such a level that the staunchest assault by the best of troops could be brought to nothing by modern weapons.

Certain thinkers did see that this was so. Engels, for example, stated flatly that:

Force is not mere act of will but calls for very real conditions before it starts to work, in particular tools, of which the perfect one overcomes the imperfect ones; that furthermore these tools must be produced, which means at the same time that the producer of more perfect tools, vulgo arms, beats the producer of more imperfect ones.

But the officers of the nineteenth century completely missed this point about the increasing dominance of the tools of war. For them war still was an act of will. Military memories and traditions had been formed in a pre–industrial age when the final bayonet or cavalry charge might be decisive. For them, in the last analysis, man was the master of the battlefield. In the military hierarchiesof Europe the traditional ideas lived on, and the whole period up to 1918 and even beyond is dominated by this basic contradiction. In a stimulating study of the fictional treatment of war at this time, I. F. Clarke is drawn to just this conclusion:

> The great paradox running through the whole of this production of imaginary wars between 1871 and 1914 was the total failure of army and navy writers to guess what would happen when the major industrial nations decided to fight it out.

In Prussia, Heros von Borcke took pains to examine many corpses and found so few stabbing wounds that he concluded that" bayonet fights rarely if ever occur, and exist only in the imagination." After spending twelve years examining the nature of modern warfare the Polish banker, Ivan Bloch, came to the conclusion that:

> War will become a kind of stalemate... . Everybody will be entrenched. It will be a great war of entrenchments. The spade would be as indispensable to the soldier as his rifle.... It will of necessity partake of the character of siege operations... . There will be increased slaughter ... on so terrible a scale as to render it impossible to get troops to push the battle

to a decisive issue. They will try to, thinking that they are fighting under the old conditions, and they will learn such a lesson that they will abandon the attempt for ever.

But such warnings fell on deaf ears. The average officer was simply not receptive to any ideas that might force him to change his comfortable habits.

The most bizarre reflection of the contradiction between the old modes of thought and the new weapons was the grim determination with which military establishments clung on to their cavalry regiments. Thus the British Cavalry Training Manual of 1907: "It must be accepted as a principle that the rifle, effective as it is, cannot replace the effect produced by the speed of the horse, the magnetism of the charge, and the terror of cold steel." Luckily for the Germans, in the First World War, they used machine guns, pill boxes and barbed wire that seem to have been immune to such awesome tactics. That it took the British generals so long to get this through their heads is partly explained by the fact that nearly all of them were cavalry men. Thus Haig, in 1904, attacked a writer who "sneers at the effect produced by sword and lance in modern war; surely he forgets that it is not the weapons carried but the moral factor on at highest speed in spite of rifle fire, which affects the nerves and aim of the ... rifleman."

It is thus hardly surprising that the general military reaction to the machine gun was something less than enthusiastic. There was some support from seemingly important quarters, but in fact such proponents of automatic weapons tended to be isolated individuals or to come from groups unable to make much impact on the orthodox military establishment. In 1882, Lord Charles Beresford asserted that: "In my opinion, machine guns, if properly worked, could decide the fate of a campaign, and would be equally useful ashore or afloat." Beresford was actually a Navy man, and he, and others, had all gained their reputations in the many colonial wars that Britain waged in the nineteenth century. Though this made them popular figures with the general public it, in fact, reduced their influence within the military hierarchy. For, in the last analysis, the majority of soldiers regarded such imperialist expeditions as mere sideshows, and concentrated their thoughts upon the possibility of a future war in Europe. So the machine gun became associated with colonial expeditions and the slaughter of natives, and was thus by definition regarded as being totally inappropriate to the conditions of regular European warfare.

The most tragic aspect of the High Commands' blindness to the power of automatic weapons was their chronic inability to recognise exactly what it meant to face up to an enemy equipped with such weapons. For all power had now passed to the defensive and the main reason for this was the presence of the machine guns. As one writer has put is: "It was as simple as this: three men and a machine gun can stop a battalion of heroes." The essential tragedy of the First World War is that the British commanders did not grasp this basic fact over three years.

The war on the ground had congealed almost immediately. The first trench warfare took place in September 1914 as the Germans on the Chemin des Dames Ridge, on the Aisne, dug in to block the Allied advance. By October 1914 one officer was able to write that: "The foremost infantry of both armies are now too securely entrenched, 200 to 400 yards apart, for attacks to have much chance of success save at prohibitive price." These were the conditions that prevailed for the next three years and more. The power of the defence, and particularly the machine gun, had rendered almost nil the chances of a successful frontal attack.

One of the first British offensives took place at Neuve Chapelle, in March 1915. The offensive was doomed to failure from the first because it was carried out with insufficient men and equipment. It had been intended that the French and the British should share the burden but Sir John French had tired of ceaseless French demands for aid in other sectors, and in a fit of pique decided to mount the attack with his own forces. The events of the first day made abundantly clear the characteristics of the new style of warfare. The actual infantry assault was preceded by a concentrated artillery barrage, intended to knock out the front line defences. When it stopped the British were to move forward. The experiences of one unit, the 2nd Scottish Rifles, in this battle have been meticulously studied, and are typical of the day's events:

> Ferrers was first out from 'B' Company, his monocle in his eye and his sword in his hand. As the guns stopped firing there was a moment of silence. Then the guns started again, firing behind the German lines… . Almost at the same moment came another noise, the whip and crack of the enemy machine guns opening up with deadly effect. From the intensity of their fire, and its accuracy, it was clear that the shelling had not been as effective as expected…. As the attack progressed the German positions which did most damage were two machine gun posts in front of the Middlesex. Not only did they virtually wipe out the 2nd Middlesex with frontal fire, but they caused many of the losses in the 2nd Scottish Rifles with deadly enfilade, or flanking fire.

In other words, two machine guns, a dozen Germans at most, brought to a halt two battalions of British infantry, or something over 1,500 men. Similar experiences were recorded all down the line of attack, and as the Germans pushed more men and machine guns into the threatened sector the attack swiftly fizzled out.

But the Allied High Command drew no lessons from this reverse. It was merely felt that the next time all that was needed was more shells, more men, and possibly just a little more offensive spirit. In September, at the Battle of Loos, exactly the same thing happened again. But still no one thought to question the British tactics. Instead they got rid of the commander–

in–chief. At the end of the year French was replaced by Haig.

Through bitter experience the machine taught that man himself was no longer master of the battlefield. The individual counted for nothing, all that mattered now was the machinery of war. If a machine gun could wipe out a whole battalion of men in three minutes, where was the relevance of the old concepts of heroism, glory and fair play between gentlemen? Lloyd George said that almost eighty per cent of the First World War casualties were caused by machine guns. In a way in which death was dealt out to so many with such mechanical casualness how could the old traditional modes of thought survive? The First World War was an event of crucial significance in the history of Western culture, a four–year trauma in which men tried to hold on to their old self–confidence in the face of horrors that would have been literally unimaginable two or three years earlier.

The confusion manifested itself in many ways. Some tried to cling on to the old modes of thought. In this respect the praise for the German machine–gunners achieves a new significance. In it one sees a desperate attempt to create new heroes in a war in which heroism was in fact irrelevant. Men tried to forget the weapons themselves, the mere machines that killed so unerringly and so indiscriminately, and remember only the men that pressed the trigger. Thus death could be made a little more acceptable.

Even those who retained their humanity and sensitivity also showed signs of the spiritual confusion that overtook those on the Western Front. Nowhere is this more clearly evidenced than in the work of the First World War poets. A poem of Siegfried Sassoon's, *The Redeemer*, shows this as well as any one poem can. Sassoon tells how he saw an English soldier struggling along with a load of planks, and in the darkness imagined for a moment that he was Christ on his cross. The last verse reads:

> He faced me, reeling in his weariness,
> Shouldering his load of planks, so hard to bear.
> I say that he was Christ, who wrought to bless
> All groping things with freedom bright as air,
> And with his mercy washed and made them fair.
> Then the flame sank, and all grew black as pitch,
> While we began to struggle along the ditch;
> And someone flung his burden in the muck,
> Mumbling: 'O Christ Almighty, now I'm stuck!'

The intentionally pathetic ending clearly reveals Sassoon's feeling that, try as he might to rekindle some belief in the old religious and ethical sureties of the days before the war, a new reality has been born in which such beliefs count for nothing besides the facts of the mud, the darkness and the heavy load. One critic has put the whole thing very well:

> The poets of World War I made it clear that man could no longer depend on his personal courage or strength for victory or even survival; mechanisation, the increased size of armies, the intensification of operations, the scientific efficiency of long–distance weapons destroyed the very elements of human individuality: courage, hope, enterprise, and a sense of the heroic possibilities in moral and physical conflict.

43

World War I: War of Attrition

Field Marshall Sir Douglas Haig:

"In the stage of the wearing-out struggle losses will necessarily be heavy on both sides, for in it the price of victory is paid. If the opposing forces are approximately equal in numbers, in courage, morale and in equipment, there is no way of avoiding payment of the price or of eliminating this phase of the struggle.

In former battles this stage of the conflict has rarely lasted more than a few days, and has often been completed in a few hours. When armies of millions are engaged, with the resources of great empires behind them, it will inevitably be long. It will include violent crises of fighting which, when viewed separately and apart from the general perspective, will appear individually as great indecisive battles. To this stage belong the great engagements of 1916 and 1917 which wore down the strength of the German armies."

General Erich von Falkenhayn on Verdun:

"We can probably do enough for our purposes with limited resources. Within our reach behind the French sector of the Western Front there are objectives for which the French General Staff would be compelled to throw in every man they have. If they do so the forces of France will bleed to death—as there can be no question of voluntary withdrawal—whether we reach our goal or not."

World War I: Battlefield Statistics

Battle of Verdun (1915):

Artillery used by both sides: ca. 2,000 guns

In four months of battle, over 24,000,000 shells had been fired by both sides

This was equivalent to 1,000 shells for each square meter of the battlefield

Battle of the Somme (1916):

27,768,076 rounds were fired in 153 days of battle by the British

This was equivalent to 181,491 rounds/day or 3,951 tons/day

which required 13 trains/day to transport

Battle of Arras (1917):

The Canadian Corps used 377 heavy guns on a front of four miles

(1 heavy for every 20 yards of front)

plus

1 field gun for every 10 yards of front

2,687,653 rounds were fired in the preliminary bombardment

4,261,500 rounds were fired during the most intensive fighting

Third Battle of Ypres (1917):

4,283,550 rounds were fired in the preliminary bombardment

World War I: Casualties

Personnel:

65,000,000 mobilized

10,000,000 soldiers died in battle

20,000,000 soldiers wounded

7,000,000 permanently disabled

20,000,000 civilians killed

Battle of Verdun: 750,000 killed and wounded

Battle of the Somme: 1,200,000 killed and wounded

One-half of all French males, 20–32 years old, killed

Statistics adapted from *White Heat: The New Warfare, 1914–1918* by John Terraine. Copyright © 1982 by Sidgwich & Jackson.

Four Empires Destroyed:

1. The German Empire
2. The Austrian Empire
3. The Russian Empire
4. The Ottoman Empire

World War I: The Cost
(Carnegie Foundation Estimate)
$400,000,000,000 (1914 dollars)

This amount could:

1. Give every family in the British Isles, Belgium, Russia,
   the U.S., Germany, Canada and Australia a $2500
   house, $1000 worth of furniture and a $500 five-acre lot,

and

2. Provide a $5,000,000 library and a $10,000,000 university
   to every community of over 20,000 people,

and

3. Create a fund to pay from interest alone 125,000 teachers
   and 125,000 nurses,

and

4. Purchase every piece of property and all the wealth of
   both England and France.

44

War in the Trenches

Eric Maria Remarque's *All Quiet on the Western Front* is the most famous example of the genre of war novels that were written in the 1920's. The purpose of these books was to bring home to the civilians what it was like to be in the trenches during the war. Remarque presents his novel as a memoir by a certain Paul Baumer, an eighteen-year-old German soldier who finds himself thrown into the abyss of war for the first time, like almost all of the soldiers in World War I.

Discussion Questions

1. How does Remarque describe the changes that men went through when they made the transition from civilian to soldier?

2. What was fighting in the trenches like?

3. What grand and noble objectives do the soldiers seem to be fighting for? If you knew about the conditions of trench warfare, would you volunteer?

4. When men kill each other in war is it murder?

5. What had happened to all the great advances of Western civilization for those who fought in the trenches? When Baumer says, "The Bushmen are primitive and naturally so, but we are primitive in an artificial sense," what does he mean?

❝ Surely Himmelstoss was a very different fellow as a postman," say I, after Albert's disappointment has subsided. "Then how does it come that he's such a bully as a drill-sergeant?"

The question revives Kropp, more particularly as he hears there's no more beer in the canteen. "It's not only Himmelstoss, there are lots of them. As sure as they get a stripe or a star they become different, as though they'd swallowed concrete."

"That's the uniform," I suggest.

"Roughly speaking it is," says Kat, and prepares long speech; "but the root of the matter lies elsewhere. For instance, if you train a dog to eat potatoes and afterwards put a piece of meat in front of him, he'll snap at it, it's his nature. And if you give a man a little bit of authority he behaves just the same way, he snaps at it too. The things are precisely the same. In himself **man is essentially a beast**, only he butters it over like a slice of bread with a little decorum. The army is based on that; one man must always have power over the other. The mischief is merely that each one has much too much power. A non-com. can torment a private, a lieutenant a non-com., a captain a lieutenant, until he goes mad. And because they know they can, they all soon acquire the habit more or less. Take a simple case: we are marching-back from the parade-ground dog-tired. Then comes the order to sing. We are glad enough to be able to trail arms but we sing spiritlessly. At once the company is turned about and has to do another hour's drill as punishment. On the march back the order to sing is given again, and once more we start. Now what's the use of all that? It's simply that the company commander's head has been turned by having so much power. And nobody blames him. On the contrary, he is praised for being strict. That, of course, is only a trifling instance, but it holds also in very different affairs. Now I ask you: Let a man be whatever you like in peace-time, what occupation is there in which he can behave like that without getting a crack on the nose? He can only do that in the army. It goes to the heads of them all, you see. And the more insignificant a man has been in civil life the worse it takes him." …

From the earth, from the air, sustaining forces pour into us—mostly from the earth. To no man does the earth mean so much as to the soldier. When he presses himself down upon her long and powerfully, when he buries his face and his limbs deep in her from the fear of death by shell-fire, then she is his only friend, his brother, his mother; he stifles his terror and his cries in her silence and her security; she shelters him and gives him a new lease of ten seconds of life, receives him again and often for ever.

Earth!—Earth!—Earth!

Earth with thy folds, and hollows and holes, into which a man may fling himself and crouch down! In the spasm of terror, under the hailing of annihilation, in the bellowing death of die explosions, O Earth, thou grantest us the great resisting surge of newwon life. Our being, almost utterly carried away by the fury of the storm, streams back through our hands from thee, and we, thy redeemed ones, bury ourselves in thee, and through the long minutes in a mute agony of hope bite into thee with our lips! …

We trudge onward in single file through the trenches and shellholes and come again to the zone of mist. Katczinsky is restive, that's a bad sign.

"What's up, Kat?" says Kropp.

"I wish I were back home." Home—he means the huts.

"It won't last much longer, Kat."

He is nervous. "I don't know, I don't know—"

We come to the communication-trench and then the open fields. The little wood reappears; we know every foot of ground here. There's the cemetery with mounds and the black crosses.

That moment it breaks out behind us, swells, roars, and thunders. We duck down—a cloud of flame shoots up a hundred yards ahead of us.

The next minute under a second explosion part of the wood rises slowly in the air, three or four trees sail up and then crash to pieces. The shells begin to hiss safety-valves—heavy fire—

"Take cover!" yells somebody, "Cover!"

The fields are flat, the wood is too distant and dangerous—the only cover is the graveyard and the mounds. We stumble across in the dark and as though spirited away every man lies glued behind a mound.

Not a moment too soon. The dark goes mad. It heaves and raves. Darknesses blacker than the night rush on us with giant strides, over us and away. The flames of the explosions light up the graveyard.

There is no escape anywhere. By the light of the shells—I try to get a view of the fields. They are a surging sea, daggers of flame from the explosions leap up like fountains. It is impossible for anyone to break through it.

The wood vanishes, it is pounded, crushed, torn to pieces. We must stay here in the graveyard.

The earth bursts before us. It rains clods. I feel a smack. My sleeve is torn away by a splinter. I shut my fist. No pain. Still that does not reassure me: wounds don't hurt till afterwards. I feel the arm all over. It is grazed but sound. Now a crack on the skull, I begin to lose consciousness. Like lightning the thought comes to me: Don't faint, sink down in the black broth and immediately come up to the top again. A splinter slashes into my helmet, but has travelled so far that it does not go through. I wipe the mud out of my eyes. A hole is torn up in front of me. Shells hardly ever land in the same hole twice, I'll get into it. With one bound I fling myself down and lie on the earth as flat as a fish; there it whistles again, quickly I crouch together, claw for cover, feel something on the left, shove in beside it, it gives way, I groan, the earth leaps, the blast thunders in my ears, I creep under the yielding thing, cover myself with it, draw it over me, it is wood, cloth, cover, cover, miserable cover against the whizzing splinters.

I open my eyes—my fingers grasp a sleeve, an arm. A wounded man? I yell to him—no answer—a dead man. My hand gropes farther, splinters of wood—now I remember again that we are lying in the graveyard.

But the shelling is stronger than everything. It wipes out the sensibilities, I merely crawl still deeper into the coffin, it should protect me, and especially as Death himself lies in it too.

Before me gapes the shellhole. I grasp it with my eyes as with fists. With one leap I must be in it. There, I get a smack in the face, a hand clamps on to my shoulder—has the dead man waked up?—The hand shakes me, I turn my head, in the second of light I stare into the face of Katczinsky, he has his mouth wide open and is yelling. I hear nothing, he rattles me, comes nearer, in a momentary lull his voice reaches me: "Gas-Gaas-Gaaas—Pass it on."

I grab for my gas-mask. Some distance from me there lies someone. I think of nothing but this: That fellow there must know Gaaas-Gaaas—

I call, I lean toward him, I swipe at him with the satchel, he doesn't see—once again,

again—he merely ducks—it's a recruit—I look at Kat desperately, he has his mask ready—I pull out mine too, my helmet falls to one side, it slips over my face, I reach the man, his satchel is on the side nearest me, I seize the mask, pull it over his head, he understands, I let go and with a jump drop back into the shellhole.

The dull thud of the gas—shells mingles with the crash of the high explosives. A bell sounds between the explosions, gongs, and metal clappers warning everyone—Gas—Gas—Gaas.

Someone plumps down behind me, another. I wipe the goggles of my mask clear of the moist breath. It is *Kat, Krop*p, and someone else. All four of us lie there in heavy, watchful suspense and breathe as lightly as possible.

These first minutes with the mask decide between life and death: is it tightly woven? I remember the awful sights in the hospital: the gas patients who in day-long suffocation cough their burnt lungs up in clots.

Cautiously, the mouth applied to the valve, I breath.

The gas still creeps over the ground and sinks into all hollows. Like a big, soft jellyfish it floats into our shellhole and lolls there obscenely. I nudge Kat, it is better to crawl out and lie on top than to stay here where the gas collects most. But we don't get as far as that; a second bombardment begins. It is no longer as though the shells roared, it is the earth itself raging.

With a crash something black bears down on us. It lands close beside us; a coffin thrown up.

I see Kat move and I crawl across. The coffin has hit the fourth man in our hole on his out-stretched arm. He tries to tear off his gas-mask with the other hand. Kropp seizes him just in time, twists the hand sharply behind his back and holds it fast... .

We have become wild beasts. We do not fight, we defend ourselves against annihilation. It is not against men that we fling our bombs, what do we know of men in this moment when Death with hands and helmets is hunting us down—now, for the first time in three days we can see his face, now, for the first time in three days we can oppose him; we feel a mad anger. No longer do we lie helpless, waiting on the scaffold, we can destroy and kill, to save ourselves, to save ourselves and be revenged.

We crouch behind every corner, behind every barrier of barbed wire, and hurl heaps of explosives at the feet of the advancing enemy before we run. The blast of the handgrenades impinges powerfully on our arms and legs; crouching like cats we run on, overwhelmed by this wave that bears us along, that fills us with ferocity, turning us into thugs, into murderers, into God only knows what devils; this wave that multiplies our strength with fear and madness and greed of life, seeking and fighting for nothing but our deliverance. If your own father came with them you would not hesitate to fling a bomb into him... .

It is nearly noon. The sun blazes hotly, the sweat stings in our eyes, we wipe it off on our sleeves, and often blood with it. At last we reach a trench that is in a somewhat better condition. It is manned and ready for the counter-attack, it receives us. Our guns open up in full blast and cut off the enemy attack.

The lines behind us stop. They can advance no farther. The attack is crushed by our artillery. We watch. The fire lifts a hundred yards and we break forward. Beside me a lance-corporal has his head torn off. He runs a few steps more while the blood spouts from his neck like a fountain.

It does not come quite to hand-to-hand fighting; they are driven back. We arrive once again at our shattered trench and pass on beyond it.

Oh, this turning back again! We reach the shelter of the reserves and yearn to creep in and disappear; but instead we must turn round and plunge again into the horror. If we were not automata at that moment we would continue lying there, exhausted, and without will. But we are swept forward again, powerless, madly savage and raging; we will kill, for they are still our mortal enemies; their rifles and bombs are aimed against us, and if we don't destroy them, they will destroy us.

The brown earth, the torn, blasted earth, with a greasy shine under the sun's rays; the earth is the background of this restless, gloomy world of automatons, our gasping is the scratching of a quill, our lips are dry, our heads are debauched with stupor—thus we stagger forward, and into our pierced and shattered souls bores the torturing image of the brown earth with the greasy sun and the convulsed and dead soldiers, who lie there—it can't be helped—who cry and clutch at our legs as we spring away over them.

We have lost all feeling for one another. We can hardly control ourselves when our hunted glance lights on the form of some other man. We are insensible, dead men, who through some trick, some dreadful magic, are still able to run and to kill... .

One morning two butterflies play in front of our trench. They are brimstone-butterflies, with red spots on their yellow wings. What can they be looking for here? There is not a plant nor a flower for miles. They settle on the teeth of a skull. The birds too are just as carefree, they have long since accustomed themselves to the war. Every morning larks ascend from No Man's Land. A year ago we watched them nesting; the young ones grew up too.

We have a spell from the rats in the trench. They are in No Man's Land-we know what for. They grow fat; when we see one we have a crack at it... .

We see men living with their skulls blown open; we see soldiers run with their two feet cut off, they stagger on their splintered stumps into the next shellhole; a lance-corporal crawls a mile and half on his hands dragging his smashed knee after him; another goes to the dressing-station and over his clasped hands bulge his intestines; we see men without mouths, without jaws, without faces; we find one man who has held the artery of his arm in his teeth for two hours in order not to bleed to death. The sun goes down, night comes, the shells whine, life is at an end.

Still the little piece of convulsed earth in which we lie is held. We have yielded no more than a few hundred yards of it as a prize to the enemy. But on every yard there lies a dead man.

* * *

A man cannot realize that above such shattered bodies there are still human faces in which life goes its daily round. And this is only one hospital, one single station; there are hundreds of thousands in Germany, hundreds of thousands in France, hundreds of thousands in Russia. How senseless is everything that can ever be written, done, or thought, when such things are possible. It must all be lies and of no account when the culture of a thousand years could not prevent this stream of blood being poured out, these torture-chambers in their hundreds of thousands. A hospital alone shows what war is.

I am young, I am twenty years old; yet I know nothing of life but despair, death, fear, and fatuous superficiality cast over an abyss of sorrow. I see how peoples are set against one another, and in silence, unknowingly, foolishly, obediently, innocently slay one another. I see that the keenest brains of the world invent weapons and words to make it yet more refined and enduring. And all men of my age, here and over there, throughout the whole world, see these things; all my generation is experiencing these things with me. What would our fathers do if we suddenly stood up and came before them and proffered our account? What do they expect of us if a time ever comes when the war is over? Through the years our business has been killing; it was our first calling in life. Our knowledge of life is limited to death. What will happen afterwards? And what shall come out of us?

* * *

Here, on the borders of death, life follows an amazingly simple course, it is limited to what is most necessary, all else lies buried in gloomy sleep;—in that lies our primitiveness and our survival. We more subtly differentiated we must long since have gone mad, have deserted, or have fallen. As in a polar expedition, every expression of life must serve only the preservation of existence, and is absolutely focussed on that. All else is banished because it would consume energies unnecessarily. That is the only way to save ourselves. In the quiet hours when the puzzling reflection of former days, like a blurred mirror, projects beyond me the figure of my present existence, I often sit over against myself, as before a stranger, and wonder how the unnameable active principle that calls itself Life has adapted itself even to this form. All other expressions lie in a winter sleep, life is simply one continual watch against the menace of death; it has transformed us into unthinking animals in order to give us the weapon of instinct—it has reinforced us with dullness, so that we do not go to pieces before the horror, which would overwhelm us if we had clear, conscious thought—it has awakened in us the sense of comradeship, so that we escape the abyss of solitude—it has lent us the indifference of wild creatures, so that in spite of all we perceive the positive in every moment, and store it up as a reserve against the onslaught of nothingness. Thus we live a closed, hard existence of the utmost superficiality, and rarely does an incident strike out a spark. But then unexpectedly a flame of grievous and terrible yearning flares up.

Those are the dangerous moments. They show us that the adjustment is only artificial, that it is not simple rest, but sharpest struggle for rest. In the outward form of our life we are hardly distinguishable from Bushmen; but whereas the latter can be so always, because they are so truly, and at best may develop further by exertion of their spiritual forces, with us it is the reverse; our inner forces are not exerted toward regeneration, but toward degeneration. The Bushmen are primitive and naturally so, but we are primitive in an artificial sense, and by virtue of the utmost effort.

And at night, waking out of a dream, overwhelmed and bewitched by the crowding face; a man perceives with alarm how slight is the support, how thin the boundary that divides him from the darkness. We are little flames poorly sheltered by frail walls against the storm of dissolution and madness, in which we flicker and sometimes almost go out. Then the muffled roar of the battle becomes a ring that encircles us, we creep in upon ourselves, and with big eyes stare into the night. Our only comfort is the steady breathing of our comrades asleep, and thus we wait for the morning… .

45

Japan at Versailles

Japan's role in the twentieth century has been a study in contrasts. Her victory over the Russians in 1905 inspired nationalists all over the world, and by World War I, Japan was in a position to demand full equality with the Western powers. However, as these readings suggest, Japan's perspective on her rights in Asia, on her relationship with the West, and her role in the Wilsonian world order, reflect potential contradictions that would lead Japan, the friend in the early twentieth century, to become Japan the foe by the 1930's.

1. What values and interests seemed to be motivating the Japanese leaders at Versailles? Were these interests markedly different from those influencing the other leaders?

2. What were Japan's main goals at Versailles? How did these differ from the aims of other countries? What potential conflicts do you see?

3. What was Japan's position towards China, and what inconsistencies do you find in her position as compared with other Japanese aims at Versailles?

Japanese Aims at the Paris Peace Conference

The Peace Conference had its origins in the idealism of American President Woodrow Wilson. The year before the war had ended Wilson had set forth in his State of the Union Message his famous Fourteen Points. Among the more important of these were the abolition of secret treaties, freedom of the seas, reduction of armaments, and specific proposals based on the self-determination of various countries. Yet another noteworthy feature was his proposal for the "establishment of a League of Nations with the aim of guaranteeing the political and territorial sovereignty of all nations, large and small alike."

Japan at the time was in the reign of the Emperor Taisho, the successor of the Emperor Meiji. The press was free, and championship of the people's rights was such that this period would later be known as that of "Taisho democracy." Government during the Meiji era had for the most part been under the strict control of the elder statesmen who had played key roles in the Meiji Restoration. However, in the Taisho era a system of government by two major parties was well on the way to establishment. The right to vote still depended upon the amount of taxes paid, but general elections were already in the cards.

The Japanese press was unanimous in its support of Wilson's proposals, and welcomed them as advancing the cause of humanity. However, the response of experienced members of the Foreign Ministry was somewhat more complex. In a word, they were perplexed. These men were accustomed to living by the rules of the jungle of international relations, where might was right and clandestine plotting

indispensable. Never before had the "ideals" that Wilson proposed been put forth as fundamental principles of international polities. While they felt they could not openly oppose Wilson's idealism, neither could they speak out with any enthusiasm in favor of it. Their hands were tied, and they feared the results would be most disadvantageous to their own country. Would this idealism ultimately become the guiding principle of the post-World War I world? Could they be assured it did not conceal a trap that would hinder the further progress of Japan?

One of the delegates to the Paris Peace Conference was Konoe Fumimaro, the eldest son of a family that for a thousand years had been closer than any other to the imperial household, and future prime minister, relinquishing his position to Tojo right before the start of World War II. He was a fair-skinned young man, only twenty-seven years old in 1919, and this philosophically-minded member of the delegation had only shortly before published an essay, "Against a Peace to the Advantage of England and America," in which he challenged openly the "ideals" of Wilson's Fourteen Points. He sharply criticized Japan's leaders for being deceived by the flowery rhetoric of English and American politicians and for endorsing the ideals of the League of Nations without noting the "egoism of England and America" that lay beneath them. Konoe saw the war in Europe as a struggle between the established powers and the as yet unestablished powers. Those nations that stood to profit most from the League and the other Fourteen Points were England and America. Japan, therefore, should, at the very least, make its participation in an alliance for peace contingent upon the following two conditions: the rejection of economic imperialism and the abolition of discrimination between the white and yellow races.

Japan, Konoe maintained, had the right to act in its own best interests. This was not to say that Japan could simply ignore other nations, but that it should see their egoism, backed by military and economic power, for what it was. And Japan should resist it for the sake of its own right to exist, which was equally defensible on the grounds of justice and humanity. To the leaders of Japan, who, since the opening of the country, had pursued a foreign policy based entirely upon learning from the West and cooperating with the West—often to their own humiliation—this was an entirely new concept. It seemed a dangerous proposition, excessively direct and naive.

However, there was one Chinese who was deeply impressed by the Konoe article. This was Sun Yat-sen, now known as the father of the Chinese revolution. When Sun saw Konoe he praised his article and predicted that "the Paris Peace Conference would decide the fate not only of Japan but of all the peoples of East Asia." Recalling the Russo-Japanese War, Sun said, "I was in Paris when I heard of Japan's victory. On the way home an Arab I met at the Suez Canal asked me if I was Japanese. I told him I was, and he said to me, 'I've seen a constant stream of wounded Russian soldiers coming through the canal lately, on their way home. That's real proof that an Asian nation can defeat Russia. And when I realized that, I was happier than if my own country had won that war.' As a fellow Asian, masquerading as a Japanese, I myself had never felt as confident as I did then."

Japan's victory in the Russo-Japanese War of 1904–1905 had been a beacon of rebellion to the people of the world who for the past three hundred years had been ruled by the West. It had aroused a desire for independence among the oppressed peoples of the world, especially in Asia. Sun Yat-sen went on to say, "Yes, until thirty years ago there wasn't a single country in Asia that was entirely independent. But now that Japan has become one of the five great powers it stands at a parting of the ways. Will it participate in the division of Asia, will it act as an agent of the enslavement of Asia; or will it lead the one billion people of Asia and fight by their side? It is unfortunate," he concluded, "that at this crucial time there is neither a true politician nor a true diplomat to be found in Japan." Konoe agreed completely.

Japan's greatest concerns at the Paris Peace Conference were, first, the inclusion of a clause in the Covenant of the League of Nations abolishing racial discrimination, and, second, the guarantee of its rights to the Shantung Peninsula in China, which had been taken from Germany in the war. Japan first acquired rights in China after the Sino-Japanese War of 1894–95, and had entered World War I after an agreement with England, America and France that Japan would receive German concessions in China, to be returned to China at some point in the future. Japanese leaders were still angered by the treatment they had gotten from Germany, Russia and France after the Sino-Japanese War, those countries arguing that Japan's possession of special rights was a threat to peace in Asia. Japan submitted to their pressure, yet immediately thereafter, those three countries, as "rewards" for their intercession, carved out territories for themselves in China. This humiliation had left an indelible impression on the minds of all Japanese, from the nation's leaders down to the humble farmer.

If these interests were to be returned to China in the near future, Wilson argued, would it not be as well to relinquish them at the conference itself? But Japan was insistent for reasons of national dignity and interest. There was a feeling among the Japanese that they were being manipulated and meddled with by the larger powers. If these interests had to be returned to China, and returned shortly, at that, Japan felt that there should be direct negotiations with China, and it wanted to hold the winning card in these negotiations.

Relations between Japan and China were extremely complex. Virtually every Japanese felt himself to be in league with the Chinese in their determination to prevent European aggression. To this end the modernization and unification of China were essential. The Sino-Japanese War in no way diminished this desire. In 1900 Japan for the first time joined forces with the Western nations in armed intervention in China; yet even then the idea of cooperation between Japan and China remained a strong current in the ideas and activities of the ordinary citizen. Many Chinese students had come to study in Japan while many Japanese military men had been involved as advisers in the modernization of China's armed forces. While Japan advanced steadily toward becoming a well-ordered modern nation, China was left behind, as disordered as ever, an insignificant state that fell prey to the European powers. Seeing this, Japan's hopes gave way to irritation, while throughout the nation contempt for the Chinese came to prevail. Japan came to feel that, if it was China's fate to be divided up among the great powers, then Japan, its neighbor, who had defended China against the encroachment of Russia, has a right to its fair share of the spoils.

World War I changed the world in two major ways. First, it gave birth to the Soviet Union, the first of the new states to be founded on the principles of communism. At the time, this suggested that armed intervention by the once-powerful Russia would diminish, but eventually the great powers came to fear that the new ideas would infiltrate their own nations and lead to revolution. Japan, although powerful, was nonetheless still unsettled internally by the process of development. As a near neighbor of Russia, it was one of the nations that felt its influence most strongly.

Secondly, there was the rise of America. America had had, until then, little power to influence international politics, but as a result of World War I it had become the richest nation in the world and the financial backer of the European nations. It not only became a formidable military power, but also acquired a powerful voice in world politics. Insofar as America often based policies upon ideals, often admittedly, to its own advantage, it had a different style of diplomacy from that of the European powers.

Europe and America had divided up the world and grown rich on its abundant resources and population. America, with much of its own vast continent still to develop, had in the name of the Monroe Doctrine barred Japanese immigrants from every country within its sphere of influence except Brazil.

Japan had two possible paths of action before it. It could stand up for justice and humanity, to which end it would have to resign itself to sacrificing its special interests in China. It might even have to run the risk of becoming a weak nation. Or, on the other hand, it could adhere to nineteenth-century principles of power, and, with the greatest caution, make its way in the world as a rival of the great powers.

Anti-Asian Discrimination and the Racial Equality Clause

As the structure of the League of Nations began to take shape under the guidance of England and America, the Japanese government, like Konoe, sensed the danger of racial bias working to Japan's disadvantage. Anti-Asian discrimination in America was great. The many Asian immigrants who endured the arduous Pacific crossing to work in the mining industries and to build the railroads that helped fuel the American industrial revolution, were now being discriminated against in many ways.

In San Francisco in October 1906, the Board of Education gave as its reason for excluding Japanese children from public schools the fact that they were "vicious, immoral, of an age and maturity too advanced for safe association with the younger American children." Discrimination against the Japanese on the West Coast was, as with the Chinese, based upon resentment of cheap labor and cultural differences, but with an additional element. As one might expect in a situation that had arisen shortly after the Russo-Japanese War, the anti-Japanese leaders on the coast covertly feared the West Coast would be "occupied" by Japan. Thus, the anti-Japanese movement was both politically motivated and well-organized.

In April of 1906, the great San Francisco earthquake occurred, and the Japanese people sent contributions totaling $245,000, more than half the amount collected throughout the world. When immediately thereafter the immigration problem arose, it was hardly surprising that the Japanese felt that America was "ungrateful." President Roosevelt, who had been upset with earlier laws discriminating against Asians, continued to voice his displeasure at Western legislators' attempts to restrict Japanese immigration, but at the same time negotiated a gentleman's agreement with the Japanese government to send no more immigrants. (In 1924 national immigration restrictions would be enacted that prohibited Japanese and Chinese immigrants from coming to the U.S.). Further demonstrations of anti-Asian sentiment would lead to a California law prohibiting Japanese from owning real estate and limiting their right to rent land to three years. Wilson, president at the time, appealed to Californians to rescind their laws, but to no avail.

England's delegate, too, felt that since equality of member nations was the fundamental spirit of the League of Nations, Japan's proposal of a racial-equality clause could hardly be denied.

However, he opposed the proposal on account of the rigid opposition of the Commonwealth prime ministers, in particular Australian Prime Minister William M. Hughes. Behind-the-scenes negotiations dragged on from the end of January until April. Makino tried every possible tactic: he repeatedly sought the support and cooperation of English and American delegates; he spoke with Henry W. Steed, the chief correspondent of the *Times*, who alerted public opinion in England through his writings; he attempted to persuade Hughes to reconsider his position. All the British Commonwealth leaders tried to persuade Hughes to change his mind, but Hughes, who feared defeat in domestic elections, threatened to withdraw his delegation and refuse to sign the treaty if Japan's proposal was included in any form whatever. South Africa's Prime Minister Louis Botha told Makino, "Strictly between ourselves, I think he is mad."

Japanese had long been working in northern Australia, planting sugar cane and gathering pearls. The first act of the newly established Commonwealth Council in 1901 was to prohibit the entry of Asians. The new immigration laws required a dictation test given in a European language, which all but completely excluded immigrants from Japan. On the other hand, illiterate Europeans could be excused from the examination at the discretion of immigration officials. Australia's Attorney General Alfred Deakin said of the law, "If restrictions were to be based on race, we would provoke the antagonism of Japan, as one of the civilized nations of the world, and we would not attain our objective." He then went on to say, "The Japanese are extremely enterprising and energetic, and moreover the standard of living they are accustomed to is low. As competitors they are the most dangerous of the Asians, and we must make every effort to keep them out. In short, we exclude the Japanese not because they are an inferior race, but because they are a superior one."

The committee that was to make the decision concerning Japan's proposal of a clause in the covenant calling for equal treatment of nations was convened on the evening of April 11. Wilson was the chairman and there were sixteen other members. The vote was divided as follows: eleven in favor, i.e., two votes each from Japan, France, and Italy, and one vote each from Greece, China, Serbia, Portugal, and Czechoslovakia; and five opposed, i.e., England, America, Poland, Brazil, and Romania. Makino had been advised in advance that because England was opposed America would join it.

Wilson declared as chairman that "since the committee could not reach a unanimous decision, the proposal cannot be adopted." Makino protested that most matters at the conference had been decided by majority vote and was supported in this by several others. However, Wilson dismissed this objection, saying, "I raised this matter on the understanding that such an important matter required the unanimous agreement of the committee, or that at least there be no opposition."

In this way Japan's racial-equality proposal was defeated. News of Japan's frustration in Paris, as well as the exclusion of the Japanese from the Pacific Coast, was reported in detail in Japan. A succession of protest meetings was held, but their efforts were thwarted by the fact that Japan's delegation in Paris could do nothing as long as England and America opposed them. The only way left open to them was to state clearly Japan's intentions for the future.

Due to Wilson's idealism it was expected that he would support the Japanese clause for racial equality at the Paris Peace Conference, and, in principle, he did. It was the English, particularly concerned over anti-Asian feeling in Australia, who persuaded Wilson to drop his support for the clause. The Japanese delegates protested that "if it is to be a principle of the League of Nations that certain peoples are not to be given just and equal treatment, this will strike those peoples as odd, and in the future, will undermine their faith in the very principles of justice and equality that are supposed to regulate relations between member nations." The Paris press was unanimous in its sharp criticism of the League rejections. One paper pointed out that "it was outrageous that although a clause recognizing America's Monroe Doctrine was included, the equal treatment amendment sought by Japan was rejected."

46

The Impact of World War I—
The Age of Anxiety

"What shall I think tomorrow?"

George Grosz, 1920

Psychology

Freud—Death Wish—Aggression Instinctual

"Men are not gentle friendly creatures, but are naturally aggressive; no man can trust another man. Man to man is a wolf."

Civilization and Its Discontents

Pavlov—Behavioral Conditioning

Art

"The Lost Generation"

Alienation, Cubism, Surrealism, Futurism, Dadaism

Anthropology

Cultural Relativism

Religion

Concept of Original Sin Reemerges

"Civilization is a disease which is almost invariably fatal , unless its course is checked in time ... If so-called civilized nations show any protracted vitality, it is because they are only civilized at the top. Ancient civilizations were destroyed by imported barbarians. We breed our own."

Dean of St. Paul's Cathedral,
"The Idea of Progress"

Science

There Are No Absolute Truths

Heisenberg—The Uncertainty Theory

Einstein—The Theory of Relativity

Curie—The Sub-Atomic (Nuclear) World

Eugenics—The science of race

History

"You are a product of your conditioning."

Philosophy

Nietzsche—Western Civilization Is Decadent

"Disintegration characterizes this time, and thus, uncertainty. Nothing stands firmly on its feet or on a hard faith in itself, one lives for tomorrow as the day after tomorrow is dubious. Everything on our way is slippery and dangerous, and the ice that still supports us has become thin: all of us feel the warm, uncanny breath of the thawing wind: where we still walk, soon no one will be able to walk."

The Will to Power

William James—Pragmatism

Sartre, Camus—Existentialism

"Existence precedes essence"

"Man is condemned to be free"

Political Ideology

Totalitarianism

Lenin—Communism

Mussolini, Hitler—Fascism

47

Lenin and Communism

In his book *State and Revolution*, written in 1917, Vladimir Lenin (1870–1924) discusses what will happen when revolution replaces the bourgeois capitalist system with a "dictatorship of the proletariat."

Discussion Questions

1. What is the link between the dictatorship of the proletariat and democracy?

2. How does communism "render the state absolutely unnecessary?" How do you think Lenin is defining the term "state?"

3. Do you agree that democracy means equality?

4. What do you think Lenin means when he implies that democracy is more a means than an end?

5. Why do you think that in Russia the dictatorship of the "proletariat" never did disappear under communism?

The dictatorship of the proletariat—*i.e.,* the organisation of the vanguard of the oppressed as the ruling class for the purpose of crushing the oppressors—cannot produce merely an expansion of democracy. *Together* with an immense expansion of democracy which *for the first time* becomes democracy for the poor, democracy for the people, and not democracy for the rich folk, the dictatorship of the proletariat produces a series of restrictions of liberty in the case of the oppressors, the exploiters, the capitalists. We must crush them in order to free humanity from wage-slavery; their resistance must be broken by force; it is clear that where there is suppression there is also violence, there is no liberty, no democracy.

Engels expressed this splendidly in his letter to Bebel when he said, as the reader will remember, that "as long as the proletariat still *needs* the state, it needs it not in the interests of freedom, but for the purpose of crushing its antagonists; and as soon as it becomes possible to speak of freedom, then the state, as such, ceases to exist." ...

Only Communism renders the state absolutely unnecessary, for there is *no one* to be suppressed—"no one" in the sense of a *class,* in the sense of a systematic struggle with a definite section of the population. We are not Utopians, and we do not in the least deny the possibility and inevitability of excesses on the part of *individual persons,* nor the need to suppress *such* excesses. But, in the first place, no special machinery, no special apparatus of repression is needed for this; this will be done by the armed people itself, as simply and as readily as any crowd of civilised people, even in modern society, parts a pair of combatants or does not allow a woman to be outraged. And, secondly, we know that the fundamental social cause of excesses which consists in violating the rules of social life is the exploitation of the masses, their want and their poverty. With the removal of this chief cause, excesses will inevitably begin to "wither away." We do not know how quickly and in what succession, but we know that they will wither away. With their withering away, the state will also wither away... .

Democracy means equality. The great significance of the struggle of the proletariat for equality, and the significance of equality as a slogan, are apparent, if we correctly interpret it as meaning the abolition of *classes.* But democracy means only *formal* equality. Immediately after the attainment of equality for all members of society *in respect* of the ownership of the means of production, that is, of equality of labour and equality of wages, there will inevitably arise before humanity the question of going further from formal equality to real equality, *i.e.,* to realising the rule, "From each according to his ability; to each according to his needs." By what stages, by means of what practical measures humanity will proceed to this higher aim—this we do not and cannot know. But it is important to realise how infinitely mendacious is the usual bourgeois presentation of Socialism as something lifeless petrified, fixed once for all, whereas in reality, it is *only* with Socialism that there will commence a rapid, genuine, real mass advance, in which first the *majority* and then the whole of the population will take part—an advance in all domains of social and individual life.

From Vladimir Lenin, *State and Revolution,* copyright © 1932 by International Publishers, New York, pp. 73, 75, 82–85. Reprinted with permission.

Democracy is a form of the state—one of its varieties. Consequently, like every state, it consists in organised, systematic application of force against human beings. This on the one hand. On the other hand, however, it signifies the formal recognition of the equality of all citizens, the equal right of all to determine the structure and administration of the state. This, in turn, is connected with the fact that, at a certain stage in the development of democracy, it first rallies the proletariat as a revolutionary class against capitalism, and gives it an opportunity to crush, to smash to bits, to wipe off the face of the earth the bourgeois state machinery—even its republican variety: the standing army, the police, and bureaucracy; then it substitutes for all this a *more* democratic, but still a state machinery in the shape of armed masses of workers, which becomes transformed into universal participation of the people in the militia... .

[Eventually] the whole of society will have become one office and one factory, with equal work and equal pay.

But this "factory" discipline, which the proletariat will extend to the whole of society after the defeat of the capitalists and the overthrow of the exploiters, is by no means our ideal, or our final aim. It is but a *foothold* necessary for the radical cleansing of society of all the hideousness and foulness of capitalist exploitation, *in order to advance further.*

From the moment when all members of society, or even only the overwhelming majority, have learned how to govern the state *themselves,* have taken this business into their own hands, have "established" control over the insignificant minority of capitalists, over the gentry with capitalist leanings, and the workers thoroughly demoralised by capitalism—from this moment the need for any government begins to disappear. The more complete the democracy, the nearer the moment when it begins to be unnecessary. The more democratic the "state" consisting of armed workers, which is "no longer a state in the proper sense of the word," the more rapidly does every state begin to wither away.

For when *all* have learned to manage, and independently are actually managing by themselves social production, keeping accounts, controlling the idlers, the gentlefolk, the swindlers and similar "guardians of capitalist traditions," then the escape from this national accounting and control will inevitably become so increasingly difficult, such a rare exception, and will probably be accompanied by such swift and severe punishment (for the armed workers are men of practical life, not sentimental intellectuals, and they will scarcely allow any one to trifle with them), that very soon the *necessity* of observing the simple, fundamental rules of everyday social life in common will have become a *habit.*

The door will then be wide open for the transition from the first phase of Communist society to its higher phase, and along with it to the complete withering away of the state.

48

Mussolini: What Is Fascism?

Benito Mussolini (1883–1945) came to power in Italy in 1922 as the leader of a new movement called Fascism (so named from the *fasces*, a bundle of sticks which was a symbol of unified power in ancient Rome—*e pluribus unum*).

The following is an article written by Mussolini for the Italian Encyclopedia in 1932.

Discussion Questions

1. Earlier in his career, Mussolini had been a socialist. What reasons does he give for turning against it?

2. What key ideas of the Enlightenment does he reject? Why?

3. Was Mussolini correct in arguing that fascism "is the characteristic doctrine of our time"?

4. What is meant by calling fascism nationalist and statist?

Benito Mussolini: What Is Fascism, 1932

Fascism, the more it considers and observes the future and the development of humanity quite apart from political considerations of the moment, believes neither in the possibility nor the utility of perpetual peace. It thus repudiates the doctrine of Pacifism—born of a renunciation of the struggle and an act of cowardice in the face of sacrifice. War alone brings up to its highest tension all human energy and puts the stamp of nobility upon the peoples who have courage to meet it. All other trials are substitutes, which never really put men into the position where they have to make the great decision—the alternative of life or death... .

...The Fascist accepts life and loves it, knowing nothing of and despising suicide: he rather conceives of life as duty and struggle and conquest, but above all for others—those who are at hand and those who are far distant, contemporaries, and those who will come after... .

...Fascism [is] the complete opposite of ... Marxian Socialism, the materialist conception of history of human civilization can be explained simply through the conflict of interests among the various social groups and by the change and development in the means and instruments of production... . Fascism, now and always, believes in holiness and in heroism; that is to say, in actions influenced by no economic motive, direct or indirect. And if the economic conception of history be denied, according to which theory men are no more than puppets, carried to and fro by the waves of chance, while the real directing forces are quite out of their control, it follows that the existence of an unchangeable and unchanging class-war is also denied—the natural progeny of the economic conception of history. And above all Fascism denies that class-war can be the preponderant force in the transformation of society... .

After Socialism, Fascism combats the whole complex system of democratic ideology, and repudiates it, whether in its theoretical premises or in its practical application. Fascism denies that the majority, by the simple fact that it is a majority, can direct human society; it denies that numbers alone can govern by means of a periodical consultation, and it affirms the immutable, beneficial, and fruitful inequality of mankind, which can never be permanently leveled through the mere operation of a mechanical process such as universal suffrage... .

...Fascism denies, in democracy, the absur[d] conventional untruth of political equality dressed out in the garb of collective irresponsibility, and the myth of "happiness" and indefinite progress... .

...Given that the nineteenth century was the century of Socialism, of Liberalism, and of Democracy, it does not necessarily follow that the twentieth century must also be a century of Socialism, Liberalism and Democracy: political doctrines pass, but humanity remains, and it may rather be expected that this will be a century of authority ... a century of Fascism. For if the nineteenth century was a century of individualism it may be expected that this will be the century of collectivism and hence the century of the State... .

The foundation of Fascism is the conception of the State, its character, its duty, and its aim. Fascism conceives of the State as an absolute, in comparison with which all individuals or groups are relative, only to be conceived of in their relation to the State. The conception of the Liberal State is not that of a directing force, guiding the play and development, both material and spiritual, of a collective body, but merely a force limited to the function of recording results: on the other hand, the Fascist State is itself conscious and has itself a will and a personality—thus it may be called the "ethic" State... .

...The Fascist State organizes the nation, but leaves a sufficient margin of liberty to the individual; the latter is deprived of all useless and possibly harmful freedom, but retains what is essential; the deciding power in this question cannot be the individual, but the State alone... .

...For Fascism, the growth of empire, that is to say the expansion of the nation, is an essential manifestation of vitality, and its opposite a sign of decadence. Peoples which are rising, or rising again after a period of decadence, are always imperialist; and renunciation is a sign of decay and of death. Fascism is the doctrine best adapted to represent the tendencies and the aspirations of a people, like the people of Italy, who are rising again after many centuries of abasement and foreign servitude. But empire demands discipline, the coordination of all forces and a deeply felt sense of duty and sacrifice: this fact explains many aspects of the practical working of the regime, the character of many forces in the State, and the necessarily severe measures which must be taken against those who would oppose this spontaneous and inevitable movement of Italy in the twentieth century, and would oppose it by recalling the outworn ideology of the nineteenth century— repudiated wheresoever there has been the courage to undertake great experiments of social and political transformation; for never before has the nation stood more in need of authority, of direction and order. If every age has its own characteristic doctrine, there are a thousand signs which point to Fascism as the characteristic doctrine of our time. For if a doctrine must be a living thing, this is proved by the fact that Fascism has created a living faith; and that this faith is very powerful in the minds of men is demonstrated by those who have suffered and died for it.

49

Hitler and Nazism

Adolf Hitler started writing his autobiography *Mein Kampf (My Struggle)* while he was in Landsberg prison after his abortive coup (putsch) in Munich in 1923. It was published in two volumes in 1925 and 1927.

Discussion Questions

1. Comparing Hitler's racism to that of H.S. Chamberlain, is there anything new?

2. What is a "folkish state" and what is its purpose?

3. What are some specific ways in which Hitler's ideas are antithetical to democracy?

Adolf Hitler: Mein Kampf

Just as little as Nature desires a mating between weaker individuals and stronger ones, far less she desires the mixing of a higher race with lower one, as in this case her entire work of higher breeding, which has perhaps taken hundreds of thousands of years, would tumble at one blow.

Historical experience offers countless proofs of this. It shows with terrible clarity that with any mixing of the blood of the Aryan with lower races the result was the end of the culture-bearer.

* * *

Excerpt from *Mein Kampf* by Adolf Hitler, translated by Ralph Manheim. Copyright © 1943, renewed 1971 by Houghton Mifflin Co. Reprinted by permission of Houghton Mifflin Co. All rights reserved.

Thus the highest purpose of the folkish State is the care for the preservation of those racial primal elements which, supplying culture, create the beauty and dignity of a higher humanity... .

The folkish State, through this realization, has to direct its entire education primarily not at pumping in mere knowledge, but at the breeding of absolutely healthy bodies. Of secondary importance is the training of the mental abilities. But here again first of all the development of the character, especially the promotion of will power and determination, connected with education for joyfully assuming responsibility, and only as the last thing, scientific schooling.

Thereby the folkish State has to start from the presumption that a man, though scientifically little educated but physically healthy, who has a sound, firm character, filled with joyful determination and will power, is of greater value to the national community than an ingenious weakling.

* * *

A view of life which, by rejecting the democratic mass idea, endeavors to give this world to the best people, that means to the most superior men, has logically to obey the same aristocratic principle also within this people and has to guarantee leadership and highest influence within the respective people to the best heads.

With this it does not build up on the idea of the majority, but on that of the personality.

* * *

After my joining the German Workers' Party, I immediately took over the management of the propaganda... . Propaganda had to precede far in advance of the organization and to win for the latter the human material to be utilized... .

The psyche of the great masses is not receptive to half measures or weakness.

Like a woman, whose psychic feeling is influenced less by abstract reasoning than by undefinable, sentimental longing for complementary strength, who will submit to the strong man rather than dominate the weakling, thus the masses love the ruler rather than the suppliant, and inwardly they are far more satisfied by a doctrine which tolerates no rival than by the grant of liberal freedom; they often feel at a loss what to do with it, and even easily feel themselves deserted... .

The great masses' receptive ability is only very limited, their understanding is small, but their forgetfulness is great. As a consequence of these facts, all effective propaganda has to limit itself only to a very few points and to use them like slogans until even the very last man is able to imagine what is intended by such a word.

50

The Hitler Myth

The following article by Ian Kershaw attempts to explain the extraordinary hold Hitler had on the German people, including his opponents, after he came to power in 1933.

Discussion Questions

1. Does Kershaw make a convincing distinction between Hitler's personality and his popular image? Is he implying that Hitler was a "phony?"

2. How was Hitler's popular image the product of certain elements in Germany's past?

3. How did non-Nazis see Hitler?

4. How did Hitler win over the masses of the German people after he was named chancellor in 1933?

5. What does Kershaw say were the seven bases of the "Hitler Myth?" Was Hitler the creation of political image-makers like more recent leaders?

6. What happened when Hitler himself succumbed to the "Hitler Myth?"

7. What lessons for all democratic societies can be learned from Hitler's political career?

For almost a decade after 1933, Hitler enjoyed a remarkable degree of popularity among the great majority of the German people. However dramatic and spectacular his political career, concentration on Hitler's character and personality—in some respects bizarre, in others downright mediocre and wholly unpleasant—can nevertheless do little to explain the magnetism of his popular appeal. Nor can his extraordinary impact on the German people in these years be accounted for satisfactorily by seeing in Hitler's personal Weltanschauung (notably in his obsessions with the "Jewish Question" and with Lebensraum) a mirror image of the motivation of Nazism's mass following. Recent research has done much to qualify such assumptions, suggesting too that even deep into the period of the dictatorship itself Hitler's own ideological fixations had more of a symbolic than concrete meaning for most Nazi supporters.

What seems necessary, therefore, is an examination not of Hitler's personality, but of his popular image—how the German people saw their leader: the "Hitler Myth." The "Hitler Myth" was a double-sided phenomenon. On the one hand, it was a masterly achievement in image-building by the exponents of the new techniques of propaganda, building upon notions of "heroic" leadership widespread in right-wing circles long before Hitler's rise to prominence. On the other hand, it has to be seen as a reflection of "mentalities," value-systems, and socio-political structures which conditioned the acceptance of a "Superman" image of political leadership. Both the active manufacture of Hitler's public image and the receptivity to it by the German people need, therefore, to be explored.

Images of "heroic" leadership were already gaining ground in populist-nationalist circles of the German Right in the late nineteenth century. Their inclusion as a growing force in the political culture of the Right in Kaiser's Germany (and there are parallels in prefascist Italy, which later gave rise to the cult of the Duce) was largely shaped by three interlinked factors: the social and political disruption accompanying a simultaneous transition to nation-state, constitutional government (if strongly authoritarian in character), and industrialised society; the deep fragmentation of the political system (reflecting fundamental social cleavages); and, not least, the spread of a chauvinistic-imperialist ideology clamouring for a rightful "place in the sun" for Germany, a "have-not" nation.

Growing disappointment on the populist Right with Wilhelm II promoted notions of a "People's Kaiser" who, embodying strength and vitality, would crush Germany's internal enemies and, at the expense of inferior peoples, would provide the new nation with greatness and would win an empire for "a people without living space."

The extreme glorification of military values before and especially during the First World War, and the Right's shock and trauma at defeat, revolution, and the victory of the hated Social Democrats, promoted the extension and partial transformation of "heroic" leadership images in the 1920s. Following the abdication of the Kaiser and the end of the old political order, ideal leadership was envisaged as being embodied in a man from the people whose qualities would reflect struggle, conflict, the values of the trenches. Hard, ruthless, resolute, uncompromising, and radical, he would destroy the old privilege- and class-ridden society and bring about a new beginning, uniting the people in an ethnically pure and socially harmonious "national community." The extreme fragmentation of Weimar politics kept such visions alive on the nationalist and völkisch Right. And by the early 1930s, perceptions of the total failure of Weimar democracy and mortal crisis of the entire political system allowed the image to move from the wings of politics to centre stage. By then, one man in particular was making a claim—accepted by increasing numbers of people—that he alone could reawaken Germany and restore the country's greatness. This was Adolf Hitler, the leader of the Nazis.

Within the Nazi Party, the beginnings of a personality cult around Hitler go back to 1922–3, when some party members were already comparing him with Napoleon or describing him as Germany's Mussolini. Of course, Hitler only gradually established an unchallengeable authority within the party, initially having to contend with some powerful factions of opposition. And although his own concept of leadership was already becoming more "heroic" in the year before his *Putsch* attempt, it was only during imprisonment following its failure that he came to believe that he himself was Germany's predestined great leader. During the following years in which the Nazis were little more than a minor irritant in German politics, the "Hitler Myth" was consciously built up within the Movement as a device to integrate the party, to fend off leadership challenges, and to win new members. The introduction in 1926 of a compulsory "*Heil Hitler*" fasciststyle greeting and salute among party members was an outward sign of their bonds with their leader. Pseudo-religious imagery and fanciful

rhetoric so ludicrous that it even occasionally embarrassed Hitler became commonplace in references to the leader in party publications.

Before 1930, the nascent *Führer* cult around Hitler found an echo among at most a few hundred thousand followers. But with the Nazi Party's breakthrough in the 1930 election (which brought it 18.3 per cent of the vote), the *Führer* cult ceased to be merely the property of a fanatical fringe party. The potential was there for its massive extension, as more and more Germans saw in Nazism—symbolised by its leader—the only hope for a way out of gathering crisis. Those now surging to join the Nazi party were often already willing victims of the "Hitler Myth." Not untypical was the new party member who wrote that after hearing Hitler speak for the first time, "there was only one thing for me, either to win with Adolf Hitler or to die for him. The personality of the *Führer* had me totally in its spell." Even for the vast majority of the German people who did not share such sentiments, there was the growing feeling—encouraged by Hitler's profile even in the non-Nazi press—that Hitler was not just another politician, that he was a party leader extraordinary, a man towards whom one could not remain neutral. He polarised feelings between bitter hatred and ecstatic devotion, but he could no longer be ignored, or shrugged off as a political nonentity.

For the thirteen million Germans who voted Nazi in 1932, Hitler symbolised—chameleon-like—the various facets of Nazism which they found appealing. In his public portrayal, he was a man of the people, his humble origins emphasising the rejection of privilege and the sterile old order in favour of a new, vigorous, upwardly-mobile society built upon strength, merit, and achievement. He was seen as strong, uncompromising, ruthless. He embodied the triumph of true Germanic virtues—courage, manliness, integrity, loyalty, devotion to the cause—over the effete decadence, corruption, and effeminate weakness of Weimar society. Above all, he represented "struggle"—as the title of his book *Mein Kampf* advertised: struggle of the "little man" against society's "big battalions," and mortal struggle against Germany's powerful internal and external enemies to assure the nation's future. More prosaically, for the many still less convinced, he headed a huge mass movement which, given the weak and divided Weimar parties, seemed to offer the only way out of all-embracing crisis.

Still, not one German in two cast a vote for Hitler's party in the March election of 1933—held five weeks after Hitler had been appointed Chancellor in an atmosphere of national euphoria coupled with terroristic repression of the Left. Most Germans remained either hostile to, or unconvinced by, their new "people's Chancellor," as the Nazi press dubbed him. Within the diehard ranks of the persecuted socialist and Communist Left, of course, the hatred of Hitler and all he stood for—which in many respects was accurately foreseen—was implacable. In Catholic quarters, deep suspicions lingered about the anti-Christian tendencies of Nazism—though there was already a growing readiness to distance Hitler himself from the "dangerous elements" in his movement. And bourgeois circles continued to see in Hitler the social upstart and vulgar demagogue, mouthpiece of the hysterical masses, the head of a party containing some wild and threatening elements—but a man, with all his faults, who could have his uses for a time. Attitudes towards Hitler in early 1933 varied greatly, therefore, and were often heatedly negative.

Three factors at least have to be taken into account in explaining how, nevertheless, the *Führer* cult could, within a strikingly short time, extend its hold to wide sections of the population, and eventually to the overwhelming majority of Germans. Of crucial significance was the widespread feeling that the Weimar political system and leadership was utterly bankrupt. In such conditions, the image of a dynamic, energetic, "youthful" leader offering a derisive change of direction and backed by an army of fanatical followers was not altogether unattractive. Many with grave doubts were prepared to give Hitler a chance. And compared with the pathetic helplessness of his predecessors as Chancellor, the apparent drive and tempo of government activity in the months after he took office seemed impressive.

Secondly, the gross underestimation of Hitler again paved the way for at first reluctant or condescending and then wholehearted, enthusiasm for the way he apparently mastered within such a short time the internal political situation which had seemed beyond the capabilities of an upstart rabblerouser. Thirdly, and most importantly, Hitler embodied an already well-established, extensive ideological consensus which also embraced most of those, except the Left, who had still not given him their vote in March 1933. Its chief elements were virulent anti-Marxism and the perceived need for a powerful counter to the forces of the Left; deep hostility towards the failed democratic system and a belief that strong, authoritarian leadership was necessary for any recovery; and a widespread feeling, even extending to parts of the Left, that Germany had been badly wronged at Versailles, and was threatened by enemies on all sides. This preexisting wide consensus offered the potential for strong support for a national leader who could appear to offer absolute commitment, personal sacrifice, and selfless striving in the cause of inner unity and outward strength.

By 1933, Nazi propaganda had been highly successful in establishing "charismatic authority" as the organisational premise of the Nazi Party, and then in portraying Hitler to Nazi sympathisers as not just another party leader, but as *the* Leader for whom the nation had been waiting—a man of incomparably different stature to contemptible party politicians. The most important propaganda step now remained to be taken: the conversion, for the "majority of the majority" that had still not supported Hitler in March 1933, of his image from that of leader of the Nazi Movement to that of national leader.

Given the fact that Nazi propaganda now enjoyed a virtual monopoly within Germany, and that those taking a less than favourable view of Hitler's qualities were now incarcerated or silenced by fear and repression, the scene was set for the rapid establishment by the end of 1934 of the full-blown *Führer* cult of an almost deified national leader. No doubt many Germans found the extremes of the now omnipresent Hitler cult nauseating. But they were for the most part coming to accept that Hitler was no ordinary head of government. Above all, one could not ignore his "achievements": "order" had been restored; unemployment was falling rapidly; the economy was picking up strongly; Germany was beginning to stand up for itself again in the world. The record seemed to speak for itself.

By 1935, Hitler could be hailed in the Nazi press—and there was by now hardly any other press to speak of inside Germany—as the "Symbol of the Nation" who, having struggled as an "ordinary worker" to establish Germany's "social freedom," had now, as a one-time ordinary "Front soldier," re-established Germany's "national freedom"—a reference to the recent reassertion of German military sovereignty. The message being conveyed was that people and nation found their identity, their "incarnation," as it was put, in the person of the *Führer*. To this weight placed upon Hitler's "achievements," Goebbels added the pathos of the human qualities of the *Führer*: his simplicity and modesty, toil and endeavour for his people, mastery of all problems facing the nation, toughness and severity, unshakable determination though flexibility of method in the pursuit of farsighted goals. With all this went

the intense loneliness and sadness of a man who had sacrificed all personal happiness and private life for his people. This extraordinary catalogue of personal virtues—making the "human" Hitler almost inhuman in the degree of his perfection was set alongside the political genius of the *Führer* as a human counterpart to the image of the lofty, distant statesman. It amounted to almost a mirror of contemporary bourgeois values—characteristics with which almost everyone could find some point of association.

Difficult though it is to evaluate, evidence of the receptivity to this image—drawn both from sources from within the regime and those hostile to the Nazi system—lends strong support to Goebbels' claim in 1941 that the creation of the "Hitler Myth" had been his greatest propaganda achievement. The powerfully integrative force of Hitler's massive popularity seems undeniable. Goebbels might have added, however, that the way had been paved for him by the constant exposure to rabid chauvinist-imperialist values pumped into the population for decades by a stridently nationalist press (excepting the publications of the Left) and by a variety of forms of "socialisation" in schools, the bourgeois youth movement, the army, and an entire panoply of "patriotic" clubs, leagues, and associations.

Of course, the political culture was far from a unitary one, and not all Germans were affected. As is well known, the socialist subculture remained relatively immune. Those schooled in the traditions of the Socialist and Communist parties continued throughout the Third Reich to be the least susceptible to the appeal of the "Hitler Myth." To a lesser extent, the Catholic subculture was also resistant to the full extremes of the *Führer* cult, though strong traditions of authoritarianism and especially endemic anti-Marxism allowed for substantial inroads. Clearly, therefore, Hitler's popularity was far from complete, the *Führer* cult far from uniform in its impact. However, detailed examination of an extensive mass of sources relating to the formation of popular opinion and attitudes in the Third Reich suggests at least seven significant bases of the "Hitler Myth" which can be singled out.

Firstly, Hitler was seen as the embodiment of strong and, where necessary, ruthless enforcement of "law and order"—the representative of "popular justice," the voice of the "healthy sentiment of the people." An example can be seen in the great gains in popularity which accrued to him in spring 1933 as a result of the brutal Nazi onslaught on the Left, "clearing away" the Socialist and Communist "enemies of the state." Even more spectacular as an illustration is the extraordinary boost to Hitler's popularity following the ruthless massacre of members of his own Movement—the leaders of the highly unpopular SA—in June 1934. In reality, the purge of the SA leadership served to crush a destabilising element in the regime and further the power-political ambitions of the army and the SS. But none of this was reflected in Hitler's image following the purge. As even opponents of the regime acknowledged, Hitler's blood-letting was hugely popular, welcomed as a blow struck for law and order—"popular justice" eradicating corruption and immorality within the Movement. The propagated image of a leader upholding public morality corresponded closely with commonly-held values and prejudices—for instance, in the condemnation of rowdiness and disorder, venal corruption and homosexuality. In what was a complete inversion of reality, Hitler was seen to be signalling a triumph for values associated with "normality."

Secondly, Hitler was seen as representing the national interest, putting the nation first before any particularist cause and wholly detached from any personal, material, or selfish motives. Crucial to this image was the way, after 1933, in which propaganda succeeded in isolating Hitler from the growing unpopularity of the Nazi Party itself. The wholly positive resonance of the portrayal of Hitler, the national leader, contrasted vividly with the sullied reputation of party functionaries, the "little Hitlers," whose corruption and greed, jumped-up arrogance and highhandedness, pettiness and hypocrisy, were a daily scandal. And whereas the local party officials bore the brunt of extensive and real daily discontent, Hitler's popularity was cushioned by the myth that he was being kept in the dark about the misdeeds of his underlings, was unaware of the just complaints of his people.

Without at least the prospect of an improved living standard, the extent of the effective integration produced by the "Hitler Myth" would have been difficult to achieve. A third, extremely important, component of the perceived *Führer* image was, therefore, that of the architect and creator of Germany's "economic miracle" of the 1930s. Part of the apologetic of the post-war era was, of course, that despite his "mistakes," Hitler had revamped the economy, rid Germany of unemployment, and built the motorways. This is itself testimony to the penetrating and enduring features of this aspect of the contemporary Hitler image. Certainly, by 1939 it was difficult to deny that economic conditions in Germany, for whatever reasons, had improved dramatically since the Depression era. However, more than in any other sphere, perceptions of Hitler's image in the context of economic and social policy were determined by experiences which divided for the most part along class lines.

The working class remained the social grouping least impressed by the "economic miracle" and *relatively* immune to the image of Hitler as the creator of Germany's striking new prosperity. After all, with their own standard of living pinned down to Depression levels in the years 1933–36, most industrial workers saw no particular reason to offer marked signs of gratitude to the *Führer*. Through repression and intimidation, low wages, and longer hours, the "economic miracle," as most realised, was being carried out on their own backs. Nevertheless, as the underground worker resistance was forced to admit, Hitler undoubtedly did gain some popularity among workers for "his" work creation and the economic recovery which "he" had brought about. And in the first years of the Third Reich in particular, the "socialist" aspect of the Hitler image also struck a chord among many of the poorer Germans who were recipients of the "Winter Aid." Even so, on the whole it appears that the image of the economic miracle-worker, the restorer of Germany's prosperity, had its greatest appeal among those sectors of the population who benefited most from the economic boom of the rearmament period: the middle class, who, despite their unceasing grumbling, continued to provide the main base of support for the regime and devotion to Hitler to at least the middle of the war.

Fourthly, in matters affecting established institutions and traditions, Hitler was seen as a "moderate," opposed to the radical and extreme elements in the Movement. An obvious example is the "church struggle." Whenever fundamental institutions or basic traditional props of both major Christian denominations were under attack—as in the Nazi attempt in 1934 to abolish surviving Protestant bishoprics with a firm tradition of independence, or to remove crucifixes, the symbol of Christianity itself, from Catholic schoolrooms in 1936 and again in 1941, Hitler was looked to as the defence against the "wild elements" in the party.

His apparent non-involvement in, or aloofness from, the bitter conflicts, before finally intervening to end the disturbance—put down to party radicals and the "new heathenism" associated above all with Rosenberg—and "restore order," left Hitler's standing among churchgoers relatively unscathed, despite the slump in popularity of the party. Grotesque as it seems, Hitler himself continued to be widely regarded as a God-fearing and deeply religious man. Even church leaders with a reputation for hostility to Nazism were persuaded of his sincerity, belief in God, and acceptance of the role of Christianity and the churches. Their public avowals of obedience to the *Führer* and recognition of his leadership and achievements played no small part in helping to give legitimation to the "Hitler Myth."

Fanatical commitment to uncompromising and ruthless action against the "enemies of the people" was a fifth crucial component of Hitler's image. But he was regarded as condoning only lawful, "rational" action, not the crude violence and public brutalities of the party's distasteful "gutter" elements. No one could have been left in any doubt, for instance, of Hitler's fanatical anti-Semitism and determination to exclude Jews from German society. And at the beginning of his career, anti-Semitism had been a keynote of almost all his speeches and must have been a dominant component of his popular image among early converts to Nazism. However, during the period of the party's major electoral successes, anti-Semitism appears to have featured less prominently in Hitler's public addresses, and was less important as an electoral drawing card than has often been presumed—tending mainly to function as a general touchstone for other propaganda themes.

After 1933, Hitler was extremely careful to avoid public association with the generally unpopular pogrom-type anti-Semitic outrages, particularly of course following the nation-wide "Crystal Night" pogrom in November 1938. In the years when his popularity was soaring to dizzy heights, moreover, Hitler's public pronouncements on the "Jewish Question" were less numerous than might be imagined, and, while certainly hate-filled, were usually couched in abstract generalities in association with western plutocracy or Bolshevism. In these terms, bolstering the passive anti-Semitism already widespread among the German people and lending support to "legal" measures—for the most part popular—excluding Jews from German society and the economy, Hitler's hatred of the Jews was certainly an acceptable component of his popular image, even if it was an element "taken on board" rather than forming a centrally important motivating factor for most Germans. Even during the war, when his vitriolic public onslaughts on the Jews came far more frequently and contained dire allusions to their physical extermination, the signs are that this was not a centrally formative factor shaping attitudes towards Hitler among the German people.

Sixthly, Hitler's public profile in the arena of foreign affairs stood in stark contrast to reality. He was commonly seen here as a fanatical upholder of the nation's just rights to territory "robbed" from Germany in the peace settlement after the First World War, a rebuilder of Germany's strength, and a statesman of genius— to which his astounding run of diplomatic coups seemed to offer ample testimony. Amid the widespread, deep fears of another war, he was also, astonishingly, seen by many as a "man of peace" who "would do everything he could to settle things peacefully" (as one then youthful observer later came to describe her feelings at the time)—a defender of German rights, not a racial-imperialist warmonger working towards a "war of annihilation" and limitless German conquest. Hitler's imposing series of "triumphs without bloodshed" directed at "peace with honour"—tearing up the Versailles settlement, winning back the Saar, restoring "military sovereignty," recovering the Rhineland, uniting Austria with Germany, and bringing the Sudetenland "home into the Reich"—won him support in all sections of the German people and unparalleled popularity, prestige, and acclaim.

Finally, there is Hitler's image, when war came, as the military strategist of genius, outwitting Germany's enemies in an unbelievable run of *Blitzkrieg* victories,

culminating in the taking of France within four weeks when a generation earlier four years had not been enough. Even after the war started to turn sour for Germany in the winter of 1941–2, the unpopularity of the party and its despised representatives at home continued for a time to stand in stark contrast to the image of the *Führer*'s devotion to duty in standing with his soldiers at the Front. However, according to Max Weber's model, "charismatic leadership" could not survive lack of success. And indeed, as "his" astonishing run of victories turned gradually but inexorably into calamitous defeat, the tide of Hitler's popularity first waned rather slowly, then ebbed sharply. The decline accelerated decisively following the catastrophe of Stalingrad, a defeat for which Hitler's personal responsibility was widely recognised.

The "Hitler Myth" was now fatally flawed. In the face of defeats, personal losses, misery, and sacrifice, the earlier successes began to be seen in a new light. Hitler was now increasingly blamed for policies which had led to war. His much vaunted strong will, resolution, unshakeable determination, and absolute fanaticism were regarded more and more not as attributes but as the main stumbling blocks to the longed-for peace. With no more successes to proclaim, Hitler was now reluctant even to speak to the German people. The new image put out by Goebbels of Hitler as a latterday Frederick the Great—distant majesty finally triumphant in the face of extreme adversity—symbolised the growing gulf.

Important reserves of popularity remained to the end. Hatred of the Allies prompted by terror bombing campaigns partially benefited Hitler and the regime for a while; some temporary vain hopes were placed in the *Führer*'s promises of new weapons which would accomplish the desired "retaliation"; a short-lived upsurge of support and proclamation of loyalty followed the attempt on his life in July 1944—an indication that a successful coup might have encountered a new version of the "stab-in-the-back" legend; and surprisingly large numbers of prisoners-of-war in the west continued till the end to avow their belief in Hitler. But the potency of the "Hitler Myth" had vanished. Eloquent commentary on this is a report on a remembrance ceremony at the war memorial in the little Bavarian alpine town of Markt Schellenberg on March 11th, 1945:

> When the leader of the *Wehrmacht* unit at the end of his speech for the remembrance called for a *"Sieg-Heil"* for the *Führer,* it was returned neither by the *Wehrmacht* present, nor by the *Volkssturm,* nor by the spectators of the civilian population who had turned up. This silence of the masses had a depressing effect, and probably reflects better than anything the attitudes of the people.

Unquestionably, the adulation of Hitler by millions of Germans who may otherwise have been only marginally committed to the Nazi ideology, or party, was a crucial element of political integration in the Third Reich. Without this mass base of support, the high level of plebiscitary acclamation, which the regime could repeatedly call upon to legitimise its actions and to take the wind out of the sails of the opposition, is unthinkable. It also enabled the specifically Nazi élite to free itself from dependence upon the support of traditional conservative ruling groups, thereby boosting the autonomy of the "wild men" in the Movement. Without the degree of popular backing which Hitler was able to command, the drive,

dynamism, and momentum of Nazi rule could hardly have been sustained.

The *Führer* cult necessarily influenced the relations of the Nazi leadership itself with Hitler, as well as those of the traditional ruling élites. Inevitably, it surrounded Hitler with toadies, flatterers, and sycophants, shielding him from rational criticism or genuine debate, and bolstered increasing detachment from reality. Nor could Hitler himself remain impervious to the extraordinary cult which had been created around him and which came to envelop him. His own person gradually became inseparable from the myth.

Hitler had to live out more and more the constructed image of omnipotence and omniscience. And the more he succumbed to the allure of his own *Führer* cult and came to believe in his own myth, the more his judgement became impaired by faith in his own infallibility and guidance "by providence," enabling him to "go his way with the certainty of a sleepwalker." His room for manoeuvre now became restricted by his own need to protect the "Hitler Myth" and sustain his prestige, aware as he was that if Nazism lost its forward momentum and stagnation set in, Hitler's own popularity and the mass base of the regime's support would be fatally undermined. To this extent, it has been claimed with some justification, that "Hitler well understood his own function, the role which he had to act out as 'Leader' of the Third Reich," that he "transformed himself into a function, the function of *Führer.*"

51

Japan's Declaration of War in 1941

The following selection is an excerpt from Tokutomi Iichiro's *Commentary on the Imperial Declaration of War*. Earlier in his career Tokutomi had been enthusiastic about Christianity and liberalism but gradually became a defender of Japanese civilization and government against the West—a not unusual course among his contemporaries. By the 1930's he had become one of the leading spokesmen for the nationalist point of view. His *Commentary* analyzes the Imperial Rescript declaring war point by point and discusses Japan's role in Asia.

Discussion Questions

1. What does Tokutomi mean by the "Imperial Way?"

2. What does he think makes Japan unique as a nation, especially compared with China and the West?

3. How is Japan to become the "Light of Asia and the world?"

Chapter IV: The Basis of the Imperial Way

The virtue of sincerity is represented by the Mirror, the virtue of love is represented by the Jewels, and the virtue of intelligence is represented by the Sword... . The interpretation given by Kitabatake Chikafusa has, indeed, grasped the true meaning. Then, it is not wrong to liken the Three Sacred Treasures to the three virtues of intelligence, love, and courage by saying that the Mirror represents the intelligence which reflects everything, the Jewels, the love which embraces everything, and the Sword, the courage which judges between justice and injustice, honesty and dishonesty.

In any case, the basis of the Imperial Way lies in truth, in sincerity, and in justice. Its range is wide and there is nothing it does not embrace. It expels evil, subjugates injustice, absolutely maintains the tenets of justice, and itself occupies a position which can never be violated. The august virtue of the divine imperial lineage has not a single instance when it did not arise from these three virtues. In other words, they form the national character of Nippon, and, at the same time, the national trait of the people of Nippon. Combining them all, we call it the Imperial Way.

The phrase "The three virtues of intelligence, love, and courage" may sound very much like a common ethical teaching, but when considered realistically, it gives us the reason why our country, under whatever circumstances, has never resorted to arms for the sake of arms alone... .

Chapter VIII: The Unique Features of the Nation of Nippon

What we should note first of all is that Nippon is not a country built upon that Western individualism patterned after the insistence on rights, nor a country built with the family as the basis as in China ... our Nippon is neither a country of individualism nor a country of the family system. In Nippon, the family is valued and good lineage is highly regarded the same as in China. However, in Nippon there is that which goes farther and which is greater than these. There is the Imperial Household. In China, there are families, but there is not the Imperial Household. In Nippon, there are families, but still, above them, there is the Imperial Household. In China, families gather to form a nation, but in Nippon the Imperial Household deigns to rule the land, and on the land the families, the members of which are subjects of the Imperial Household, flourish.

That is why, in China, one speaks first of the family and then next of the nation, but, in Nippon, the nation comes first and next the family. In China, if it is to be asked which is valued higher, the nation or the family, it must be answered that, under whatever circumstances, the family is valued first and next the nation. In the West, the individual is valued first, and next the family, and last the nation. In Nippon, the nation is valued first, then next the family, and last the individual. The order of the West is absolutely reversed in Nippon... .

Chapter XLVIII: Three Qualifications of the Leader of Greater East Asia

Now that we have risen up in arms, we must accomplish our aim to the last. Herein lies the core of our theory. In Nippon resides a destiny to become the Light of Greater East Asia and to become ultimately the Light of the World. However, in order to become the Light of Greater East Asia, we must have three qualifications. The first is, as mentioned previously, strength. In other words, we must expel Anglo-Saxon influence from East Asia with our strength.

To speak the truth, the various races of East Asia look upon the British and Americans as superior to the Nippon race. They look upon Britain and the United States as more powerful nations than Nippon. Therefore, we must show our real strength before all our fellow-races of East Asia. We must show them an object lesson. It is not a lesson in words. It should be a lesson in facts.

In other words, before we can expel the Anglo-Saxons and make them remove all their traces from East Asia, we must annihilate them. In this way only will the various fellow races of Greater East Asia look upon us as their leader. I believe that the lesson which we must first show to our fellow-races in Greater East Asia is this lesson of cold reality.

The second qualification is benevolence. Nippon must develop the various resources of East Asia and distribute them fairly to all the races within the East Asia Co-Prosperity Sphere to make them share in the benefits. In other words, Nippon should not monopolize the benefits, but should distribute them for the mutual prosperity of Greater East Asia.

We must show to the races of East Asia that the order, tranquillity, peace, happiness, and contentment of East Asia can be gained only by eradicating the evil precedent of the encroachment and extortion of the Anglo-Saxons in East Asia, by effecting the real aim of the co-prosperity of East Asia, and by making Nippon the leader of East Asia.

The third qualification is virtue. East Asia embraces various races. Its religions are different. Moreover, there has practically been no occasion when these have mutually united to work for a combined aim. It was the favorite policy of the Anglo-Saxons to make the various races of East Asia compete and fight each other and make them mutually small and powerless. We must, therefore, console them, bring friendship among them, and make them all live in peace with a boundlessly embracing virtue.

In short, the first is the Grace of the Sacred Sword, the second, the Grace of the Sacred Mirror, and the third, the Grace of the Sacred Jewels. If we should express it in other words, we must have courage, knowledge, and benevolence. If Nippon should lack even one of the above three, it will not be able to become the Light of Asia.

52

The Bombing of Hiroshima

The following selections present recent historical and moral perspectives on the use of atomic weapons in World War II. A summary of the deliberations leading up to the bombing of Hiroshima and Nagasaki are presented in the first reading, with particular attention given to the prevailing attitudes that existed in 1945 towards weapons of mass destruction. Included in the first piece is also a discussion of the alternatives to the use of the bomb, why those alternatives were discarded, and what the advocates of the bomb's use hoped to achieve. The second reading introduces a number of ways to look at the moral issues raised by the introduction of atomic weapons into war, with a reminder that, more than fifty years after the event, the issue raises as many questions as it answers.

Discussion Questions

1. Are Hiroshima and Nagasaki "landmarks on the mental and moral geography of the United States"? What is their meaning to us today? What do you think they will mean to the citizens of the U.S. in 2045?

2. What are the key reasons that the atomic bomb was used in World War II? Do you find Bernstein's arguments convincing? What do you think would have been the "right" decision regarding the use of atomic weapons?

3. Hiroshima and Nagasaki have been called "an end and a beginning." What do you think is meant by this statement, and would you agree after reading these articles?

4. Though Auschwitz and Hiroshima have been compared in another reading, are there similarities between Pearl Harbor and Hiroshima today, as well as historically?

The Debate Over Hiroshima

Fifty years later, the question will not be put to rest. What went into the decision to drop the atomic bomb?

The debate is about morality as well as history, but often the history is written as though it settled the morality. Opinions collide, for example, over how many American lives President Harry S. Truman and other high officials thought might be lost if the Allies had invaded Japan. Estimates from American military sources from before August 1945 range from 16,000 to 46,000 deaths, with four times as many wounded.

Writing after the bomb was dropped (on Hiroshima on Aug. 6 and Nagasaki on Aug. 9), Truman said he had feared 500,000 deaths and Secretary of War Henry Stimson said he had envisioned more than one million casualties.

The unstated moral premise in much of this historical fencing is this: the right decision would have been what brought victory with the least loss of life.

* * *

But not everyone agrees that this principle was the essential one. Survey the literature, or simply listen to a dinner conversation where Hiroshima and Nagasaki are considered more compelling topics than Hugh Grant, and at least five basic moral arguments are heard:

All war is wrong. For the pacifist, it does not matter whether killing is done by a bomb, a bayonet or a bow, or whether the victim is a pediatrician or a pilot. The atomic bomb simply made clear on a horrific scale the evil of all war.

Nuclear arms are different. They represent a quantum leap in destructiveness. From the beginning, some scientists and statesmen sensed that to develop and then to use weapons was to sign a pact with the devil. Nothing should be done to diminish the taboo surrounding these weapons or the dread they inspire, not even suggesting that they fall within our normal rules of morality.

Civilians are different. It is immoral to attack, directly and indiscriminately, civilian populations of men, women and children, the young and the old, the healthy and the disabled. This is the principle that condemns terrorism, that declares passengers on a subway or families in a restaurant not fair targets, no matter the justice of the cause. In World War II, first the Germans, then the Allies had already crossed this line, Hiroshima and Nagasaki were massive, singlebomb versions of the fire-bombings of Dresden, Hamburg, Tokyo and scores of smaller Japanese cities. The atomic bomb represented not so much the evil of all war as the evil of total war.

Do the least harm possible. Death, casualties and destruction should be no more than necessary and somehow proportionate to the objective. The distinction between civilian and combatant is not essential in this argument: A life is a life. Less clear is how enemy lives are weighed against one's own, but presumably they are part of the calculation. If dropping the atomic bombs was likely to save lives, not dropping them would have been the immoral deed. This is the principle that fuels the debate between those who defend the bombing and those who maintain it was unnecessary or disproportionate.

War is hell. No nation should go to war except as a last resort, but once in war, morality gives way to efficiency. Minimize one's own losses, whatever it takes. Condemnation of what happens in the heat of battle—indeed, any notion that the reality of war can be squeezed into moral boundaries—is home-front hypocrisy, an effort to prettify the horror with armchair ethics.

After 50 years, does it matter which of these arguments we embrace? Are we doing anything more than still trying to convict or acquit Truman?

Yet the debate matters because nations and civilizations, like individuals, do not live by abstract principles. Moral principles arise from experience; they are tested and revised in the face of new experience, and they must be embodied in experience and the collective memories that result.

Children may learn to be good by heeding the Ten Commandments or the Five Precepts of Buddhism. But long before that, they learn goodness by modeling themselves on parents, teachers, saints and heroes.

Nations, likewise, live by formative events far more than by formal principles. Americans imbibe their fierce attachment to self-determination and redress of rights with their accounts of the Revolution. The principles of nationhood and equality are embodied in the Civil War; appeasement, in Munich; radical evil, in the Holocaust; Western resolve, in the Berlin airlift; adroit crisis diplomacy, in the Cuban missile crisis, and tragic overreaching in Vietnam. These events are landmarks on the mental and moral geography of the United States and of the West in general.

And Hiroshima and Nagasaki?

In 1945, in the midst of the great national sigh of relief that the war was over, only a few public voices denounced the atomic bombings. Polls showed that not only did the vast majority of Americans approve of the bombings, but also that those who questioned them or thought the bomb should have been dropped first on an unpopulated area as a demonstration were outnumbered by those who wished that more atomic bombs could have been dropped on Japan before it had a chance to surrender.

* * *

Many of those protesting voices were religious: the liberal Protestant weekly The Christian Century, theologians like Reinhold and H. Richard Niebuhr, leading Roman Catholic journals like Commonweal and The Catholic World and, somewhat later, America. They spoke in terms of sin, shame, guilt and contrition.

But widespread moral misgivings did not really begin until August 1946, when The New Yorker published John Hersey's understated but excruciatingly detailed account of the human devastation at Hiroshima.

Those misgivings, even a half century later, have never jelled into a consensus, as proved by the inability of the National Air and Space Museum to mount an exhibition that raised serious questions about the bombing. Will the United States ever integrate the bombs of August into its moral self-understanding? Or will they continue to haunt and torment us like ghosts?

53

Witness to the Holocaust: Auschwitz

The Nazi genocide of twelve million people during World War II, what is now known as the Holocaust, is examined in this set of readings from the perspective of survivors of the killing camps. The first excerpt is from the noted writer Primo Levi, an Italian Jew who was deported to Auschwitz, one of the extermination camps constructed for mass, industrial death. At the Nuremberg Trials following World War II, the testimony of Marie-Claude Vaillant-Coutrier, a French Jew who arrived at Auschwitz in 1943, bears further witness to genocide.

Discussion Questions

1. Both Levi and Vaillant-Coutrier are "haftling." What did that mean and was that a key to their survival?

2. How would you describe the level of planning that existed at Auschwitz? Based on the survivors' accounts, would you say that the camps were central to the German war effort?

3. How did Primo Levi learn how to survive at Auschwitz and what did he learn? How does Levi's experience compare with that of Vaillant-Coutrier?

4. What is meant by "the Lager," "Arbeit Macht Frei," and "selection?"

5. When Levi writes about "the demolition of a man," and "hollow man," what does he mean? When he states that 'extermination camp' has a double meaning, what is he suggesting?

6. Do you agree with Levi that "It was better not to think" in their situation? Do you think that Levi and Vaillant-Coutrier actually did that? If you had been in either of their shoes, would you have come to some of the same conclusions?

7. What do you think is the historical value of personal accounts such as those of Levi and Vaillant-Coutrier?

Survival in Auschwitz

The journey did not last more than twenty minutes. Then the lorry stopped, and we saw a large door, and above it a sign, brightly illuminated (its memory still strikes me in my dreams): *Arbeit Macht Frei*, work gives freedom.

We climb down, they make us enter an enormous empty room that is poorly heated. We have a terrible thirst. The weak gurgle of the water in the radiators makes us ferocious; we have had nothing to drink for four days. But there is also a tap – and above it a card which says that it is forbidden to drink as the water is dirty. Nonsense. It seems obvious that the card is a joke, 'they' know that we are dying of thirst and they put us in a room, and there is a tap, and *Wassertrinken Verboten*. I drink and I incite my companions to do likewise, but I have to spit it out, the water is tepid and sweetish, with the smell of a swamp.

This is hell. Today, in our times, hell must be like this. A huge, empty room: we are tired, standing on our feet, with a tap which drips while we cannot drink the water, and we wait for something which will certainly be terrible, and nothing happens and nothing continues to happen. What can one think about? One cannot think any more, it is like being already dead. Someone sits down on the ground. The time passes drop by drop.

We are not dead. The door is opened and an SS man enters, smoking. He looks at us slowly and asks, '*Wer kann Deutsch*?' One of us whom I have never seen, named Flesch, moves forward: he will be our interpreter. The SS man makes a long calm speech; the interpreter translates. We have to form rows of five, with intervals of two yards between man and man; then we have to undress and make a bundle of the clothes in a special manner, the woollen garments on one side, all the rest on the other; we must take off our shoes but pay great attention that they are not stolen.

Stolen by whom? Why should our shoes be stolen? And what about our documents, the few things we have in our pockets, our watches? We

---

all look at the interpreter, and the interpreter asks the German, and the German smokes and looks him through and through as if he were transparent, as if no one had spoken.

I had never seen old men naked. Mr Bergmann wore a truss and asked the interpreter if he should take it off, and the interpreter hesitated. But the German understood and spoke seriously to the interpreter pointing to someone. We saw the interpreter swallow and then he said: 'The officer says, take off the truss, and you will be given that of Mr Coen.' One could see the words coming bitterly out of Flesch's mouth; this was the German manner of laughing.

Now another German comes and tells us to put the shoes in a certain corner, and we put them there, because now it is all over and we feel outside this world and the only thing is to obey. Someone comes with a broom and sweeps away all the shoes, outside the door in a heap. He is crazy, he is mixing them all together, ninety-six pairs, they will be all unmatched. The outside door opens, a freezing wind enters and we are naked and cover ourselves up with our arms. The wind blows and slams the door; the German reopens it and stands watching with interest how we writhe to hide from the wind, one behind the other. Then he leaves and closes it.

Now the second act begins. Four men with razors, soap-brushes and clippers burst in; they have trousers and jackets with stripes, with a number sewn on the front; perhaps they are the same sort as those others of this evening (this evening or yesterday evening?); but these are robust and flourishing. We ask many questions but they catch hold of us and in a moment we find ourselves shaved and sheared. What comic faces we have without hair. The four speak a language which does not seem of this world. It is certainly not German, for I understand a little German.

Finally another door is opened: here we are, locked in, naked, sheared and standing, with our feet in water – it is a shower-room. We are alone. Slowly the astonishment dissolves, and we speak, and everyone asks questions and no one answers. If we are naked ia a shower-room, it means that we will have a shower. If we have a shower it is because they are not going to kill as yet. But why then do they keep us standing, and give us nothing to drink, while nobody explains anything, and we have no shoes or clothes, but we are all naked with our feet in the water, and we have been travelling five days and cannot even sit down.

And our women?

Mr Levi asks me if I think that our women are like us at this moment, and where they are, and if we will be able to see them again. I say yes, because he is married and has a daughter; certainly we will see them again. But by now my belief is that all this is a game to mock and sneer at us. Clearly they will kill us, whoever thinks he is going to live is mad, it means that he has swallowed the bait, but I have not; I have understood that it will soon all be over, perhaps in this same room, when they get bored of seeing us naked, dancing from foot to foot and trying every now and again to sit down on the floor. But there are two inches of cold water and we cannot sit down.

We walk up and down without sense, and we talk, everybody talks to everybody else, we make a great noise. The door opens, and a German enters; it is the officer of before. He speaks briefly, the interpreter translates. 'The officer says you must be quiet, because this is not a rabbinical school.' One sees the words which are not his, the bad words, twist his mouth as they come out, as if he was spitting out a foul taste. We beg him to ask what we are waiting for, how long we will stay here, about our women, everything; but be says no, that he does not want to ask. This Flesch, who is most unwilling to translate into Italian the hard cold German phrases and refuses to turn into German our questions because he knows that it is useless, is a German Jew of about fifty, who has a large scar on his face from a wound received fighting the Italians on the Piave. He is a closed taciturn man, for when I feel an instinctive respect as I feel that he has begun to suffer before us.

The German goes and we remain silent, although we are a little ashamed of our silence. It is still night and we wonder if the day will ever come. The door opens again, and someone else dressed in stripes comes in. He is different from the others, older, with glasses, a more civilized face, and much less robust. He speaks to us in Italian.

By now we are tired of being amazed. We seem to be watching some mad play, one of those plays in which the witches, the Holy Spirit and the devil appear. He speaks Italian badly, with a strong foreign accent. He makes a long speech, is very polite, and tries to reply to all our questions.

We are at Monowitz, near Auschwitz, in Upper Silesia, a region inhabited by both Poles and Germans. This camp is a work-camp, in German one says *Arbeitslager*; all the prisoners (there are about ten thousand) work in a factory which produces a type of rubber called Buna, so that the camp itself is called Buna.

We will be gives shoes and clothes – no, not our own – other shoes, other clothes, like his. We are naked now because we are waiting for the shower and the disinfection, which will take place immediately after the reveille, because one cannot enter the camp without being disinfected.

Certainly there will be work to do, everyone must work here. But there is work and work: he, for example, acts as doctor. He is a Hungarian doctor who studied in Italy and he is the dentist of the Lager. He has been in the Lager for four and a half years (not in this one: Buna has only been open for a year and a half), but we can see that he is still quite well, not very thin. Why is he

in the Lager? Is he Jewish like us? 'No,' he says simply, 'I am a criminal.'

We ask him many questions. He laughs, replies to some and not to others, and it is clear that he avoids certain subjects. He does not speak of the women: he says they are well, that we will see them again soon, but he docs not say how or where. Instead he tells us other things, strange and crazy things, perhaps he too is playing with us. Perhaps he is mad – one goes mad in the Lager. He says that every Sunday there are concerts and football matches. He says that whoever boxes well can become cook. He says that whoever works well receives prize-coupons with which to buy tobacco and soap. He says that the water is really not drinkable, and that instead a coffee substitute is distributed every day, but generally nobody drinks it as the soup itself is sufficiently watery to quench thirst. We beg him to find us something to drink, but he says he cannot, that he has come to see us secretly, against SS orders, as we still have to be disinfected, and that he must leave at once; he has come because he has a liking for Italians, and because, he says, he 'has a little heart'. We ask him if there are other Italians in the camp and he says there are some, a few, he does not know how many; and he at once changes the subject. Meanwhile a bell rang and he immediately hurried off and left us stunned and disconcerted. Some feel refreshed but I do not. I still think that even this dentist, this incomprehensible person, wanted to amuse himself at our expense, and I do not want to believe a word of what he said.

At the sound of the bell, we can hear the still dark camp waking up. Unexpectedly the water gushes out boiling from the showers – five minutes of bliss; but immediately after, four men (perhaps they are the barbers) burst in yelling and shoving and drive us out, wet and steaming, into the adjoining room which is freezing; here other shouting people throw at us unrecognizable rags and thrust into our hands a pair of broken-down boots with wooden soles: we have no time to understand and we already find ourselves in the open, in the blue and icy snow of dawn, barefoot and naked, with all our clothing in our hands, with a hundred yards to run to the next hut. There we are finally allowed to get dressed.

When we finish, everyone remains in his own corner and we do not dare lift our eyes to look at one another. There is nowhere to look in a mirror, but our appearance stands in front of us, reflected in a hundred livid faces, in a hundred miserable and sordid puppets. We are transformed into the phantoms glimpsed yesterday evening.

Then for the first time we became aware that our language lacks words to express this offence, the demolition of a man. In a moment, with almost prophetic intuition, the reality was revealed to us: we had reached the bottom. It is not possible to sink lower than this; no human condition is more miserable than this, nor could it conceivably be so. Nothing belongs to us any more: they have taken away our clothes, our shoes, even our hair; if we speak, they will not listen to us, and if they listen, they will not understand. They will even take away our name: and if we want to keep it, we will have to find ourselves the strength to do so, to manage somehow so that behind the name something of us, of us as we were, still remains.

We know that we will have difficulty in being understood, and this is as it should be. But consider what value, what meaning is enclosed even in the smallest of our daily habits, in the hundred possessions which even the poorest beggar owns: a handkerchief, an old letter, the photo of a cherished person. These things are part of us, almost like limbs of our body; nor is it conceivable that we can be deprived of them in our world, for we immediately find others to substitute the old ones, other objects which are ours in their personification and evocation of our memories.

Imagine now a man who is deprived of everyone he loves, and at the same time of his house, his habits, his clothes, in short, of everything be possesses: he will be a hollow man, reduced to suffering and needs, forgetful of dignity and restraint, for he who loses all often easily loses himself. He will be a man whose life or death can be lightly decided with no sense of human affinity, in the most fortunate of cases, on the basis of a pure judgement of utility. It is in this way that one can understand the double sense of the term 'extermination camp', and it is now clear what we seek to express with the phrase: 'to lie on the bottom'.

Häftling*: I have learnt that I am Häftling. My number is 174517; we have been baptized, we will carry the tattoo on our left arm until we die.

The operation was slightly painful and extraordinarily rapid: They placed us all in a row, and one by one, according to the alphabetical order of our names, we filed past a skillful official, armed with a sort of pointed tool with a very short needle. It seems that this is the real, true initiation: only by 'showing one's number' can one get bread and soup. Several days passed, and not a few cuffs and punches, before we became used to showing our number promptly enough not to disorder the daily operation of food-distribution: weeks and months were needed to learn its sound in the German language. And for many days, while the habits of freedom still led me to look for the time on my wristwatch, my new name ironically appeared instead, a number tattooed in bluish characters under the skin.

Only much later, and slowly, a few of us learnt something of the funereal science of the numbers of Auschwitz, which epitomize the stages of

---

* Prisoner.

destruction of European Judaism. To the old hands of the camp, the numbers told everything: the period of entry into the camp, the convoy of which one formed a part, and consequently the nationality. Everyone will treat with respect the numbers from 30,000 to 80,000: there are only a few hundred left and they represented the few survivals from the Polish ghettos. It is as well to watch out in commercial dealings with a 116,000 or a 117,000: they now number only about forty, but they represent the Greeks of Salonica, so take care they do not pull the wool over your eyes. As for the high numbers they carry an essentially comic air about them, like the words 'freshman' or 'conscript' in ordinary life. The typical high number is a corpulent, docile and stupid fellow: he can be convinced that leather shoes are distributed at the infirmary to all those with delicate feet, and can be persuaded to run there and leave his bowl of soup 'in your custody'; you can sell him a spoon for three rations of bread; you can send him to the most ferocious of the Kapos to ask him (as happened to me!) if it is true that his is the *Kartoffelschalenkommando*, the 'Potato Peeling Command', and if one can be enrolled in it.

In fact, the whole process of introduction to what was for us a new order took place in a grotesque and sarcastic manner. When the tattooing operation was finished, they shut us in a vacant hut. The bunks are made, but we are severely forbidden to touch or sit on them: so we wander around aimlessly for half the day in the limited space available, still tormented by the parching thirst of the journey. Then the door opens and a boy in a striped suit comes in, with a fairly civilized air, small, thin and blond. He speaks French and we throng around him with a flood of questions which till now we had asked each other in vain.

But he does not speak willingly; no one here speaks willingly. We are new, we have nothing and we know nothing; why waste time on us? He reluctantly explains to us that all the others are out at work and will come back in the evening. He has come out of the infirmary this morning and is exempt from work for today. I asked him (with an ingenuousness that only a few days later already seemed incredible to me) if at least they would give us back our toothbrushes. He did not laugh, but with his face animated by fierce contempt, he threw at me '*Vous n'etes pas à la maison.*' And it is this refrain that we hear repeated by everyone: you are not at home, this is not a sanatorium, the only exit is by way of the Chimney. (What did it mean? Soon we were all to learn what it meant.)

And it was in fact so. Driven by thirst, I eyed a fine icicle outside the window, within hand's reach. I opened the window and broke off the icicle but at once a large, heavy guard prowling outside brutally snatched it away from me. '*Warum?*' I asked him in my poor German. '*Hier ist kein warum*' (there is no why here), he replied, pushing me inside with a shove.

The explanation is repugnant but simple: in this place everything is forbidden, not for hidden reasons, but because the camp has been created for that purpose. If one wants to live one must learn this quickly and well:

> 'No Sacred Face will help thee here! it's not
> A Serchio bathing-party...'

Hour after hour, this first long day of limbo draws to its end. While the sun sets in a tumult of fierce, blood-red clouds, they finally make us come out of the hut. Will they give as something to drink? No, they place us in line again, they lead us to a huge square which takes up the centre of the camp and they arrange us meticulously in squads. Then nothing happens for another hour: it seems that we are waiting for someone.

A band begins to play, next to the entrance of the camp: It plays Rosamunda, the well known sentimental song, and this seems so strange to us that we look sniggering at each other; we feel a shadow of relief, perhaps all these ceremonies are nothing but a colossal farce in Teutonic taste. But the band, on finishing *Rosamunda*, continues to play other marches, one after the other, and suddenly the squads of our comrades appear, returning from work. They walk in columns of five with a strange, unnatural hard gait, like stiff puppets made of jointless bones; but they walk scrupulously in time to the band.

They also arrange themselves like us in the huge square, according to a precise order; when the last squad has returned, they count and recount us for over an hour. Long checks are made which all seem to go to a man dressed in stripes, who accounts for them to a group of SS men in full battle dress.

Finally (it is dark by now, but the camp is brightly lit by headlamps and reflectors) one hears the shout '*Absperre*!' at which all the squads break up in a confused and turbulent movement. They no longer walk stiffly and erectly as before: each one drags himself along with obvious effort. I see that all of them carry in their hand or attached to their belt a steel bowl as large as a basin.

We new arrivals also wander among the crowd, searching for a voice, a friendly face or a guide. Against the wooden wall of a hut two boys are seated on the ground: they seem very young, sixteen years old at the outside, both with their face and hands dirty with soot. One of the two, as we are passing by, calls me and asks me in German some questions which I do not understand; then he asks where we come from. '*Italien*,' I reply; I want to ask him many things, but my German vocabulary is very limited.

'Are you a Jew?' I asked him.

'How long have you been in the Lager?'

'Three years,' and he lifts up three fingers. He must have been a child when he entered, I think with horror; on the other hand this means that at least some manage to live here.

'What is your work?'

'*Schlosser*,' he replies. I do not understand.

'*Eisen, Feuer*' (iron, fire), he insists, and makes a play with his hands of someone beating with a hammer on an anvil. So he is an ironsmith.

'*Ich Chemiker*,' I state; and he nods earnestly with his head, '*Chemiker gut*.' But all this has to do with the distant future: what torments me at the moment is my thirst.

'Drink, water. We no water,' I tell him.

He looks at me with a serious face, almost severe, and states clearly: 'Do not drink, water, comrade,' and then other words that I do not understand.'

'*Warum*?'

'*Geschwollen*,' he replies cryptically. I shake my head, I have not understood. '*Swollen*,' he makes me understand, blowing out his cheeks and sketching with his hands a monstrous tumefaction of the face and belly. '*Warten bis heute Abend*.' 'Wait until this evening,' I translate word by word.

Then he says: '*Ich Schlome. Du?*' I tell him my name, and he asks me: 'Where your mother?'

'In Italy.' Schlome is amazed: a Jew in Italy? 'Yes,' I explain as best I can, 'hidden, no one knows, run away, does not speak, no one sees her.' He has understood; he now gets up, approaches me and timidly embraces me. The adventure is over, and I feel filled with a serene sadness that is almost joy. I have never seen Schlome since, but I have not forgotten his serious and gentle face of a child, which welcomed me on the threshold of the house of the dead.

We have a great number of things to learn, but we have learnt many already. We already have a certain idea of the topography of the Lager; our Lager is a square of about six hundred yards in length, surrounded by two fences of barbed wire, the inner one carrying a high tension current, It consists of sixty wooden huts, which are called Blocks, ten of which are in construction. In addition, there is the body of the kitchens, which are in brick; an experimental farm, run by a detachment of privileged Häftlinge; the huts with the showers and the latrines, one for each group of six or eight Blocks. Besides these, certain Blocks are reserved for specific purposes. First of all, a group of eight, at the extreme eastern end of the camp, forms the infirmary and clinic; then there is Block 24 which is the *Krätzeblock*, reserved for infectious skin-diseases; Block 7 which no ordinary Häftling has ever entered, reserved for the '*Prominenz*', that is, the aristocracy, the internees holding the highest posts; Block 47, reserved for the *Reichsdeutsche* (the Aryan Germans, 'politicals' or criminals); Block 49, for the Kapos alone; Block 12, half of which, for use of the *Reichsdeutsche* and the Kapos, serves as canteen, that is, a distribution centre for tobacco, insect powder and occasionally other articles; Block 37, which formed the Quartermaster's office and the Office for Work; and finally, Block 29, which always has its windows closed as it is the *Frauenblock*, the camp brothel, served by Polish Häftling girls, and reserved for the *Reichsdeutsche*.

The ordinary living Blocks are divided into two parts. In one *Tagesraum* lives the head of the hut with his friends. There is a long table, seats, benches, and on all sides a heap of strange objects in bright colours, photographs, cuttings from magazines, sketches, imitation flowers, ornaments; on the walls, great sayings, proverbs and rhymes in praise of order, discipline and hygiene; in one corner, a shelf with the tools of the *Blockfrisör* (official barber), the ladles to distribute the soup, and two rubber truncheons, one solid and one hollow, to enforce discipline should the proverbs prove insufficient. The other part is the dormitory: there are only one hundred and forty-eight bunks on three levels, fitted close to each other like the cells of a beehive, and divided by three corridors so as to utilize without wastage all the space in the room up to the roof.

Here all the ordinary Häftlinge live, about two hundred to two hundred and fifty per hut. Consequently there are two men in most of the bunks, which are portable planks of wood, each covered by a thin straw sack and two blankets.

The corridors are so narrow that two people can barely pass together; the total area of the floor is so small that the inhabitants of the same Block cannot all stay there at the same time unless at least half are lying on their bunks. Hence the prohibition to enter a Block to which one does not belong.

In the middle of the Lager is the roll-call square, enormous, where we collect in the morning to form the work-squads and in the evening to be counted. Facing the roll-call square there is a bed of grass, carefully mown, where the gallows are erected when necessary.

We had soon learned that the guests of the Lager are divided into three categories: the criminals, the politicals and the Jews. All are clothed in stripes, all are Häftlinge, but the criminals wear a green triangle next to the number sewn on the jacket; the politicals wear a red triangle; and the Jews, who form the large majority, wear the Jewish star, red and yellow. SS men exist but are few and outside the camp, and are seen relatively infrequently. Our effective masters in practice are the green triangles, who have a free hand over us, as well as those of the other two categories who are ready to help them - and they are not few.

And we have learnt other things, more or less quickly, according to our intelligence: to reply '*Jawohl*', never to ask questions, always to pretend to understand. We have learnt the value of food; now we also diligently scrape the bottom of the bowl after the ration and we hold it under our chins when we eat bread so as not to lose the crumbs. We, too, know that it is not the same thing to be given a ladleful of soup from the top or from the bottom of the vat, and we are already able to judge, according to the capacity of the various vats, what is the most suitable place to try and reach in the queue when we line up.

We have learnt that everything is useful: the wire to tie up our shoes, the rags to wrap around our feet, waste paper to (illegally) pad out our jacket against the cold. We have learnt, on the other hand, that everything can be stolen, in fact is automatically stolen as soon as attention is relaxed; and to avoid this, we had to learn the art of sleeping with our head on a bundle made up of our jacket and containing all our belongings, from the bowl to the shoes.

We already know in good part the rules of this camp, which are incredibly complicated. The prohibitions are innumerable: to approach nearer to the barbed wire than two yards; to sleep with one's jacket, or without one's pants, or with one's cap on one's head; to use certain washrooms or latrines which are '*nur für Kapos*' or '*nur für Reichsdeutsche*'; not to go for the shower on the prescribed day, or to go there on a day not prescribed; to leave the hut with one's jacket unbuttoned, or with the collar raised; to carry paper or straw under one's clothes against the cold; to wash except stripped to the waist.

The rites to be carried out were infinite and senseless: every morning one had to make the 'bed' perfectly flat and smooth; smear one's muddy and repellent wooden shoes with the appropriate machine grease; scrape the mudstains off one's clothes (paint, grease and rust-stains were, however, permitted); in the evening one had to undergo the control for lice and the control of washing one's feet; on Saturday, have one's beard and hair shaved, mend or have mended one's rags; on Sunday, undergo the general control for skin diseases and the control of buttons on one's jacket, which had to be five.

In addition, there are innumerable circumstances, normally irrelevant, which here become problems. When one's nails grow long, they have to be shortened, which can only be done with one's teeth (for the toenails, the friction of the shoes is sufficient); if a button comes off, one has to tie it on with a piece of wire; if one goes to the latrine or the washroom, everything has to be carried along, always and everywhere, and while one washes one's face, the bundle of clothes has to be held tightly between one's knees: in any other manner it will be stolen in that second. If a shoe hurts, one has to go in the evening to the ceremony of the changing of the shoes: this tests the skill of the individual who, in the middle of the incredible crowd, has to be able to choose at an eye's glance one (not a pair, one) shoe, which fits. Because once the choice is made, there can be no second change.

And do not think that shoes form a factor of secondary importance in the life of the Lager. Death begins with the shoes; for most of us, they show themselves to be instruments of torture, which after a few hours of marching cause painful sores which become fatally infected. Whoever has them is forced to walk as if he was dragging a convict's chain (this explains the strange gait of the army which returns every evening on parade); he arrives last everywhere, and everywhere he receives blows. He cannot escape if they run after him; his feet swell and the more they swell, the more the friction with the wood and the cloth of the shoes becomes insupportable. Then only the hospital is left: but to enter the hospital with a diagnosis of '*dicke Füsse*' (swollen feet) is extremely dangerous, because it is well known to all, and especially to the SS, that here there is no cure for that complaint.

And in all this we have not yet mentioned the work, which in its turn is a Gordian knot of laws, taboos and problems.

We all work, except those who are ill (to be recognized as ill implies in itself an important equipment of knowledge and experience).

Every morning we leave the camp in squads for the Buna; every evening, in squads, we return. As regards the work, we are divided into about two hundred *Kommandos*, each of which consists of between fifteen and one hundred and fifty men and is commanded by a Kapo. There are good and bad Kommandos; for the most part they are used as transport and the work is quite hard, especially in the winter, if for no other reason merely because it always takes place in the open. There are also skilled Kommandos (electricians, smiths, brick-layers, welders, mechanics, concrete-layers, etc.), each attached to a certain workshop or department of the Buna, and depending more directly on civilian foremen, mostly German and Polish. This naturally only applies to the hours of work; for the test of the day the skilled workers (there are no more than three or four hundred in all) receive no different treatment from the ordinary workers. The detailing of individuals to the various Kommandos is organized by a special office of the Lager, the *Arbeitsdienst*, which is in continual touch with the civilian direction of the Buna. The *Arbeitsdienst* decides on the basis of unknown criteria, often openly on the basis of protection or corruption, so that it anyone manages to find enough to eat, he is practically certain to get a good post at Buna.

The hours of work vary with the season. All hours of light are working hours: so that from a minimum winter working day (8–12 a.m. and 12.30–4 p.m.) one rises to a maximum summer one (6.30–12 a.m. and 1 6 p.m.). Under no excuse are the Häftlinge allowed to be at work during the hours of darkness or when there is a thick fog, but they work regularly even if it rains or snows or (as occurs quite frequently) if the fierce wind of the Carpathians blows; the reason being that the darkness or fog might provide opportunities to escape.

One Sunday in every two is a regular working day; on the so-called holiday Sundays, instead of working at Buna, one works normally on the upkeep of the Lager, so that days of real rest are extremely rare.

Such will be our life. Every day, according to the established rhythm, *Ausrücken* and *Einrücken*, go out and come in; work, sleep and eat; fall ill, get better or die.

…And for how long? But the old ones laugh at this question. they recognize the new arrivals by this question. They laugh and they do not reply. For months and years, the problem of the remote future has grown pale to them and has lost all intensity in face of the far more urgent and concrete problems of the near future: how much one will eat today, if it will snow, if there will be coal to unload.

If we were logical, we would resign ourselves to the evidence that our fate is beyond knowledge, that every conjecture is arbitrary and demonstrably devoid of foundation. But men are rarely logical when their own fate is at stake; on every occasion, they prefer the extreme positions. According to our character, some of us are immediately convinced that all is lost, that one cannot live here, that the end is near and sure; others are convinced that however hard the present life may be, salvation is probable and not far off, and if we have faith and strength, we will see our houses and our dear ones again. The two classes of pessimists and optimists are not so clearly defined, however, not because there are many agnostics, but because the majority, without memory or coherence, drift between the two extremes, according to the moment and the mood of the person they happen to meet.

Here I am, then, on the bottom. One learns quickly enough to wipe out the past and the future when one is forced to. A fortnight after my arrival I already had the prescribed hunger, that chronic hunger unknown to free men, which makes one dream at night, and settles in all the limbs of one's body. I have already learnt not to let myself be robbed, and in fact if I find a spoon lying around, a piece of string, a button which I can acquire without danger of punishment, I pocket them and consider them mine by full right. On the back of my feet I already have those numb sores that will not heal. I push wagons, I work with a shovel, I turn rotten in the rain, I shiver in the wind; already my own body is no longer mine: my belly is swollen, my limbs emaciated, my face is thick in the morning, hollow in the evening; some of us have yellow skin, others grey. When we do not meet for a few days we hardly recognize each other.

We Italians had decided to meet every Sunday evening in a corner of the Lager, but we stopped it at once, because it was too sad to count our numbers and find fewer each time, and to see each other ever more deformed and more squalid. And it was so tiring to walk those few steps and then, meeting each other, to remember and to think. It was better not to think.

Extract from Evidence Given at the Nuremberg Trials on the Auschwitz Extermination Camp[*]

M. DUBOST: What do you know about the Jewish transport that arrived from Romainville about the same time as you?

VAILLANT-COUTURIER: When we left Romainville the Jewish women who were together with us remained behind. They were sent to Drancy, and finally arrived in Auschwitz, where we saw them again three weeks later. Of 1,200 who left, only 125 arrived in the camp. The rest were taken to the gas chambers immediately, and of the 125 not a single one was left by the end of a month.

The transports were carried out as follows: at the beginning, when we arrived, when a Jewish transport came there was a "selection." First the old women, the mothers and the children. They were told to get on trucks, together with the sick and people who looked weak. They kept only young girls, young women and young men; the latter were sent to the men's camp. In general, it was rare for more than 250 out of a transport of 1,000 to 1,500 to reach the camp, and that was the maximum; the others were sent to the gas chambers straight away.

At this "selection" healthy women between 20 and 30 years old were also chosen, and sent to the Experimental Block. Girls and women, who were a little older or not chosen for this purpose, were sent to the camp and, like us, had their heads shaved and they were tattooed.

In the spring of 1944 there was also a block for twins. That was at the time of the immense transport of Hungarian Jews, about 700,000[*] persons. Dr. Mengele, who was carrying out the experiments, kept back the twin children from all transports, as well as twins of any age, so long as both twins were there. Both children and adults slept

---

[*] The correct number of Hungarian Jews sent to Auschwitz was about 430,000.

on the floor in this block. I don't know what experiments were made apart from blood tests and measurements.

M. DUBOST: Did you actually see the "selection" when transports arrived?

VAILLANT-COUTURIER: Yes, because when we were working in the Sewing Block in 1944, the block in which we lived was situated just opposite the place where the trains arrived. The whole process had been improved: Instead of carrying out the "selection" where the trains arrived, a siding took the carriages practically to the gas chamber, and the train stopped about 100 m. from the gas chamber. That was right in front of our block, but of course there were two rows of barbed wire between.

Then we saw how the seals were taken off the trucks and how women, men and children were pulled out of the trucks by soldiers. We were present at the most terrible scenes when old couples were separated. Mothers had to leave their daughters because they were taken to the camp, while the mothers and children went to the gas chambers. All these people knew nothing of the fate that awaited them. They were only confused because they were being separated from each other, but they did not know that they were going to their death.

To make the reception pleasanter there was then—in June and July 1944, that is—an orchestra made up of prisoners, girls in white blouses and dark blue skirts, all of them pretty and young, who played gay tunes when the trains arrived, the "Merry Widow," the Barcarolle from the 'Tales of Hoffmann," etc. They were told it was a labor camp, and as they never entered the camp they saw nothing but the small platform decorated with greenery, where the orchestra played. They could not know what awaited them.

Those who were taken to the gas chambers—that is, the old people, children and others—were taken to a red brick building.

M. DUBOST: Then they were not registered?

VAILLANT-COUTURIER: No.

M. DUBOST: They were not tattooed?

VAILLANT-COUTURIER: No, they were not even counted.

M. DUBOST: Were you yourself tattooed?

VAILLANT-COUTURIER: Yes.

(The witness shows her arm)

They were taken to a red brick building with a sign that said Baths. There they were told to get undressed and given a towel before they were taken to the so-called shower room. Later, at the time of the large transports from Hungary, there was no time left for any degree of concealment. They were undressed brutally. I know of these particulars because I was acquainted with a little Jewess from France, who had lived on the Place de la Republique.... .

M. DUBOST: In Paris?

VAILLANT-COUTURIER: In Paris, she was known as "little Marie" and was the only survivor of a family of nine. Her mother and her seven sisters and brothers had been taken to the gas chambers as soon as they arrived. When I got to know her she worked on undressing the small children before they were taken into the gas chamber.

After the people were undressed they were taken into a room that looked like a shower room, and the capsules were thrown down into the room through a hole in the ceiling. An SS man observed the effect through a spy-hole. After about 5 to 7 minutes, when the gas had done its job, be gave a signal for the opening of the doors. Men with gas-masks, these were prisoners too, came in and took the bodies out. They told us that the prisoners must have suffered before they died, because they clung together in bunches like grapes so that it was difficult to separate them.... .

World War II—Major Consequences

1. End of the European Age

2. Rise of the U.S. and the U.S.S.R. to Superpower Status

3. Emergence of the Cold War

4. The Nuclear Age

5. Rise of Nationalism and Independence Movements

6. Rise of Social Movements—Women, Youth, Human Rights, Ethnic, Religious, and Cultural Minorities

7. Internationalism—United Nations, IMF, World Bank

Definition of the Cold War

"A worldwide struggle for power between the United States and the Soviet Union ... [which led to the creation of a bipolar world.] ... It never resulted in direct military conflict between the two superpowers, but it did lead to competition on all fronts: ideological, diplomatic, economic, military ... [and cultural.] Each nation felt besieged by the other."

The West and the World Since 1945

Cold War Historiography

	Personal Leadership	Domestic Pressures	International Issues
It Was the Soviets' Cold War	Stalin as paranoid; seized East Europe to shore up power at home. (Adam Elam)	Communist system as requiring a foreign enemy to justify totalitarian rule. (Brzezinski)	Russian and/or Communist bid for Eurasian hegemony forced Western powers into containment. (Kissinger)
It Was the Americans' Cold War	Truman as insecure, ignorant bully; "if only FDR had lived." (Diane Clemens)	"Open door" capitalist imperialism and US military-industrial complex threatened USSR. (Lloyd Gardner)	US came out of WWII with hegemonic power, forced Soviet bloc to resist and defend itself. (Martin Sherwin)
The Deterministic View of the Cold War: It Was Inevitable	Stalin and Truman both scared and suspicious, applied lessons of 1930's and 1940's, and came from opposite backgrounds; agreement impossible. (Robert Divine)	It was the wartime alliance that was the aberration, and after 1945 the cold war between a Wilsonian and Leninist system that dated from 1917 resumed. (Stephen Ambrose)	It was the case of an elephant and a whale; US and USSR posed Asymmetrical threats, each viewed the other as a potential "Nazi Germany," and each feared sneak attack. (Walter McDougall)

"Cold War Historiography" by Walter McDougall from a handout prepared for an FPRI History Institute for Teachers on The Cold War Revisited. Copyright © 1998 by Foreign Policy Research Institute, www.fpri.org. Reprinted with permission.

56

Vietnamese Declaration of Independence, 1945

The author of this document, Ho Chi Minh, was the leader of the Vietnamese independence movement at the Versailles Conference, where he would present a petition for independence. Ho, who established the Vietnamese Communist Party in 1930 in Paris, would later form the Viet Minh, a coalition of nationalists that would use guerrilla tactics to fight the French, the Japanese, the Americans and the South Vietnamese before Vietnam reunified the country by driving out the Americans and their allies in 1974. When Ho proclaimed the Democratic Republic of Vietnam on September 2, 1945, he consciously modeled his declaration on the American one hoping for U. S. support of its claim to independence. Vietnam had been a colony of France since the 1860s, along with Cambodia and Laos, in what was called French Indochina. The Japanese displaced the French during World War II, which Ho Chi Minh described as another form of imperialism. After the war, there were great hopes from colonized people throughout the world that the European powers would finally relinquish their control, but France, like others, chose to return. American officials ultimately supported the French attempt to reclaim their colony, resulting in the First Indochina War. France would be defeated in 1954, resulting in the division of Vietnam into North and South, and followed by the Second Indochina War, waged by Americans who feared that a communist Vietnam would be the first in a series of "falling dominoes" that would make all of Southeast Asia communist.

Discussion Questions

1. What similarities to the U.S. Declaration of Independence (RGH # 7) can you find? What differences?

2. What are the main charges against the French and the Japanese that Ho makes? Are Ho's claims similar to those of other independence leaders?

3. How does this document reflect Enlightenment principles as well as the ideology of nationalism?

Vietnamese Declaration of Independence, 1945

" All men are created equal. They are endowed by their Creator with certain inalienable rights; among these are Life, Liberty, and the pursuit of Happiness."

This immortal statement was made in the Declaration of Independence of the United States of America in *1776*. In a broader sense, this means: All the peoples on the earth are equal from birth, all the peoples have a right to live, to be happy and free.

The Declaration of the French Revolution made in *1791* on the Rights of Man and the Citizen also states: "All men are born free and with equal rights, and must always remain free and have equal rights."

Those are undeniable truths.

Nevertheless, for more than eighty years, the French imperialists, abusing the standard of Liberty, Equality, and Fraternity, have violated our Fatherland and oppressed our fellow-citizens. They have acted contrary to the ideals of humanity and justice.

In the field of politics, they have deprived our people of every democratic liberty.

They have enforced inhuman laws; they have set up three distinct political regimes in the North, the Center, and the South of Vietnam in order to wreck our national unity and prevent our people from being united.

They have built more prisons than schools. They have mercilessly slain our patriots; they have drowned our uprisings in rivers of blood.

They have fettered public opinion; they have practiced obscurantism against our people.

To weaken our race they have forced us to use opium and alcohol.

In the field of economics, they have fleeced us to the backbone, impoverished our people, and devastated our land.

They have robbed us of our rice fields, our mines, our forests, and our raw materials. They have monopolized the issuing of banknotes and the export trade.

They have invented numerous unjustifiable taxes and reduced our people, especially our peasantry, to a state of extreme poverty.

They have hampered the prospering of our national bourgeoisie; they have mercilessly exploited our workers.

In the autumn of 1940, when the Japanese Fascists violated Indochina's territory to establish new bases in their fight against the Allies, the French imperialists went down on their bended knees and handed over our country to them.

Thus, from that date, our people were subjected to the double yoke of the French and the Japanese. Their sufferings and miseries increased. The result was that from the end of last year to the beginning of this year, from Quang Tri province to the North of Vietnam, more than two million of our fellow citizens died from starvation. On March 9, the French troops were disarmed by the Japanese. The French colonialists either fled or surrendered showing that not only were they incapable of "protecting" us, but that, in the span of five years, they had twice sold our country to the Japanese.

On several occasions before March 9, the Vietminh League urged the French to ally themselves with it against the Japanese. Instead of agreeing to this proposal, the French colonialists so intensified their terrorist activities against the Vietminh members that before fleeing they massacred a great number of our political prisoners detained at Yen Bay and Caobang.

Notwithstanding all this, our fellow-citizens have always manifested toward the French a tolerant and humane attitude. Even after the Japanese putsch of March 1945, the Vietminh League helped many Frenchmen to cross the frontier, rescued some of them from Japanese jails, and protected French lives and property.

From the autumn of 1940, our country had in fact ceased to be a French colony and had become a Japanese possession.

After the Japanese had surrendered to the Allies, our whole people rose to regain our national sovereignty and to found the Democratic Republic of Vietnam.

The truth is that we have wrested our independence from the Japanese and not from the French.

The French have fled, the Japanese have capitulated, Emperor Bao Dai has abdicated. Our people have broken the chains which for nearly a century have fettered them and have won independence for the Fatherland. Our people at the same time have overthrown the monarchic regime that has reigned supreme for dozens of centuries. In its place has been established the present Democratic Republic.

For these reasons, we, members of the Provisional Government, representing the whole Vietnamese people, declare that from now on we break off all relations of a colonial character with France; we repeal all the international obligation that France has so far subscribed to on behalf of Vietnam and we abolish all the special rights the French have unlawfully acquired in our Fatherland.

The whole Vietnamese people, animated by a common purpose, are determined to fight to the bitter end against any attempt by the French colonialists to reconquer their country.

We are convinced that the Allied nations, which at Tehran and San Francisco have acknowledged the principles of self-determination and equality of nations, will not refuse to acknowledge the independence of Vietnam.

A people who have courageously opposed French domination for more than eight years, a people who have fought side by side with the Allies against the Fascists during these last years, such a people must be free and independent.

For these reasons, we, members of the Provisional Government of the Democratic Republic of Vietnam, solemnly declare to the world that Vietnam has the right to be a free and independent country—and in fact is so already. The entire Vietnamese people are determined to mobilize all their physical and mental strength, to sacrifice their lives and property in order to safeguard their independence and liberty.

Ho Chi Minh, "Declaration of Independence of the Democratic Republic of Vietnam," *Selected Writings* (Hanoi: Foreign Languages Publishing House, 1977), pp. 53–56.

Third World/Developing Nations, 1945–2000

Decolonization, Independence, Revolution, Development

China	India	Africa	Middle East	Latin America
Revolutions 1911—Republican Revolution. —Sun Yatsen, 3 Principles 1919—May 4th Movement 1930–1949—Mao vs. Jiang—Civil War —People's Liberation Army —Long March—1934 —Guerrilla War	Independence: —Modernizers/Traditionalists —Indian National Congress —Partition of Bengal —swaraj—self-rule —Amritsar Massacre —Gandhi and Nehru	Independence (Uhuru) Examples: —Nkrumah-Ghana —Kenyatta-Kenya —Nyerere-Tanzania —Lumumba-Congo	Arab nationalism —Ottoman decline —Arab brotherhood —World War I—created the modern Middle East	Revolutions —Guatemala—1954 —Cuba—1959 —Dom. Rep.—1965 —Jamaica—1977 —Nicaragua—1979 —Mexico—1990's (Chiapas)
Mao Zedong 1949–1976 —People's Republic of China—10/1.49 —rapid incustrialization —literacy and social reforms —Sino-Soviet split—1959 —Taiwan and the Nationalists	Satyagraha-Soul Force— —Salt March —Civil disobedience —Nonviolent resistance —Non-cooperation —Social reforms, untouchables —Self-reliance	Strategies in Decolonization— —Nationalist movements —Western-educated leaders —One-party states —Social reforms—education, health, economic development	Arab-Israeli Conflict— —Zionism-Jewish nationalism —1948—State of Israel —Wars—1948, 1956, 1967, 1973, Intifadas —PLO—Arafat, Hamas —Camp David, Oslo, Wye Accords, Roadmap	Cuba and Castro— —Communism —Anti-Americanism —Bay of Pigs—1961 —Missile Crisis—1962 —Elian—2000 —Embargo
Continuous Revolution—Using ideas to move the masses: —Great Leap Forward —Cultural Revolution—Red Guards	Hindu-Muslim Split— —Jinnah and Pakistan —Partition 1947—Pakistan and India 1971—Bangladesh —Kashmir	Social and Political: —Negriude—African identity —Pan-Africanism —Role of women in development	New States/New Leaders: —Egypt-Nasser (Arab Socialism) —Syria-Assad —Iraq-Hussein (Ba'ath Party) —Jordan-Hussein	Human Rights— —Chile—1973 —Argentina—1977 —El Salvador—1984 —Desaperacidos —Haiti—1990's
Deng Xiaoping 1978–1997 —"To get rich is glorious" —Market totalitarianism —Tiananmen—1989	India after independence— —Nonalignment —1970's—Indira Gandhi —Socialism	South Africa— —Apartheid —African National Congress —Mandela —Majority rule—1994	Political Developments: —Turkey—secular state —Iran-Islamic theocracy—1979 —Saudi Arabia—Wahabism	Economic Development— —Brazil, Chile, Argentina, Mexico— —Colombia, Panama—"narcodemocracies" —NAFTA, Globalization
China Today— —"Fang shcu"—relaxation and control —Great power status —Olympics—2008 —Friend or foe? —Impact of globalization	India Today— —Hindu nationalism (BJP) —Nuclear weapons —Economic development —Most populous democracy —Hindu-Muslim conflict —Impact of globalization	Africa Today— —Ethnic conflict —Weak governments —AIDS —Poverty —Economic dependence —Impact of globalization	Middle East Today— —Authoritarian states —Conflict, terrorism —Cultural heterogeneity —Outside intervention —Fundamentalism —Oil and economics	Latin America Today— —Constitutionally weak states —Economic dependence —Drug Trade —Poverty —Democratization —Impact of globalization

Chinese Chronology: 1911–1949

1911	End of Manchu Dynasty REPUBLICAN REVOLUTION (Sun Yatsen)
	Period of Yuan Shih-kai
1916	
1919	May Fourth Movement
1921	Chinese Communist Party (CCP) Founded
1923	
	First United Front
1927	Great Northern Expedition: GMT-CCP split NATIONALIST REVOLUTION (Jiang Jieshi)
1931	Japan seizes Manchuria
1934	Communist Long March to Yanan
1937	Full-scale Japanese War on China
1942	Second United Front
1945	End of World War II
1946	
1947	
	Open Civil War: Nationalists vs. Communists
1949	COMMUNIST REVOLUTION (Mao Zedong)

Warlord Era

Nationalist Era
(Guomintang - GMT)

59

The Peasant Movement in Hunan

In this document, Mao Zedong reported on his investigation of the progress of the communist movement among the peasants of Hunan, his native province, in March of 1927. His emphasis on organizing the peasants of the countryside went against the mainstream of Chinese communists who followed the Marxist-Leninist doctrine that communism must take root among the industrial workers in the cities. In April of 1927 Jiang Jieshi purged the communists in the Guomintang, thus ending the first period of cooperation, or united front, between the right and left within the party. A long period of self-examination among the communists, who had fled to the more remote areas of Jiangsi and Hunan after their expulsion and persecution, eventually led to the adoption of Mao's ideas concerning the importance of the peasantry and a new lease on life for his movement.

Discussion Questions

1. Do you get the impression from Mao's essay that the peasant movement was spontaneous or carefully planned and organized?

2. Who are the objects of the wrath of the peasants? Do they deserve this treatment?

3. How does Mao justify the violence ("going too far") of the peasants?

4. Who are the most revolutionary people?

5. What does he say are the achievements of the peasants?

6. Do you think the peasants believe in "democracy?"

March 1927

The development of the peasant movement in Hunan may be divided roughly into two periods with respect to the counties in the province's central and southern parts where the movement has already made much headway. The first, from January to September of last year, was one of organization. The second period, from last October to January of this year, was one of revolutionary action. The membership of the associations jumped to two million and the masses directly under their leadership increased to ten million.

The main targets of attack by the peasants are the local tyrants, the evil gentry and the lawless landlords, but in passing they also hit out against patriarchal ideas and institutions, against the corrupt officials in the cities and against bad practices and customs in the rural areas.

In a few months the peasants have accomplished what Dr. Sun Yat-sen wanted, but failed to accomplish in the forty years he devoted to the national revolution. Countless thousands of the enslaved—the peasants—are striking down the enemies who battened on their flesh. What the peasants are doing is absolutely right; what they are doing is fine! "It's fine!" is the theory of the peasants and of all other revolutionaries. Every revolutionary comrade should know that the national revolution requires a great change in the countryside. The Revolution of 1911 did not bring about this change, hence its failure. This change is now taking place, and it is an important factor for the completion of the revolution. Every revolutionary comrade must support it, or he will be taking the stand of counter-revolution.

A revolution is an insurrection, an act of violence by which one class overthrows another. A rural revolution is a revolution by which the peasantry overthrows the power of the feudal landlord class. Without using the greatest force, the peasants cannot possibly overthrow the deeprooted authority of the landlords which has lasted for thousands of years. The rural areas need a mighty revolutionary upsurge, for it alone can rouse the people in their millions to become a powerful force. Proper limits have to be exceeded in order to right a wrong, or else the wrong cannot be righted. Those who talk about the peasants "going too far" seem at first sight to be different from those who say "It's terrible!"; but in essence they proceed from the same standpoint and likewise voice a landlord theory that upholds the interests of the privileged classes. Since this theory impedes the rise of the peasant movement and so disrupts the revolution, we must firmly oppose it.

According to the survey of Changsha County, the poor peasants comprise 70 per cent, the middle peasants 20 per cent, and the landlords and the rich peasants 10 per cent of the population in the rural areas. The 70 per cent, the poor peasants, may be sub-divided into two categories, the utterly destitute and the less destitute. The utterly destitute, comprising 20 per cent, are the completely dispossessed, that is, people who have neither land nor money, are without any means of livelihood, and are forced to leave home and become mercenaries or hired laborers or wandering beggars. The less destitute, the other 50 per cent, are the partially dispossessed, that is, people with just a little land or a little money who eat up more than they earn and live in toil and distress the year round, such as the handicraftsmen, the tenant-peasants (not including the rich tenant-peasants) and the semi-owner-peasants. This great mass of poor peasants, or altogether 70 per cent of the rural population, are the backbone of the peasant associations, the vanguard in the overthrow of the feudal forces and the heroes who have performed the great revolutionary task which for long years was left undone. Without the poor peasant class (the "riffraff," as the gentry call them), it would have been impossible to bring about the present revolutionary situation in the countryside, or to overthrow the local tyrants and evil gentry and complete the democratic revolution. The poor peasants, being the most revolutionary group, have gained the leadership of the peasant associations. Leadership by the poor peasants is absolutely necessary. Without the poor peasants there would be no revolution. To deny their role is to deny the revolution. To attack them is to attack the revolution. They have never been wrong on the general direction of the revolution. They have beaten down the local tyrants and evil gentry, big and small, and kept them underfoot.

Most critics of the peasant associations allege that they have done a great many bad things. The peasants' attack on the local tyrants and evil gentry is entirely revolutionary behavior and in no way blameworthy. The peasants have done a great many things, and in order to answer people's criticism we must closely examine all their activities, one by one, to see what they have actually done. I have classified and summed up their activities of the last few months; in all, the peasants under the leadership of the peasant associations have the following great achievements to their credit.

1. Organizing the Peasants into Peasant Associations

This is the first great achievement of the peasants. In counties like Hsiangtan, Hsianghsiang and Hengshan, nearly all the peasants are organized and there is hardly a remote corner where they are not on the move. By the end of January the membership must have reached at least two million. As a family generally enters only one name when joining and has an average of five members, the mass following must be about ten million. This astonishing and accelerating-rate of expansion explains why the local tyrants, evil gentry and corrupt officials have been isolated, why the public has been amazed at how completely the world has changed since the peasant movement, and why a great revolution has been wrought in the countryside. This is the first great achievement of the peasants under the leadership of their associations.

2. Hitting the Landlords Politically

Once the peasants have their organization, the first thing they do is to smash the political prestige and power of the landlord class, and especially of the local tyrants and evil gentry, that is, to pull down landlord authority and build up peasant authority in rural society. This is a most serious and vital struggle. It is the pivotal struggle in the second period, the period of revolutionary action. Without victory in this struggle, no victory is possible in the economic struggle to reduce rent and interest, to secure land and other means of production, and so on.

3. Hitting the Landlords Economically

Prohibition on sending grain out of the area, forcing up grain prices, and hoarding and cornering. This is one of the great events of recent months in the economic struggle of the Hunan peasants. Since last October the poor peasants have prevented the outflow of the grain of the landlords and rich peasants and have banned the forcing up of grain prices and hoarding and cornering. As a result, the poor peasants have fully achieved their objective; the ban on the outflow of grain is watertight, grain prices have fallen considerably, and hoarding and cornering have disappeared.

Prohibition on increasing rents and deposits; agitation for reduced rents and deposits. Last July and August, when the peasant associations were still weak, the landlords, following their long-established practice of maximum exploitation, served notice one after another on their tenants that rents and deposits would be increased. But by October, when the peasant associations had grown considerably in strength and had all come out against the raising of rents and deposits, the landlords dared not breathe another word on the subject. From November onwards, as the peasants have gained ascendancy over the landlords they have taken the further step of agitating for reduced rents and deposits.

Prohibition on canceling tenancies. In July and August of last year there were still many instances of landlords canceling tenancies and re-letting the land. But after October nobody dared cancel a tenancy. Today, the canceling of tenancies and the re-letting of land are quite out of the question.

4. Overthrowing the Feudal Rule of the Local Tyrants and Evil Gentry

The evil gentry who ran these organs were virtual monarchs of the countryside. Comparatively speaking, the peasants were not so much concerned with the president of the Republic, the provincial military governor or the county magistrate; their real "bosses" were these rural

monarchs. A mere snort from these people, and the peasants knew they had to watch their step. As a consequence of the present revolt in the countryside the authority of the landlord class has generally been struck down.

5. Overthrowing the Political Power of the County Magistrate and His Bailiffs

In a county where power is in the hands of the local tyrants and evil gentry, the magistrate, whoever he may be, is almost invariably a corrupt official. In a county where the peasants have risen there is clean government, whoever the magistrate.

6. Overthrowing the Clan Authority of the Ancestral Temples and Clan Elders, the Religious Authority of Town and Village Gods, and the Masculine Authority of Husbands

A man in China is usually subjected to the domination of three systems of authority: (1) the state system (authority), ranging from the national, provincial and county government down to that of the township; (2) the clan system (clan authority), ranging .from the central ancestral temple and its branch temples down to the head of the household; and (3) the supernatural system (religious authority), ranging from the King of Hell down to the town and village gods belonging to the nether world, and from the Emperor of Heaven down to all the various gods and spirits belonging to the celestial world. As for women, in addition to being dominated by these three systems of authority, they are also dominated by the men (the authority of the husband). These four authorities political, clan, religious and masculine are the embodiment of the whole feudal patriarchal system and ideology, and are the four thick ropes binding the Chinese people, particularly the peasants.

While I was in the countryside, I did some propaganda against superstition among the peasants. I said:

"The gods? Worship them by all means.

But if you had only Lord Kuan and the Goddess of Mercy and no peasant association, could you have overthrown the local tyrants and evil gentry? The gods and goddesses are indeed miserable objects. You have worshipped them for centuries, and they have not overthrown a single one of the local tyrants or evil gentry for you! Now you want to have your rent reduced. Let me ask, how will you go about it? Will you believe in the gods or in the peasant association?"

My words made the peasants roar with laughter.

7. Spreading Political Propaganda

The spread of political propaganda throughout the rural areas is entirely an achievement of the Communist Party and the peasant associations. Simple slogans, cartoons and speeches have produced such a widespread and speedy effect among the peasants that every one of them seems to have been through a political school.

8. Peasant Bans and Prohibitions

When the peasant associations, under Communist Party leadership, establish their authority in the countryside, the peasants begin to prohibit or restrict the things they dislike. Gaming, gambling and opium-smoking are the three things that are most strictly forbidden.

Gaming. Where the peasant association is powerful, mahjong, dominoes and card games are completely banned.

The peasant association in the 14th District of Hsianghsiang burned two basketfuls of mahjong sets.

If you go to the countryside, you will find none of these games played; anyone who violates the ban is promptly and strictly punished.

Gambling. Former hardened gamblers are now themselves suppressing gambling; this abuse, too, has been swept away in places where the peasant association is powerful.

Opium-smoking. The prohibition is extremely strict. When the peasant association orders the surrender of opium pipes, no one dares to raise the least objection. In Liling County one of the evil gentry who did not surrender his pipes was arrested and paraded through the villages.

9. Eliminating Banditry

Wherever the peasant associations are powerful, there is not a trace of banditry. Surprisingly enough, in many places even the pilfering of vegetables has disappeared. In other places there are still some pilferers. But in the counties I visited, even including those that were formerly bandit-ridden, there was no trace of bandits.

10. The Movement for Education

In China education has always been the exclusive preserve of the landlords, and the peasants have had no access to it. But the landlords' culture is created by the peasants, for its sole source is the peasants' sweat and blood. In China 90 per cent of the people have had no education, and of these the overwhelming majority are peasants. The moment the power of the landlords was overthrown in the rural areas, the peasants' movement for education began. See how the peasants who hitherto detested the schools are today zealously setting up evening classes!

Now the peasants are enthusiastically establishing evening classes, which they call peasant schools. Some have already been opened, others are being organized, and on the average there is one school per township. The peasants are very enthusiastic about these schools, and regard them, and only them, as their own. The funds for the evening schools come from the "public revenue from superstition," from ancestral temple funds, and from other idle public funds or property.

11. The Cooperative Movement

The peasants really need cooperatives, and especially consumers', marketing and credit cooperatives. When they buy goods, the merchants exploit them; when they sell their farm produce, the merchants cheat them; when they borrow money or rice, they are fleeced by the usurers; and they are eager to find a solution to these three problems.

All the deeds enumerated above have been accomplished by the peasants under the leadership of the peasant associations. Would the reader please think it over and say whether any of them is bad in its fundamental spirit and revolutionary significance? Only the local tyrants and evil gentry, I think, will call them bad.

60

The Communist Political Thesis

In the period after the Long March (1934–5), from their headquarters in Yenan, Mao and the communists engaged in a village-by-village transformation that would gain them the loyalty of many, if not most, Chinese peasants in the northern and central regions of eastern China—areas that were mostly under Japanese control after 1937. In their book *Thunder Out of China*, Theodore H. White and Annalee Jacoby explain the appeal of the communists to the peasants.

Discussion Questions

1. What did the communists do for the peasants?

2. Is it possible to understand the success of the communists over the long run?

3. How did the communists' approach differ from that of the Guomindang as seen in the U.S. Foreign Service officers' reports?

The entire Communist political thesis could be reduced to a single paragraph: If you take a peasant who has been swindled, beaten, and kicked about for all his waking days and whose father has transmitted to him an emotion of bitterness reaching back for generations—if you take such a peasant, treat him like a man, ask his opinion, let him vote for a local government, let him organize his own police and gendarmes, decide on his own taxes, and vote himself a reduction in rent and interest—if you do all that, the peasant becomes a man who has something to fight for, and he will fight to preserve it against any enemy, Japanese or Chinese. If in addition you present the peasant with an army and a government that help him harvest, teach him to read and write, and fight off the Japanese who raped his wife and tortured his mother, he develops a loyalty to the army and the government and to the party that controls them. He votes for that party, thinks the way that party wants him to think, and in many cases becomes an active participant... .

61

Communism Comes to a Chinese Village

Once Mao Zedong and the Chinese communists decided that the future of China lay with the majority peasant class, the question of how to "convert" the peasants to communism came to the fore. Their approach, pioneered in Jiangsi and southern Hunan provinces before the Long March, was refined during the Yanan period (1935–1947). The situation was complicated by the full-scale invasion of China by Japan in 1937 and continued fighting with the Guomindang of Jiang Jieshi. In the following selection, William Hinton describes how the communists, on a village-by-village basis, gained the support of the peasantry in the countryside.

Discussion Questions

1. What was the strategy used by the communists to gain the confidence of the peasants? What were the difficulties?

2. What were the main fears of the peasants?

3. What role did the Japanese play?

4. Would you call this a "popular" revolution?

Fanshen

A Documentary of Revolution in a Chinese Village

At Yellow Dog Kuo's suggestion, T'ien-ming called all the active young cadres and militiamen of Long Bow together and announced to them the policy of the county government, which was to confront all enemy collaborators and their backers at public meetings, expose their crimes, and turn them over to the county authorities for punishment. He proposed that they start with Kuo Te-yu, the puppet village head. Having moved the group to anger with a description of Te-yu's crimes, T'ien-ming reviewed the painful life led by the poor peasants during the occupation and recalled how hard they had all worked, and how as soon as they harvested a little grain the puppet officials, backed by army bayonets, took what they wanted, turned over huge quantities to the Japanese devils, forced the peasants to haul it away, and flogged those who refused.

The young men agreed to conduct a public meeting of the whole population the very next day.

And so it was that Kuo Te-yu, running dog of the landlords, informer, torturer, grafter, and enemy stooge, found himself standing before a crowd of several hundred stolid peasants whom he had betrayed. His face was ashen, his tunic shabby and soiled. A stranger might well have taken him for a thief caught stealing melons, hardly for a village tyrant.

As the silent crowd contracted toward the spot where the accused man stood, T'ien-ming stepped forward.

"Comrades, countrymen," he began. Immediately his short, handsome figure became the center of attention. Was this dark, assured young man with the quick, piercing eyes the same T'ien-ming they had seen running barefoot and ragged in the streets only a few bitter years ago? Was this the reticent laborer they had all stood guarantor for? Who would have thought a few days earlier that he could speak before a crowd? Yet now his words came naturally, passionately: "This is our chance. Remember how we were oppressed. The traitors seized our property. They beat us and kicked us. Now the whole world is ours. The government and the Eighth Route Army stand behind us. Let us speak out the bitter memories of the past. Let us see that the blood debt is repaid."

He paused for a moment. The peasants were listening to every word but gave no sign as to how they felt.

"In the past we were despised. Who did not feel it every day? Only now can we hold our heads up and speak like men. Look, the village is ours." He swept his arm in a wide arc that took in the crowd clad in dark cloth all patched and faded, the crumbling compound walls that bounded the square, the pond green with slime, the sagging doors on the weathered brick church, the partly caved-in roof of the Buddhist temple, the rutted street leading out to the fields, and the fields themselves with their crops trampled in the rainy season mud as a result of the battle—a vista of neglect, collapse, and decay universal enough to discourage even the stoutest heart, the most optimistic spirit. "What is there to be afraid of? When we beat down the traitors, we can stand up. We can divide the fruits of their corruption and start a new life."

He spoke plainly. His language and his accent were well understood by the people among whom he had been raised, but no one moved and no one spoke.

"Come now, who has evidence against this man?"

Again there was silence.

Kuei-ts'ai, the new vice-chairman of the village, found it intolerable. He jumped up, struck Kuo Te-yu on the jaw with the flat of his hand. "Tell the meeting how much you stole," he demanded.

The blow jarred the ragged crowd. It was as if an electric spark had tensed every muscle. Not in living memory had any peasant ever struck an official. A gasp, involuntary and barely audible, came from the people and above it a clear sharp "Ah" from an old man's throat.

Te-yu, in a spasm of fear, could utter only a few incoherent sentences. This so angered Kuei-ts'ai that he struck him again.

"One bag of tax grain..." Only those who were standing very close could hear Te-yu's hoarse whisper.

"One bag! You took only one bag?" shouted Kuei-ts'ai.

"But it was not my fault. There were seven pecks..."

"Now you deny it. Not even one bag. It was not my fault..." Kuei-ts'ai strode back and forth in front of Te-yu and mimicked his words.

Kuei-ts'ai, like T'ien-ming, was short and husky, but he could not be called handsome. He had a heavy brow, and a high-bridged nose that made his eyes appear extraordinarily deep-set. Now his whole face was contorted with anger like the head of a war god on a New Year's poster.

"Don't lie to us," he shouted, shaking his fist in the cringing man's face. The cry was taken up by the rest of the militiamen who had moved in behind Te-yu: "Don't lie to us."

This frightened the village head still more. Words gagged in his throat. Further blows only made him cringe. He bowed his head low before the meeting but revealed nothing of the graft he had wallowed in.

The people in the square waited fascinated, as if watching a play. They did not realize that in order for the plot to unfold they themselves had to mount the stage and speak out what was on their minds. No one moved to carry forward what Kuei-ts'ai had begun.

T'ien-ming was upset. Without the participation of hundreds the record could never be set straight. He called a hasty conference of his fellow village officers. They decided to put off the meeting until the next day. In the interim they hoped to mobilize at least a dozen people who would speak out and lead the way.

When T'ien-ming announced the postponement a murmur went through the crowd, but it was difficult to say whether it was a murmur of approval or a murmur of disappointment. Kuo Te-yu was led away to the village lockup, a crowd of small boys following closely on his heels. Slowly the people in the square dispersed until only a small knot of cadres and militiamen remained in front of the inn. There they vigorously discussed the failure of the people to step forward, until their children came to call them home for supper.

That evening T'ien-ming and Kuei-ts'ai called together small groups of poor peasants from various parts of the village and sought to learn what it was that was really holding them back. They soon found that the root of the trouble was fear. The landlords and the Kuomintang Party organization of the district, headed by Wang En-pao, son of the Carry-On Society's chairman, Wang Kuei-ching, already had a fairly clear idea of what was coming and had taken vigorous steps to forestall and divert the attack. They spread rumors to the effect that Yen Hsi-shan, with the help of the Japanese Army, would soon be back. That this was no idle boast had been made clear by Yen's acts. The old warlord had no sooner re-entered his old capital, Tai-yuan, than he ordered General Roshiro Sumita, Commander of all the Japanese forces in Shansi, to re-occupy his imposing wartime headquarters and mastermind the campaign for the recovery of the Liberated Areas. General Sumita threw 40,000 men into the battle. Lest anyone have the nerve to act in the face of this offensive, the gentry also let it be known that lists were being drawn up of active revolutionaries who were to be dispatched by firing squads when Yen's troops returned. Along with these threats went a campaign to discredit the resistance movement; rumors were spread that women were nationalized in the Liberated Areas, ancestral graves violated, and all peasants forced to eat *ta kuo fan* or "food out of one big pot." The other side of this coin was the claim that collaboration had really been resistance, that by bending temporarily to Japan's will the puppets had worked for national salvation along a curved path. Was not the final surrender of the Japanese proof of this?

All this activity was not without effect. Many peasants who might have been eager to strike a blow against collaborators hesitated. They were afraid to act. They had little confidence that the Eighth Route Army, soldiers without boots, without helmets, and without heavy weapons could hold the region. Fighting was still heavy around Changchih, only ten miles away. Who could tell? Perhaps the "sky would change again" and the old regime would return with fire and sword. Was it not better to lie low and see how things turned out? The old reluctance to move against the power of the gentry, the fear of ultimate defeat and terrible reprisal that had been seared into the consciousness of so many

generations lay like a cloud over their minds and hearts.

The mere collapse of the fort and the arrest of the puppet leaders were clearly not enough to bring the peasants of Long Bow into action. The mobilization of the population could spread only slowly and in concentric circles like the waves on the surface of a pond when a stone is thrown in. The stone in this case was the small group of *chi chi fen-tse* or "activists," as the cadres of the new administration and the core of its militia were called.

That evening they talked plain facts to the selected people in the small groups that they had called together. They discussed "change of sky." Could the Kuomintang troops or the Japanese ever come back? "Even if they do," T'ien-ming said, "we younger men can go off to the higher mountains with the Eighth Route Army, so why be afraid? If we don't move now, the chance will be lost." He reviewed again the evil record of the traitor clique, the death of So-tzu and Lai-pao, and the beatings suffered by himself, Fu-yuan, and countless others, the seized grain, the forced labor.

Emboldened by T'ien-ming's words, other peasants began to speak out. They recalled what Te-yu had done to them personally. Several vowed to speak up and accuse him in the morning. After the meetings broke up, the passage of time worked its own leaven. In many a hovel and tumble-down house talk continued well past midnight. Some people were so excited they did not sleep at all. As the village cocks began to crow they found themselves still discussing whether or not to act, and if so, how.

On the following day the meeting was livelier by far. It began with a sharp argument as to who would make the first accusation and T'ien-ming found it difficult to keep order. Before Te-yu had a chance to reply to any questions a crowd of young men, among whom were several militiamen, surged forward ready to beat him.

At this crucial moment the district leader, Yellow Dog Kuo, strode between the young men and their victim. He blocked the assault with his own body and then explained to the crowd that the puppet leader was but a "dog's leg"—a poor peasant who had been used. To kill him would gain them nothing. It was the manipulators behind him who had to be exposed.

"Let him tell what he knows," Kuo urged. "Let him expose the others."

Once again T'ien-ming demanded that the prisoner talk.

This time Te-yu finally found his tongue and spoke out so that the whole gathering could hear him, but he rambled so much in his explanation, and went into such detail making clear the extenuating circumstances of his every act that no coherent account of money and grain emerged. Furthermore his own statements and the memory of his accusers conflicted. The cadres decided to charge him with ten hundredweight of grain for good measure and set his case aside for the time being. They searched his home for the grain that same afternoon and swapped it in Lucheng for four rifles for the militia.

With this inconclusive action the local struggle was called off for a few days while the more important and notorious puppet leaders of the district were brought before large representative meetings. Shih Jen-pao, of the Fourth Column, had unfortunately escaped, but Wen Ch'i-yung, commander of the puppet garrison in Long Bow fort, Shen Chi-mei, head of the Fifth District police, and Ch'ing T'ien-hsing, his assistant, were brought face to face with 190 peasants from all over the district—more than ten from each village—who came together in Long Bow's square as delegates from their respective communities. These were the people who had suffered the most from puppet depredations, whose homes had been looted, whose sons and husbands had been killed, whose wives and daughters had been seduced or raped.

Hundreds of accusations were made that day against the leading traitors and all those who worked with them. A Long Bow woman told how her son, Chin-mao, had been killed. When she came to the part where the police threw him, gagged and bound, into a well, she broke down weeping and could not go on. Many in the crowd wept with her. Shen Ch'uan-te, also of Long Bow, charged the puppet regime with the death of his brother. "My brother was killed by the Eighth Route soldiers," he said, "but they killed him because he was carrying a message for the traitors. The traitors forced him to carry it. Why didn't they carry their own messages? They are the real killers."

Yellow Dog Kuo finally asked, "What is the origin of these murders? Who stood back of these puppets? How was it possible for their puny troops to have such power? Who served as their eyes and ears? Who informed on the peasants and exposed them to attack?"

Many then spoke out and said it was Shen Chi-mei and the landlords who backed him that lay at the root of the disaster that had befallen them. Before the meeting ended, Commander Wen and Police Officer Shen were condemned to death. They were taken to an empty field at the edge of the village and there, in sight of the fort they had done so much to build and to defend, they were shot. While the dead Shen Chi-mei lay still warm on the ground where he fell, a Long Bow militiaman, Yu-hsing, stripped a sweater off his corpse. Someone else took off his shoes. They left the body to his relatives to bury as they would.

Ch'ing T'ien-hsing, the third prisoner, was not sentenced that day. He was handed over to the County Court at Lucheng for investigation. He escaped from the lockup in the middle of the night but the militiamen from Long Bow who had taken him to Lucheng the day before, hunted him down, caught him in Horse Square, and killed him on the spot.

During the next few days the militia led thousands of people in a search for all the property that the soldiers of the Fourth Column had stolen. The loot had been placed in various village homes for safekeeping. Many families volunteered information that led to its discovery. Several hundred suits of clothes, several thousand feet of cloth, and many other valuable household articles were recovered and returned to their rightful owners. A large cache of this looted property was found in Landlord Wang Lai-hsun's home. The land, tools, stock, and household effects of the executed men were confiscated.

62

U.S. Reports on China

During World War II John S. Service and John Paton Davies, Foreign Service officers for the State Department stationed in Chungking, offered realistic, if pessimistic, accounts of the position of Jiang Jieshi and the Guomintang (GMT). Their analysis was not limited to the situation within Chiang's government but also its prospects for dealing with the communists after the war was over.

Discussion Questions

1. What factors endangered the base of the GMT among the people?

2. How were Chiang and the GMT trying to deal with the problems they faced? Would you agree with Service that their policies were suicidal?

3. Why did Service and Davies seem to think that a communist victory was inevitable? Was there any realistic hope that Chiang could prevail?

4. With this background in mind, what do you think would have been the position of the United States if Chiang had managed to hold out in some region of China? Could the U.S. have guaranteed a GMT victory over the communists?

U.S. Foreign Service Officer Reports

John S. Service and John Paton Davies

June 20, 1944 (Service)

The position of the Kuomintang and the Generalissimo is weaker than it has been for the past ten years. China faces economic collapse. This is causing disintegration of the army and the government's administrative apparatus. It is one of the chief causes of growing political unrest. The Generalissimo is losing the support of a China which, by unity in the face of violent aggression, found a new and unexpected strength during the first two years of the war with Japan. Internal weaknesses are becoming accentuated and there is taking place a reversal of the process of unification.

1. Morale is low and discouragement widespread. There is a general feeling of hopelessness.

2. The authority of the Central Government is weakening in the areas away from the larger cities. Government mandates and measures of control cannot be enforced and remain ineffective. It is becoming difficult for the Government to collect enough food for its huge army and bureaucracy.

3. The governmental and military structure is being permeated and demoralized from top to bottom by corruption, unprecedented in scale and openness.

4. The intellectual and salaried classes, who have suffered the most heavily from inflation, are in danger of liquidation. The academic groups suffer not only the attrition and demoralization of economic stress; the weight of years of political control and repression is robbing them of the intellectual vigor and leadership they once had.

5. Peasant resentment of the abuses of conscription, tax collection and other arbitrary impositions has been widespread and is growing. The danger is ever-increasing that past sporadic outbreaks of banditry and agrarian unrest may increase in scale and find political motivation... .

9. The Kuomintang is losing the respect and support of the people by its school policies and its refusal to heed progressive criticism. It seems unable to revivify itself with fresh blood, and its unchanging leadership shows a growing ossification and loss of a sense of reality. To combat the dissensions and cliquism within the Party, which grow more rather than less acute, the leadership is turning toward the reactionary and unpopular Chen brothers clique.

10. The Generalissimo shows a similar loss of flexibility and a hardening of narrowly conservative views: His growing megalomania and his unfortunate attempts to be "sage" as well as leader—shown, for instance, by "China's Destiny" and his

From "U.S. Foreign Service Officer Reports," by John S. Service and John Paton Davies from *United States Relations With China*, with Special Reference to the period 1944–1949. Published by the U.S. Department of State, Washington, D. C., 1949.

book on economics—have forfeited the respect of many intellectuals, who enjoy in China a position of unique influence. Criticism of his dictatorship is becoming outspoken.

In the face of the grave crisis with which it is confronted the Kuomintang is ceasing to be the unifying and progressive force in Chinese society, the role in which it made its greatest contribution to modern China... .

On the internal political front the desire of the Kuomintang leaders to perpetuate their own power overrides all other considerations. The result is the enthronement of reaction.

The Kuomintang continues to ignore the great political drive within the country for democratic reform. The writings of the Generalissimo and the Party press show that they have no real understanding of that term. Constitutionalism remains an empty promise for which the only "preparation" is a halfhearted attempt to establish an unpopular and undemocratic system of local self-government based on collective responsibility and given odium by Japanese utilization in Manchuria and other areas under their control.

Questions basic to the future of democracy such as the form of the Constitution and the composition and election of the National Congress remain the dictation of the Kuomintang. There is no progress toward the fundamental conditions of freedom of expression and recognition of non-Kuomintang groups. Even the educational and political advantages of giving power and democratic character to the existing but impotent Peoples Political Council are ignored.

The Kuomintang shows no intention of relaxing the authoritarian controls on which its present power depends. Far from discarding reducing the paraphernalia of a police state— the multiple and omnipresent secret police organizations, the Gendarmerie, and so forth—it continues to strengthen them as its last resort for internal security... .

These apparently suicidal policies of the Kuomintang have their roots in the composition and nature of the Party.

In view of the above it becomes pertinent to ask *why* the Kuomintang has lost its power of leadership; *why* it neither wishes actively to wage war against Japan itself nor to cooperate whole-heartedly with the American Army in China; and *why* it has ceased to be capable of unifying the country.

The answer to all these questions is to be found in the present composition and nature of the Party. Politically, a classical and definitive American description becomes ever more true; the Kuomintang is a congerie of conservative political cliques interested primarily in the preservation of their own power against all outsiders and in jockeying for position among themselves. Economically, the Kuomintang rests on the narrow base of the rural-gentry-landlords and militarists, the higher ranks of the government bureaucracy, and merchant bankers having intimate connections with the government bureaucrats. This base has actually contracted during the war. The Kuomintang no longer commands, as it once did, the unequivocal support of China's industrialists, who as a group have been much weakened economically, and hence politically, by the Japanese seizure of the coastal cities... .

December 9, 1944 (Davies)

...The Generalissimo realizes that if he accedes to the Communist terms for a coalition government, they will sooner or later dispossess him and his Kuomintang of power. He will therefore not, unless driven to an extremity, form a genuine coalition government. He will seek to retain his present government, passively wait out the war and conserve his strength, knowing that the Communist issue must eventually be joined.

The Communists, on their part, have no interest in reaching an agreement with the Generalissimo short of a genuine coalition government. They recognize that Chiang's position is crumbling, that they may before long receive substantial Russian support and that if they have patience they will succeed to authority in at least North China... .

The Communists would, inevitably, win such a war because the foreign powers, including the United States, which would support the Government, could not feasibly supply enough aid to compensate for the organic weaknesses of the Government.

January 23, 1943 (Service)

...Assuming that open hostilities are for the time being averted, the eventual defeat and withdrawal of the Japanese will leave the Kuomintang still confronted with the Communists solidly entrenched in most of North China (East Kansu, North Shensi, Shansi, South Chahar, Hopei, Shantung, North Kiangsu and North Anhwei). In addition the Communists will be in a position to move into the vacuum created by the Japanese withdrawal from Suiyan, Jehol and Manchuria, in all of which areas there is already some Communist activity. In the rest of China they will have the sympathy of elements among the liberals, intellectuals, and students.

...There is undoubtedly a strong revulsion in the mind of the average, non-party Chinese to the idea of renewed civil war and the Kuomintang may indeed have difficulty with the loyalty and effectiveness of its conscript troops.

October 9, 1944 (Service)

Just as the Japanese Army cannot crush these militant people now, so also will Kuomintang force fail in the future. With their new arms and organization, knowledge of their own strength, and determination to keep what they have been fighting for, these people—now some 90 million and certain to be many more before the Kuomintang can reach them—will resist oppression. They are not Communists. They do not want separation or independence. But at present they regard the Kuomintang—from their own experience—as oppressors; and the Communists as their leaders and benefactors.

With this great popular base, the Communists likewise cannot be eliminated. Kuomintang attempts to do so by force must mean a complete denial of democracy. This will strengthen the ties of the Communists with the people: a Communist victory will be inevitable... .

From the basic fact that the Communists have built up popular support of a magnitude and depth which makes their elimination impossible, *we must draw the conclusion that the Communists will have a certain and important share in China's future... .* I suggest the future conclusion that unless the Kuomintang goes as far as the Communists in political and economic reform, and otherwise proves itself able to contest this leadership of the people (none of which it yet shows signs of being willing or able to do), the Communists will be the dominant force in China within a comparatively few years.

63

The Foolish Old Man Who Removed the Mountains

During the last months of World War II in the Pacific, Mao Tse-tung (Mao Zedong) wrote the following brief article during a meeting of the Communist Party Congress. In it he explains what had been accomplished and what remained to be done. He also addresses the role of the United States on the scene in China. This article quickly became a classic of Chinese communist literature and was especially popular among the Red Guards during the Cultural Revolution after 1966.

Discussion Questions

1. What spirit do you think Mao was trying to encourage among the Chinese people with the age-old story of the foolish old man?

2. What do you think he meant by the phrase "self-criticism?"

3. Mao alludes to the democratic forces and the reactionary counter-current in the world—what or whom is he referring to?

4. Toward the end of the article he mentions "three major contradictions in the old world;" what are the three contradictions and what is the old world?

June 11, 1945

We have had a very successful congress. We have done three things. First, we have decided on the line of our Party, which is boldly to mobilize the masses and expand the people's forces so that, under the leadership of our Party, they will defeat the Japanese aggressors, liberate the whole people and build a new-democratic China. Second, we have adopted the new, Party Constitution. Third, we have elected the leading body of the Party—the Central Committee. Henceforth our task is to lead the whole membership in carrying out the Party line. Ours has been a congress of victory, a congress of unity. The delegates have made excellent comments on the three reports. Many comrades have undertaken self-criticism; with unity as the objective unity has been achieved through selfcriticism. This congress is a model of unity, of self-criticism and of inner-Party democracy.

When the congress closes, many comrades will be leaving for their posts and the various war fronts. Comrades, wherever you go, you should propagate the line of the congress and, through the members of the Party, explain it to the broad masses.

Our aim in propagating the line of the congress is to build up the confidence of the whole Party and the entire people in the certain triumph of the revolution. We must first raise the political consciousness of the vanguard so that, resolute and unafraid of sacrifice, they will surmount every difficulty to win victory. But this is not enough; we must also arouse the political consciousness of the entire people so that they may willingly and gladly fight together with us for victory. We should fire the whole people with the conviction that China belongs not to the reactionaries but to the Chinese people. There is an ancient Chinese fable called "The Foolish Old Man Who Removed the Mountains." It tells of an old man who lived in northern China long, long ago and was known as the Foolish Old Man of North Mountain. His house faced south and beyond his doorway stood the two great peaks, Taihang and Wangwu, obstructing the way. With great determination, he led his sons in digging up these mountains hoe in hand. Another graybeard, known as the Wise Old Man, saw them and said derisively, "How silly of you to do this! It is quite impossible for you few to dig up these two huge mountains." The Foolish Old Man replied, "When I die, my sons will carry on; when they die, there will be my grandsons, and then their sons and grandsons, and so on to infinity. High as they are, the mountains cannot grow any higher and with every bit we dig, they will be that much lower. Why can't we clear them away?" Having refuted the Wise Old Man's wrong view, he went on digging every day, unshaken in his conviction. God was moved by this, and he sent down two angels, who carried the mountains away on their backs. Today, two big mountains lie like a dead weight on the Chinese people. One is imperialism, the other is feudalism. The Chinese Communist Party has long made up its mind to dig them up. We must persevere and work unceasingly, and we, too, will touch God's heart. Our God is none other than the masses of the Chinese people. If they stand up and dig together with us, why can't these two mountains be cleared away?

Yesterday, in a talk with two Americans who were leaving for the United States, I said that the U.S. government was trying to undermine us and this would not be permitted. We oppose the U.S. government's policy of supporting Chiang Kai-shek against the Communists. But we must draw a distinction, firstly, between the people of the United States and their government and, secondly, within the U.S. government between the policy-makers and their subordinates. I said to these two Americans, "Tell the policy-makers in your government that we forbid you Americans to enter the Liberated Areas because your policy is to support Chiang Kai-shek against the Communists, and we have to be on our guard. You can come to the Liberated Areas if your purpose is to fight Japan, but there must first be an agreement. We will not permit you to nose around everywhere. Since Patrick J. Hurley has publicly declared against co-operation with the Chinese Communist Party, why do you still want to come and prowl around in our Liberated Areas?"

The U.S. government's policy of supporting Chiang Kai-shek against the Communists shows the brazenness of the U.S. reactionaries. But all the scheming of the reactionaries, whether Chinese or foreign, to prevent the Chinese people from achieving victory is doomed to failure. The democratic forces are the main current in the world today, while reaction is only a counter-current. The reactionary counter-current is trying to swamp the main current of national independence and people's democracy,

but it can never become the main current. Today, there are still three major contradictions in the old world, as Stalin pointed out long ago: first, the contradiction between the proletariat and the bourgeoisie in the imperialist countries; second, the contradiction between the various imperialist powers; and third, the contradiction between the colonial and semicolonial countries and the imperialist metropolitan countries. Not only do these three contradictions continue to exist but they are becoming more acute and widespread. Because of their existence and growth, the time will come when the reactionary anti-Soviet, anti-Communist and anti-democratic counter-current still in existence today will be swept away.

At this moment two congresses are being held in China, the Sixth National Congress of the Kuomintang and the Seventh National Congress of the Communist Party. They have completely different aims: the aim of one is to liquidate the Communist Party and all the other democratic forces in China and thus to plunge China into darkness; the aim of the other is to overthrow Japanese imperialism and its lackeys, the Chinese feudal forces, and build a new-democratic China and thus to lead China to light. These two lines are in conflict with each other. We firmly believe that, led by the Chinese Communist Party and guided by the line of its Seventh Congress, the Chinese people will achieve complete victory, while the Kuomintang's counterrevolutionary line will inevitably fail.

64

Gandhi: Indian Home Rule

Hind Swaraj (Indian Home Rule) was Gandhi's first complete statement of his social and political ideals. It was written in 1909 in the form of an imagined dialogue between Gandhi [Editor] and a skeptical friend [Reader]. Major themes presented in the excerpts below are the contrast between India and England, the nature of modern civilization and the technique of passive resistance.

Discussion Questions

1. What does Gandhi mean by "civilization?"

2. What does he think are the evils which have grown out of modern civilization? Why does he think it is doomed?

3. Why does Gandhi think that the force of arms is not the best way to achieve home rule?

4. How does he define "passive resistance?" Why does he think it is the only path to follow?

Editor: Let us first consider what state of things is described by the word "civilization." Its true test lies in the fact that people living in it make bodily welfare the object of life. We will take some examples. The people of Europe today live in better-built houses than they did a hundred years ago. This is considered an emblem of civilization, and this is also a matter to promote bodily happiness. Formerly, they wore skins, and used spears as their weapons. Now, they wear long trousers, and, for embellishing their bodies, they wear a variety of clothing, and, instead of spears, they carry with them revolvers containing five or more chambers. If people of a certain country, who have hitherto not been in the habit of wearing much clothing, boots, etc., adopt European clothing, they are supposed to have become civilized out of savagery. Formerly, in Europe, people plowed their lands mainly by manual labor. Now, one man can plow a vast tract by means of steam engines and can thus amass great wealth. This is called a sign of civilization. Formerly, only a few men wrote valuable books. Now, anybody writes and prints anything he likes and poisons people's minds. Formerly, men traveled in wagons. Now, they fly through the air in trains at the rate of four hundred and more miles per day. This is considered the height of civilization. It has been stated that, as men progress, they shall be able to travel in airships and reach any part of the world in a few hours. Men will not need the use of their minds and feet. They will press a button, and they will have their clothing by their side. They will press another button, and they will have their newspaper. A third, and a motor-car will be in waiting for them. They will have a variety of delicately dished up food. Everything will be done by machinery. Formerly, when people wanted to fight with one another, they measured between them their bodily strength; now, it is possible to take away thousands of lives by one man working behind a gun from a hill. This is civilization. Formerly, men worked in the open air only as much as they liked. Now thousands of workmen meet together and for the sake of maintenance work in factories or mines. Their condition is worse than that of beasts. They are obliged to work, at the risk of their lives, at most dangerous occupations, for the sake of millionaires. Formerly, men were made slaves under physical compulsion. Now they are enslaved by temptation of money and of the luxuries that money can buy. There are now diseases of which people never dreamt before, and an army of doctors is engaged in finding out their cures, and so hospitals have increased. This is a test of civilization. Formerly, special messengers were required and much expense was incurred in order to send letters; today, anyone can abuse his fellow by means of a letter for one penny. True, at the same cost, one can send one's thanks also. Formerly, people had two or three meals consisting of home-made bread and vegetables; now, they require something to eat every two hours so that they have hardly leisure for anything else. What more need I say? All this you can ascertain from several authoritative books. These are all true tests of civilization. And if anyone speaks to the contrary, know that he is ignorant. This civilization takes note neither of morality nor of religion. Its votaries calmly state that their business is not to teach religion. Some even consider it to be a superstitious growth. Others put on the cloak of religion, and prate about morality. But, after twenty years' experience, I have come to the conclusion that immorality is often taught in the name of morality. Even a child can understand that in all I have described above there can be no inducement to morality. Civilization seeks to increase bodily comforts, and it fails miserably even in doing so.

This civilization is irreligion, and it has taken such a hold on the people in Europe that those who are in it appear to be half-mad. They lack real physical strength or courage. They keep up their energy by intoxication. They can hardly be happy in solitude. Women, who should be the queens of households, wander in the streets or they slave away in factories. For the sake of a pittance, half a million women in England alone are laboring under trying circumstances in factories or similar institutions. This awful fact is one of the causes of the daily growing suffragette movement.

This civilization is such that one has only to be patient and it will be self-destroyed. According to the teaching of Mahomed this would be considered a Satanic Civilization. Hinduism calls it the Black Age. I cannot give you an adequate conception of it. It is eating into the vitals of the English nation. It must be shunned. Parliaments are really emblems of slavery. If you will sufficiently think over this, you will entertain the same opinion and cease to blame the English. They rather deserve our sympathy. They are a shrewd nation and I therefore believe that they will cast off the evil. They are enterprising and industrious, and their mode of thought is not inherently immoral. Neither are they bad at heart. I therefore respect them. Civilization is not an incurable disease,

but it should never be forgotten that the English people are at present afflicted by it.

Reader: I cannot follow this. There seems little doubt that we shall have to expel the English by force of arms. So long as they are in the country we cannot rest... .

Editor: ...I believe that you want the millions of India to be happy, not that you [merely] want the reins of government in your hands. If that be so, we have to consider only one thing: how can the millions obtain self-rule? You will admit that people under several Indian princes are being ground down. The latter mercilessly crush them. Their tyranny is greater than that of the English, and if you want such tyranny in India, then we shall never agree. My patriotism does not teach me that I am to allow people to be crushed under the heel of Indian princes if only the English retire. If I have power, I should resist the tyranny of Indian princes just as much as that of the English. By patriotism I mean the welfare of the whole people, and if I could secure it at the hands of the English, I should bow down my head to them. If any Englishman dedicated his life to securing the freedom of India, resisting tyranny, and serving the Indians, I should welcome that Englishman as an Indian.

Again [you say that] India can fight ... only when she has arms. You have not considered this problem at all. The English are splendidly armed; that does not frighten me, but it is clear that, to pit ourselves against them in arms, thousands of Indians must be armed. If such a thing be possible, how many years will it take? Moreover, to arm India on a large scale is to Europeanize it. Then her condition will be just as pitiable as that of Europe. This means, in short, that India must accept European civilization, and if that is what we want, the best thing is that we have among us those who are so well trained in that civilization. We will then fight for a few rights, will get what we can and so pass our days. But the fact is that the Indian nation will not adopt arms, and it is well that it does not.

> Introducing the concept of "soul-force" or "passive resistance," Gandhi argued that it is the only method by which home rule can be regained.

Thousands, indeed tens of thousands, depend for their existence on a very active working of this force. Little quarrels of millions of families in their daily lives disappear before the exercise of this force. Hundreds of nations live in peace. History does not and cannot take note of this fact. History is really a record of every interruption of the even working of the force of love or of the soul. Two brothers quarrel; one of them repents and reawakens the love that was lying dormant in him; the two again begin to live in peace; nobody takes note of this. But if the two brothers, through the intervention of solicitors or some other reason, take up arms or go to law—which is another form of the exhibition of brute force—their doings would be immediately noticed in the press, they would be the talk of their neighbors and would probably go down to history. And what is true of families and communities is true for nations. There is no reason to believe that there is one law for families and another for nations. History, then, is a record of an interruption of the course of nature. Soulforce, being natural, is not noted in history.

Reader: According to what you say, it is plain that instances of this kind of passive resistance are not to be found in history. It is necessary to understand this passive resistance more fully. It will be better, therefore, if you enlarge upon it.

Editor: Passive resistance is a method of securing rights by personal suffering; it is the reverse of resistance by arms. When I refuse to do a thing that is repugnant to my conscience, I use soul-force. For instance, the government of the day has passed a law which is applicable to me. I do not like it. If by using violence I force the government to repeal the law, I am employing what may be termed body-force. If I do not obey the law and accept the penalty for its breach, I use soul-force. It involves sacrifice of self.

Everybody admits that sacrifice of self is infinitely superior to sacrifice of others. Moreover, if this kind of force is used in a cause that is unjust, only the person using it suffers. He does not make others suffer for his mistakes. Men have before now done many things which were subsequently found to have been wrong. No man can claim that he is absolutely in the right or that a particular thing is wrong because he thinks so, but it is wrong for him so long as that is his deliberate judgment. It is therefore meet that he should not do that which he knows to be wrong, and suffer the consequence whatever it may be. This is the key to the use of soulforce.

Reader: You would then disregard laws— this is rank disloyalty. We have always been considered a law-abiding nation. You seem to be going even beyond the extremists. They say that we must obey the laws that have been passed, but that if the laws be bad, we must drive out the lawgivers even by force.

Editor: Whether I go beyond them or whether I do not is a matter of no consequence to either of us. We simply want to find out what is right and to act accordingly. The real meaning of the statement that we are a law-abiding nation is that we are passive resisters. When we do not like certain laws, we do not break the heads of law-givers but we suffer and do not submit to the laws. That we should obey laws whether good or bad is a new-fangled notion. There was no such thing in former days. The people disregarded laws they did not like and suffered the penalties for their breach. It is contrary to our manhood if we obey laws repugnant to our conscience. Such teaching is opposed to religion and means slavery. If the government were to ask us to go about without any clothing, should we do so? If I were a passive resister, I would say to them that I would have nothing to do with their law. But we have so forgotten ourselves and become so compliant that we do not mind any degrading law.

A man who has realized his manhood, who fears only God, will fear no one else. Manmade laws are not necessarily binding on him. Even the government does not expect any such thing from us. They do not say: "You must do such and such a thing," but they say: "If you do not do it, we will punish you." We are sunk so low that we fancy that it is our duty, and our religion to do what the the law lays down. If man will only realize that it is unmanly to obey laws that are unjust, no man's tyranny will enslave him. This is the key to self-rule or home-rule.

It is a superstition and ungodly thing to believe that an act of a majority binds a minority. Many examples can be given in which acts of majorities will be found to have been wrong and those of minorities to have been right. All reforms owe their origin to the initiation of minorities in opposition to majorities. If among a band of robbers a knowledge of robbing is obligatory, is a pious man to accept the obligation? So long as the superstition that men should obey unjust laws exists, so long will their slavery exist. And a passive resister alone can remove such a superstition.

To use brute-force, to use gunpowder, is contrary to passive resistance, for it means that we want our opponent to do by force that which we desire but he does not. And if such a use of force is justifiable, surely he is entitled to do likewise by us. And so we should never come to an agreement. We may simply fancy, like the blind horse moving in a circle round a mill, that we are making progress. Those who believe that they are not bound to obey laws which are repugnant to their conscience have only the

remedy of passive resistance open to them. Any other must lead to disaster.

Reader: From what you say I deduce that passive resistance is a splendid weapon of the weak, but that when they are strong they may take up arms.

Editor: This is gross ignorance. Passive resistance, that is, soul-force, is matchless. It is superior to the force of arms. How, then, can it be considered only a weapon of the weak? Physical-force men are strangers to the courage that is requisite in a passive resister. Do you believe that a coward can ever disobey a law that he dislikes? Extremists are considered to be advocates of brute force. Why do they, then, talk about obeying laws? I do not blame them. They can say nothing else. When they succeed in driving out the English and they themselves become governors, they will want you and me to obey their laws. And that is a fitting thing for their constitution. But a passive resister will say he will not obey a law that is against his conscience, even though he may be blown to pieces at the mouth of a cannon.

What do you think? Wherein is courage required—in blowing others to pieces from behind a cannon, or with a smiling face to approach a cannon and be blown to pieces? Who is the true warrior—he who keeps death always as a bosom-friend, or he who controls the death of others? Believe me that a man devoid of courage and manhood can never be a passive resister.

This however, I will admit: that even a man weak in body is capable of offering this resistance. One man can offer it just as well as millions. Both men and women can indulge in it. It does not require the training of an army; it needs no jiu-jitsu. Control over the mind is alone necessary, and when that is attained, man is free like the king of the forest and his very glance withers the enemy.

Passive resistance is an all-sided sword, it can be used anyhow; it blesses him who uses it and him against whom it is used. Without drawing a drop of blood it produces far-reaching results. It never rusts and cannot be stolen. Competition between passive resisters does not exhaust. The sword of passive resistance does not require a scabbard. It is strange indeed that you should consider such a weapon to be a weapon merely of the weak.

65

Imperialism: The Civilizing Mission

One of the ideological motives for imperialism in the 19th and 20th centuries was what has been called the "civilizing mission." Western nations, believing themselves to be superior societies, felt it was their duty to bring civilization to other regions of the world. The following selection analyzes the success, or non-success, of these missions.

Already right after World War I, some British questioned the ability of Europeans to attain their goals.

One British correspondent for The Times of London in 1919 wrote:

"Many people 'think the local inhabitants will welcome us because we have saved them' and that the country only needs developing to repay our expenditure, but this is clearly wrong, since 'we are asking the Arab to exchange his pride and independence for a little Western civilization'."

T.E. Lawrence, a key British figure in the Middle East, said in 1920:

"in Iraq we have been 'led into a trap from which it will be hard to escape with dignity and honor. …Things have been far worse than we have been told, our administration more bloody and inefficient than the public knows. …We are today not far from disaster'."

Discussion Questions

1. What are the difficulties in implementing a "civilizing mission" in the non-Western world?

2. What are the differences between direct and indirect rule? What are the difficulties involved in each?

3. This article was written in March of 2003 when the American invasion of Iraq had just begun. Have the Americans and their coalitions allies been more successful than the British in the early 20th century?

Lessons of 'Civilizing Missions' Are Mostly Unlearned

According to the latest official reports, the United States envisages a short, "necessary occupation" in Iraq, lasting months and intends to have "the structure of a post-Saddam society in place within a year." If this occurs, the world will witness an exercise in social engineering on a scale of intensity never before contemplated, still less achieved.

Unfortunately, history demonstrates that there is room for skepticism. In the 19th century, when Europe's great modern empires were assembled, Britain and France formulated "civilizing missions" that were equally wide ranging and optimistic. Having invaded occupied and annexed, they too had a peace to win.

Everything we know about the "civilizing mission" of the 19th century reveals how difficult it was to convert others to different ways of thinking, and how consistently the difficulties were underestimated.

After defeating Napoleon in 1815, Britain emerged as the strongest power of the day, and proceeded to launch the world's first comprehensive development plan. The liberal ideals of free trade and constitutional government would transform the world. The British expected that, by showing the light, others in foreign lands would surely follow the way. Yet establishing a liberal, progressive order, even among congenial partners in areas of European settlement — like Canada, Australia and New Zealand — was an arduous task that took generations.

Elsewhere, in the non-Western world, optimism that the moral force of Victorian values would easily convert others, if not to Christianity then to free trade and constitutional government, faded as the century advanced.

When disillusion set in, the recipients were blamed, but never the plan. States that failed to conform were cordoned off or incorporated according to estimates of value and cost. The Ottoman Empire, which sprawled across the greater part of the Middle East, was one example of disappointed expectations. The Ottomans were exposed to the benefits of free trade and offered a program of what today would be called structural adjustment.

But the chance was missed. The empire fell into debt and became the "sick man of Europe." It was propped up by the great powers, and staggered on until World War I brought its demise. The alternative was thought to be anarchy, which would have damaged foreign interests in the region.

Across the globe, brief occupations had the habit of becoming long-term commitments. Early in the 19th century, Egypt had pushed through a program of modernization that promoted export development and secured greater political autonomy from its Ottoman overlords. But the white hope of European improvers became a white elephant in 1876, when Egypt was unable to service its foreign debt.

Unlike the rest of the Ottoman empire, however, Egypt was judged to have potential that could be realized at little cost. In 1882 the British moved in for what was to be a short stay. They claimed to be reluctant to act, but had been compelled by irresponsible elements in Egypt that threatened the onward march of civilization.

Britain's proclaimed motives were phrased in high-minded generalities. Prime Minister William Gladstone once said this was a "just war, a holy war." Regime change was quick and easy. But the brief occupation lasted three-quarters of a century, and Britain's initially limited aims reached the point where the security of Egypt required annexation of the Sudan too.

Even when installed, colonial rulers too often lacked legitimacy. They could command acquiescence but not consent. The gratitude they expected for bringing the benefits of the West to the Rest was either not forthcoming or was short-lived. So they devised alternative means of control.

One strategy, direct rule, had a strong military component; another, indirect rule, relied on local collaborators. Direct rule, which was more likely to be oppressive, usually created a focus for resistance, and even terrorism. It was also costly.

Indirect rule was less visible and far cheaper, but it obliged the colonial authorities to meddle in local society and to juggle endlessly with landlords, warriors, bureaucrats, merchants and peasants.

After a full century of endeavor, Britain's development plan was no more than a qualified success, even when viewed in a good light. And by the middle of the 20th century, when the idea of empire was fading, it was apparent that the coercion and the juggling had ignited the forces of opposition that fed into colonial nationalism.

It does not follow that the difficulties experienced by Britain's attempt to manage the world will apply to the United States Time and circumstance are different. The most striking difference is the unprecedented military might of the world's first hyperpower. It might be concluded that the United States possesses a level of technology and know-how that will enable it to overcome the obstacles that hampered the civilizing missions of the European empires.

But the problem can be looked at from a different angle. Recent experience does not suggest that the United States has developed a talent for bringing freedom and democracy to subject peoples. Reconstruction in Afghanistan still has a long way to go, and has run into familiar difficulties.

The same may be true of Iraq. Whatever the initial reception, it is inevitable that foreign rule will be resented, especially a postcolonial world. Proclamations of democracy and freedom may satisfy the public at home but will be meaningless unless made to work in Iraq.

How should this be done? Direct rule, as the British found, can be costly. Moreover, people cannot be forced into freedom: they have to grow into it. Opting for indirect rule will drag the United States into the complexities of local politics and will compromise the principles of reconstruction.

When the British occupied Iraq in 1918 and then ruled it under a mandate from the League of Nations, they quickly realized that they needed to cooperate with the Sunni minority, which had filled the senior ranks of the military and civil service. The British merely took over from the Ottomans; the United States may find itself reinventing Britain's formula for indirect rule.

It is also important to consider the interests as well as the principles of the ruling power. Large contracts for reconstruction have reportedly already been issued to American companies. It is inconceivable that these companies will invest heavily in Iraq without adequate political security. That must come either from direct rule by Washington, which would be unpopular, or from a compliant government.

Can a compliant government also be a democratic one? If democracy means, minimally, one person one vote, then power is likely to shift away from the Sunni minority and toward the Shiites and the Kurds. The problem here is that the Shiites have close affiliations with Iran, which is on the axis of evil, and that the Kurds have their own agenda — and oil resources.

With its occupation of Iraq, the United States faces some longstanding imperial problems. Since it has yet to announce any novel solutions, is it possible that some of the old imperial remedies will be applied?

66

The Search for Peace in the Middle East

The following selection presents a succinct, yet balanced view of the long conflict between the Arabs and the Jews. While this pamphlet, first published in 1966, does not include some of the recent developments with regards the Palestinian issue, it does explain the fundamental historical, political, religious and economic grievances of each side in the dispute. As you read, consider those elements that the antagonists have in common, as well as those which divide them.

Discussion Questions

1. Of the claims that each side makes to its right to Palestine, which is most convincing to you and why? Which of the claims seems the least valid? Why?

2. What events, agreements, organizations and personalities would you identify as being the most important in understanding the background of the Arab-Israeli conflict?

3. Have any of the claims mentioned in the selection been addressed, or is no longer in dispute? What additional arguments would you add to each side?

Background

The Jews and the Arabs are ancient and long-suffering peoples, and their sufferings continue. Both have been cruelly dealt with by peoples of other cultures, and both are still subject to manipulation by forces beyond their control. Both are distrustful of other peoples and of each other, as they seek to establish their own identity, their right to respect, freedom and national self-development.

It is one of the great ironies of history that the roots of the present Arab-Jewish struggle should have grown, not in a poisoned soil of ancient mutual animosities, but in the mistreatment each has received at the hands of others. The Jews and the Arabs are Semitic cousins, share cultural traits and traditions, and through long centuries lived in relative peace with one another even during periods when Jews were subject to sustained persecution by the Christian West. At a time when Europeans tended to confine Jews to money-lending and certain other commercial trades, Jews served as physicians, government officials, philosophers, and scholars in Muslim-controlled societies from Moorish Spain across North Africa to the borders of India. The cultural vitality of the Islamic world, which kept alive Graeco-Roman culture and made fresh advances in mathematics, medicine, science, and philosophy while Christian Europe was struggling through the Dark Ages, was in part attributable to the enlightened policies Islamic rulers followed concerning their able Jewish subjects. Maimonides, the most famous of the medieval Jewish physician-philosophers, was both religious leader of the Jewish community and court physician to Saladin, the Kurdish general who unified a vast expanse of the Muslim world in the twelfth century. In more modern times, many Jews achieved high social, cultural, and financial position in Egypt where they were prominent in the civil service, and some received titles of "Bey" and "Pasha." One of these, Cattaui Pasha, was Minister of Finance to King Fouad less than fifty years ago.

The intensified struggle of Jews and Arabs has come since the end of World War I and most intensely since the end of World War II, as the two peoples, in their own ways, finally sought to put an end to persecution and to their common status as subject peoples—and ran head on into each other.

Zionism, the most dynamic force of nineteenth-century Jewish nationalism, burst upon the world scene just as Arab nationalism was beginning to rise from the dying Turkish Empire. These simultaneously emerging nationalisms, unfortunately, were destined to fight for possession of the same territory in the Holy Land of Palestine.

The nineteenth century, which saw the rapid spread of science, technology, and parliamentary concepts of political freedom over vast areas of the world, also witnessed the rise of the most vicious persecution of the Jews since the Romans drove them from Palestine in A.D. 135. Pogroms in Czarist Russia and in other parts of Eastern Europe in the 1880's raised again the fears which had intermittently assailed the Jews through many centuries of partial assimilation into various European societies. Numerous Jewish groups intensified efforts in Western Europe and America to promote migration away from their tormentors. Some settled in Western Europe, others in Canada and South Africa. The largest groups, by far, came to the United States. About 135,000 Eastern European Jews found new homes in the United States during the 1880's, another 280,000 in the 1890's, and the movement continued into the first part of the twentieth century. Other thousands were caught up in the dream of resettlement as farmers, and Jewish agricultural colonies were planted in Manitoba, Argentina, Australia, and South Africa.

Beginning in the 1860's, there were groups of European Jews who preached the then improbable dream of migration to the Holy Land of Palestine. An imaginative and determined Central European journalist, Theodor Herzl, took up this idea and in 1897, at Basle, Switzerland, challenged the First World Zionist Congress to develop a program for creating a Jewish homeland. He suggested how this should be achieved in a pamphlet entitled *The Jewish State.*

The Zionist movement quickly became a widely debated issue in world Jewry. Some Jewish philanthropists gave it limited support, some intellectual and religious leaders attacked it as both impractical and contrary to the interests of Jewish communities already established in Western countries. The strongest support came from among the Jewish masses seeking to flee from Eastern Europe, even though most of them chose, as the opportunity became available, to migrate to the United States. Around 1903, Herzl began to despair of establishing a homeland in Palestine and seriously raised the question of accepting a British offer to provide lands for Jewish settlement in the temperate highlands of the new British colonial territories in East Africa. At another time, Argentina was considered. All such proposals were, however, firmly rejected by the rank-and-file of Zionists, in favor of a "return" to the Holy Land.

Throughout the centuries of the Jewish diaspora, a small contingent of Jews had clung tenaciously to the city of Jerusalem. However, by the end of the 1880's, there were estimated to be only about 30,000 to 40,000 Jews in Palestine, or about five per cent of the total population. This was, of course, before political Zionism, as such, began. By the end of World War I, colonies of Jewish settlers, primarily from Russia, had brought the Jewish population of Palestine to approximately 60,000 or about ten per cent of the total.

Initial negotiations for Jewish settlement in Palestine were carried on with the authorities of the Ottoman Empire which had control of Palestine and the adjoining Arab territories. Land for the Jewish newcomers was acquired by purchase from Arab landowners. Peaceful coexistence was stressed by the promoters of the new settlements, and initially there was little difficulty with Arab neighbors. However, certain kinds of friction arose. At the human level, the sale of land sometimes meant that Arab farm workers were turned out without provision for resettlement or absorption into a new society, and this practice produced bitterness, On the broader, political level, it became increasingly clear to the more educated and sophisticated Arabs that these Jewish settlements were eventually going to be welded into some form of political entity to be carved out of Palestine, or that Jewish immigration might reach such a level that the Arabs would become a minority in their homeland. With that realization began the dark fears that produced a growing Arab determination to oppose by any means the Zionist dream.

These apprehensions among the Palestinian Arabs came very much to the fore after the Balfour Declaration was issued by the British Foreign Minister in 1917, and particularly after that document was incorporated into the

Versailles peace agreements and the League of Nations Mandates. The Balfour Declaration was simply a one-page letter which Lord Balfour wrote to Lord Rothschild stating that "His Majesty's Government view with favor the establishment in Palestine of a national home for the Jewish people." Coupled with that statement was a gesture of reassurance to the Palestinian Arabs to the effect "that nothing shall be done which may prejudice the civil and religious rights of the existing non-Jewish communities in Palestine." The Arabs, at that time, outnumbered the Jews by almost ten to one. The Balfour Declaration could be interpreted in several ways. Some Zionists saw it as a promise that the Jews of the world would be given all of Palestine and allowed to create there a sovereign state. Others interpreted it as a guarantee of unlimited Jewish immigration, but with no assurance that a Jewish state, as such, would ever be established. For years, bitter debates raged inside and outside Zionist circles over whether full-fledged political statehood was the goal. At various times, some Zionist leaders undertook to calm Arab and other critics by statements denying any ambition to create a Jewish state.

Meanwhile, as was later revealed, the British and the French had in 1916 entered into the secret Sykes-Picot agreement under which these two major powers were to divide between themselves control of much of the Arab world as soon as the Turkish empire could be destroyed. That arrangement was translated into the League of Nations Mandate system under which Britain took over the supervision of Palestine, Trans-Jordan, and Iraq, while France acquired dominance in Lebanon and Syria. As this arrangement was being worked out, during and immediately after World War I, the British, through Lawrence of Arabia and others, were making promises to Arab nationalists and to individual Arab chieftains that the dreams of Arab national statehood (and of expanded power

for particular leaders) would be fulfilled as the Turkish overlords could be driven out. These promises lay at the basis of the British-supported uprisings which culminated in the liberation of Jerusalem, Damascus and other ancient cities long controlled by the Turks.

By the mid-1920's, with British administrators and occupation forces installed in Palestine, a seemingly irreconcilable conflict was emerging. The Holy Land was claimed by a growing group of Jewish newcomers, gathering in from many parts of the world. It was also claimed by the long-settled Arab (Muslim and Christian) majority who took it for granted that they should in time control their own political destiny. Both sides became increasingly concerned to rid the land of British mandatory control and to establish their "rightful" claims on their own.

Competing Claims to Palestine

After the passage of these years, it is still impossible to get agreement on the relative merits of the rival claims to Palestine. Even to try to state what those claims are is to bring down on one's head (as the authors of this statement have discovered) the denunciation of either side, or both. Yet there are two sides to the argument. The Jews base their claim to the Holy Land on these contentions:

1. Their ancestors controlled Jerusalem and territories to the north and south of that city more than two thousand years ago.
2. In the Scriptures, Jehovah promised this entire land to Abraham and his "seed."
3. The ancient Jewish kingdom was the only independent, indigenous state that area ever had prior to the present day.
4. Though driven out in cruel attacks by the Romans, a remnant of Jews always remained in the Holy land and, for the past century, constituted a majority in the city of Jerusalem.

5. Through all the centuries of the diaspora, Jews maintained their cultural attachment to their ancestral homeland and regularly reaffirmed that attachment through prayers of "next year in Jerusalem."

6. Modern Jewish resettlement in Palestine was on the basis of peaceful purchases of land, with approval of the only legitimate authorities with whom the Zionist leadership could at the time deal: first, the Turkish Sultan and, later, the British mandatory officials.

7. The Palestinian Arabs were late-comers to the area, a migratory people, and never had a Palestinian Arab state.

8. Centuries of persecution, culminating in the holocaust of the Hitler era, drove the Jews to seek and to create a secure national haven as a matter of survival. Such a haven for the Jews could be provided only in Palestine, whereas the Arabs have abundant lands stretching over vast areas in the region which are, or could be, open to the Palestinians.

9. The Jews offered to live at peace with their Arab neighbors either in a shared state or in a partitioned state, but the Arabs refused either solution and, following their own foolhardy resort to violence and subsequent defeats, have forfeited all claim to Palestine.

10. The enormous and effective investment of Jewish labor and capital in developing the land, its agriculture and industry, has established through creative use an indisputable Jewish right.

11. The superior technological and financial resources of the Jews allow them to develop the area, not only for themselves, but also for the Palestinian Arabs and other peoples of the region; it is toward that sort of constructive sharing, not racial aggrandizement, that the humanistic spirit of Zionism is directed.

The Arabs base their claims to Palestine and their opposition to a Jewish state on these contentions:

1. The Arabs as a people have lived on the land of Palestine and had unbroken use of its soil for more than 1,300 years.

2. Accepting the mixing of ethnic strains, which has been going on throughout the Euro-Asian land mass through history, there are no pure races in the Middle East. Among the Arab population there are many who have just as good a claim to descent from the indigenous people of Judea and Samaria from 2,000 years ago—are just as truly among "the seed of Abraham"—as any of the Jews, and have a great deal better ethnic claim than can be put forward by most European Jews with their mixed ancestry.

3. In the course of the assorted empires which ruled over the area, Palestinian Arabs participated, at various levels, in administration of the region, even if there was no specific Palestinian Arab state; even under the Turkish empire there was substantial local self-government on a religious "community" basis.

4. The British promised during World War I that they would assist the Arabs to achieve national identity and independence through the creation of appropriate nation-states. The Palestinian Arabs have as much claim on that assistance as any other people of the Arab world.

5. Following the First World War, self-determination was promised to all the subject peoples ruled by the Central Powers, and that promise applied as much to the Palestinian Arabs as to any other people. This principle was violated when the promise was given to support the creation of a Jewish homeland in Palestine without consulting the Palestinian Arabs,

who were then an overwhelming majority of the people.

6. The Palestinian Arabs, though originally welcoming Jewish settlers when they quietly bought land and moved in, never agreed to become a minority in their own homeland.

7. Although some Arab leaders initially believed that Jewish immigration could be accepted on a basis which would not lead to displacement of the Arabs, from the time of World War I onward Palestinian Arab nationalists argued that the Zionist movement would eventually mean control over Palestine by the Jews and expulsion or subjection of the Arabs.

8. The influx of European Jews has threatened the basic cultural character of Palestine as part of Levantine society. Where Palestinian Arabs and Oriental (or Arabized) Jews have little difficulty adjusting to each other, the Western Jews undermined the hope for any kind of equitable Arab-Jewish partnership.

9. Zionism is another manifestation of Western imperialism. Arabs inevitably must fear the power represented by links between Jewish settlers and the world Zionist movement and the influence of that relationship with and upon Western governments.

10. Continuing Jewish expansionism is proclaimed by some elements in the world Zionist movement and by some political factions in Israel. The Arabs can never accept in their midst a Jewish state which appears to have no fixed conception its territorial boundaries and pursues an aggressive policy trying to stimulate unlimited immigration from all over the world. If successful, that policy would almost certainly create *Lebensraum* demands for the annexation of still more Arab territory.

11. The idea that the Palestinian Arabs should give up their homeland to Jews and move to other Arab lands because there is space for resettlement is rejected as illogical and inhuman; every people has a right to remain on the lands they have long held as their own.

Growth of the Yishuv

Between World War I and World War II, parallel but complete separate and distinct national communities emerged in Palestine: the *Yishuv*, or Jewish community, and the Palestine Arab community. Each had its educational system in which its children were taught to become supporters of the respective national causes. Each developed its political system with its own Arab or Jewish parties; Arab and Jewish social and economic organizations provided for the needs of their respective communities from birth to burial in separate Muslim, Christian or Jewish cemeteries. Arabs and Jews organized security and underground military or paramilitary forces. During this era, the *Yishuv* grew from a few token settlements constituting a mere ten per cent of the population to an effective and strong national community, with nearly a third of the population, but in many respects far stronger than the poorly organized and divided Arab community which opposed its growth.

The Palestinian Arabs did not succeed in their efforts to stop Zionism. Beginning in the 1920's, accelerating in the 1930's and 1940's, the violent struggle of Arab against Jew and Jew against Arab repeatedly broke the calm which the British mandate government tried to maintain. Well warned though the British and the world were by these disorders, no solution to the problem was found. Study commission followed study commission, but the international community paid little attention to what was happening then and gave scant thought to what might happen later.

With Hitler's rise, his assault against Europe and his evil campaign to exterminate the Jews, the flight from Europe became for many European Jews a matter of life or death. Here again, before and after World War II, the Christian West was weighed and found wanting. Instead of opening wide their gates to refugees from Nazi persecution—and perhaps saving millions of lives—the free nations vacillated, took half measures, and waited. In the end, Western Europe and America, plus the Soviet Union, fought and at great cost won a war for their own survival against the Nazi military machine while an estimated six million Jews were murdered. When the fighting ceased, the remnant of continental Jews could, for the most part, think only of getting away from Europe as quickly as possible. With Jewish settlements already well established in Palestine, with a vigorous World Zionist Organization working to assist in resettlement, the movement to Palestine of concentration camp survivors and Jews from other countries grew in size and urgency. The British mandate government tried to impose controls upon that movement but succeeded only partially and in the end abandoned the struggle to administer Palestine, as the flow of immigrants continued and inter-communal violence mounted.

How many of the Jews who went to Palestine in the 1930's and 1940's would have migrated to some other country if they had been given encouragement cannot be known. In any case, the Christian West was able to escape in large measure from its accumulated centuries of anti-Semitic guilt, by cooperating with the dedicated Zionist leadership in helping displaced Jews find refuge in a predominantly Arab land.

At the time the UN partition was adopted, the Jewish third of the population of Palestine owned about six per cent of the land. The Arab two-thirds of the population owned about a third of the land, and felt they had good claim on that major portion of public lands

listed as government domain. At partition, the Palestinian Arabs saw themselves being forced to give up much of their lands, private and communal, to Jewish settlers as part of a grand-scale international effort at restitution and compensation to the Jews. The Palestinian Arabs, chiefly a Muslim people, concluded that they were being required to pay for the anti-Semitic sins of the Christian West.

This is obviously a simplified and only partial explanation of how the Zionist movement and the present state of Israel came to gain broad Western support, but it will be impossible to understand current Arab attitudes apart from this unflattering interpretation of why the United States and Western Europe gave support to the creation of Israel and have continued to support it. In fact, some Arabs came to feel that in Western nations pro-Zionism for Jews abroad was the natural corollary of continued anti-Semitism at home.

Partition and War

One of the first great problems faced by the infant United Nations was the collapse of the British mandate and the necessity to find some internationally acceptable solution to the Arab-Jewish conflict in Palestine. The UN study commission recommended partition as the only solution with any hope of success. This plan called for the creation of separate Jewish and Arab states and the acceptance of international status for Jerusalem with free access for all races and religions.

This United Nations plan was approved by a two-thirds vote of its then members—and made possible by agreement-for-the-moment of the United States and the Soviet Union. Partition was never accepted by the local Palestinian Arabs nor by any of the neighboring Arab states. The Jews did accept partition and prepared to proclaim the state of Israel at the earliest possible moment, May 14, 1948. Long before the partition plan could go into effect, however, clashes developed between underground groups and paramilitary units already active on both sides. Arab terrorists, linked to the so-called Arab Liberation Army, attacked Jewish farm settlements, offices, factories, buses, and isolated individuals. Jewish terrorists inflicted similar blows upon the Arabs. On the night of April 9, 1948, Jewish extremist paramilitary groups killed 254 men, women and children in the Arab village of Deir Yassin—as some of the participants in the massacre later said, "to persuade the Arabs to get moving." On April 12, a reprisal by the Arabs resulted in the deaths of 77 Jewish doctors, nurses, university teachers and students travelling in a Red Cross convoy to Hadassah Hospital near Jerusalem.

Thus a state of civil war had already developed in Palestine over the period from December, 1947, following adoption of the UN partition plan, right through the final weeks of the British Mandate. Within hours after Dr. Chaim Weizmann and his Zionist colleagues proudly raised the Star of David flag and launched the Jewish state, military units from Jordan, Syria, Egypt, Lebanon and Iraq began an open assault upon Israel. After some initial successes for Arab arms, the Israeli forces rallied, broke the siege of Jewish West Jerusalem, and occupied substantial areas in the north of Palestine and in the south which had been assigned to Arab control under the UN partition plan. Israel wound up holding a third more territory than it would have held had the Arabs accepted the original UN partition plan.

A series of armistice agreements finally terminated hostilities in 1949. But peace did not come. Organized fighting was replaced by a propaganda war that has never ceased—and by innumerable acts of terror and counter-terror.

The Palestinian Arab state called for in the UN partition resolution was never created. Instead Jordan annexed the West Bank, including the Eastern sector of Jerusalem. Egypt

assumed a kind of protectorate control over the Gaza Strip. Israel, in turn, absorbed Jewish West Jerusalem, the Negev and parts of Galilee.

The Arabs had been beaten and humiliated but neither the Israeli nor the United Nations could compel them to make peace. In the absence of peace, Israel held on to its territorial gains, as did Jordan. In the closing phases of the war of 1948–49 it became clear how weak and disorganized the Arab forces were, how competent and determined were the Israelis. Despite the disparity between the total numbers of people on the two sides, vastly favoring the Arab countries over Israel, the actual military superiority of Israel over all its Arab neighbors was made clear through the Israeli victory in early 1949. That dominance has persisted through the intervening years. It has been convincingly demonstrated by Israel's ability to strike quickly and to win spectacular victories over the Arab states in the wars of 1956 and 1967, and to dominate the military situation along the cease-fire lines and in the air to this day.

The general response of the Arabs to the establishment and consolidation of a Jewish state in their midst has continued to be one of bitterness, frustration, and a sense of humiliated impotence. Their chief satisfaction for a long time has come in a war of propaganda rarely matched in passion and vituperation and in a kind of mystical faith that in time, somehow, the Arabs would achieve the military power with which to destroy Israel. The Arabs in defeat remained weak and disorganized. But they have believed that their cause was just and that it would prevail in the end. Meanwhile, the United Nations set up machinery and provided funds to care for the minimal subsistence needs of nearly a million Arab refugees scattered across Gaza, Jordan, Syria, Lebanon, and Egypt. Out of these refugee camps and from other Palestinians in exile came increasing cries for revenge and for a chance "to go home." Thus, through the 1940's and well into the 1950's, there seemed no hope for a resolution of the conflict. There remained only an uneasy truce, broken occasionally by acts of terror and counter-terror. Moreover, the Arabs stepped up their propaganda war into more and more blood-curdling threats of eventual revenge against Israel, a state whose very existence Arabs refused to concede. The Arabs insisted on the maintenance of belligerency against Israel and a boycott against an trade and communications across the common boundaries.

67

The First Arab Students' Congress, 1938

World War I transformed the Middle East in several ways. The Ottoman Empire, which had controlled much of the Middle East, disintegrated as a consequence of its support of the Central Powers. As a result, much of the territory in the Middle East was up for grabs, and several of the European powers, chief among them the British and the French, were interested in laying claim. In fact, under the terms of the Sykes-Picot agreement, secretly negotiated between the two countries during World War I, a division of Arab lands had already been worked out. However, this agreement conflicted with the promise of independence to Arab leaders as a condition for Arab support of the Entente powers. This much-coveted territory was also the focus of the activities of the Zionists, whose support of the Entente powers had won them support within the British government for a "national homeland" in Palestine. Finally, the League of Nations would establish mandates for the newly-created countries of Palestine, Transjordan, Syria and Iraq. Not too surprisingly, the British and French overlooked earlier promises made to both Arabs and Jews, the French moving into Syria and Iraq, and Britain controlling Palestine and Transjordan. While Egypt and Iraq would win independence during the 1930's, most of the area remained under European control until after World War II, stimulating an Arab nationalism that differed from country to country. In this selection the manifesto of the first congress of Arab student nationalists, held in Paris in 1938, sets forth their demands.

Discussion Questions

1. How do the students define what it means to be an Arab? Is is similar to the way the Jews define what it means to be Jewish? Other ethnic groups, past or present?

2. Are the aims of the Arab nationalists similar to other nationalist groups you've studied? Similar to the Zionists? What differences exist?

3. Why do the Arab students oppose the Jews in Palestine? What is their objection to the Italians and the French? Have any of their demands been met?

Our National Pact

I am an Arab, and I believe that the Arabs constitute one nation. The sacred right of this nation is to be sovereign in her own affairs. Her ardent nationalism drives her to liberate the Arab homeland, to unite all its parts, and to found political, economic, and social institutions more sound and more compatible than the existing ones. The aim of this nationalism is to raise up the standard of living and to increase the material and the spiritual good of the people; it also aspires to share in working for the good of the human collectivity; it strives to realize this by continuous work based on national organization.

I pledge myself to God, that I will strive in this path to my utmost, putting the national interest above any other consideration.

First Principles

The Arabs: All who are Arab in their language, culture, and loyalty, … those are the Arabs. The Arab is the individual who belongs to the nation made up of those people.

The Arab Homeland: It is the land which has been, or is, inhabited by an Arab majority, in the above sense, in Asia and Africa. As such it is a whole which cannot be divided or partitioned. It is a sacred heritage no inch of which may be trifled with. Any compromise in this respect is invalid and is national treason.

Arab Nationalism: It is the feeling for the necessity of independence and unity which the inhabitants of the Arab lands share. … It is based on the unity of the homeland, of language, culture, history, and a sense of the common good.

The Arab Movement: It is the new Arab renaissance which pervades the Arab nation. Its motive force is her glorious past, her remarkable vitality and the awareness of her present and future interests. This movement strives continuously and in an organized manner toward well-defined aims. These aims are to liberate and unite the Arab homeland, to found political, economic, and social organizations more sound than the existing ones, and to attempt afterward to work for the good of the human collectivity and its progress. These aims are to be realized by definite means drawn from the preparedness of the Arabs and their particular situation, as well as from the experience of the West. They will be realized without subscribing to any particular creed of the modern Western ones such as Fascism, Communism, or Democracy.

The Arab National Idea: It is a national idea which proscribes the existence of racial, regional, and communal fanaticisms. It respects the freedom of religious observance, and individual freedoms such as the freedom of opinion, work, and assembly, unless they conflict with the public good. The Arab national idea cannot be contradictory to the good of real racial and religious minorities; it aims rather at treating all sincere patriots on the principle of equality of rights and duties.

Foreign Elements in the Arab Countries

We have said that the Arab countries belong to the Arabs and that benefits therefrom must accrue to them. By Arabs we mean those whom the political report has included under this appellation. As for those elements who are not Arabized and who do not intend to be Arabized but are, rather, intent on putting obstacles in the way of the Arab nation, they are foreign to the Arab nation. The most prominent problem of this kind is that of the Jews in Palestine.

If we looked at the Jews in Palestine from an economic angle we would find that their economy is totally incompatible with the Arab economy. The Jews are attempting to build up a Jewish state in Palestine and to bring into this state great numbers of their kind from all over the world. Palestine is a small country, and they will therefore have to industrialize it so that this large number of inhabitants can find subsistence. And in order to make their industry a success they will have to find markets for their products. For this they depend on the Arab market; their products will therefore flood the Arab countries and compete with Arab industries. This is very harmful to the Arabs.

Moreover, Palestine, placed as it is between the Arab countries in Asia and Africa, occupies an important position in land, sea, and air communications. A foreign state in Palestine will impede these communications and have a harmful effect on commerce. And even if the Jews in Palestine presented no danger other than the economic, this would be enough for us to oppose them and to put an end to their intrigues, so that we may ensure for our country a happy and glorious future.

Among the dangerous alien elements in the Arab countries are the foreign colonies such as the Italians in Tripolitania, the French, and the Frenchified Jews in Tunisia, Algeria, and Morocco. The danger of these elements is akin to that of the Jews in Palestine, even though less prominent and less critical.

68

The Palestinian National Covenant, 1968

The document you will be reading was drawn up in the immediate aftermath of the 1967 Six Day War, in which the Arab nations were humiliated by the Israelis. The crushing defeat of Arab armies was compounded by Israeli occupation of Arab lands, including the Gaza Strip and the Sinai in Egypt; Jerusalem and the West Bank in Jordan, the home of large numbers of Palestinians; and the Golan Heights in Syria. While many Israelis believed that their victory would lead to the recognition by their opponent that only a negotiated settlement of their differences would bring peace, Palestinians were of a different mind altogether. Until 1967 many Palestinians had relied on the Arab states of Egypt, Syria, Jordan and Iraq to fight for their rights, but after the 1967 war that was no longer a reality. Therefore, one important consequence of the 1967 War was a growing sense of Palestinian nationalism and identity. The Palestine Liberation Organization (PLO), formed in 1964, would issue this covenant in a statement of their consciousness, goals, and strategies in the ongoing conflict with Israel, with al-Fatah developing as the most important group within the PLO and Yasser Arafat, its leader since 1969, an important spokesman. The excerpts presented here reflect the aspirations of the Palestinians at an important moment in the Arab-Israeli Conflict.

Discussion Questions

1. What is Palestine and what is a Palestinian? What distinction does the covenant make between Palestinians and Jews, or Israelis?

2. What do the Palestinians want? Would it be possible to achieve their goals without infringing on the rights of the Israelis?

3. What is meant by self-determination, mentioned in Article 19? Where have you seen this term used before?

4. How does the description of Zionism compare with other readings in the RGH and in your text?

5. How were the fedayeen (guerrilla fighters) to wage the struggle with the Israelis, and what would their relationship with Arab states be?

6. How do you think Israelis reacted to the covenant? The U.S.? Other Arab states? Which provision do you think is the most inflammatory from the Israeli point of view?

The Palestinian National Covenant, 1968 [Excerpts]

This Covenant will be called The Palestinian National Covenant *(al-mithaq al-watani al-filastini)*.

Article 1: Palestine is the homeland of the Palestinian Arab people and an integral part of the great Arab homeland, and the people of Palestine is a part of the Arab nation.

Article 2: Palestine with its boundaries that existed at the time of the British mandate is an integral regional unit.

Article 3: The Palestinian Arab people possesses the legal right to its homeland, and when the liberation of its homeland is completed it will exercise self-determination solely according to its own will and choice.

Article 4: The Palestinian personality is an innate, persistent characteristic that does not disappear, and it is transferred from fathers to sons. The Zionist occupation, and the dispersal of the Palestinian Arab people as a result of the disasters which came over it, do not deprive it of its Palestinian personality and affiliation and do not nullify them.

Article 5: The Palestinians are the Arab citizens who were living permanently in Palestine until 1947, whether they were expelled from there or remained. Whoever is born to a Palestinian Arab father after this date, within Palestine or outside it, is a Palestinian.

Article 6: Jews who were living permanently in Palestine until the beginning of the Zionist invasion will be considered Palestinians. [For the dating of the Zionist invasion, considered to have begun in 1917.]

Article 7: The Palestinian affiliation and the material, spiritual and historical tie with Palestine are permanent realities. The upbringing of the Palestinian individual in an Arab and revolutionary fashion, the undertaking of all means of forging consciousness and training the Palestinian, in order to acquaint him profoundly with his homeland, spiritually and materially, and preparing him for the conflict and the armed struggle, as well as for the sacrifice of his property and his life to restore his homeland, until the liberation of all this is a national duty.

Article 8: The phase in which the people of Palestine is living is that of national *(watani)* struggle for the liberation of Palestine. Therefore, the contradictions among the Palestinian national forces are of secondary order which must be suspended in the interest of the fundamental contradiction between Zionism and colonialism on the one side and the Palestinian Arab people on the other. On this basis, the Palestinian masses, whether in the homeland or in places of exile *(mahajir),* organizations and individuals, comprise one national front which acts to restore Palestine and liberate it through armed struggle.

Article 9: Armed struggle is the only way to liberate Palestine and is therefore a strategy and not tactics. The Palestinian Arab people affirms its absolute resolution and abiding determination to pursue the armed struggle and to march forward towards the armed popular revolution, to liberate its homeland and return to it [to maintain] its right to a natural life in it, and to exercise its right of self-determination in it and sovereignty over it.

Article 10: Fedayeen action forms the nucleus of the popular Palestinian war of liberation. This demands its promotion, extension and protection, and the mobilization of all the masses and scientific capacities of the Palestinians, their organization and involvement in the armed Palestinian revolution and cohesion in the national *(watani)* struggle among the various groups of the people of Palestine, and between them and the Arab masses, to guarantee the continuation of the revolution, its advancement and victory... .

Article 13: Arab unity and the liberation of Palestine are two complementary aims. Each one paves the way for realization of the other.

Arab unity leads to the liberation of Palestine, and the liberation of Palestine leads to Arab unity. Working for both goes hand in hand... .

Article 15: The liberation of Palestine, from an Arab viewpoint, is a national *(qawmi)* duty to repulse the Zionist, Imperialist invasion from the great Arab homeland and to purge the Zionist presence from Palestine. Its full responsibility falls upon the Arab nation, peoples and governments, with the Palestinian Arab people at their head.

Article 16: The liberation of Palestine, from a spiritual viewpoint, will prepare an atmosphere of tranquility and peace for the Holy Land in the shade of which all the Holy Places will be safeguarded, and freedom of worship and visitation to all will be guaranteed, without distinction or discrimination of race, colour, language or religion. For this reason, the people of Palestine looks to the support of all the spiritual forces in the world.

Article 17: The liberation of Palestine, from a human viewpoint, will restore to the Palestinian man his dignity, glory and freedom. For this, the Palestinian Arab people looks to the support of those in the world who believe in the dignity and freedom of man... .

Article 19: The partitioning of Palestine in 1947 and the establishment of Israel is fundamentally null and void, whatever time has elapsed, because it was contrary to the wish of the people of Palestine and its natural right to its homeland, and contradicts the principles embodied in the Charter of the UN, the first of which is the right of self-determination.

Article 20: The Balfour Declaration, the Mandate document, and what has been based upon them are considered null and void. The claim of a historical or spiritual tie between Jews and Palestine does not tally with historical realities nor with the constituents of statehood in their true sense. Judaism, in its character as a religion of revelation, is not a nationality with an independent existence. Likewise, the Jews are not one people with an independent personality. They are rather citizens of the states to which they belong.

Article 21: The Palestinian Arab people, in expressing itself through the armed Palestinian revolution, rejects every solution that is a substitute for a complete liberation of Palestine, and rejects all plans that aim at the settlement of the Palestine issue or its internationalization.

Article 22: Zionism is a political movement organically related to world Imperialism and hostile to all movements of liberation and progress in the world. It is a racist and fanatical movement in its formation: aggressive, expansionist and colonialist in its aims; and fascist and Nazi in its means. Israel is the tool of the Zionist movement and a human and geographical base for world Imperialism. It is a concentration and jumping-off point for Imperialism in the heart of the Arab homeland, to strike at the hopes of the Arab nation for liberation, unity and progress... .

Article 24: The Palestinian Arab people believes in the principles of justice, freedom, sovereignty, self-determination, human dignity and the fight of people to exercise them... .

Article 27: The Palestine Liberation Organization will cooperate with all Arab States, each according to its capacities, and will maintain neutrality in their mutual relations in the light of and on the basis of, the requirements of the battle of liberation and will not interfere in the internal affairs of any Arab State.

Article 28: The Palestinian Arab people insists upon the originality and independence of its national *(wataniyya)* liberation and rejects every manner of interference, guardianship and subordination... .

Article 33: This covenant cannot be amended except by a two-thirds majority of all the members of the National Assembly of the Palestine Liberation Organization in a special session called for this purpose.

69

Key Themes of Middle East Politics

The Middle East encompasses some 20 countries situated on the three continents of Europe, Asia, and Africa. Its current importance on the world scene is not new, for it has long been a strategic crossroads where countless cultures have met, exchanged ideas and goods, fought, and coexisted. In the brief article that follows, Adam Garfinkle provides an introduction to some important realities of the Middle Eastern past and present.

Discussion Questions

1. What is the importance of traditional (old) social, political and economic customs on the present day Middle East?

2. How does Garfinkle describe most Middle Eastern political systems, and what role has nationalism played in this process?

3. What kinds of divisions exist within Middle Eastern states, and what impact have these divisions had for political and economic stability?

4. What does Garfinkle mean when he talks about outside intervention in the Middle East in the form of "two overlapping cold wars?" How has the situation changed today?

Key Themes of Middle East Politics

Adam Garfinkle

S cholarly approaches to the study of the modern Middle East vary, but most reputable experts agree on the following basic themes, even if they differ on particulars.

1. Old Civilizations, New States

For the most part, the modern Middle East consists of old societies organized under new states. The Middle East is one of the oldest human habitats on earth, and its ancient civilizations among the most grand and influential. Civilizations in Egypt, Mesopotamia (present day Iraq), ancient Israel, Persia, North Africa, and Anatolia (present day Turkey) gave rise to cultural and social patterns that persist in many ways still today. The rise first of Christianity and then of Islam in the 7th century added other very significant overlays to these ancient legacies. So did the Ottoman Turkish rule of the Middle East, which lasted for 400 years—until the end of World War I.

When the Ottoman Empire ended and European control and influence receded some thirty years later, the landscape revealed mostly recognizable societies, but few if any of those societies were organized in the territorial state of the Western model. (In this respect, the Middle East is more like East Asia as it emerged into the twentieth century, and less like sub-Saharan Africa as it emerged halfway through

the same century.) The borders of the modern Middle East, then, correspond at least roughly to historic frontiers—Yemen is where Yemen was, Egypt is where Egypt was, Iraq is where Babylon/Mesopotamia was, modern Turkey is where the center of Suleyman the Magnificent's empire was, Iran is where the Persia of Cyrus the Great was, the State of Israel is where the kingdoms of David and Solomon were, and so forth.

More important, however, the political systems of most Middle Eastern states are new, arising out of the post-Ottoman period. Not a single state in the region can boast a continuous political regime that predates this century, and the great majority date from after 1946.

What we have then, in most cases, is a relatively recent political system, whose formal structures are mostly borrowed from the West, superimposed upon old and deeply rooted social and political patterns. These patterns, in turn, are rooted in extended family (or clan, or tribe) and communities of faith (sectarian identification). The reason for this has mainly to do with the reaction of local societies over time to life under foreign domination. Today, then, political authority competes with the often conflicting authority that emanates from religious and tribal institutions.

In short, most Middle East states, and particularly the Arab states, exhibit much transparency; formal government structure tends to fold into pre-existing socioeconomic patterns because that is the best, and sometimes the only way short of outright coercion, that the state apparatus can function, or can itself survive. (Israel is the biggest exception to this pattern, Turkey is a partial exception, and Iran is a still lesser one.)

Recent Middle Eastern experience exhibits several patterns, but all come back one way or another to the tension between strong, deeply rooted social authority revolving around extended family (hamula) and religious sectarianism.

Some states, such as Syria, Algeria, Egypt after 1952, and Iraq after July 1958, have tried to accumulate and consolidate power through revolutionary transformations directed from the top down. These political authorities often set themselves up against religious authority and often against the power of the old, aristocratic family networks.

In many cases, Egypt being a good example, accommodation with religious authority rather than repression of it has become the prevalent pattern, with the mammoth state bureaucracy being penetrated by social realities as well as the other way around. In other states, such as Iraq and Syria, a virtual policestate emerged. In virtually none have institutional links developed between state and society to the extent that the majority of people assume the natural, organic social legitimacy of the government.

Other states have taken the more traditional route, trying more patiently to amass state authority by associating themselves with traditional authority patterns. The monarchies of the region, from Morocco to Jordan to Saudi Arabia, are the best examples of such an approach. Some scholars have referred to such states as really only "families with flags," and, they might have added, with mosques. The evidence thus far suggests that the more traditionally-minded states have fared better in creating social stability, and in maintaining a sense of legitimacy and limited political participation. This is not at all what Western and local regional analysts in the 1950s and 1960s expected or predicted.

Nonetheless, the tension between weak polities and strong societies persists in virtually all Middle Eastern states. Governments naturally appeal to and try to build up local versions of nationalism based around the state (wataniya), but find competing realities and aspirations that are both "too small," (hamula, extended family) and "too large" (qawmiya, Pan-Arabism; or pan-Islamism). Thus, as political sociologists might put it, Middle Eastern—especially Arab—polities have relatively weak cores and strong peripheries.

Correspondingly, the prominence of faith and family as forms of legitimate social authority have made it hard for national political institutions, including political parties, to take root in society. As a result, political pluralism of the sort familiar in the West and elsewhere is very weak in the Middle East, excepting Israel and Turkey, which are functioning democracies. The political mobilization that does occur does so most often according to sectarian or regional tribal affiliation rather than along the lines of a national agenda that cuts across such groupings. Whereas some countries may be only "families with flags," almost all political parties in the region (again, excepting Turkey and Israel) are families or mosque-based groups with "programs" and "banners."

2. Cultural Heterogeneity

The weakness of the Middle Eastern state is also a function of divisions within societies. Not only is the region as a whole diverse, but so are many of the societies within themselves.

As to the region as a whole, there are, first of all, cultural divisions along religious lines: between Muslim and Christian (and Jew), and within Islam between Sunni and various heterodox Shi'a groupings. There are also ethnographic/linguistic divisions, between Arab and Persian and Turk, with many smaller demographic groups also of relevance in certain states (for example, Kurds in Iran, Iraq, and Turkey; Berbers and Tuareg in Algeria; Beja/Nubian peoples in the Sudan; Armenians in Lebanon).

There are also divisions between rich states and poor states, between those with dominant traditions of sedentary agriculture and those with traditions of pastoral nomadism of one degree or another, and between, finally, those states that are internally homogeneous and those that are internally heterogeneous—which brings us back to questions of internal political organization, stability, and governmental competency and effectiveness.

In general, all else being equal, the more homogeneous a Middle Eastern state in terms of ethno-linguistic and religious diversity, the easier to govern well and with a benign hand. No Middle Eastern State is completely homogeneous, so we speak in relative terms, but Egypt, Tunisia, and Saudi Arabia are to be counted among the most homogeneous (despite 6 million Christians [Copts] in Egypt and many Shi'a in the al-Hasa province of Saudi Arabia). Syria, Iraq, and Lebanon are among the most heterogeneous, some mainly along sectarian lines (like Syria), and some combinations of ethno-linguistic and sectarian lines (like Iraq).

There are also intermediate cases: Jordan is almost all Sunni Muslim (only 3 percent are Christian and fewer still are Circassian), but it is divided between East Banker and Palestinian identifications; Sudan's Arabs are a relatively homogeneous group but the state includes large numbers of Beja/Nubian peoples who

are neither Arab nor Muslim. These divisions, on the top of weak central state authority, tend to undermine the sense of the state as a single community. They have been the root cause of repression, violence, and even civil war in several countries.

3. Institutional Weaknesses and External Influences

Because of the relative weakness of the state in the Middle East—even those attempting revolution from above and the concomitant bureaucratization of society—many countries in the region have been particularly vulnerable to external influences. These external influences have come in basically two forms: intra-regional and extra-regional.

Over most of the last 40 years, the Middle East has experienced not just one but two overlapping cold wars. Division and conflict among the states of the region (Arab vs. Israel, Arab vs. Iran, and Arab vs. Arab as well) has been the more important of the two. The Yemeni and Lebanese civil wars stand as excellent examples, as do the efforts of the larger regional states (Egypt, Syria, Iraq) to influence political dynamics in Jordan and among the Palestinians.

Nevertheless, the regional cold war drew in the United States and the Soviet Union—and to a lesser extent also Europe, China, Pakistan, and India. Sometimes local states that were locked in protracted regional disputes invited these influences by turning to external powers for weapons, economic aid, and diplomatic support.

Great power conflict that was played out through Middle Eastern proxies sometimes magnified, prolonged, and intensified the violence of local conflicts, but in other cases or at other levels probably helped keep local conflicts from getting out of hand. With the end of the Cold War, the collapse of the Soviet

Union and the retreat of Russian power from the region, these dynamics have changed dramatically. In some respects, the considerable success of the Arab-Israeli peace process owes its progress to such changes.

For a bibliography on the Middle East, contact FPRI at 215-732-3774, ext. 201, or email ms@fpri.org.

70

Islamic Jihad

An important, though minority, feature of recent Islamic fundamentalism has been the use of the concept of jihad. Traditionally this idea has been seen in two ways: as the Greater Jihad and as the Lesser Jihad. The Greater Jihad is the struggle within every individual Muslim to bring his or her will into conformity with the will of God. The Lesser Jihad refers to a "holy war," or morally justifiable war. The role of jihad in Islam has had a variable history; there have been times when it was hardly mentioned at all and other times when it became more prominent, but it was usually seen as defensive (of the faith or the territory of the faith). Normally a jihad, or a fatwa calling for a jihad or anything else, was the prerogative of some recognized authority such as a learned scholar or even a Muslim government.

The following selection is the fatwa proclaimed by Osama bin Laden and four other Islamic radicals in 1998 in reaction to the presence of American troops in Saudi Arabia.

Discussion Questions

1. What is the significance of bin Laden's use of the term "crusade?"

2. What was bin Laden's justification for calling for a jihad against the Americans?

3. What does he say is the purpose of a jihad?

4. How would you put this kind of appeal in a global and historical context? How does it relate to reading #18—the World Revolution of Westernization?

Praise be to God, who revealed the Book, controls the clouds, defeats factionalism, and says in His Book "But when the forbidden months are past, then fight and slay the pagans wherever ye find them, seize them, beleaguer them, and lie in wait for them in every stratagem (of war)"; and peace be upon our Prophet, Muhammad Bin-'Abdallah, who said "I have been sent with the sword between my hands to ensure that no one but God is worshipped, God who put my livelihood under the shadow of my spear and who inflicts humiliation and scorn on those who disobey my orders."

The Arabian Peninsula has never—since God made it flat, created its desert, and encircled it with seas—been stormed by any forces like the crusader armies now spreading in it like locusts, consuming its riches and destroying its plantations. All this is happening at a time when nations are attacking Muslims like people fighting over a plate of food. In the light of the grave situation and the lack of support, we and you are obliged to discuss current events, and we should all agree to settle the matter.

No one argues today about three facts that are known to everyone; we will list them, in order to remind everyone:

First, for over seven years the United States has been occupying the lands of Islam in the holiest of places, the Arabian Peninsula, plundering its riches, dictating to its rulers, humiliating its people, terrorizing its neighbors, and turning its bases in the Peninsula into a spearhead through which to fight the neighboring Muslim peoples.

If some people have formerly debated the fact of the occupation, all the people of the Peninsula have now acknowledged it. The best proof of this is the Americans' continuing aggression against the Iraqi people using the Peninsula as a staging post, even though all its rulers are against their territories being used to that end, still they are helpless.

Second, despite the great devastation inflicted on the Iraqi people by the crusader-Zionist alliance, and despite the huge number of those killed, in excess of 1 million... despite all this, the Americans are once again trying to repeat the horrific massacres, as though they are not content with the protracted blockade imposed after the ferocious war or the fragmentation and devastation.

So here they come to annihilate what is left of this people and to humiliate their Muslim neighbors.

Third, if the Americans' aims behind these wars are religious and economic, the aim is also to serve the Jews' petty state and divert attention from its occupation of Jerusalem and murder of Muslims there. The best proof of this is their eagerness to destroy Iraq, the strongest neighboring Arab state, and their endeavor to fragment all the states of the region such as Iraq, Saudi Arabia, Egypt, and Sudan into paper statelets and through their disunion and weakness to guarantee Israel's survival and the continuation of the brutal crusader occupation of the Peninsula.

All these crimes and sins committed by the Americans are a clear declaration of war on God, his messenger, and Muslims. And *ulema* have throughout Islamic history unanimously agreed that the *jihad* is an individual duty if the enemy destroys the Muslim countries.

On that basis, and in compliance with God's order, we issue the following fatwa to all Muslims:

The ruling to kill the Americans and their allies—civilians and military—is an individual duty for every Muslim who can do it in any country in which it is possible to do it, in order to liberate the al-Aqsa Mosque and the holy mosque [in Mecca] from their grip, and in order for their armies to move out of all the lands of Islam, defeated and unable to threaten any Muslim. This is in accordance with the words of Almighty God, "and fight the pagans all together as they fight you all together," and "fight them until there is no more tumult or oppression, and there prevail justice and faith in God."

This is in addition to the words of Almighty God "And why should ye not fight in the cause of God and of those who, being weak, are ill-treated and oppressed—women and children, whose cry is 'Our Lord, rescue us from this town, whose people are oppressors; and raise for us from thee one who will help!' "

We—with God's help—call on every Muslim who believes in God and wishes to be rewarded to comply with God's order to kill the Americans and plunder their money wherever and whenever they find it. We also call on Muslim *ulema*, leaders, youths, and soldiers to launch the raid on Satan's U.S. troops and the devil's supporters allying with them, and to displace those who are behind them so that they may learn a lesson.

Almighty God said "O ye who believe, give your response to God and His Apostle, when He calleth you to that which will give you life. And know that God cometh between a man and his heart, and that it is He to whom ye shall all be gathered."

Almighty God also says "O ye who believe, what is the matter with you, that when ye are asked to go forth in the cause of God, ye cling so heavily to the earth! Do ye prefer the life of this world to the hereafter? But little is the comfort of this life, as compared with the hereafter. Unless ye go forth, He will punish you with a grievous penalty, and put others in your place; but Him ye would not harm in the least. For God hath power over all things."

Almighty God also says "So lose no heart, nor fall into despair. For ye must gain mastery if ye are true in faith."

> Shaykh Usamah Bin-Muhammad Bin-Laden
>
> Ayman al-Zawahiri, *Amir* of the *Jihad* Group in Egypt
>
> Abu-Yasir Rifa'i Ahmad Taha, Egyptian Islamic Group
>
> Shaykh Mir Hamzah, secretary of the Jamiat-ul-Ulema-e-Pakistan
>
> Fazlur Rahman, *Amir* of the *Jihad* Movement in Bangladesh

71

Islamic Fundamentalism

One of the most widespread phenomena of the twentieth century (and today) is what is often called "Fundamentalism." In this selection, Karen Armstrong, one of the most prominent scholars of religion, places fundamentalism in its modern context and then turns to a brief discussion of its Islamic variant.

(She refers to "Afghani," a late 19th century Iranian activist who feared the encroachment of the modern West, and to "al-Nasser" who was the ruler of Egypt in the 1950s and 1960s.)

Discussion Questions

1. Why is fundamentalism a distinctively modern idea? Where did it start?

2. What do all fundamentalists have in common?

3. What forms has Islamic fundamentalism taken?

4. Is fundamentalism, generally, destined to succeed or fail? Why?

Islamic Fundamentalism

Karen Armstrong

The Western media often give the impression that the embattled and occasionally violent form of religiosity known as "fundamentalism" is a purely Islamic phenomenon. This is not the case. Fundamentalism is a global fact and has surfaced in every major faith in response to the problems of our modernity. There is fundamentalist Judaism, fundamentalist Christianity, fundamentalist Hinduism, fundamentalist Buddhism, fundamentalist Sikhism and even fundamentalist Confucianism. This type of faith surfaced first in the Christian world in the United States at the beginning of the twentieth century. This was not accidental. Fundamentalism is not a monolithic movement, each form of fundamentalism, even within the same tradition, develops independently and has its own symbols and enthusiasms, but its different manifestations all bear a family resemblance. It has been noted that a fundamentalist movement does not arise immediately, as a knee-jerk response to the advent of Western modernity, but only takes shape when the modernization process is quite far advanced. At first religious people try to reform their traditions and effect a marriage between them and modern culture, as we have seen the Muslim reformers do. But when these moderate measures are found to be of no avail, some people resort to more extreme methods, and a fundamentalist movement is born. With hindsight, we can see that it was only to be expected that fundamentalism should first make itself known in the United States, the showcase of modernity, and only appear in other parts of the world at a later date. Of the three monotheistic religions, Islam was in fact the last to develop a fundamentalist strain, when modern culture began to take root in the Muslim world in the late 1960s and 1970s. By this date, fundamentalism was quite well established among Christians and Jews, who had had a longer exposure to the modern experience.

Fundamentalist movements in all faiths share certain characteristics. They reveal a deep disappointment and disenchantment with the modern experiment, which has not fulfilled all that it promised. They also express real fear. Every single fundamentalist movement that I have studied is convinced that the secular establishment is determined to wipe religion out. This is not always a paranoid reaction. We have seen that secularism has often been imposed very aggressively in the Muslim world. Fundamentalists look back to a "golden age" before the irruption of modernity for inspiration, but they are not atavistically returning to the Middle Ages. All are intrinsically modern movements and could have appeared at no time other than our own. All are innovative and often radical in their reinterpretation of religion. As such, fundamentalism is an essential part of the modern scene. Wherever modernity takes root, a fundamentalist movement is likely to rise up alongside it in conscious reaction. Fundamentalists will often express their discontent with a modern development by overstressing those elements in their tradition that militate against it. They are all—even in the United States—highly critical of democracy and secularism. Because the emancipation of women has been one of the hallmarks of modern culture, fundamentalists tend to emphasize conventional, agrarian gender roles, putting women back into veils and into the home. The fundamentalist community can thus be seen as the shadow-side of modernity; it can also highlight some of the darker sides of the modern experiment.

Fundamentalism, therefore, exists in a symbiotic relationship with a coercive secularism. Fundamentalists nearly always feel assaulted by the liberal or modernizing establishment, and their views and behavior become more extreme as a result. After the famous Scopes Trial (1925) in Tennessee, when Protestant fundamentalists tried to prevent the teaching of evolution in the public schools, they were so ridiculed by the secularist press that their theology became more reactionary and excessively literal, and they turned from the left to the extreme right of the political spectrum. When the secularist attack has been more violent, the fundamentalist reaction is likely to be even greater. Fundamentalism therefore reveals a fissure in society, which is polarized between those who enjoy secular culture and those who regard it with dread. As time passes, the two camps become increasingly unable to understand one another. Fundamentalism thus begins as an internal dispute, with liberalizers or secularists within one's own culture or nation. In the first instance, for example, Muslim fundamentalists will often oppose their fellow countrymen or fellow Muslims who take a more positive view of modernity, rather than such external foes as the West or Israel. Very often, fundamentalists begin by withdrawing from mainstream culture to create an enclave of pure faith (as, for example, within the ultra-Orthodox Jewish communities in Jerusalem or New York). Thence they will sometimes conduct an offensive which can take many forms, designed to bring the mainstream back to the right path and resacralize the world. All fundamentalists feel that they are fighting for survival, and because their backs are to the wall, they can believe that they have to fight their way out of the impasse. In this frame of mind, on rare occasions, some resort to terrorism. The vast majority, however, do not commit acts of violence, but simply try to revive their faith in a more conventional, lawful way.

Fundamentalists have been successful in so far as they have pushed religion from the sidelines and back to center stage, so that it now plays a major part in international affairs once again, a development that would have seemed inconceivable in the mid-twentieth century when secularism seemed in the ascendant. This has certainly been the case in the Islamic world since the 1970s. But fundamentalism is not simply a way of "using" religion for a political end. These are essentially rebellions against the secularist exclusion of the divine from public life, and a frequently desperate attempt to make spiritual values prevail in the modern world. But the desperation and fear that fuel fundamentalists also tend to distort the religious tradition, and accentuate its more aggressive aspects at the expense of those that preach toleration and reconciliation.

Muslim fundamentalism corresponds very closely to these general characteristics. It is not correct, therefore, to imagine that Islam has within it a militant, fanatic strain that impels Muslims into a crazed and violent rejection of modernity. Muslims are in tune with fundamentalists in other faiths all over the world, who share their profound misgivings about modern secular culture. It should also be said that Muslims object to the use of the term "fundamentalism," pointing out quite correctly that it was coined by American Protestants as a badge of pride, and cannot be usefully translated into Arabic. *Usul*, as we have seen, refers to the fundamental principles of Islamic jurisprudence, and as all Muslims agree on these, all Muslims could be said to subscribe to *usuliyyah* (fundamentalism). Nevertheless, for all its shortcomings, "fundamentalism" is the only term we have to describe this family of embattled religious movements, and it is difficult to come up with a more satisfactory substitute.

One of the early fundamentalist idealogues was Mawdudi, the founder of the Jamaat-i Islami in Pakistan. He saw the mighty power of the West as gathering its forces to crush Islam. Muslims, he argued, must band together to fight this encroaching secularism, if they wanted their religion and their culture to survive. Muslims had encountered hostile societies before and had experienced disasters but, starting with Afghani, a new note had crept into Islamic discourse. The Western threat had made Muslims defensive for the first time. Mawdudi defied the whole secularist ethos: he was proposing an Islamic liberation theology. Because God alone was sovereign, nobody was obliged to take orders from any other human being. Revolution against the colonial powers was not just a right but a duty. Mawdudi called for a universal *jihad*. Just as the Prophet had fought the *jahiliyyah* (the "ignorance" and barbarism of the pre-Islamic period), Muslims must use all means in their power to resist the modern *jahiliyyah* of the West. Mawdudi argued that *jihad* was the central tenet of Islam. This was an innovation. Nobody had ever claimed before that *jihad* was equivalent to the five Pillars of Islam, but Mawdudi felt that the innovation was justified by the present emergency. The stress and fear of cultural and religious annihilation had led to the development of a more extreme and potentially violent distortion of the faith.

But the real founder of Islamic fundamentalism in the Sunni world was Sayyid Qutb (1906–66), who was greatly influenced by Mawdudi. Yet he had not originally been an extremist but had been filled with enthusiasm for Western culture and secular politics. Even after he joined the Muslim Brotherhood in 1953 he had been a reformer, hoping to give Western democracy an Islamic dimension that would avoid the excesses of a wholly secularist ideology. However, in 1956 he was imprisoned by al-Nasser for membership of the Brotherhood, and in the concentration camp he became convinced that religious people and secularists could not live in peace in the same society. As he witnessed the torture and execution of the Brothers, and reflected upon al-Nasser's avowed determination to cast religion into a marginal role in Egypt, he could see all the characteristics of *jahiliyyah*, which he defined as the barbarism that was for ever and for all time the enemy of faith, and which Muslims, following the example of the Prophet Muhammad, were bound to fight to the death. Qutb went further than Mawdudi, who had seen only non-Muslim societies as *jahili*. Qutb applied the term *jahiliyyah*, which in conventional Muslim historiography had been used simply to describe the pre-Islamic period in Arabia, to contemporary Muslim society. Even though a ruler such as al-Nasser outwardly professed Islam, his words and actions proved him to be an apostate and Muslims were duty-bound to overthrow such a government, just as Muhammad had forced the pagan establishment of Mecca (the *jahiliyyah* of his day) into submission.

The violent secularism of al-Nasser had led Qutb to espouse a form of Islam that distorted both the message of the Quran and the Prophet's life. Qutb told Muslims to model themselves on Muhammad: to separate themselves from mainstream society (as Muhammad had made the *bijrah* from Mecca to Medina), and then engage in a violent *jihad*. But Muhammad had in fact finally achieved victory by an ingenious policy of non-violence; the Quran adamantly opposed force and coercion in religious matters, and its vision—far from preaching exclusion and separation—was tolerant and inclusive. Qutb insisted that the Quranic injunction to toleration could occur only *after* the political victory of Islam and the establishment of a true Muslim state. The new intransigence sprang from the profound fear that is at the core of fundamentalist religion. Qutb did not survive. At al-Nasser's personal insistence, he was executed in 1966.

72

The Modern Islamic Revival

Sayyid Qutb (1906–1966) was a leader of the Egyptian Muslim Brotherhood which supported the 1952 revolt by Gamal Abdal Nasser against Egypt's monarchy which was subservient to the British. But the Brotherhood soon became disillusioned with Nasser's secularism and socialism and turned against him. Qutb increasingly came to see Nasser's Egypt, and the world as a whole, as equivalent to the jahiliyya, the period of Arab history before the arrival of Muhammad—a period characterized as ignorant and barbaric. He wrote his "Milestones" while in prison in 1964 and called for force to create a state based on Islamic ideals as found in the Quran. Nasser had him executed in 1966.

Discussion Questions

1. Why did Qutb think that "mankind today is on the brink of a precipice?"

2. Why did he see the leadership of the West in decline?

3. What did he think was wrong with the Islam of his own day? What needs to be done?

Corruptions of the Modern World

Mankind today is on the brink of a precipice, not because of the danger of complete annihilation... but because humanity is devoid of those vital values which are necessary not only for its healthy development but also for its real progress. Even the Western world realizes that Western civilization is unable to present any healthy values for the guidance of mankind.

Democracy in the West has become infertile to such an extent that it is borrowing from the systems of the Eastern bloc, especially in the economic system, under the name of socialism. It is the same with the Eastern bloc. Its social theories, foremost among which in Marxism, in the beginning attracted not only a large number of people from the East but also from the West, as it was a way of life based on a creed. But now Marxism is defeated on the plane of thought, and if it is stated that not a single nation in the world is truly Marxist, it will not be an exaggeration. On the whole this theory conflicts with man's nature and its needs. This ideology prospers only in a degenerate society or in a society which has become cowed as a result of some form of prolonged dictatorship. But now, even under these circumstances, its materialistic economic system is failing, although this was the only foundation on which its structure was based. Russia, which is the leader of the communist countries, is itself suffering from shortages of food. Although during the times of the Tsars Russia used to produce surplus food, it now has to import food from abroad and has to sell its reserves of gold for this purpose. The main reason for this is the failure of the system of collective farming, or one can say, the failure of a system which is against human nature.

It is essential for mankind to have new leadership!

The leadership of mankind by Western man is now on the decline, not because Western culture has become poor materially or because its economic and military power has become weak. The period of the Western system has come to an end primarily because it is deprived of those life-giving values which enabled it to be the leader of mankind.

It is necessary for the new leadership to preserve and develop the material fruits of the creative genius of Europe, and also to provide mankind with such high ideals and values as have so far remained undiscovered by mankind, and which will also acquaint humanity with a way of life which is harmonious with human nature.

Islam is the only system which possesses these values and this way of life.

The period of the resurgence of science has also come to an end. The period, which began with the Renaissance in the sixteenth century after Christ and reached its zenith in the eighteenth and nineteenth centuries, does not possess a reviving spirit.

All nationalistic and chauvinistic ideologies which have appeared in modern times, and all the movements and theories derived from them, have also lost their vitality. In short, all man-made individual or collective theories have proved to be failures.

At this crucial and bewildering juncture, the turn of Islam and the Muslim community

From Milestones by Sayyid Qutb

has arrived—the turn of Islam, which does not prohibit material inventions.

Islam cannot fulfill its role except by taking concrete form in a society, rather, in a nation; for man does not have to listen, especially in this age, to an abstract theory which is not seen materialized in a living society. From this point of view, we can say that the Muslim community has been extinct for a few centuries.... The Muslim community with these characteristics vanished at the moment the laws of God became suspended on earth.

If Islam is again to play the role of the leader of mankind, then it is necessary that the Muslim community be restored to its original form.

It is necessary to revive that Muslim community which is buried under the debris of the man-made traditions of several generations, and which is crushed under the weight of those false laws and customs which are not even remotely related to the Islamic teachings, and which, in spite of all this, calls itself the "world of Islam."

I am aware that between the attempt at "revival" and the attainment of "leadership" there is a great distance, as the Muslim community has long ago vanished from existence and from observation, and the leadership of mankind has long since passed to other ideologies and other nations, other concepts and other systems. This was the era during which Europe's genius created its marvelous works in science, culture, law and material production, due to which mankind has progressed to great heights of creativity and material comfort. It is not easy to find fault with the inventors of such marvelous things, especially since what we call the "world of Islam" is completely devoid of all this beauty.

But in spite of all this, it is necessary to revive Islam. The distance between the revival of Islam and the attainment of world leadership may be vast, and there may be great difficulties on the way; but the first step must be taken for the revival of Islam.

The Muslim community today is neither capable of nor required to present before mankind great genius in material inventions, which will make the world bow its head before its supremacy and thus re-establish once more its world leadership. Europe's creative mind is far ahead in this area, and at least for a few centuries to come we cannot expect to compete with Europe and attain supremacy over it in these fields.

Hence we must have some other quality, that quality which modern civilization does not possess.

But this does not mean that we should neglect material progress.... [I]t is an essential condition for our very existence; and Islam... makes material progress obligatory for us.

To attain the leadership of mankind, we must have something to offer besides material progress, and this other quality can only be a faith and a way of life which on the one hand conserves the benefits of modern science and technology, and on the other fulfills the basic human needs on the same level of excellence as technology has fulfilled them in the sphere of material comfort, And then this faith and way of life must take concrete form in a human society—in other words, in a Muslim society.

If we look at the sources and foundations of modern ways of living, it becomes clear that the whole world is steeped in *Jahiliyyah* and all the marvelous material comfort and high-level inventions do not diminish this ignorance. This *Jahiliyyah* is based on rebellion against God's sovereignty on earth. It transfers to man one of the greatest attributes of God, namely sovereignty, and makes some men lords over others. It...takes the form of claiming that the right to create values, to legislate rules of collective behavior, and to choose any way of life rests with men, without regard to what God has prescribed. The result of this rebellion against the authority of God is the oppression of His creatures. Thus the humiliation of the common man under the communist systems and the exploitation of individuals and nations due to greed for wealth and imperialism under the capitalist systems are but a corollary of rebellion against God's authority and the denial of the dignity of man given to him by God.

[W]e need to initiate the movement of Islamic revival in some Muslim country. Only such a revivalist movement will eventually attain to the status of world leadership, whether the distance is near or far.

How is it possible to start the task of reviving Islam?

It is necessary that there should be a vanguard which sets out with this determination and then keeps walking on the path, marching through the vast ocean of Jahiliyyah which has encompassed the entire world. During its course, it should keep itself somewhat aloof from this all-encompassing *Jahiliyyah* and should also keep some ties with it.

It is necessary that this vanguard should know the landmarks and the milestones of the road toward this goal so that they may recognize the starting place, the nature, the responsibilities and the ultimate purpose of this long journey. Not only this, but they ought to be aware Of their position as opposed to this *Jahiliyyah*, which has struck its stakes throughout the earth: when to co-operate with others and when to separate from them; what characteristics and qualities they should cultivate, and with what characteristics and qualities the *Jahiliyyah* immediately surrounding them is armed; how to address the people of *Jahiliyyah* in the language of Islam, and what topics and problems ought to be discussed; and where and how to obtain guidance in all these matters.

The milestones will necessarily be determined by the light of the first source of this faith—the Holy *Qur'an*—and from its basic teachings, and from the concept which it created in the minds of the first groups of Muslims, those whom God raised to fulfill His will, those who once changed the course of human history in the direction ordained by God.

73

"The Gentlemen of the Jungle"

The following famous story by Jomo Kenyatta (the "father" of independent Kenya), from his book *Facing Mt. Kenya*, presents us with a fable meant to illustrate the nature of colonialism in Africa. It should be compared with the Lugard selection on the Dual Mandate.

Discussion Questions

1. What is the point of the story?

2. What arguments do the animals use to dispossess the man?

3. Why is the man so apparently helpless?

4. What recourse did the man have in dealing with the animals? Is this an argument for the use of terrorism?

Once upon a time an elephant made a friendship with a man. One day [when] a heavy thunderstorm broke out, the elephant went to his friend, who had a little hut at the edge of the forest, and said to him: "My dear good man, will you please let me put my trunk inside your hut to keep it out of this torrential rain?" The man, seeing what situation his friend was in, replied: "My dear good elephant, my hut is very small, but there is room for your trunk and myself. Please put your trunk in gently." The elephant thanked his friend, saying: "You have done me a good deed and one day I shall return your kindness." But what followed? As soon as the elephant put his trunk inside the hut, slowly he pushed his head inside, and finally flung the man out in the rain, and then lay down comfortably inside his friend's hut, saying: "My dear good friend, your skin is harder than mine, and as there is not enough room for both of us, you can afford to remain in the rain while I am protecting my delicate skin from the hailstorm."

The man, seeing what his friend had done to him, started to grumble; the animals in the nearby forest heard the noise and came to see what was the matter. All stood around listening to the heated argument between the man and his friend the elephant. In the turmoil the lion came along roaring, and said in a loud voice: "Don't you all know that I am the King of the jungle? How dare anyone disturb the peace of my kingdom?" On hearing this the elephant, who was one of the high ministers in the jungle kingdom, replied in a soothing voice, and said: "My lord, there is no disturbance of the peace in your kingdom. I have only been having a little discussion with my friend here as to the possession of this little hut which your lordship sees me occupying." The lion, who wanted to have "peace and tranquillity" in his kingdom, replied in a noble voice, saying: "I command my ministers to appoint a Commission of Inquiry to go thoroughly into this matter and report accordingly." He then turned to the man and said: "You have done well by establishing friendship with my people, especially with the elephant, who is one of my honorable ministers of state. Do not grumble any more, your hut is not lost to you. Wait until the sitting of my Imperial Commission and there you will be given plenty of opportunity to state your case. I am sure that you will be pleased with the findings of the Commission." The man was very pleased by these sweet words from the King of the jungle, and innocently waited for his opportunity, in the belief that, naturally, the hut would be returned to him.

The elephant, obeying the command of his master, got busy with other ministers to appoint the Commission of Inquiry. The following elders of the jungle were appointed to sit in the Commission: (1) Mr. Rhinoceros; (2) Mr. Buffalo; (3) Mr. Alligator; (4) The Rt. Hon. Mr. Fox to act as chairman; and (5) Mr. Leopard to act as Secretary to the Commission. On seeing the personnel, the man protested and asked if it was not necessary to include in this Commission a member from his side. But he was told that it was impossible, since no one from his side was well enough educated to understand the intricacy of jungle law. Further, that there was nothing to fear, for the members of the Commission were all men of repute for their impartiality in justice, and as they were gentlemen chosen by God to look after the interests of races less adequately endowed with teeth and claws, he might rest assured that they would investigate the matter with the greatest care and report impartially.

The Commission sat to take the evidence. The Rt. Hon. Mr. Elephant was first called. He came along with a superior air, brushing his tusks with a sapling which Mrs. Elephant had provided, and in an authoritative voice said: "Gentlemen of the jungle, there is no need for me to waste your valuable time in relating a story which I am sure you all know. I have always regarded it as my duty to protect the interests of my friends, and this appears to have caused the misunderstanding between myself and my friend here. He invited me to save his hut from being blown away by a hurricane. As the hurricane had gained access owing to the unoccupied space in the hut, I considered it necessary, in my friend's own interests, to turn the undeveloped space to a more economic use by sitting in it myself; a duty which any of you would undoubtedly have performed with equal readiness in similar circumstances."

After hearing the Rt. Hon. Mr. Elephant's conclusive evidence, the Commission called Mr. Hyena and other elders of the jungle, who all supported what Mr. Elephant had said. They then called the man, who began to give his own account of the dispute. But the Commission cut him short, saying: "My good man, please confine yourself to relevant issues. We have already heard the circumstances from various unbiased sources; all we wish you to tell us is whether the undeveloped space in your hut was occupied by anyone else before Mr. Elephant assumed his position?" The man began to say: "No, but—" at this point the Commission declared that they had heard sufficient evidence from both sides and retired to consider their decision. After enjoying a delicious meal at the expense of the Rt. Hon. Mr. Elephant, they reached their verdict, called the man, and declared as follows: "In our opinion this dispute has arisen through a regrettable misunderstanding due to the backwardness of your ideas. We consider that Mr. Elephant has fulfilled his sacred duty of protecting your interests. As it is clearly for your good that the space should be put to its most economic use, and as you yourself have not yet reached the stage of expansion which would enable you to fill it, we consider it necessary to arrange a compromise to suit both parties. Mr. Elephant shall continue his occupation of your hut, but we give you permission to look for a site where you can build another hut more suited to your needs, and we will see that you are well protected."

The man, having no alternative, and fearing that his refusal might expose him to the teeth and claws of members of the Commission, did as they suggested. But no sooner had he built another hut than Mr. Rhinoceros charged in with his horn lowered and ordered the man to quit the hut. A Royal Commission was again appointed to look into the matter, and the same finding was given. This procedure was repeated until Mr. Buffalo, Mr. Leopard, Mr. Hyena, and the rest were all accommodated with new huts. Then the man decided that he must adopt an effective method of protection, since Commissions of Inquiry did not seem to be of any use to him. He sat down and said: "*Ng'enda thi ndeagaga motegi*," which literally means "there is nothing that treads on the earth that cannot be trapped," or in other words, you can fool people for a time, but not forever.

Early one morning, when the huts already occupied by the jungle lords were all beginning to decay and fall to pieces, he went out and build a bigger and better hut a little distance away. No sooner had Mr. Rhinoceros seen it than he came rushing in, only to find that Mr. Elephant was already inside, sound asleep. Mr. Leopard next came in at the window, Mr. Lion, Mr. Fox, and Mr. Buffalo entered the doors, while Mr. Hyena howled for a place in the shade and Mr. Alligator basked on the roof. Presently they all began disputing about their rights of penetration, and from disputing they came to fighting, and when they were all embroiled together the man set the hut on fire and burnt it to the ground, jungle lords and all. Then he went home saying: "Peace is costly, but it's worth the expense," and lived happily ever after.

74

The Motion of Destiny

On July 10, 1953, Kwame Nkrumah delivered the following speech before the House of Assembly of the Gold Coast in which he argued for its independence from Great Britain. Independence was granted in 1957—the first British colony south of the Sahara to achieve that status. The former Gold Coast was renamed Ghana after the great empire that went back as far as the fourth century.

Discussion Questions

1. What advantages did Nkrumah believe the Gold Coast had for becoming an independent nation?

2. Why did he think independence would be beneficial to the British themselves?

3. How did he think that history justified independence?'

The right of a people to decide their own destiny, to make their way in freedom, is not to be measured by the yardstick of color or degree of social development. It is an inalienable right of peoples which they are powerless to exercise when forces, stronger than they them whatever means, for whatever reasons, take this right away from them. If there is to be a criterion of a people's preparedness for self-government, then I say it is their readiness to

From Kwame Nkrumah, *Ghana: The Autobiography of Kwame Nkrumah*, copyright © Panaf Books Ltd., an imprint of Zed Press Ltd., 57 Caledonian Road, London N19BU, UK.

assume the responsibilities of ruling themselves. For who but a people themselves can say then they are prepared?...

There is no conflict that I can see between our claim and the professed policy of all parties and governments of the United Kingdom. We have here in our country a stable society. Our economy is healthy, as good as any for a country of our size. In many respects, we are very much better off than many Sovereign States. And our potentialities are large. Our people are fundamentally homogeneous, nor are we plagued with religious and tribal problems. And, above all, we have hardly any color bar. In fact, the whole democratic tradition of our society precludes the *herrenvolk* doctrine. The remnants of this doctrine are now an anachronism in our midst, and their days are numbered.

We have traveled long distances from the days when our fathers came under alien subjugation to the present time. We stand now at the threshold of self-government and do not waver. The paths have been tortuous, and fraught with peril, but the positive and tactical action we have adopted is leading us to the New Jerusalem, the golden city of our hearts desire!...

Today, more than ever before, Britain needs more "autonomous communities freely associated." For freely associated communities make better friends than those associated by subjugation. We see today how much easier and friendlier are the bonds between Great Britain and her former dependencies of India, Pakistan and Ceylon. So much of the bitterness that poisoned the relations between these former colonies and the United Kingdom has been absolved by the healing power of a better feeling so that a new friendship has been cemented in the free association of autonomous communities... .

In the very early days of the Christian era, long before England had assumed any importance, long even before her people had united into a nation, our ancestors had attained a great empire, which lasted until the eleventh century, when it fell before the attacks of the Moors of the North. At its height that empire stretched from Timbuktu to Bamako, and even as far as the Atlantic... .

Thus may we take pride in the name of Ghana, not out of romanticism, but as an inspiration for the future. It is right and proper that we should know about our past. For just as the future moves from the present, so the present has emerged from the past. Nor need we be ashamed of our past. There was much in it of glory. What our ancestors achieved in the context of their contemporary society gives us confidence that we can create, out of that past, a glorious future, not in terms of war and military pomp, but in terms of social progress and of peace. For we repudiate war and violence. Our battles shall be against the old ideas that keep men trammeled in their own greed; against the crass stupidities that breed hatred, fear and inhumanity. The heroes of our future will be those who can lead our people out of the stifling fog of disintegration through serfdom, into the valley of light where purpose, endeavor and determination will create that brotherhood which Christ proclaimed two thousand years ago, and about which so much is said, but so little done... .

75

Dawn in the Heart of Africa

The author of this poem, Patrice Lumumba, was the Prime Minister of the newly independent Republic of the Congo when he was assassinated in 1961. He tried to forge a multiethnic national party based on many of the principles made popular by the nationalist leader of Ghana, Kwame Nkrumah, and was winning converts to his cause when he was killed. The former Belgian Congo had suffered long during the years of colonization, and would face years of turmoil before some stability resulted. The following selection reflects both the burdens of imperialism and the promise of independence so much a part of the African nationalist message.

Discussion Questions

1. What or who does Lumumba blame for the thousand years of suffering? What or who does he say is changing things?

2. How do his words compare with those of Nkrumah, Kenyatta and other nationalist leaders? Are there differences? If so, why do you suppose those differences exist?

3. If Lumumba were living today, how do you think he would view events in Africa?

Dawn in the Heart of Africa

Patrice Lumumba

For a thousand years, you, African, suffered like a beast,
Your ashes strewn to the wind that roams the desert.
Your tyrants built the lustrous, magic temples
To preserve your soul, preserve your suffering.
Barbaric right of fist and the white right to whip,
You had the right to die, you also could weep.
On your totem they carved endless hunger, endless bonds,
And even in the cover of the woods a ghastly cruel death
Was watching, snaky, crawling to you
Like branches from the holes and heads of trees
Embraced your body and your ailing soil.
Then they put a treacherous big viper on your chest:
On your neck they laid the yoke of firewater,
They took your sweet wife for glitter of cheap pearls,
Your incredible riches that nobody could measure.
From you hut, the tom-toms sounded into dark of night
Carrying cruel laments up might black rivers

About abused girls, streams of tears and blood,
About ships that sailed to countries where the little man
Wallows in an anthill and where the dollar is king,
To that damned land which they called a motherland.
There your child, your wife were ground, day and night,
In a frightful, merciless mill, crushing them in dreadful pain.
You are a man like others. They preach you to believe
That good white God will reconcile all men at last.
By fire you grieved and sang the moaning songs
Of a homeless beggar that stinks at strangers' doors.
And when a craze possessed you
And your blood boiled through the night
You danced, you moaned, obsessed by father's passion.
Like fury of a storm to lyrics of a manly tune
From a thousand years of misery a strength burst out of you
In metallic voice of jazz, in uncovered outcry
That thunders through the continent like gigantic surf.
The whole world, surprised, wakes up in panic

To the violent rhythm of blood, to the violent rhythm of jazz,
The white man turning pallid over this new song
That carries torch of purple through the dark of night
The dawn is here, my brother! Dawn! Look in our faces,
A new morning breaks in our old Africa.
Ours alone will now be the land, the water, mighty rivers
Poor African surrendered for a thousand years.

Hard torches of the sun will shine for us again
They'll dry the tears in eyes and spittle on your face.
The moment when you break the chains, the heavy fetters,
The evil, cruel times will go never to come again.
A free and gallant Congo will arise from black soil,
A free and gallant Congo—black blossom from black seed!

76

Africa: Imperialism and the Present

As African nations won their independence in the 1960's there was much optimism that, freed from their colonial yoke, they would blossom into modern, economically dynamic nation-states. That has not largely occurred, and, today, much of Africa can be characterized as a region of failed states, disease, ethnic conflict, and environmental devastation. Yet the continent houses some of the oldest and richest civilizations, possesses vast resource wealth, and its young population has great potential. The central theme of this reading is to document the role that imperialism played in contributing to the problems of present-day Africa.

Discussion Questions

1. What has been the legacy of "indirect rule," "hasty decolonization," and "decentralized despotism" for today's African states?

2. What specific examples of European imperialism are presented in the reading and which African countries are highlighted? Are these countries still seeing the long-term effects of the policies put in place by the Europeans during the imperialist period?

3. What is meant by "the iron grid of colonialism," and what does it mean for today's Africa?

4. How is Africa's imperial experience similar and different from that of other regions of the world mentioned in the reading?

5. How would you answer the question raised in the reading by Kenyan scholar, Makau wa Mutua, who asks how Europeans would have reacted "if an African imperial army had marched into Europe in the Middle Ages and required Germany, France and England to live together by force of arms?"

6. How helpful is it to "play the blame game" when it comes to examining the impact of imperialism on the present situation in Africa? If you were sitting in judgment of the New Imperialism, would you find it guilty of wrongdoing to Africa (and the rest of the world for that matter)?

The African Question: Who Is to Blame?

By the late 1960's, scarcely a decade after Africa's great independence wave had begun, many of the continent's new political creations had already begun to resemble disasters. With no ready answers to their problems, many African leaders struck upon a new strategy for explaining their failings to impatient populations while simultaneously drawing more outside aid: blaming the European colonizers for Africa's seemingly intractable difficulties.

But if this approach was at least temporarily successful in many cases, the increasing stridency of the claims made against the West, set against the backdrop of the growing despotism of the new leaders, quickly backfired, as both foreign sympathy and assistance dwindled.

For the next two decades or so, conventional wisdom largely rejected African assertions of outside responsibility for the continent's problems, and many in the West argued, often with a growing vehemence of their own, that Africa's bad leaders were primarily to blame rather than any European legacy.

In the closing years of this century, though, historians, political scientists and other students of African affairs have begun a searching re-examination of the continent's recent past. Increasingly they have concluded that many of its most persistent curses — from the plague of ethnic hatred widely known as tribalism to endemic official corruption — have powerful roots that are at least partly traceable to European subjugation and rule.

Among the writings that helped forge this reconsideration are works like "Citizen and Subject: Contemporary Africa and the Legacy of Late Colonialism," by the Ugandan scholar Mahmood Mamdani. Mr. Mamdani's 1996 book draws extensively on colonial records to show how Europeans administered their new subjects through a deliberately authoritarian form of indirect rule — for which the author coined the term "decentralized despotism" — that greatly reinforced or even created notions of ethnicity, helping set the stage for the tribal conflict that wracks the continent today.

Another work, Basil Davidson's "Black Man's Burden Africa and the Curse of the Nation-State," depicts the European process of decolonization in Africa as one of hasty, even offhand decision-making filled with a disdain for Africans and their history and an unquestioning arrogance that assumed that the political structures of the West were appropriate for Africans even when they had been given no preparation for making them work.

In these and other scholarly works, African specialists have made the point that the example left by European rule was one of politics by sheer domination and not democracy. Then, as is so often the case now, African states were run with little thought to the benefit of their subjects.

Perhaps no country in Africa today displays the consequences of Europe's African past as harshly as Congo, where the three-decade-old Mobutu dictatorship was violently over-thrown in 1997, only to be followed by a bumbling new authoritarian figure, Laurent Kabila, and more recently by a succession of new rebellions that are tearing his vast country apart.

Shortly before suddenly granting independence in 1960, amid a wave of simultaneous African independence ceremonies, Belgian colonial planners still spoke dreamily of holding onto their possession — a country 77 times as large as their own — for decades more.

At independence, Congo entered the modern era, nominally at least, with only a few score high school graduates and less than 500 miles of paved road. The country's first university had been created by the Belgians only six years before.

"The colonial history of the Congo has inclined that country in a more tragic direction than even most other African countries," said Zine Magubane, a South African professor of sociology and African studies at the University of Illinois at Urbana. "The Belgians had no interest in establishing any sort of permanency or any true state. The country was instead run by a series of companies that had a free hand at pillaging the land."

Other African scholars place an emphasis even further back, on the last decades of the 19th century, when Europe's imperial powers divided up the continent and defined the borders that remain today.

"What you had before the imposition of this great iron grid of colonialism was an extraordinarily variegated network of cultures," said Rene Lamarchand, a professor emeritus of the University of Florida at Gainesville and a lifelong student of Africa. "That certainly included some rather extensive and elaborate kingdoms — take the case of Ashanti, of Buganda, of Kongo or of the Zulu.

"When the iron grid was removed," he continued, "what resurfaced were residues of traditional systems, and in many cases precolonial antagonisms resurfaced."

What is worse, many Africanists say, colonial subjugation brutally ended Africa's sovereign evolution toward modern nation-states, a gradual process of conquest and agglomeration that has occurred throughout history around the world.

In the Americas, native populations were exterminated by arriving Europeans or saw their cultures marginalized by the makers of new states. In India and many other parts of Asia, conquering Europeans imposed their new colonial order on states that had already begun to coalesce to one degree or another around an idea of national identity.

In Africa, meanwhile, Europeans carved out new frontiers as a function of the existing power balance among themselves, giving an occasional nod to natural features of the continent, like broad rivers, but almost never paying heed to the chosen identities of Africans themselves or to the political systems already in place.

"The example I like to think of is if an African imperial army had marched into Europe in the Middle Ages and required Germany, France and England to live together by force of arms," said Makau wa Mutua, a Kenyan scholar who teaches law at the State University at Buffalo. "It would have unleashed untold mayhem, and not to excuse the villainies of Africa's subsequent leaders, that is precisely what happened when Europe did this to Africa in the span of 30 years by destroying Africa's existing political structures, some of them powerful and far-ranging kingdoms, and imposing its own borders, religions and administration."

In cataloguing and later registering their African subjects, Europeans everywhere reinforced and sometimes completely invented ethnic distinctions that Africans themselves had hitherto managed with far greater suppleness.

The most famous case of this now is that of the Hutu and Tutsi who predominate in Rwanda and Burundi and are a small minority in Congo. For centuries the two groups had coexisted peaceably, marrying, sharing a language and a king. When Belgium imposed its administration, however, it glorified the minority Tutsi peoples for their supposedly more European features, creating a de facto ethnic underclass of the majority Hutu and sowing the seeds of the cycles of mass killings that have afflicted the two groups since.

Similarly, almost every time the Europeans created a state, ethnic groups or previously existing African polities were split by the new borders, undermining the new states' claims to legitimacy in the eyes of their inhabitants.

The emerging African nations' first brush with legitimacy came with the independence movements that swept the continent in the 1950's. But in the case of Congo, as with many other countries, the nationalism of the leader who best channeled pro-independence sentiment, Patrice Lumumba, was quickly seen as a threat by Belgium and by a cold-war-driven United States.

Both countries worked to undermine and ultimately overthrow Lumumba, who was subsequently assassinated under murky circumstances. The man they helped replace him with was Mobutu Sese Seko, the dictator who ruled ruinously over Africa's third largest country with strong Western backing for 32 years. For most of that period Mobutu loomed over his country and over the continent's affairs. The West had decided that Zaire, as he renamed his country, with its borders with nine other African countries, was of strategic importance. And acting on behalf of his foreign sponsors, Mobutu intervened freely in his neighbors' affairs.

With the end of the cold war, however, Western interest in propping up Mobutu, indeed Western interest in Africa generally, evaporated. It was then, through the collapse of Mobutu and the crumbling of a dozen or more countries that the myth of the modern African state began to crumble.

For Mobutu the end came quickly at the hands of Mr. Kabila, long an obscure and inconsequential rebel leader who this time had the critical backing of Rwanda and Uganda, two neighbors that decided to pursue their own security interests in Congo aggressively.

Shorn of foreign assistance, the Mobutu Government, a creation of the West, could not pay its civil servants, equip its army or even move its ill-disciplined troops from one part of the country to another when war came.

Now Congo, which owed its definition and preservation to the outside world, is being dismembered by its neighbors while the West averts its suddenly disinterested gaze.

The first to feast on Central Africa's largest piece of real estate have been Uganda and Rwanda, two of Africa's Western favorites now.

Following the lead of these two nations, which have already carved out large spheres of interest for themselves in the country's eastern regions, other neighbors, some less favored by the West, are aggressively asserting their interests too.

Zimbabwe and Angola, Congo's southern neighbors, have rushed to Mr. Kabila's defense, invoking the principle of territorial integrity as they position themselves to profit from the country's immense mineral wealth.

"States which are more stable and can project more economic or military power are going to interfere more readily in the affairs of their neighbors," Mr. Mutua said.

A century after Europe created the edifice of African nation-states many observers of the continent's affairs say they foresee a potentially perilous period in which the structure progressively crumbles, with no one quite sure what to expect next.

77

Imperialism: Africa

The debate on the impact of European imperialism on Africa continues today. This reading sheds light on the experiences of the Bamoun people in present-day Cameroon, who created a 600 year-old culture and kingdom prior to German, then French control.

Discussion Questions

1. How would you describe the kingdom of Bamoun and its king, Njoya, before the arrival of the Europeans?

2. What do some of the speakers in the article identify as the "major colonial damage" done as a result of European imperialism? Were there any positive interactions between the Africans and the Europeans?

3. African intellectuals ask, "what if" the kingdom's indigenous culture had not been destroyed by the Europeans. What is your opinion?

4. How does the example of the Bamoun people help to expand our understanding of African history before, during, and after the European imperialism of the late 19th century?

5. Along with the reading, "The African Question: Who Is to Blame," what lessons does this example of imperialism suggest for Africans today?

Inheritors of an African Kingdom, Come and Gone

Surrounded by praise-singers who strive to outdo one another in chanting his virtues, court attendants who wave fans to preserve him from the heat and musicians who blow shrill six-foot-long trumpets toward an incandescent sky, Sultan Ibrahim Mbombo Njoya takes half an hour to walk the stone's throw from the central mosque to his imposing palace.

The spectacle is repeated every Friday at the end of the midday Muslim prayers in this town, tucked in equatorial mountain country where pine trees outnumber palms. But people of the Bamoun ethnic group still enthusiastically crowd the path for the entire 200-yard route, bowing or ululating as their sovereign slowly passes, a serene smile his only acknowledgment of their salute.

Aside from the introduction of Islam early in this century, the rituals of the Bamoun people would seem little changed in the 600 years of recorded history of their royalty. But for many visitors here, what is most impressive about this culture is not the colorful ceremonies repeated week after week, or even the longevity of the royal line, but the intellectual and historical treasures proudly guarded inside the palace.

There, under the impassive gaze of the current sultan's grandfather, the first King Ibrahim Njoya, who is immortalized in a huge black-and-white photograph, are housed the achievements of a small but impressive civilization. These clash sharply with common stereotypes of a continent's dark and savage history.

By almost any standard, the original Ibrahim Njoya was a Renaissance man who, Jeffersonlike, drew up plans and oversaw construction of a three-story mud-brick palace of vaulted ceilings and elaborately engraved wooden shutters.

Historians say the building was first envisioned in 1904 after King Njoya visited the German governor's mansion in the coastal city of Buea and insisted that his culture could produce better.

The cavernous interior, which now serves as a museum, houses King Njoya's meticulously kept administrative records and legal codes. A poetic treatise on esthetics providing nearly 200 criteria for appraising the beauty of women, an elaborate volume on pharmacopoeia and a detailed history of the Bamoun Kingdom were all written by the ruler.

By itself, the creation of such works in turn-of-the-century equatorial Africa would be remarkable. But the brightest jewel in the collection is not a document at all. It is an alphabet and writing system unique to the Bamoun, who number 570,000.

The first Njoya was born into the Bamoun royal line in 1875. Twenty years later, when the country that would become known as Cameroon had just beep named a German protectorate, Njoya, responding to a dream, began work on one of the rare sub-Saharan writing systems that do not borrow from Arabic or Roman characters. Known as Shumom, it evolved during his 32-year rule from a sprawling system of ideographs to a concise syllabic alphabet.

As the use of written documents spread, mostly in the court and administration, Njoya built a printing press, and soon a royal library of works in Shumom began to grow.

"He was one of me first sub-Saharan Africans to build a museum," said Dayirou Ngouchemo, a palace guide. "He created a writing system when he was 25 years old. This man was a genius to whom Cameroon and Africa owe a great deal."

Njoya's creations did not escape intact from the colonial collision of European and African cultures.

When France took over most of what is now Cameroon from a defeated Germany after World War I, the French sought to impose their language and administration throughout the territory. They were suspicious of the astute sultan, who they feared might form an alliance with the part of the country controlled by the British.

It was, inevitably, an uneven match. And although the French takeover of the Bamoun Kingdom was relatively peaceful, indigenous schools were destroyed, the printing press was smashed and, in 1931. King Njoya was exiled to the city of Yaounde, where he died, humiliated, two years later.

"We had our own culture, our own script, our own army and our own institutions," said Adamou Ndam Njoya, a Cameroonian opposition politician and lawyer descended from the exiled King. "The Germans didn't have enough time to destroy our civilization, but when the French arrived, they abolished everything."

In less than 100 years, from the time of widespread European penetration to formal colonialism early in the century, similar bouts of destruction doomed impressive civilizations throughout Africa.

The names of some of the larger nation-states, places like Ashanti, Benin, Kongo and Dahomey, still carry an echo of grandeur for some. But outside a small circle of experts, few are aware of the extent of their accomplishments—from postal systems and tax imposition to uniformed police forces, diplomats and courts of law—or of the violent end they met at the hands of Europeans with a supposedly civilizing mission.

For many African intellectuals today, there is a bitter twinge of conjecture that lingers, an eternally unanswerable "what if," that looks at a continent scarred by misery and war, and asks whether much of Africa would not be better off if its home-grown institutions had not been destroyed by outsiders.

As Maurice Tadadjeu, a Cameroonian linguist, put it: "The major colonial damage is that, after the destruction of what we were building, Africans were brainwashed to the point where they looked down on their past as nothing more than backwardness. Why should we even bother with something like Shumom? It is to remind ourselves that we have many things to be proud of."

"Believe it or not," he added, "until 1972 we had a national anthem that said, 'In the time of our ancestors, we lived in barbarism.'"

78

Revolution in Modern Latin America

Fidel Castro's revolution in Cuba in 1959 signaled the beginning of a new stage in Latin America's struggle for independence from the developed Western nations—especially economically. Stimulated by Marxist ideas during the Cold War, Castro attempted to participate in what he thought was a global fight for freedom by the less-developed countries from economic exploitation by the "rich countries."

Discussion Questions

1. What does Castro see as the motivating force for the invasion by European countries into the Americas?

2. What have been the results of Western imperialism in Latin America and the rest of the world?

3. What does Castro think are the foundations of revolution in the Americas?

4. Why does Castro think that the revolution by the poor and exploited will be successful?

Fidel Castro: Second Declaration of Havana, 1962

he Cuban Revolution of 1959 was a broadly based nationalist revolution against a corrupt government. It was a revolution facilitated by the long Cuban revolutionary tradition. [There had been major disturbances in the Ten Years' War (18681878), a failed attempt to break with Spain; during the war of independence that began in 1895 but which resulted only independence on the U.S.; and the revolution of 1933, which tried to restore constitutional order and democracy.] In the 1933 events Fulgencio Batista, an army sergeant, emerged and he dominated Cuba for decades. Cuban nationalists, with some reason, blamed U.S. foreign policy for Cuba's problems.

The revolution in 1959 was led by Fidel Castro. He apparently had the support of most Cubans in his broad based "provisional government". Castro turned to the Cuban Communist Party for support in internal struggles. By 1962, after the US began to give "covert" assistance to Cuban exiles oppoing the revolution, Castro had adopted Marxism Leninism as the ideology of the Cuban Revolution. This can be seen in the Second Declaration of Havana, delivered on February 4, 1962.

What is Cuba's history but that of Latin America? What is the history of Latin America but the history of Asia, Africa, and Oceania? And what is the history of all these peoples but the history of the cruelest exploitation of the world by imperialism?

At the end of the last century and the beginning of the present, a handful of economically developed nations had divided the world among themselves subjecting two thirds of humanity to their economic and political domination Humanity was forced to work for the dominating classes of the group of nations which had a developed capitalist economy.

The historic circumstances which permitted certain European countries and the United States of North America to attain a high industrial development level put them in a position which enabled them to subject and exploit the rest of the world.

What motives lay behind this expansion of the industrial powers? Were they moral, "civilizing" reasons, as they claimed? No. Their motives were economic.

The discovery of America sent the European conquerors across the seas to occupy and to exploit the lands and peoples of other continents; the lust for riches was the basic motivation for their conduct. America's discovery took place in the search for shorter ways to the Orient, whose products Europe valued highly.

A new social class, the merchants and the producers of articles manufactured for commerce, arose from the feudal society of lords and serfs in the latter part of the Middle Ages.

The lust for gold promoted the efforts of the new class. The lust for profit was the incentive of their behavior throughout its history. As industry and trade developed, the social influence of the new class grew. The new productive forces maturing in the midst of the feudal society increasingly clashed with feudalism and its serfdom, its laws, its institutions, its philosophy, its morals, its art, and its political ideology... .

Since the end of the Second World War, the Latin American nations are becoming pauperized constantly. The value of their capita income falls. The dreadful percentages of child death rate do not decrease, the number of illiterates grows higher, the peoples lack employment, land, adequate housing, schools, hospitals, communication systems and the means of subsistence. On the other hand, North America investments exceed 10 billion dollars. Latin America, moreover, supplies cheap raw materials and pays high prices for manufactured articles. Like the first Spanish conquerors, who exchanged mirrors and trinkets with the Indians for silver and gold, so the United States trades with Latin America. To hold on to this torrent of wealth, to take greater possession of America's resources and to exploit its longsuffering peoples: this is what is hidden behind the military pacts, the military missions and Washington's diplomatic lobbying… .

Wherever roads are closed to the peoples, where repression of workers and peasants is fierce, where the domination of Yankee monopolies is strongest, the first and most important lesson is to understand that it is neither just nor correct to divert the peoples with the vain and fanciful illusion that the dominant classes can be uprooted by legal means which do not and will not exist. The ruling classes are entrenched in all positions of state power. They monopolize the teaching field. They dominate all means of mass communication. They have infinite financial resources. Theirs is a power which the monopolies and the ruling few will defend by blood and fire with the strength of their police and their armies.

The duty of every revolutionary is to make revolution. We know that in America and throughout the world the revolution will be victorious. But revolutionaries cannot sit in the doorways of their homes to watch the corpse of imperialism pass by. The role of Job does not behoove a revolutionary. Each year by which America's liberation may be hastened will mean millions of children rescued from death, millions of minds, freed for learning, infinitudes of sorrow spared the peoples. Even though the Yankee imperialists are preparing a bloodbath for America they will not succeed in drowning the people's struggle. They will evoke universal hatred against themselves. This will be the last act of their rapacious and caveman system… .

Fidel Castro: On The Export of Revolution

To the accusation that Cuba wants to export its revolution, we reply: Revolutions are not exported, they are made by the people…

What Cuba can give to the people, and has already given, is its example.

And what does the Cuban Revolution teach? That revolution is possible, that the people can make it, that in the contemporary world there are no forces capable of halting the liberation movement of the peoples.

Our triumph would never have been feasible if the Revolution itself had not been inexorably destined to arise out of existing conditions in our socio-economic reality, a reality which exists to an even greater degree in a good number of Latin American countries.

It inevitably occurs that in the nations where the control of the Yankee monopolies is strongest, the exploitation of the oligarchy cruelest, and the situation of the laboring and peasant masses most unbearable, the political power appears most solid. The state of siege becomes habitual. Every manifestation of discontent by the masses is repressed by force. The democratic path is closed completely. The brutal character of dictatorship, the form of rule adopted by the ruling classes, reveals itself more clearly than ever. It is then that the revolutionary explosion of the peoples becomes inevitable.

Although it is true that in those underdeveloped countries of America the working class is generally relatively small, there is a social class which, because of the subhuman conditions in which it lives, constitutes a potential force that, led by the workers and the revolutionary Intellectuals, has a decisive importance in the struggle for national liberation-the peasants.... .

In our countries are two conditions: an underdeveloped industry and an agrarian regime of feudal character. That is why, with all the hardships of the conditions of life of the urban workers, the rural population lives in even more horrible conditions of oppression and exploitation; but it is also, with exceptions, the absolute majority sector, at times exceeding seventy per cent of the Latin American population.

Discounting the landlords, who often reside in the cities, the rest of that great mass gains its livelihood working as peons on the *haciendas* for the most miserable wages, or work the land under conditions of exploitation which in no manner puts the Middle Ages to shame. These circumstances determine that in Latin America the poor rural population constitutes a tremendous potential revolutionary force.

The armies, built and equipped for conventional war, which are the force on which the power of the exploiting classes rests, become absolutely impotent when they have to confront the irregular struggle of the peasants on their own terrain. They lose ten men for each revolutionary fighter who falls. Demoralization spreads rapidly among them from having to face an invisible and invincible enemy who does not offer them the opportunity of showing off their academy tactics and their braggadocio which they use so much in military displays to curb the city workers and the students.

The initial struggle by small combat units is incessantly fed by new forces, the mass movement begins to loosen its bonds, the old order little by little begins to break into a thousand pieces, and that is the moment when the working class and the urban masses decide the battle.

What is it that from the beginning of the struggle of those first nuclei makes them invincible, regardless of the numbers, power, the resources of their enemies? It is the aid of the people, and they will be able to count on that help of the people on an ever-growing scale.

79

The Declaration of Human Rights, 1948

In 1948 the newly established United Nations approved a sweeping set of proposals known as the Universal Declaration of Human Rights. Forty-eight nations voted for the document, with only eight abstentions and no vetoes. The document that follows contains the original list of rights worked out by the General Assembly in 1948, though provisions expanding the list have been added over time. Scholars have often divided the U. N. Declaration of Human Rights into three categories, civil and political rights, social and economic rights, and solidarity rights. This third category includes provisions that would require the cooperation of the global community, such as is reflected in Article 28. While there continues to be much controversy over the implementation of these rights, there is general agreement that every human being possesses certain basic rights, and that gross crimes like genocide and torture are clear violations. As the Tibetan spiritual and human rights leader, the Dalai Lama maintains, "the responsibility that we all have for each other and for all sentient beings and also for all of Nature," is key to peace in the 21st century. As this century progresses, the issue of human rights will continue to be an important component of the global community.

Discussion Questions

1. Do you think there is such a thing as universal human rights, or does each society have a unique set of rights? If you believe the latter, is the U.N. document unworkable?

2. Which of the rights belong in category one, civil and political rights? Category two, social and economic rights? Category three, solidarity rights? Are there some that are overlapping?

3. Are there any provisions of this declaration that you find either offensive, unrealistic, or contrary to U.S. principles? Are there any principles that have been omitted from this list that should be included?

4. Do you think human rights have expanded since 9/11, or has the war against terrorism led to a diminishment of some of these rights?

5. Do you agree with the Dalai Lama that we must be global citizens with responsibilities for the environment and animals, as well as humans?

Universal Declaration of Human Rights, 1948

Preamble

Whereas recognition of the inherent dignity and of the equal and inalienable rights of all members of the human family is the foundation of freedom, justice and peace in the world, Whereas disregard and contempt for human rights have resulted in barbarous acts which have outraged the conscience of mankind, and the advent of a world in which human beings shall enjoy freedom of speech and belief and freedom from fear and want has been proclaimed as the highest aspiration of the common people,

Whereas it is essential, if man is not to be compelled to have recourse, as a last resort, to rebellion against tyranny and oppression, that human rights should be protected by the rule of law,

Whereas it is essential to promote the development of friendly relations between nations,

Whereas the peoples of the United Nations have in the Charter reaffirmed their faith in fundamental human rights, in the dignity and worth of the human person and in the equal rights of men and women and have determined to promote social progress and better standards of life in larger freedom,

Whereas Member States have pledged themselves to achieve, in co-operation with the United Nations, the promotion of universal respect for and observance of human rights and fundamental freedoms, Whereas a common understanding of these rights and freedoms is of the greatest importance for the full realization of this pledge,

Now, therefore,

The General Assembly

Proclaims this Universal Declaration of Human Rights as a common standard of achievement for all peoples and all nations, to the end that every individual and every organ of society, keeping this Declaration constantly in mind, shall strive by teaching and education to promote respect for these rights and freedoms and by progressive measures, national and international, to secure their universal and effective recognition and observance, both among the peoples of Member States themselves and among the peoples of territories under their jurisdiction.

Article 1

All human beings are born free and equal in dignity and rights. They are endowed with reason and conscience and should act towards one another in a spirit of brotherhood.

Article 2

Everyone is entitled to all the rights and freedoms set forth in this Declaration, without distinction of any kind, such as race, color, sex, language, religion, political or other opinion, national or social origin, property, birth or other status. Furthermore, no distinction shall be made on the basis of the political, jurisdictional or international status of the country or territory to which a person belongs, whether it be independent, trust, non-self-governing or under any other limitation of sovereignty.

Article 3

Everyone has the right to life, liberty and the security of person.

Article 4

No one shall be held in slavery or servitude; slavery and the slave trade shall be prohibited in all their forms.

Article 5

No one shall be subjected to torture or to cruel, inhuman or degrading treatment or punishment.

Article 6

Everyone has the right to recognition everywhere as a person before the law.

Article 7

All are equal before the law and are entitled without any discrimination to equal protection against any discrimination in violation of this Declaration and against any incitement to such discrimination.

Article 8

Everyone has the right to an effective remedy by the competent national tribunals for acts violating the fundamental rights granted him by the constitution or by law.

Article 9

No one shall be subjected to arbitrary arrest, detention or exile.

Article 10

Everyone is entitled in full equality to a fair, and public hearing by an independent and impartial tribunal, in the determination of his rights and obligations and of any criminal charge against him.

Article 11

1. Everyone charged with a penal offence has the right to be presumed innocent until proven guilty according to law in a public trial at which he has had all the guarantees necessary for his defence.
2. No one shall be held guilty of any penal offence on account of any act or ommision which did not constitute a penal offence, under national or international law, at the time when it was committed. Nor shall a heavier penalty be imposed than the one that was applicable at the time the penal offence was committed.

Article 12

No one shall be subjected to arbitrary interference with his privacy, family, home or correspondence, nor to attacks upon his honour and reputation. Everyone has the right to the protection of the law against such interference or attacks.

Article 13

1. Everyone has the right to freedom of movement and residence within the borders of each State.
2. Everyone has the right to leave any country, including his own, and to return to his country.

Article 14

1. Everyone has the right to seek and to enjoy in other countries asylum from persecution.
2. This right may not be invoked in the case of prosecutions genuinely arising from non-political crimes or from acts contrary to the purposes and principles of the United Nations.

Article 15

1. Everyone has the right to a nationality.
2. No one shall be arbitrarily deprived of his nationality nor denied the right to change his nationality.

Article 16

1. Men and women of full age, without any limitation due to race, nationality or religion, have the right to marry and to found a family. They are entitled to equal rights as to marriage, during marriage and at its dissolution.
2. Marriage shall be entered into only with the free and full consent of the intending spouses.
3. The family is the natural and fundamental group unit of society and is entitled to protection by society and the State.

Article 17

1. Everyone has the right to own property alone as well as in association with others.
2. No one shall be arbitrarily deprived of his property.

Article 18

Everyone has the right to freedom of thought, conscience and religion; this right includes freedom to change his religion or belief, and freedom, either alone or in community with others and in public or private, to manifest his religion or belief in teaching, practice, worship and observance.

Article 19

Everyone has the right to freedom of opinion and expression; this right includes freedom to hold opinions without interference and to seek, receive and impart information and ideas through any media and regardless of frontiers.

Article 20

1. Everyone has the right to freedom of peaceful assembly and association.
2. No one may be compelled to belong to an association.

Article 21

1. Everyone has the right to take part in the government of his country, directly or through freely chosen representatives.
2. Everyone has the right of equal access to public service in his country.
3. The will of the people shall be the basis of the authority of government; this will shall be expressed in periodic and genuine elections which shall be by universal

and equal suffrage and shall be held by secret vote or by equivalent free voting procedures.

Article 22

Everyone, as a member of society, has the right to social security and is entitled to realization, through national effort and international co-operation and in accordance with the organization and resources of each State, of the economic, social and cultural rights indispensable for his dignity and the free development of his personality.

Article 23

1. Everyone has the right to work, to free choice of employment, to just and favourable conditions of work and to protection against unemployment.
2. Everyone, without any discrimination, has the right to equal pay for equal work.
3. Everyone who works has the right to just and favourable remuneration ensuring for himself and his family an existence worthy of human dignity, and supplemented, if necessary, by other means of social protection.
4. Everyone has the right to form and to join trade unions for the protection of his interests.

Article 24

Everyone has the right to rest and leisure, including reasonable limitation of working hours and periodic holidays with pay.

Article 25

1. Everyone has the right to a standard of living adequate for the health and well-being of himself and of his family, including food, clothing, housing and medical care and necessary social services, and the right to security in the event of unemployment, sickness, disability, widowhood, old age or other lack of livelihood in circumstances beyond his control.
2. Motherhood and childhood are entitled to special care and assistance. All children, whether born in or out of wedlock, shall enjoy the same social protection.

Article 26

1. Everyone has the right to education. Education shall be free, at least in the elementary and fundamental stages. Elementary education shall be compulsory. Technical and professional education shall be made generally available and higher education shall be equally accessible to all on the basis of merit.
2. Education shall be directed to the full development of the human personality and to the strengthening of respect for human rights and fundamental freedoms. It shall promote understanding, tolerance and friendship among all nations, racial or religious groups, and shall further the activities of the United Nations for the maintenance of peace.
3. Parents have a prior right to choose the kind of education that shall be given to their children.

Article 27

1. Everyone has the right freely to participate in the cultural life of the community, to enjoy the arts and to share in scientific advancement and its benefits.
2. Everyone has the right to the protection of the moral and material interests resulting from any scientific, literary or artistic production of which he is the author.

Article 28

Everyone is entitled to a social and international order in which the rights and freedoms set forth in this Declaration can be fully realized.

Article 29

1. Everyone has duties to the community in which alone the free and full development of his personality is possible.
2. In the exercise of his rights and freedoms, everyone shall be subject only to such limitations as are determined by law solely for the purpose of securing due recognition and respect for the rights and freedoms of others and of meeting the just requirements of morality, public order and the general welfare in a democratic society.
3. These rights and freedoms may in no case be exercised contrary to the purposes and principles of the United Nations.

Article 30

Nothing in this Declaration may be interpreted as implying for any State, group or person any right to engage in any activity or to perform any act aimed at the destruction of any of the rights and freedoms set forth herein.